D0085328

Urban Life in Mediterranean Europe

Urban Life
in Mediterranean Europe:
Anthropological Perspectives

Edited by
Michael Kenny and David I. Kertzer

University of Illinois Press
Urbana   Chicago   London

WILLIAM MADISON RANDALL LIBRARY UNC AT WILMINGTON

© 1983 by the Board of Trustees of the University of Illinois

Manufactured in the United States of America

This book is printed on acid-free paper.

Library of Congress Cataloging in Publication Data

Main entry under title:

Urban Life in Mediterranean Europe.

   Includes bibliographies and index.
   1. Cities and towns—Europe, Southern.
2. Urban anthropology.   I. Kenny, Michael,
1923–   II. Kertzer, David I., 1948–
HT131.U69   307.7′64′094   82–1890
ISBN 0-252-00958-4 (c1)   AACR2
ISBN 0-252-00990-8 (pbk)

HT131
.U69
1983

Contents

236512

Foreword

This book meets a need long felt by those interested in Mediterranean Europe. More than 20 years ago the grand old man of Mediterraneanists, Julio Caro Baroja, advised his younger colleagues, "It is impossible to conceive of the social structure of the peoples of the Mediterranean which does not investigate the role of the city" (1963:27). This was noted with approval, for all had observed the importance of the city in the Mediterranean. Yet they continued to explore rural society. The city was looked at only from the outside. Urban life was left unexplored.

But why should anthropologists study urban life in Mediterranean Europe? Quite simply because, as Donald Pitkin observed, Mediterranean Europe is "essentially urban in its overall orientation" (1963:120). Physically, culturally, politically, and economically cities have formed the central points of reference in the area. Physically even the smallest villages in southern Europe are cities writ small. Cities, towns, and villages have concentric structures. They focus inward on the central temple or church on the main square, the *piazza, plaza,* or *aghora.* Facing this are buildings that house the elite and the powerful institutions they run, the municipal offices, police station and banks, the political and social clubs, and the coffee houses. As one moves away from the center, the less urbane and urban the surroundings become. Eventually the increasing presence of livestock, peasant implements, farmyard sounds and smells, and the shanties of immigrants signal the periphery. Here urban life gives way to rural life, sometimes with remarkable abruptness. If the opulent buildings that flank the square epitomize the civilization, wealth, status, and power associated with urban life, the humble dwellings of laborers at the edge of town signal its mirror image, the toil, poverty, and dependence of the country. This concentric settlement pattern, basic to both Hellenic and Roman cities, has been replicated for centuries in city, town, and village of Mediterranean Europe (Pitkin 1963:127, Blok 1972:116–17).

Urban life has also provided a cultural point of reference. It is associated with "civilization," with education, power, and wealth. For Italians the quintessence of an urban way of life, characterized by a distinct style in residence, speech, clothing, manners, and occupation, is expressed in the term *civiltà.* It signifies the opposite of the rural lifestyle. Throughout most of southern Europe there has been and still is a distinct distaste for the life, and especially the manual work, associated with the country. "Being civilized and being urbanized were almost identical" (Blok 1972:119; cf. Redfield 1956, Pitkin 1963:128, and, especially, Silverman 1975:1–11). Urban culture, then, provided the yardstick of civilization.

Politically and economically the city has also dominated the country-side of Mediterranean Europe, and has done so for centuries. The domina-tion of Hellenic city-states was replaced by that of Rome, later forced to share with Byzantium. But by the end of the fourteenth century the Medi-terranean once again "belonged to its towns, the city-states scattered around its shores" (Braudel 1973:657). Even when the slowly growing territorial states began to usurp the power of Mediterranean city-states, they con-tinued to dominate the area. Not only did towns house the fiscal, military, and administrative machinery of the region but they also accommodated the landlords who owned most of the countryside and who spent the surplus ex-tracted from the peasants on urban life. Wealth, like dependence and food, moved from the countryside to the city, from the periphery to the core.

Given the central role of the city in the life of Mediterranean Europe and the fact that more than half the population of the area live in urban settle-ments, it is indeed strange that we have had to wait so long for this book on urban life. As the editors show, the work of anthropologists who have stud-ied the Mediterranean area has been overwhelmingly concerned with the countryside. Rural, not urban, life has been the principal object of study. Moreover, until a few years ago anthropologists knew far more about Afri-can cities than about those in the Mediterranean. Even today there are no anthropological studies of south European cities that can compare with the detailed monographs of African urban life by Epstein (1958), Mayer (1961), and Pons (1969). In fact, more was known about how Italians lived in North American than in Italian cities (Whyte 1943, Gans 1962, Boissevain 1970).

The rural bias among Mediterraneanist anthropologists is not only the result of the monopoly that classicists, historians, and sociologists exercised over European urban studies, and especially the activities of the elite, as the editors suggest. Rural bias is inherent to anthropology. Just as anthropolo-gists with a head start of a generation followed African migrants from the country to mining compounds and cities, so the next generation followed migrating Mediterranean countrymen, first to the cities of the New World and then, as the economies of their own countries improved, to their own cities. The link between migration and urban life is explicit in this book, as is the concern for the lifestyle of the urban poor, of which migrants form such an important part. There are sound reasons for this bias.

Anthropologists who began to work in Europe following World War II sought out areas neglected by their numerous colleagues in other disciplines. These, by and large, had focused on the lives of the elite and the cities, civili-zations, and trading empires they had built. They cared little for the history and culture of the common men and women who had provided the labor to produce the food, build the cities, sail the ships, and fight the wars that made possible the glorious episodes of Mediterranean history they studied. Mediterranean anthropologists thus focused on these neglected areas, with considerable effect. Anthropologists have gone a long way toward extending our knowledge of neglected marginal groups. In short, this concern with common people has been one of the principal features of Mediterranean anthropology.[1] It is a bias we need not be ashamed of.[2] Historians like Le Roy Ladurie have come to share it.

This book is thus a welcome extension of an established tradition. The authors discuss both urban development in southern Europe and various aspects of city life there. These include family, kin and sex roles, religion and the church, politics and associations, and neighborhood and social identity. The focus, as maintained, is most clearly directed at the lifestyle of migrants and the urban poor. Future studies must deal with the lifestyle of the urban elite, who have yet to be studied by anthropologists. The world view, kinship patterns, and customs of the urban-dwelling captains of industry, professional politicians, and barons of the arts, universities, and media must also be studied. This elite controls the lives, molds the opinions, and influences the culture of the people of the Mediterranean. Yet very little is known about them.

Clearly anthropological research into urban life in Mediterranean Europe has well and truly begun. It is vital that it continues to develop.

Jeremy Boissevain

NOTES

1. In contrast, perhaps, to some African anthropology, which has been accused of a pro-elite orientation (Brown 1979:536–37).
2. Nor is it unscientific, as Thomas Crump appeared to think when he caustically wrote, "Now when it comes to Italy too many scholars appear to assume that the canons of *anthropological science* are satisfied by forcing the Italian population through a sort of sieve to leave only a residue of relatively isolated, partly illiterate, technically retarded, rural communities" (1975:20).

REFERENCES

Blok, Anton
    1972   Reflections on city-hinterland relations in Mediterranean Europe. *Sociologische Gids* 19:115–24.
Boissevain, Jeremy
    1970   *The Italians of Montreal: Immigrant adjustment in a plural society.* Ottawa: Information Canada.
Braudel, Fernand
    1973   *The Mediterranean and the Mediterranean world in the age of Phillip II,* vol. 2. London: Collins.

Brown, Richard
    1979   Passages in the life of a white anthropologist: Max Gluckman in northern
            Rhodesia. *Journal of African History* 20:525–41.
Caro Baroja, Julio
    1963   The city and the country: Reflections on some ancient commonplaces. In
            Julian A. Pitt-Rivers, ed., *Mediterranean countrymen: Essays in the social an-
            thropology of the Mediterranean.* Paris: Mouton, pp. 27–40.
Crump, Thomas
    1975   The context of European anthropology: The lesson from Italy. In Jeremy
            Boissevain and John Friedl, eds., *Beyond the community: Social process in Eu-
            rope.* The Hague: Department of Education and Science for the European
            Mediterranean Study Group of the University of Amsterdam, pp. 18–28.
Epstein, A. L.
    1958   *Politics in an urban African community.* Manchester: Manchester University
            Press.
Gans, Herbert J.
    1962   *The urban villagers.* New York: Free Press.
Mayer, Philip
    1961   *Townsmen or tribesmen: Conservatism and the process of urbanization in a South Af-
            rican city.* Cape Town: Oxford University Press.
Pitkin, Donald S.
    1963   Mediterranean Europe. *Anthropological Quarterly* 36:120–29.
Pons, Valdo
    1969   *Stanleyville: An African urban community under Belgian administration.* London:
            Oxford University Press for the International African Institute.
Redfield, Robert
    1956   *Peasant society and culture.* Chicago: University of Chicago Press.
Silverman, Sydel F.
    1975   *Three bells of civilization: The life of an Italian hill town.* New York: Columbia
            University Press.
Whyte, William F.
    1943   *Street corner society.* Chicago: University of Chicago Press.

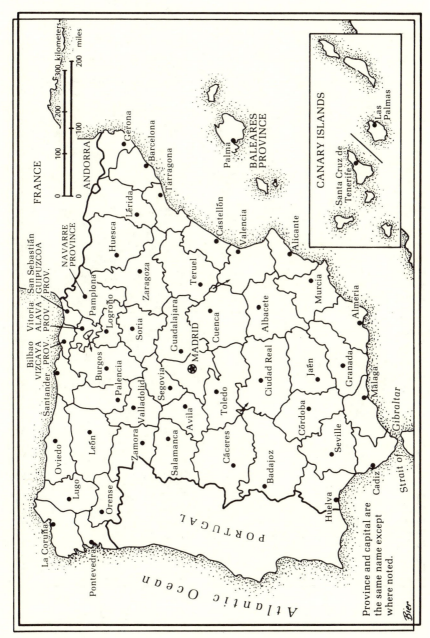

Spain

Province and capital are the same name except where noted.

FRANCE
ANDORRA

NAVARRE PROVINCE

San Sebastián GUIPUZCOA PROV.
Vitoria ALAVA PROV.
Bilbao VIZCAYA PROV.
Santander

La Coruña
Pontevedra
Lugo
Oviedo
Orense
León
Zamora
Pamplona
Logroño
Burgos
Palencia
Valladolid
Soria
Zaragoza
Huesca
Lérida
Gerona
Barcelona
Tarragona
Segovia
Avila
Salamanca
Guadalajara
MADRID
Cuenca
Teruel
Castellón
Valencia
Cáceres
Toledo
Ciudad Real
Albacete
Alicante
Murcia
Badajoz
Córdoba
Jaén
Granada
Almería
Seville
Huelva
Málaga
Cadiz
Gibraltar
Strait of Gibraltar

Atlantic Ocean
PORTUGAL

BALEARES PROVINCE
Palma

CANARY ISLANDS
Santa Cruz de Tenerife
Las Palmas

300 kilometers
200 miles
200
100
0
100
0

Bier

Italy

AUSTRIA

HUNGARY

0   100   200 kilometers

0   50   100   150 miles

Ljubljana
SLOVENIA

Zagreb
CROATIA

Karlovac

VOJVODINA

ROMANIA

Novi Sad

BELGRADE

Tuzla

BOSNIA-
HERZEGOVINA

SERBIA

Sarajevo

Kragujevac

Adriatic Sea

Split

Mostar

Niš

Nikšić

Priština

MONTENEGRO

KOSOVO-
METOHIJA

BULGARIA

Dubrovnik

Kotor
Cetinje

Titograd

ITALY

Skopje

MACEDONIA

Austro-Hungarian
Italian
Byzantine-Ottoman
Serbian
Montenegrin

ALBANIA

GREECE

Bier

Yugoslavia

Greece

Urban Life in Mediterranean Europe

Introduction

Michael Kenny and David I. Kertzer

What do anthropologists have to contribute to our understanding of urban life in Mediterranean Europe? And how do their studies promote the larger goal of anthropology in illuminating sociocultural processes? The chapters in this book provide some answers to these questions by identifying the results of urban anthropological investigation in four countries — Spain, Italy, Yugoslavia, and Greece — and by relating these to research being conducted by scholars in other disciplines.

There is now a well-established tradition of anthropological research in Mediterranean Europe, reflected in a body of literature that is remarkable both for its rich ethnographic qualities and for its heavily rural slant. There is a variety of reasons for this rural focus, which we discuss below. But it is this definition of anthropology's role in Mediterranean study that we intend to help alter through the publication of this volume. We believe that anthropologists can make an important contribution to our knowledge of urban life in Mediterranean Europe, and that anthropologists can no longer afford to ignore urban life in an area which has become heavily urban and which has, indeed, a long urban tradition.

In this introduction we first discuss the role of the anthropologist in urban study in Mediterranean Europe. We then turn to the substantive issues where we think anthropology is most likely to contribute. Finally, by highlighting the common issues that emerge in the various chapters of this book, we can identify and assess the significance of patterns of sociocultural homogeneity and diversity in the cities of Mediterranean Europe. We hope these 12 papers, written especially for this volume, will provide the basis for further efforts at comparison within Mediterranean Europe and beyond.

METHODOLOGICAL ISSUES IN URBAN ANTHROPOLOGICAL STUDY

There is certainly no dearth of research and writings on the cities of Mediterranean Europe. Indeed, the historical literature alone is massive, and the craft of local history has for centuries been a thriving enterprise in hundreds of urban centers throughout the area. Libraries are cluttered with works focusing on a single city alone. Nor are the historians alone. In recent years urban studies by sociologists, demographers, political scientists, urban planners, geographers, and others have appeared at a formidable rate. Given this large and growing corpus, and the anthropologists' role as new-comers on the urban "block," it is appropriate for those who champion urban anthropological research in Mediterranean Europe to justify their joining the scholarly crowd.[1]

Until World War II the study of the life of Mediterranean peoples was largely the preserve of the classicist and the classical archeologist. For that tradition we may perhaps thank, or blame, such diverse characters as Napo-leon and Lord Elgin, who were more concerned with pyramids and Grecian marbles than the contemporary descendants of the peoples who built them. For a variety of historical and political reasons, social scientific study devel-oped slowly in this part of the world; the nationally trained Mediterranean anthropologist is still a recent and uncommon phenomenon. For their part, foreign anthropologists were constrained by the mystique of "other cultures" and thus reluctant to study peoples who seemed much like themselves.

Even when this mystique began to fade and the emphasis on studying "primitives" or tribal peoples waned, foreign anthropologists (themselves generally the product of urban middle classes)[2] sought out marginal areas populated by nomads or peasants for their fieldwork in the Mediterranean. As was the case in other parts of the world (e.g. Africa and Latin America), anthropologists only began exploring the cities of the area in pursuit of the large numbers of their traditional peasant subjects who were themselves mi-grating to cities, or whose ties with the urban centers could no longer be ignored.

The first generation of anthropologists to undertake fieldwork in Medi-terranean Europe in the post–World War II years faced the skepticism of members of a discipline who regarded fieldwork as a period of professional initiation involving "roughing it" in technologically primitive societies radi-cally different from their own. From this perspective, it should not be sur-prising that the choice of an urban locale for research — a place viewed by other anthropologists as more suited for a vacation than an investigation — was either absent from or low on the list of potential research sites. Those few anthropologist precursors who did undertake urban fieldwork in the Mediterranean found themselves confronting not only the unfamiliar com-plexities of city research but also the dismal realization that they were inade-quately trained for urban study. Thus they suffered their own form of priva-tion; in their methodological desert they fabricated their own labyrinth of professional loneliness.

Over the past two decades urban study in anthropology has developed from the status of a stigmatized stepchild to the maturity of a recognized subfield in the discipline. In this process, which has developed further in the

Americas and in Africa than it has in continental Europe, the kinds of contributions that anthropologists can make to urban study have become clearer. These contributions derive both from anthropology's distinctive methodological heritage and from a body of sociocultural issues that has been analyzed in nonurban settings by anthropologists for several decades.

The promise of a distinctive anthropological contribution to urban research is in good part linked to our belief that participant observation as a basic anthropological field technique is not by its nature limited to the study of small-scale societies. This question has been heatedly argued elsewhere (Fallers 1974:19, Hannerz 1969:14, Gallin and Gallin 1974, Plotnicov 1973). Others (see, e.g., Sweet 1980) decry the technique as overrated, as an anthropological "fetish" resulting in parochialism and often ignoring context and history. More than programmatic statements of the appropriateness of participant observation to urban research, such incisive studies as Cohen's (1969) in Nigeria and Stack's (1974) in the United States have gone far toward proving the point. We refer, of course, to intensive fieldwork carried out over a lengthy and preferably continuous period, not "nine to five" or weekend anthropology. Moreover, we maintain that participant observation — however basic — is but the contextual aspect of a battery of such techniques with which the urban fieldworker should commit himself to the field. These techniques still need much refinement, though some (e.g., the ethnoscience variety and network analysis) are already in extensive use.

What the good participant observation study does is to provide a view of how people's lives are actually lived. This may seem simple and obvious enough, yet it is far from a common approach to urban study. The local sociocultural context is rarely investigated by scholars from other disciplines, except in highly partial and abstract ways. Heavy reliance by sociologists on survey, formal inverview, ecological and attitudinal approaches has meant that few sociologists have systematically explored the sociocultural context of Mediterranean life. Political scientists, even within their more restricted substantive focus, have likewise tended to slight the way in which political processes are enmeshed in locally based social relations, concentrating instead on more institutionally focused research, complemented by attitudinal surveying and electoral analysis. Their emphasis is generally on vertical ties as opposed to the anthropologist's concern with horizontal multifaceted relationships.

Through participant observation anthropologists are able to relate what people say they think and what they say they do with the ways in which they actually behave. Here again, the more commonly found survey and other interview techniques provide a more limited portrait of social life, and one that has few meaningful controls on validity. Indeed, one of the most important areas of anthropological research is just this relationship between what people state as their beliefs and norms and the ways in which they really act. This question is hardly less important in understanding urban social life than it is in understanding life in rural areas.

Participant observation research must be employed in the proper context, however, or the emerging view of social life will be misleading and the value of the observations limited for any explanation of behavior. If much of urban anthropology so far has been disappointingly parochial in scope, this is not the fault of anthropological technique as such but, rather, its misuse or lack of refinement. Whether studying life in a city or in a small hamlet, it is inadequate to confine the analysis to the locality. People's lives may be physically lived within the borders of a town (though often they are lived over thousands of kilometers of territory through time), yet extralocal processes have an impact on their lives. To argue for the value of participant observation studies, then, is not to defend the concept of community studies as these were originally conceived and carried out.[3] The linkages between the people being studied and the larger economic, political, and sociocultural system in which they are enmeshed must be traced out and understood if we are ever to achieve a satisfactory explanation of their own behavior and perceptions.

Given the vast number of such extralocal linkages found in the urban context, it is necessary to focus any urban anthropological research on a limited series of problems. One possible approach is to conceive of the city as a metroplex (a complex of urban systems), as outlined by Leonard Duhl (1969) in *The Urban Condition*. In this framework the city can be viewed as a problem-producing environment (e.g., mental illness) on the one hand, and a resource provider (e.g., structured leisure) on the other.[4] Such strategies enable us to fractionalize our holistic perspective without having to compartmentalize our foci into the limited frames of single disciplines. They also nudge us toward concepts of community considerably different from those traditionally used in community study. Rather than conceiving of a community as territorially based, it is perceived as a communicative community — more often than not dispersed — whose bounds are limited by a social, not a territorial, field. Compare the difference between a community of the faithful (in the sense of a dispersed religious denomination) and a community of friars (in a monastery).

Whether we call these units of study "communities" or "organized social groups" or "associations" is largely a matter of approach. A typology of such "open" fluid communities would be characterized by variables like specificity of purpose, role and norm diversity, or varying degrees of access to power structures, all familiar enough in sociological theory. Yet since these are not the natural communities we are used to studying but are often intentionally planned, we must study the reasons why they are united, how they are united (e.g., coalitions, formal associations, networks, patronage groups) and the occasions on which they unite (thus requiring situational or event analysis) within the particular contextual framework of the city. How such formal and informal groupings and networks operate in a struggle for economic privilege and political power provides one of the most challenging questions for the urban anthropologist.[5]

Does a shift in anthropological attention to urban life mean giving up all pretense at striving for an unattainable holistic view of social life? This question has generated considerable polemic in recent years, since some anthropologists have argued that it is only by retaining such holism and dealing with cities as social-cultural units that anthropology can make a meaningful contribution to urban study. This position has perhaps been most forcefully articulated by Richard Fox, who has chastised anthropologists for focusing on life in the city rather than on the city itself as a subject of study: "For the anthropologist interested in cross-cultural comparison or analysis of urban development, the city becomes only one of the many institutions such as kinship, value systems, and subsistence activity which he has always treated as parts of a sociocultural whole. This 'super-organic' approach to urbanism absolves the anthropologist of the psychological and sociological reductionism implicit in studying city men, families, and associations on urban streets and corners" (1972:47). Far from establishing a unique anthropological approach to urban study, we would argue that such a focus risks retreading the path pursued for several decades by urban sociologists and, more recently, by political economists in characterizing the nature of cities and the relationship of cities to the societies of which they are a part. The fact that these macrolevel issues have already been undertaken by other disciplines would prove no bar to a fresh anthropological approach if anthropologists were particularly suited to such study. Yet so far we have seen no convincing demonstration that, as a discipline, anthropology has a major contribution to make to the study of cities as units of social organization.

Related to this issue is the complaint by Leeds (1968) that anthropologists have used the city simply as a research locale and have not attended to the question of how social processes are influenced by the city. Thus he castigates anthropologists for asking "How is kinship operating in the city?" and not "What is the effect of cityness on the operation of kinship?" (1968:31). Cohen takes issue with this position, maintaining that the city is important to anthropological research not as an object of special study but as a rich ground of diverse sociocultural elements, affording "ideal 'laboratory' conditions" for cultural study. He argues that "the search for *special principles* governing urban life is a blind alley for sociological research. A great deal of what is called 'urban sociology' is not sociology but is mainly a description of human ecology. When, on the other hand, an urban study *is* sociological, then it is no longer necessarily urban, but is just sociological. As Mitchell points out, the town should be treated as *a social field,* not as a single social system" (1969:214).

While Fox's treatment of the city as an institution on the order of kinship leaves us unconvinced, there is something to be said for the analysis of the sociocultural impact of urban living as *one* of the questions anthropologists working on urban life might investigate. In such study, nevertheless, the various elements that together are identified with urban life (e.g., density, economic activity, political position) must be untangled and their separate and interacting effects on urban life examined. Even so, the point must be made here, and later, that urban anthropology is surely something more than the study of a city.

Whether or not anthropologists formally collaborate with scholars from other disciplines, they must rely heavily on the work of those other disciplines if their work is to have any value. The anthropological tradition, developed in field situations far removed from that of other scholars, all too often casts the anthropologist as the sole academic authority on "his" society. In the cities of Mediterranean Europe such an attitude would be highly presumptuous, to say the least. The anthropologist studying the relationship between economic change and family life, for example, must rely on both economists and demographers to provide the necessary data and complementary perspectives. Again, no study of patronage can afford to ignore the work done by political scientists on the political system at both national and local levels. In turn, other scholars must surely welcome the sensitive quality of the primary data gathered by the urban anthropologist, as seen in Part Three of this volume.

The relationship between anthropologists and historians deserves special consideration here, for the past decade has seen exciting rapprochement of these two disciplines. In the past, European historiography — both rural and urban — depended heavily on the study of the elites and the institutions chronicled by the elite. Over the past two decades, however, there has been a growing shift in emphasis, a strong revisionist movement focusing on social history. This movement itself is composed of multivarious components, but its general unifying thread is the goal of revealing how common people have lived in the past, whether they be rural peasants or urban proletarians. It is of no small significance that in article after article and book after book to come out of this initiative, particularly in France and Britain, historians are called upon by their colleagues to look to anthropology for guidance.

At the same time, anthropologists have grown increasingly sensitive to the historical dimension as they have moved from a more static structural functionalism to questions of sociocultural change, conflict, and materialist explanations of society. Not only are anthropologists in Mediterranean Europe paying more attention to the historical documentation related to understanding contemporary ethnographic observations, but more and more they are seeing the entire historical record as a source of ethnographic data to be examined. The by now all too familiar charge that anthropologists working in the Mediterranean have ignored history (see, e.g., Davis 1977) is no longer an accurate characterization of anthropological work in this area. For example, since 1972, on Italy alone, at least eight anthropologists have published exclusively urban research; none of these appear in the Davis (1977) collection. All of them (though varied in their use of historical sources) are discussed in this volume, as are others appropriate to Spain, Greece, and Yugoslavia.

CITY LIFE IN MEDITERRANEAN EUROPE

The extent to which the nations of southern Europe share an urban tradition is very much an open question. These nations were exposed through the centuries to many of the same historical forces — the Greek and Roman empires, the expansion of Catholicism and Islam, the impact of eastern and northern invasions, and the development of world trade markets — yet these cultural influences affected each of these lands in different ways. Indeed, even within the bounds of what are now the nation-states of the area there are dramatic regional differences in urban development and urban life. The nature of these differences is made evident through reading the chapters in Parts One and Two of this volume; here we draw out for emphasis some of the salient elements.

Owing to the ravages of foreign occupiers, both Greece and Yugoslavia were overwhelmingly rural in population until the past century. Indeed, as late as 1832 there were no large cities at all in Greece, while in 1867 Belgrade had but 24,000 inhabitants. With the lengthy Ottoman control of the urban centers in Yugoslavia, the native population had long taken to the hinterland, leaving the small cities to become largely foreign enclaves until the nineteenth century. Only in 1976 did Yugoslavia's largest city, Belgrade, reach the total of one million inhabitants.

By contrast, both Spain and Italy have had more continuous urban traditions, though in each case there was (and there remains) considerable regional concentration of rural and urban populations. Of all the nations considered in this volume, Italy has the greatest proliferation and the widest distribution of urban centers, though the industrial cities of Italy are concentrated in the northwest (both Spain and Italy have their respective industrial urban triangles mainly in the northwest regions). Greece provides the classic case of a primate city in Athens, wherein one-third of the population of the nation is now congregated, while only two other cities in Greece have as many as 100,000 inhabitants. Yugoslavia's situation reflects longstanding regional and ethnic polarities, with two dominant cities: Belgrade, the capital of Serbia and now political center of the nation, and Zagreb, capital of Croatia and economic nodal point of the nation. Long one of Europe's most rural areas, and as late as 1921 having 87% of its population living in villages of fewer than 20,000 people, Yugoslavia today is rapidly approaching the day when half of its population will be living in urban localities. Spain had already reached the point of becoming a predominantly urban country in the 1960s. Thus today there is much less disparity between the two western and the two eastern nations of Mediterranean Europe than had been the case half a century ago. Indeed, the four countries have shared the common experience over the past three decades of the progressive depopulation of the rural hinterland as large numbers of rural dwellers have crowded into the nations' urban centers.

The Rural-Urban Dichotomy

Given the tremendous urban growth in these countries, it is tempting to view the city as representing the antithesis of "traditional" rural life, as a sophisticated, cosmopolitan center standing in social and cultural opposition to its rural hinterland. In its classic conception this is the image of the historical *polis*—the characteristic physical and social unit of civilization, the locus of "Great Traditions," the home of the "cultured" *urbanus et instructus* gentleman-scholar. But, as the authors of the chapters in this volume make clear, this burdensome heritage of earlier conceptual models based on a rural-urban dichotomy has given us a static and homogeneous view of these misleadingly contrasted poles. This has held true even when the model of urbanization was extended to include not only processes operative in the city (i.e., urbanism) but also those influences extended to the implanting of the urban model in the countryside (see, e.g., the idea of the agro-town). These conceptual and methodological blinders were not conducive to studies of processual links between country and town, nor did they foster clear perception of the very diversity of urbanism that exerted differential impact on dependent rural hinterlands. It is notable in this regard that few have thought to study the demise of cities (e.g., Tangiers) as well as their growth.

In fact, differences in social experience are often greater within the city than between the city and the rural hinterland. Moreover, in countries such as Italy some rural areas are much more heavily industrialized than are many cities. Likewise, the importance of voluntary associations, a classic feature of urbanism in the rural-urban literature (Wirth 1938), is often greater in rural communities than in cities (e.g., compare the wealth of communist- and Church-related associational life in the small *paesi* of northern and central Italy with the dearth of associational life among the poor of southern Italian cities).

Therefore, we must deplore a regrettable tendency among scholars in the Mediterranean and elsewhere to equate urban anthropology with the study of the city alone. The nucleated settlement pattern and the "urban" quality of even village life there confound any facile rural-urban dichotomy. But it also confirms our view that the development of urban anthropological theory must be founded on a conceptualization of the "urban" which goes beyond the margins of a place we call a city or town into the very complexities of Mediterranean society at large.

This viewpoint has particular implications for the role of anthropological research in urban Mediterranean study. The goal is not to establish a distinctively urban societal type but to investigate the variations in social life throughout the area and to determine how important the rural-urban distinction is. This issue is also very much a matter of the people's own image of their social universe, for the rural-urban distinction gives rise to many invidious social judgments made by the people of the area themselves (witness the ubiquitous sociocentrism and the scornful group pejoratives that derive from this). The fact that inhabitants of a population center of less than one thousand can conceive of themselves as representatives of the urban *civitas* in central Italy (Silverman 1975) should alert us to the fact that the rural-urban contrast made by demographers and others may lead us to ignore — however inadvertently — much of the latent cultural meaning of "urban" in this part of the world.

Urban Study by Indigenous Anthropologists

In all four countries considered here, modern social anthropology has been rather slow to develop. Its development has clearly been hampered by the recent political history of the nations in question, for authoritarian governments are seldom conducive to an independent social science. Greek social science still finds itself in an early period of development, with little institutionalization of social scientific research, teaching, and publication. In Italy the fascist period certainly had an inhibiting effect on social science, but the barriers to the development of an empirical sociology and anthropology went beyond this to the Crocian idealism permeating intellectual life. The exile of many scholars and intellectuals after the Civil War in Spain (1936–39) and subsequent strict censorship resulted in what Spanish sociologists call "the underground years" for much of the Franco regime (1939–75). Field study enjoyed little professional stature, and the emphasis by budding anthropologists was on social history and folklore or archeology.

While anthropology developed slowly in these countries, it was generally less hampered by any perceived necessity for going outside the home country to conduct research than was found in the world's major anthropological centers. This attitude can be linked, perhaps, to the absence of colonial outposts for Greece and Yugoslavia and to the limited colonial spheres of Italy and Spain. It seems that only in the case of Spain, with its Latin American connection, was fieldwork largely identified with non-national research sites. The Italians made the most of their minuscule African empire, but from its beginning anthropological fieldwork was carried out within the nation-state.

One final but important point about indigenous anthropology and the social sciences in Mediterranean Europe should be made. In all four countries marxian perspectives have come to play a major role. This is obvious in the case of Yugoslavia, but, as the authors of Part One show, the new guard of social science scholars in Spain, Italy, and Greece are also heavily influenced by marxism. Anthropologists in these countries are not unique in this regard, for much of intellectual life in these nations revolves around marxian thought. Such an intellectual stance plays an important role in the development of urban anthropological studies in this area, with heavy emphasis going to issues directly related to class struggle; thus many of the more traditional anthropological topics, less obviously linked to class conflict (e.g., family, religion), receive little attention. It is a curious fact that while this marxian approach also comes partly as a reaction against the elitist idealism which had been intellectually ascendant in academic circles in these countries, many (but not all) of the marxian scholars share with the earlier idealist scholars a reluctance for, if not an aversion to, prolonged fieldwork and a lack of interest in ethnography, urban or otherwise.

Cultural Norms of the City People

In evaluating the extent to which urban dwellers in Mediterranean Europe partake of a culture distinct from that of their rural countrymen, some comparison must be made of the principal values informing life in the city and life in the country. Insofar as anthropologists and others have painted rural Mediterranean life as dominated by the concern for one's family and kin group, however defined, the question is posed as to whether the classic conception of the city as embodying more universalistic values is accurate for this part of the world. Put in terms of the Weberian ideal of modernism, do the people of the cities have a more "modern" cultural orientation? Are they less familistically oriented than rural dwellers?

This issue is treated, in one way or another, by many of the contributors to this volume. The Yugoslav literature, as both Spangler and Simić point out, emphasizes the lack of any such cultural differentiation between city and village. The title of Simić's book on Belgrade, *The Peasant Urbanites,* emphasizes this claim that the cities have been infused with a rural-based culture in which the values of kinship and personalistic bases of recruitment and interaction take precedence over more universalistic principles. Sutton tells us that, owing to their long history of oppression, the urban Greeks continue to rely heavily on their families for material and emotional assistance, and remain suspicious in dealing with non-kinsmen. Belmonte, working in a slum of Naples, has identified a similar pattern of permanent suspicion toward nonfamily members, and ties this to a larger cultural pattern of the Mediterranean. For Belmonte, however, the family cannot be seen as a haven from this hostile world, because the family itself may be fraught with tensions. The myth of the united and strong family unit in the Mediterranean does not, of course, exclude but frequently masks serious divisions within its ranks. Yet this reality does not necessarily reflect a "breakdown" of the family directly related to urban life as classically portrayed in the Wirthian analysis of the 1930s.

At this early point in urban anthropological study in Mediterranean Europe, perhaps anthropology's most palpable contribution has been the empirical questioning of widely held assumptions about the traditional-modern, rural-urban polarity. It can no longer be easily assumed that city life is based on more universalistic values than those found outside the cities. However, we now need to go beyond these preliminary warning flags to get to the requisite level of detail. What is the role of one's economic position within the city in determining universalism of values? What differences are found among different types of cities (e.g., commercial versus administrative, mining or company town versus agro-town) in this characteristic? What processes are operating to erode the personalist or familist value system in the cities? Are these any different from the processes of change found in the countryside today?

Urban Social Organization

The strength, sometimes the weakness, but always the importance of the family unit in the cities of Mediterranean Europe are illustrated throughout this book. The stage of premarital independence from one's family of origin, common in the United States, for example, is not a characteristic of these societies. Young men and especially young women are expected to continue co-residing with their parents until their marriage. Nor is marriage contracted at an early age as it often is in America.

Despite the centrality of family life in this area and the fact that the family is idealized by the people themselves, we know precious little empirically about family interaction and the life-course experiences of people in the family context as they and their parents age and their own children are born and grow older. In Italy, for example, the family is widely seen as the cornerstone of social life, yet we do not even have good data on the patterns and personalities involved in co-residence. What happens, for example, when a woman becomes a widow? Where does she go to live? Who supports her? Similarly, while much has been written about parents' relations with their young children, we have virtually no life-course studies of how these relations change as the children become adults and the parents become elderly. Generational and gerontological studies are notable for their absence in the Mediterranean.

It is also clear from the chapters in this book that relations with kinsmen beyond the household, outside the immediate family, can be of extreme importance. This is most strikingly seen in Yugoslavia, where in the past the traditional patrilineage was the focus of social control. Here we have a case where traditional kinship principles have been not abandoned but, rather, adapted in the city to meet the challenges of the new environment. Hence, while the patrilineage itself has become less influential as the dominant organizational form, bilateral kinship relations are much more often resorted to. Ironically, then, kinship ties outside the patrilineal reckoning (i.e., with those related through one's mother and one's affines) have become more important in the city than they were traditionally in many rural areas. In a similar vein, rural migrants to the city, confronting a tight or expensive housing market, may be more likely to call on kinsmen for immediate aid than they would be in their home village.

Another related issue attracting considerable recent attention is the status of women in the city. The question of women's status has held a special place in the Mediterranean anthropological literature, especially through the debate on honor and shame as cultural characteristics of the area. The honor and shame constructs, however, are rooted in a model of rural social organization that by no means appears to be always applicable to city life.[6] To what extent are urban family units preoccupied with the "purity" of their women? More broadly and more fundamentally, how are women's lives constrained by cultural conceptions of women's roles and how are their behavior and their life choices constrained by various structural obstacles they confront in the city?

One key question concerns the participation of women in the labor force. In Spain, Italy, and Greece young women commonly find extra-domestic employment during the years before their marriage or their first pregnancy, but generally drop out of the labor force at that point. Here we find regional differences within countries as well; for example, women in northern regions are more likely to go back to work as their children grow older (or not to leave work in the first place) than are women in southern regions. In Yugoslavia, where state policy encourages sexual equality in the workplace, this pattern is apparently less marked, though we need more study of just what cultural norms are operative here.

It is not clear that urban women lead more "liberated" lives than do their rural counterparts in Mediterranean Europe. In Greece the arranged marriage and the dowry are apparently no less common in the city than in the countryside. Vermeulen and Hirschon even suggest that in some ways the sexual dichotomy is more "traditional" in the city than in rural Greece, a point similarly made for Seville in Spain. Industrial work has not, so far at least, led to female emancipation.

The organization of leisure time activities outside the circle of kinsmen appears to be undergoing a change in Mediterranean European cities. Here the classic social gathering place in the city as in the countryside was the café, a center for adult male socializing but also for conducting much business. Conspicuous, sedentary leisure in the urban center was *the* essential element in the Spanish concept of "the good life." A number of social changes have taken place, however, that threaten and fragment this pattern, ranging from television to the efforts of various organizations to organize leisure time activities more formally. The advent of high-rise developments also seems to threaten the residential neighborhood as a unit of social identity and interaction. However, new forms of neighborhood organization have sprung up too, as the Spanish case of tenants' and squatters' associations demonstrates. The local capillary organization of political parties in Spain, Italy, and Greece provides another mechanism for the reorganization of neighborhood life and the institutionalization of neighborhood distinctions.

These parties represent another phenomenon of interest to those seeking out the differences between rural and urban life, for in them are found the possibilities for patron-client relations in the city. This brings us back again to the issue of universalism versus particularism in the city. Urban research has clearly demonstrated that the anthropologist's tendency to identify patron-client relations with rural social organization may be misleading. In the cities of Spain, Italy, Greece, and Yugoslavia the art of clientelism continues to flourish. There is no evidence that patron-client relations are any the less important to the urbanite than to the rural dweller. The nature and importance of the local and national bureaucracies in these countries are such that life without the "proper" connections can be difficult. Yet we would expect there to be differences among the economic strata of the city in how such ties are used and differences within and between countries in the nature of these ties. Again, however, the sources of variation have less to do with the rural-urban distinction than with such factors as the political identity of the locally ascendant party.

Migration

As the chapters in Part Two of this volume make clear, rural-urban migration in the countries of Mediterranean Europe has had a massive social impact in the post–World War II period. The cities of both Greece and Yugoslavia are still today largely inhabited by people born and reared in rural areas. Yet it should also be clear that migration is not a new phenomenon in these countries. Legion are the accounts of foreign invasion, warfare, plagues, and economic changes that have led to large-scale migration in past centuries. Moreover, in the rural sector in many areas *rural-rural* migration was an economic necessity. These patterns of migration continue to change, as we see from the increasing *urban-urban* migration of the 1970s. While in the 1950s migration was largely internal, much of the rural-urban migration in the 1960s and 1970s was directed toward the richer countries of northern Europe, with Spanish, Italian, Greek, and Yugoslav migrants flooding into the factories and construction sites of France, Germany, Switzerland, and other European countries.

What is striking about the analyses of rural-urban migration we find in these chapters is the similarity of experience among migrants in these different countries, and the many characteristics they share with migrants in other parts of the world. The initial decision to move and choice of destination are largely conditioned by the presence of kinsmen and, secondarily, *paesani* (fellow villagers or countrymen) in the city of destination. Ties with these kinsmen and countrymen are utilized to help get settled in the city through the classic form of chain migration. Even when, as in the majority of cases today, the migrant will never return to his hometown, contacts with the hometown are nevertheless maintained and utilized for a variety of purposes. Regular visits are made to the hometown, often on ritually prescribed occasions (e.g., Christmas, Easter, and the community's patron saint fiestas), and property ownership in the hometown is common. Migrants from the village may become the most important political personages in village life, given their contacts with the bureaucracies that control the lifeblood of the rural communities.

The extent to which this also means that people's lives in the cities are organized around hometown ties is variable. In Athens some of the cafés are identified with particular rural areas, and regional associations are organized to work on behalf of the village. This is remarkably similar to the pattern found in a number of Latin American countries. In Italy southern migrants to the cities of the north face local prejudice and, in confronting it, turn to ties with *paesani* as well as with their kin. Similarly, migrants from the agricultural south of Spain to Catalonia and the Basque country in the industrial northwest must face additional discrimination for not knowing the regional language.

RATIONALE AND OVERVIEW

The motives for composing this volume in its present form and organization are uncomplicated but require explanation. It is not for us here to justify the Mediterranean as a discrete entity, as a coherent and distinctive culture area, or as a specific field of interaction with a characteristic history of conquest and commerce. Attempts on this score have been amply discussed elsewhere (see, e.g., Ehrich 1956, Davis 1977, Boissevain 1979) and will always excite controversial debate. While the term "circum-Mediterranean" connoted a specific and common area of concern for the professional anthropologist since at least the 1950s, its emphasis lay more in the content and culture within its boundaries rather than in its interaction with other culture areas. While the materialist parameters of sea, climate, terrain, and mode of production, " . . . placed in a comparative historical framework, provide a basis on which various differences and similarities characteristic of Mediterranean societies may be usefully compared . . . " (Boissevain 1979), a

fashionable conceptual model of the 1970s (see Pi-Sunyer 1974) preferred to view the Mediterranean in terms of dependency theory and its increasing marginalization vis-à-vis Europe proper. Nevertheless, a treatment of the culture area as a whole is beyond the scope of this volume.

That we have limited our coverage to four countries only is not simply a question of budgeted space. The four countries that we chose — Spain, Italy, Greece, and Yugoslavia — are not merely those most representative of the European Mediterranean but are the ones for which we have available the more voluminous and informative studies of the *urban* scene. Thus to the question of size we add the consideration of balance; we wanted a set, not a mere collection of papers.

To that end, in the design of this volume we have interrelated three complementary foci in such a way that a common format reflects a similar treatment for each of the four countries. This format comprises a national survey of urban research, a national survey of internal rural-urban migration research, and a case study for each country illustrating the quality of urban life in a specific town or city — Naples in Italy, Seville in Spain, Athens-Piraeus in Greece, and Zelena jama in Yugoslavia.

The reader will note that the four chapters in Part Three not only provide geographic diversity by focusing on individual cities but also reflect a broad spectrum of anthropological approaches to urban Mediterranean study. These approaches range from the historical-ethnological tradition developed in central Europe, demonstrated in Kremenšek's study of a Ljubljana suburb, to the British-inspired social organizational approach so well exemplified in Hirschon's study of marriage in Piraeus. For their part, both Gregory and Belmonte provide perspectives on the cultural creation of reality in the city. Yet Gregory's study of Seville also attempts to examine the city as a whole in changing political and economic terms, whereas Belmonte is more concerned with providing a vivid image of the quality of life as experienced in a single Neapolitan neighborhood. We do not here intend to express our own preferences for one or another of these approaches; our views are made clear in Chapters 1 and 2. In fact, the disagreements are merely variants of methodological and theoretical divergences common to anthropology in general. By presenting the range of approaches that we do in this book, we hope to contribute to the ongoing debate about the means by which anthropologists can make the most valuable contribution to urban study.

It is clear that our contributors have made good use of studies by other disciplines and that anthropologists in general must continue to do so, yet not solely in order to complement their highly qualitative microdata with a quantitative macrobase. Urban anthropologists should resist the temptation to concentrate only on urban exotica and marginals, to substitute the "sensational" in the city for the erstwhile "exotic" in the tribe, to exhaust their professional energies on the exposé more characteristic of investigative journalism. They must lift their eyes from the local scene blinkered, perhaps, in the past by the classic community approach. As they do, so too their comparative and analytical frame will widen to include a truly pan-Mediterranean perspective. In order to achieve this wider compass, a closer collaboration with their social science colleagues and national anthropologists in Mediterranean countries must surely ensue. Whether or not this collaboration will inevitably result in team research as such on the urban scene, the urban anthropologist will indulge more in a consortium of effort than his traditional lone-wolf pursuits of the past have allowed for. Before urban anthropologists can have a significant impact on their social science colleagues, they will need to clarify the goals and methods of their own sub-discipline as well as their personal involvement in fieldwork.

Until quite recently the anthropologist exercised a plentiful freedom of choice in selecting his topic of research. This is less true of the urban anthropologist today. Constraints imposed by colleagues and demands by the people to be studied in the urban Mediterranean will grow, channeled perhaps in some cases into "contractual" anthropology or public anthropology lines of research. A new accountability will accompany this opening up of anthropology. Willy-nilly, as they move into action anthropology, urban fieldworkers are directed more and more into participant *intervention* rather than the classic but passive participant *observation*, whether as "passionate partisans" or involved professionals. Choice of both topic and method will therefore narrow further.

Explicitly or by implication, the authors in this volume have highlighted a number of topics that cry out for further study by the urban anthropologist. They include many related to a now dominant trend in urbanization, such as the growth and impact of new middle classes, leisure patterns, cultures of the poor and the newly rich, new forms of association such as neighborhood councils and housing cooperatives. Others are related more to rapid social change occurring in the cities: the growth of Protestant sects in Catholic countries such as Spain and Italy, the changing bases for *campanilismo* and chauvinism in metropolitan neighborhoods such as in Madrid or Naples. Some of these topics and others, such as the emergence of new political forms and parties or the consolidation of power by trade unions, were impossible as feasible research subjects until recent years, given the presence of authoritarian governments. Still more may be subsumed in the context of modernization, commercialization, increasing marginality, and emancipation that Boissevain (1974:26) claims are characteristic of the contemporary Mediterranean. Thus he would also advocate the anthropology of development, the impact of long-term processes of industrialization, tourism, and regional protest (and, we would add, its by-product, terrorism). Boissevain (1979) points the way to a specific and fruitful topic for future research when he speaks of the general shift from patronage to brokerage roles as governments, parties, unions, and industries grow powerful and complex and thus become the focus of lengthening chains of intermediaries mobilized to gain access to the resources they control. Such topics straddle various subareas of the Mediterranean more effectively. The Spanish sociologists Linz and Miguel (1966) have shown us the way with a typology of regions within a nation-state (Spain) that facilitates comparison with similar regions in other Mediterranean countries. Few anthropologists have attempted anything of this order, although Gellner (1968), Wolf (1969), Schneider (1971), and Boissevain (1976) are commendable exceptions.

Problems of poverty, violence, oppression, racism, alienation, and disease and their manifestation in class differences, educational systems, and values, are also rampant in all metropolises. They are no less prevalent in the Mediterranean. They, like the above, urgently claim the professional attention and compassion of the urban anthropologist.

NOTES

1. Our views here have been stimulated — and contended — by such colleagues as Julian Pitt-Rivers, Ernestine Friedl, and Louise Sweet. We thank them for their helpful comments, but our position here should not be taken as necessarily representing their views.
2. But not necessarily a product of the structural-functionalist tradition in anthropology. In fact, the presence of the earliest fieldworkers in the Mediterranean could be taken as evidence of their disapproval of traditionalist strictures, as Pitt-Rivers (1979:89) points out.
3. The literature attacking community studies on these grounds is prodigious. For a flavor of some of the most recent polemic in a European context, see Boissevain (1979) and Brandes (1979).
4. Of course, rural communities could also be conceptualized in similar terms.
5. This point is forcibly expressed in Cohen (1974).
6. The applicability of the honor/shame concept to rural Mediterranean life itself is a matter of debate; see, for example, Kenny and Knipmeyer in this volume and also Herzfeld (1980:339–51), who maintains that they are inefficient English-language glosses for a wide variety of indigenous terminological systems and therefore inadequate for the purposes of cross-cultural analysis.

REFERENCES

Boissevain, Jeremy
    1974   *Friends of friends.* Oxford: Basil Blackwell.
    1976   Uniformity and diversity in the Mediterranean: An essay in interpretation. In John G. Peristiany, ed., *Kinship and modernization.* Rome: Center for Mediterranean Studies, American Universities Field Staff, pp. 1–11.
    1979   Towards a social anthropology of the Mediterranean. *Current Anthropology* 20:81–93.

Brandes, Stanley H.
    1979   Comment. *Current Anthropology* 20:86.
Cohen, Abner
    1969   *Custom and politics in urban Africa.* Berkeley: University of California Press.
    1974   *Two-dimensional man.* Berkeley: University of California Press.
Davis, John
    1977   *People of the Mediterranean. An essay in comparative social anthropology.* London:
            Routledge and Kegan Paul.
Duhl, Leonard
    1969   *The urban condition.* New York: Simon and Schuster.
Ehrich, Robert W.
    1956   Culture area and culture history in the Mediterranean and Middle East.
            In Saul S. Weinberg, ed., *The Aegean and the Near East,* New York:
            Augustine.
Fallers, Lloyd A.
    1974   *The social anthropology of the nation state.* Chicago: Aldine.
Fox, Richard G.
    1972   Rationale and romance in urban anthropology. *Urban Anthropology*
            1:205–33.
Gallin, Bernard, and Rita Schlesinger Gallin
    1974   The rural-to-urban migration of an anthropologist in Taiwan. In George
            M. Foster and Robert V. Kemper, eds., *Anthropologists in cities.* Boston:
            Little, Brown, pp. 223–48.
Gellner, Ernest
    1968   Sanctity, puritanism, secularization, and nationalism in North Africa. In
            John G. Peristiany, ed., *Contributions to Mediterranean sociology.* The
            Hague: Mouton, pp. 31–48.
Hannerz, Ulf
    1969   *Soulside.* New York: Columbia University Press.
Herzfeld, Michael
    1980   Honour and shame: Problems in the comparative analysis of moral
            systems. *Man* 15:339–51.
Leeds, Anthony
    1968   The anthropology of cities: Some methodological issues. In Elizabeth M.
            Eddy, ed., *Urban anthropology.* Southern Anthropological Society Pro-
            ceedings, vol. 2. Athens: University of Georgia Press, pp. 31–47.
Linz, Juan J., and Amando de Miguel
    1966   Within-nation differences and comparisons: The eight Spains. In
            Richard L. Merritt and Stein Rokkan, eds., *Comparing nations: The use of
            quantitative data in cross-cultural research.* New Haven, Conn., Yale Univer-
            sity Press, pp. 267–319.
Pi-Sunyer, Oriol
    1974   Elites and noncorporate groups in the European Mediterranean: A
            reconsideration of the Catalan case. *Comparative Studies in Society and
            History* 16:117–31.
Pitt-Rivers, Julian A.
    1979   Comment. *Current Anthropology* 20:89
Plotnicov, Leonard
    1973   Anthropological field work in modern and local urban contexts. *Urban
            Anthropology* 2:248–64.

Schneider, Jane
  1971   Of vigilance and virgins. *Ethnology* 9:1–24.
Silverman, Sydel F.
  1975   *Three bells of civilization: The life of an Italian hill town.* New York: Columbia
            University Press.
Stack, Carol B.
  1974   *All our kin.* New York: Harper and Row.
Sweet, Louise
  1980   Personal communication.
Wirth, Louis
  1938   Urbanism as a way of life. *American Journal of Sociology* 44:1–24.
Wolf, Eric R.
  1969   Society and symbols in Latin Europe and in the Islamic Near East: Some
            comparisons. *Anthropological Quarterly* 42:287–301.

PART ONE: CITIES AND URBAN RESEARCH

Chapter **1**

Urban Research in Spain:
Retrospect and Prospect

Michael Kenny and Mary C. Knipmeyer

The Romanization of Hispania in the third century B.C. has been described as " . . . a cultural saturation that was more complete and enduring than elsewhere in the Empire, other than in Italy" (Violich 1962:171).[1] That this cultural transplant was achieved unilaterally through a remarkable system of cities should not blind us to the fact that the three million or so Celtiberians then in the Iberian peninsula had their own indigenous urban settlements. Pockets of Greek immigrants, too, founded their *polis* (e.g., Ampuries, on the Mediterranean coast) as early as the sixth century B.C. Our first theme meriting emphasis, therefore, is the long tradition of this nucleated clustering, an "urbanism" notable even in the connotation of the term "pueblo," and evident in the so-called agro-towns. Yet not until 1970 A.D. did a majority (55% +) of the total population (some 35 million Spaniards) live in cities of over 20,000 people, with more than 37% living in cities of over 100,000 (Keefe *et al.* 1976:78–79). The accelerated rate of urbanization in Spain has been dramatic and recent.

Our second theme must emphasize the sociological opposition and political imbalance created by Roman urban transplants within an already markedly diverse regionalism. This imbalance between city and countryside in Spain continues to exist as merely one factor in the many varieties of urbanism. We shall be concerned in this essay to interweave these themes as we trace urban development in more recent times. By this means we expect to reveal the heritage and *raison d'etre* for the types of urban studies we survey and discuss. Against this backdrop we then assess the anthropological contribution and suggest future lines of research.

The main traditions that influenced urban development in Spain may be identified as Roman, Visigothic, Moslem, reconquest Christian, and postreconquest colonial.

While it is true that Rome ruled Iberia through its urban centers and maximum local responsibility (a syncretism composed of some six types of municipal governments), the Roman city in Spain was an "open" city. Clearly, specific ports (e.g., Cartagena) or inland cities (e.g. Toledo — for

arms manufacture) were more geared to conquest and dominion. Yet classically Roman cities such as Merida (*Emerita Augusta*) and Saragossa (*Caesar
Augusta*), formally laid out in the grid pattern inherited by the Romans from
the Greeks, were planned with entertainment and sanitation rather than defense in mind—hence the profusion of theaters, stadia, arenas, aqueducts,
and baths. Much of the urban heritage in Iberia manifests this need of the
Roman conqueror to urbanize a hostile rural population, and divert them.
Ponderous and impressive walls circling the city were not usually necessary
in Roman times where there was little fear of attack.

Social historians are quick to point out that as a result of the deterioration of the urban system under the agriculturally oriented Visigoths, the autonomy of local rule, if not governmental structure, was intensified. At the
same time, the emergent Christian churches forged a ubiquitous and common religious organization that fostered this ardent sociocentrism, known
variously as *campanilismo* or *el* "patriachiquismo," so that people came to have
a deeply committed sense of membership in their local community.

The different waves of Moslems who later occupied most of Spain for
nearly 800 years (711–1492 A.D.) were not builders of cities. Nevertheless,
they reconstructed the ones they took in order to conform to an ethic of en-
closure (for privacy and defense), on the one hand, and to the two focal
points of community life—the mosque and the bazaar—on the other. "Laby-
rinthine" and "unsymmetric" describe their introverted form, a turning in-
wards to patios and courts quite contrastive to the facades and general exte-
riority of Christian cities to the north. Within this Moslem influence one
finds a curious juxtaposition of urban style; the defensive element of tower
and turret seems almost inconsistent with the contemplative ambiance of
garden and fountain. These characteristics of Moslem urbanism are seen at
their best in the major centers of transplanted Islamic culture: Toledo, Cordoba, Seville, and Granada.

The frontier spirit was already apparent in the reconquest push south
by Christians who brought with them an essentially northern European way
of urban life and urban form. The resettlement process of formerly Moorish-
occupied towns and cities demanded an elevated degree of local responsibility, recognition of which remains somewhat incongruously today in the *fue-
ros* (local municipal bounties and privileges). It was this system of local government, based on municipalities combining a rural area with an urban
core, which later became the administrative arm of the colonial government
in the Americas, a local power much weakened by central bureaucracies
after independence in Latin America in the early 1800s.

Yet is should be recalled that at the time of the final defeat of the Moslems in Granada, their last stronghold, and the opening up of the New World,
Spain was little more than a loosely federated collection of autonomous city-

states, pulled together under a roving monarchical court. Madrid did not become the permanent central capital until the transfer from Toledo (in 1561) nearly a hundred years after settlement was established in the New World.

During this period a gradual transition was made from a lord-follower relationship to a king-subject relationship. Accompanying this transition was a corresponding shift from the ethic of the typical castle-dominated Castilian town or fortified community to the stability and ideology represented by the cathedral city and its public monuments. The model of church and state in dominant accord, caught in the grid town centered around the plaza complex dominated by cathedral and municipal palace, and so common still in Spain today, became the standardized urban form for Spanish America.

The change from medieval localism to baroque centralism has been neatly summed up by the urban historian Mumford (1938:77) as a movement "from the absolutism of God and the Roman Catholic Church to absolutism of the temporal sovereign and the national state." It was, of course, symbolized by the prestige-building of the Bourbon kings typified perhaps in the neoclassical beautification of the capital, Madrid. If the Bourbons could be said to have an urban policy, then it would be one couched in the framework of national reconstruction that reached its climax under Carlos III. Yet if the overcentralization of eighteenth-century "enlightened despotism" served to heighten the imbalance between town and country, even so it can be argued that this was not achieved at the price of standardization in urban form and planning as seems to be the case today.

Granted that the Roman policy was to impose a calculated homogeneity in urban culture, the Romans nevertheless sought within that policy a viable syncretism, where appropriate, with local varieties. The Moslems, for their part, with a greater flexibility of urban development and no systematic urban policy, allowed wider variation from city to city. Neither influence negated the pattern in development " . . . of strong urban centers, each a focal point of regional economic activities" (Violich 1962:178), under a loose central framework that did not stifle local initiative and autonomy. We might ponder the trend in the 1980s whereby, despite the emergence of a long-overdue regional autonomy and, thereby, diversity in the political sense, Spain at large is committing itself to an encroaching standardization in urban culture and form. The hasty redevelopment and consequent urban blight, the erratic zoning and the proliferating high-speed boulevards, parking lots displacing historic plazas, banks nudging out theaters and seigneurial mansions — in short, most of the familiar urban "benefits" catering to a now dedicated consumer society — are all here. Much of this standardization is planned beyond the boundaries of Spain, and promoted by a global corporate world of multinationals that increasingly control not only the means of production and forms of distribution but also the patterns of consumption at national levels.

In considering these seemingly inevitable trends, we shall recall more vividly the fact that urban development cannot be analyzed separately from the social and economic changes of which it forms an integral part.

It is an accepted fact that change in Spain has been, and continues to be, uneven. In accounting for this irregular development that affects the urban scene, one must have recourse to two levels of opposition. On the one hand, we must refer to the internal geographical and cultural diversity that an early national unification (in the year 1515) could not modify. Spanish observers (e.g., Linz and Miguel 1966:277) have suggested that the late (industrial) economic development in Spain has perhaps made that diversity even more acute. At the political level a traditional tension between center and periphery ensured that whenever the center (Madrid) was weakened, regionalism and separatism — especially when supported by linguistic differences (Basques, Catalans, Galicians) — waxed strong. While it was always admitted that for practical reasons "one must fight the bulls in *Madrid*"(signifying the essential role of the capital), the cultural rivalry between such cities as Madrid and Barcelona was notorious.

Yet such geographical opposition is matched by another, deeper antagonism that has occasioned the term "two Spains," a designation that gained currency among the regenerationists and the intellectual "Generation of 98" (i.e. 1898) who sought to reassess Spain and bring her more closely into the European frame by educational and agrarian reform as well as by industrialization. The concern at the turn of the century, when the nation was shaken and disenchanted by economic and ideological crises, was to explain the historical enigma of an unintegrated "backward" Spain, the "poor relation" of Europe. Catholic traditionalists were adamantly opposed to reforms. In this context there arose the image of the two Spains, an ideological split between Spain and the anti-Spain — reactionary versus liberal, Catholic versus anticlerical, authoritarian versus anarchist, the backward rural versus the modern metropolitan. Larra's famous phrase "Here lies half of Spain, it died at the hands of the other half" was coined in 1836 in reference to the Carlist succession wars, but it could equally refer to the Civil War of 1936.

Cultural heterogeneity, regional economic imbalance, and the aforementioned antagonism of world views largely account for the lack of integration and social cohesion in the Iberian peninsula. The anthropologist Lisón Tolosana has described regional identification and loyalty as having an almost poetic unity. Such symbols as Guadalupe, Montserrat, and the tree of Guernica represent unifying myths for the region. Yet at the politico-administrative level it can be seen how different relationships with the power center — the capital, Madrid — in specific periods conditioned the level of regionalist intensity (Lisón Tolosana 1972:373). Governing was localized rather than government being decentralized. An oligarchic system based on regional political elites who exercised a personalistic power over coalitions of clients — the *caciquismo* so vibrantly analyzed by Joaquin Costa (1902) — was the norm. *Caciquismo* was such a powerful institution that, at the turn of the century, rural areas and small towns were much better represented at the national level than were the larger towns and cities. It is by no means defunct in the 1980s when it has adopted urban forms, e.g., among squatters. Without a profound industrial and bourgeois revolution, Spain could not and did not produce those new urban middle classes and proletariats more characteristic of northern Europe. The inequitable distribution of resources in the 1960s can be seen in the difference in income in 1961–62 between the region of Madrid (index 164), the richest, and inland Galicia (index 60; 100 is the national average), the poorest (FOESSA 1970:264). Bitterly divided urban strata, as well as the slow and regionally uneven economic development, were also important factors in the 1930s that sensibly contributed to social unrest and conflict, including the Civil War of 1936–39.

A certain artificial boost to the economy was provided by the establishment of U.S. military bases (and all that went with them) in 1952. Yet not until the 1960s were policies of regional development put into action by the Spanish government (e.g., *I Plan de Desarrollo* in 1964, and *II* in 1969). The dilemma consisted in whether to develop centers (*polos*) that were already strong or to induce development from new bases. Apologists for Catalonia favored the former policy, offering to absorb the surplus work force from weaker regions (Trías Fargas 1968:96). Under the plan of 1964 only seven *polos* of development were designated: La Coruña, Vigo, Burgos, Valladolid, Saragossa, Seville, and Huelva; four others — Granada, Cordoba, Oviedo, and Logroño — were designated in the plan of 1969. The regions (and of course their urban centers) most favored were coastal Galicia, Castile, and the two Andalusias. Hence it is claimed that the development policy was clearly aimed at breaking the virtual industrial pre-eminence of the three classical nuclei — Barcelona, Basque country, and Madrid. Nevertheless these three regions, and their respective metropolitan centers (Barcelona, Bilbao, Madrid), continued to exert a powerful attraction for migrants from other regions, as they did also for return migrants from northern Europe (FOESSA 1970:274–76).

Demographers and sociologists worked toward more and more precise definitions of urbanism and urbanization and created explanatory typologies of urbanism as massive movements from the countryside began to aggrandize the cities in the 1950s and 1960s. Definitions were arrived at by employing a range of criteria relating to demography (e.g., total population 10,000-plus), economics (e.g., over 50% of the active working population in nonagricultural occupations), density (e.g., 60-plus inhabitants per square

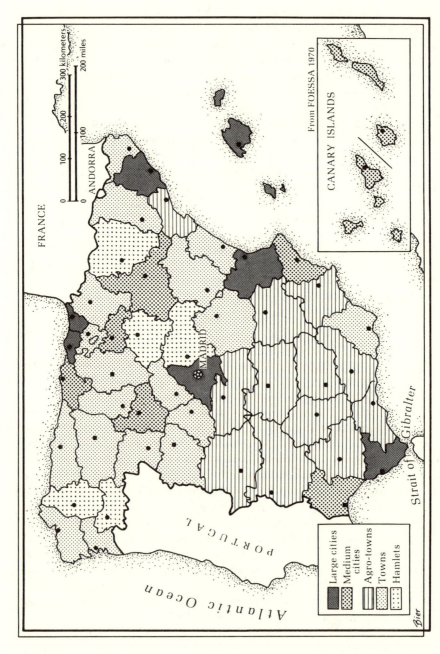

Figure 1. Types of Urbanism in 1950

kilometer), and lifestyle (Díez Nicolás 1969:12–13). Correlations were made between types of urbanism, index of urbanization, and levels of migration, so that the range (in 1950) could be designated in rank order from *grandes eludades* ("large cities," e.g., Madrid, Barcelona, Guipúzcoa, Valencia, Cadiz, Baleares) to *cuidades medias* ("medium cities," e.g., Alicante, Saragossa, Las Palmas, Valladolid, Logroño, Huelva) to *agro-ciudades* ("agro-towns," e.g., Cordoba, Granada, Jaén, Cáceres, Ciudad Real, Toledo, Seville) to *pueblos* ("towns," but often elsewhere translated as "villages," e.g., Avila, Burgos, Segovia, Oviedo, Castellón) to *aldeas* (here referring to "urban places" but elsewhere often translated as "hamlets," e.g., Guadalajara, Orense, Soria, Lugo, Huesca).

The sources of heterogeneity have been analyzed by sociologists, who have emerged with the concept of "eight Spains" distinguished by social structure (Linz and Miguel 1966). They also point to the paradox in the recent history of Spain whereby the most developed regions (e.g., the Basque provinces and Catalonia) have felt alienated from the nation-state, in contrast to the norm in other countries where usually the undeveloped areas (Quebec in Canada, Bavaria in Germany, Sicily in Italy) have manifested separatist or sectional tendencies (Linz and Miguel 1966:278).

In such a typology (of eight Spains) Barcelona and Bilbao are classified as typical of "bourgeois" (or "industrial") Spain. Whereas Madrid in the 1950s, under this classification, would be referred to as *clases medias* (literally, "middle classes"), it grew to merit a unique metropolitan category of its own because of its dramatic demographic and industrial transformation in the 1960s. "Gentry Spain" includes many of the "agricultural towns" (agro-towns), some of 20,000 or more population, and other cities passing the 100,000 mark (e.g., Albacete, Granada, Seville, Badajoz, Malaga, Murcia) that lacked modern industry in the 1960s. "Gentry Spain in transition" refers to provinces on whose capitals (like Valladolid and Valencia) a growing industry and labor-intensive commercial agriculture were dependent. *"Clases medias* in transition" refers to areas with a certain industrialization but no rural proletariat such as the less industrial towns of Catalonia, the Balearic Islands, and Saragossa (e.g., Tarragona, Palencia, Castellón, Teruel). "Proletarian in transition," a more residual and heterogeneous category, includes a variety of cities such as Santander and Cadiz.

Such typologies serve a most useful purpose in ordering the mass of data in such a way that new relationships between variables may become apparent. It is difficult, however, for typologies to be both explanatory and dynamic, and all such typologies were in danger of being confounded by the revitalization of city life in the 1960s and 1970s.

In those two decades three types of movement on a massive scale helped to cause an urban transformation that continues apace: (1) rural migrants flocked to the cities (with the exception of Madrid, the movement tended to

be from the center to the periphery, especially the Mediterranean and Cantabrian coasts); (2) some 10% of the entire Spanish population emigrated to
other countries, mainly northern Europe; and (3) a yearly influx of foreign
tourists, almost equal in numbers to the total Spanish population, flooded
into Spain bringing their cultural baggage with them and radically changing
by their presence the Spanish cityscape, especially along the Mediterranean
coast.

The transfer of a huge labor force from the fields (and later the cities) of
southern Europe to the factories of northern Europe has been likened to a
second Marshall Plan (Martinez-Mari 1966). So, too, the industrial triangle
in Spain — Madrid, Bilbao, Barcelona — has profited from this "Marshall
Plan" for many years thanks to domestic in-migration from poorer regions
in Spain (the first big wave occurred far earlier, in the 1920s). "Overseas"
migrants are in the unenviable position of having been considered a *problem*
when they left in the 1950s and 1960s (because of unemployment etc.) and a
solution in the 1970s and 1980s (when they are expected, as returnees, to contribute to development). While it can be argued that migration played a conservative role and that it is a myth that the returnee has promoted economic
development in Spain (see Cases Mendez and Cabezas Moro 1976:134–57),
it cannot be denied that Spanish governments depended very heavily on emigrant remittances and tourist hard currency (see Kenny 1972). Only a
minor percentage of emigrants returned definitively to their villages, preferring instead the nearest town or regional capital; in turn, those who had emigrated from small towns tended to settle on their return in larger cities or the
metropolises, where they invested their savings in apartments and small
businesses.

Rural migrants in Spain produced their own impact in the cities, the
most poverty-stricken creating "squatments" or moonlight-shack settlements
(*villas miseria* or *chabolas* in Madrid and Bilbao, *barracas* in Barcelona) on the
fringes of town. We might note here the contrast to the pattern in the United
States of inner-city ghettos and affluent suburbs (whereas the Spanish *sub-
urbios* refers to the slums that circle the city at its fringes). Despite their almost total lack of urban services and facilities, and the jerry-built nature of
their construction from odds and ends and poor-quality materials dubiously
acquired, the slums persist. Curiously enough, on the rare occasions when
blocks of new dwellings are built specifically to house these marginal populations, an enviable social integration achieved in the slums is usually broken
(Ministerio de la Vivienda 1969).

In surveying urban development in Spain, we have stressed its venerable tradition and the variety of process (urbanization) and type (urbanism.
Anthropologists, however, were too busy forging a tradition of peasant
studies in Spain in the 1950s to worry about research in the urban scene. Not
only were they ill equipped conceptually and methodologically to grapple

with an "urban" anthropology, but it is doubtful that they could have kept pace with the dizzy rate of change in the cities. It is sobering to think that in the year 1800 there did not exist a city of a million inhabitants and that now we are faced with the megalopolis. Bearing in mind this awesome complexity and rapidity of change — the "speeding up of time" — we turn now to the choices made by researchers for urban study.

Since World War II a new generation of scholar-intellectuals has arisen in Spain fundamentally comprised by sociologists, social psychologists, economists, and anthropologists. These are the ones who are shifting the emphasis away from studies of Spain as an historical enigma, and are now approaching Spanish society in a more sociological framework. Along with this shift goes the correspondent need for analysis of objective data (not the erstwhile impressionistic essay) culled from an increasingly *urban* population. This change should be understood in terms of the exigencies of particular decades — post–Civil War recovery of the 1940s, North American military installations and aid of the 1950s, large-scale social mobility, economic development and migration of the 1960s, and the economic crises, rapid social change, and political innovation of the 1970s. So, too, the temper of the times, the Europeanization and general "opening up" of Spain as well as the recent but rapid growth of the social sciences there, have influenced the type and number of urban studies. The simple fact of accelerated and irreversible urbanization ensured that by the 1960s nearly half of the total population of Spain was living in metropolises and regional capitals; in the decade 1960–70 alone truly phenomenal growth rates were experienced in Valladolid (56%), Las Palmas (48%), Saragossa (47%), Palma de Mallorca (47%), Madrid (39%), and Bilbao (38%) (Instituto Nacional de Estadística 1972:12–13).

What can we say about the place for anthropological research in urban studies in Spain (Kenny 1971)?

One might claim that, given the propensity for Spaniards to cluster into nucleated settlements (*pueblos*), anthropologists were in fact studying urban phenomena, unless they devoted themselves specifically to scattered-on-the-land hamlets. Yet if we accept the contemporary criteria (FOESSA 1970: 1193) for defining "urban" (i.e., 10,000-plus population, 100,000-plus for metropolitan, 50%-plus of active working population in nonagricultural occupations, 65%-plus for a Standard Urbanized Area metropolitan density of at least 60-plus inhabitants per square kilometer, as well as other criteria of lifestyle, etc.), then it is clear that few anthropologists have so far studied such units.

Much urban sociology is carried out in Spain under the banner of what we would call "regional sciences." Despite the early initiation of regional studies in the 1930s by the economist Román Perpiñá Grau (1954) and later by the economic historian Jaime Vicens Vives (1948), such studies remained comparatively underdeveloped until the 1970s (e.g., FOESSA 1970, Fraga Iribarne 1972, Miguel and Salcedo 1972), except for notable contributions by geographers. The significance of regional studies to our urban interest here lies in dependency and development theory, the product of regional industrial growth since the 1960s. Some observers, e.g., the economist Salcedo (1977:2), forthrightly maintain that the few existing urban sociologists have limited themselves, in large part, to legitimizing the wheeling and dealing of an unbridled urban speculation by acting as consultants in the service of realtors and developers, financial cartels, or state and administrative agencies controlled by these, e.g., COPLACO, Direción-General de Urbanismo, Diputación Provincial de Barcelona, and the like. But this critical attitude belittles the monumental work of scholars like Amando de Miguel and Juan J. Linz, who, however, do not regard themselves as strictly *urban* sociologists. Nevrtheless, we look in vain for a solid body of theory emanating from this "school," or for areas of declared mutual interest and overlap wherein anthropologists might fruitfully join. One exception, perhaps, lies in the concept and study of the so-called agro-towns (e.g., Cáceres, Badajoz, Toledo, Jaén, Ciudad Real, Albacete, etc.) wherein, despite an "urban" density, there is still a predominantly rural lifestyle. In fact, a goodly proportion of regional science studies limit themselves to "techniques of classification and description of urban structure" (Salcedo 1977:2), typologies and the like, or functional analyses of urban occupations and activities. Useful though such studies might be for clearing the ground, they were on the one hand clearly apolitical — opportunely so at a time when General Franco was firmly in command — and on the other hand did not reach to the heart of urban problems. Even so, for the anthropologist who was village-bound and blinkered by localisms, they could serve to raise higher his regional sights. And indeed they did, at a time in the late 1960s when urban sociology, urbanization, and migration studies also began what can be described as a "take-off stage."

Until then it would be fair to say that urbanology was not formally developed in Spain, despite such studies as Adolfo Gonzalez Posada's *La ciudad moderna* in 1915 (Real Academia de Ciencias Morales y Políticas) and the early studies on the housing situation of the working class in the 1920s by the Instituto de Reforma Social (directed by Azcárate).

There followed the social unrest and conflict of the 1930s, the fall of the monarchy and the institution of the Second Republic, and the Civil War, hardly a propitious decade for the development of any academic discipline. Sociologists themselves (Miguel and Moyer 1979:19) have characterized the subsequent period 1940–56 as the "underground years"; the exile of many scholars and intellectuals because of the Civil War, the lack of international communication and participation by Spanish scholars, and strict censorship were all important factors inhibiting the growth of the social sciences in general.

Perhaps the potential for development of "urbanology" was also diffused too thinly (in our view) among a variety of localized research institutions, like the Instituto de Estudios Madrileños or the Instituto de Estudios de Administración Local. The studies they produced (e.g., *Resumen histórico del urbanismo en España* by L. Torres Balbas *et al.* and a later one of the same title by Antonio Garcia Belludo *et al.* in 1968, Instituto de Estudios de Administración Local, Madrid 1954) looked back in time rather than analyzing the present or predicting the future. They were more concerned with housing and urban development/planning, urban clustering, and demographic growth than with the social change that accompanied these physical phenomena, with the evolution of architectural style rather than with the symbolic value of a city's monuments and artifacts and their relation to the social structure, as anthropologists might be.

In that regard, Barcelona, with a longer traditional concern for bourgeois architecture and style (see, e.g., the architect Gaudi) than most cities in Spain, has had a longer tradition of overlapping disciplinary concern with urban studies. Even now the so-called Group R, which holds seminar/*tertulias* outside the university forum, brings together architects, urban scholars, and even philosophers.

A number of academics in Barcelona (e.g., Jordi Borja and Josep Olives) and Western Europe at large (e.g., Juan Salcedo in England) seem to be constituting at least a following if not a "school" of the empirical marxism of Manuel Castells in Paris. Castells's studies (1974) deal with urban class struggles and movements by applying some of the basic postulates of historical materialism to urban conflicts. Thus his theory of urban social movements (Castells 1974b) sees the spatial distribution of the urban population not as a result of a "functional distribution of functions" (as does Juan Díez Nicolás 1972) but, rather, as a precarious balance struck by the struggle between social groups competing for the scarce urban resource of "buildable land." He is lauded for the explicative potential of his theory of imperialistic urbanization compared to the more traditional descriptive functionalism (Salcedo 1977:3).

Finally, one may detect another critical trend in urban sociology in the work of M. Gaviría (1968, 1970), who has now turned to studies of leisure and tourism (Alicante).

Clearly the boom in urban sociology is appropriately related to the comparatively recent but dramatically rapid urbanization since the 1960s, especially in the so-called industrial triangle (Madrid-Vizcaya-Barcelona). Because of the physical and demographic growth of these metropolises, sociological analysis tended to center on changes in urban structure, problems of

housing, and the integration of migrants. In short, two main approaches —
the functional and the critical — are evident in two of the major sociological
specializations — regional and urban studies — in the last 20 years (Miguel
and Moyer 1979:101–2).

Regional and urban studies also greatly benefited from the approach of
the human geographers in Spain, who in the main followed either a sociological perspective (see, e.g., Terán 1964) in the French tradition or an ecological perspective (see, e.g., Vila Valenti and Capel 1970). Few anthropologists have seen the need to develop these traditions, yet in many ways the
work of urban geographers has been far ahead of that of the anthropologists.
In the early 1960s Bosque Maurel (1962) had already produced a pioneer
and comprehensive study of Granada. Similarly, geographers were active in
the 1950s and 1960s with studies in Madrid of urban structure (Chueca Goitia 1951), spatial development (Terán 1961), and population distribution
(Trías Beltran 1964). It would appear that urban geographers were able,
quite early on, to link their interests and talents to the need for urban planning. This concern for urban form was taken up by foreign geographers and
city planners (e.g., Stanislawski 1946, Violich 1962) and by at least one foreign anthropologist (Foster 1960) whose principal interest lay in exploring
the Spanish origins of Latin American urban structure; it was not so taken
up by anthropologists for Spain itself as a fruitful source for study.

We should not ignore a highly fruitful but also entertaining source of
material for the urban anthropologist — the novelist. Suffice it here to mention the names of (Leopoldo Alas) "Clarín" (see, e.g., his *La regenta* in the
early 1900s, which deals with the bourgeois of Oviedo), Pío Baroja (see his
trilogy *La lucha por la vida*), and B. Pérez Galdós, himself influenced by
Charles Dickens and whom we think of as the Spanish Oscar Lewis of the
nineteenth century (see, e.g., his *Nazarín, Halma,* and his last novel *Misercor-
dia*). Both Pío Baroja and Pérez Galdós wrote vividly and movingly of the
poor, the down-and-outs and beggars in Madrid, and each in his own way
did his fieldwork. All three, in different measure, gave us sharply etched pic-
tures of "Spanish" character and the social and political vices and virtues of
Spanish society in their time. We have much to learn from them, for nearly a
hundred years ago they were asking, as novelists, some of the same kinds of
questions that we, as social scientists, expect to be funded for today.

Beside the panorama revealed by the novel lie other sources, in poetry,
song, and festival, rich in potential for use by the urban anthropologist.
Through the pen of the poet, the voice of the balladeer, and the drama of the
festival are reflected the temper of the times, the values and social structure
of the day. Even in the gradual displacement of epic poetry (*cantares de gesta*)
by the ballad we can see the growth of urbanism and an urban ethic (e.g.,
the courtly love of the town dweller); the ballad was a medieval medium
that, like our news media today, lends itself to an analysis of the times and

their concerns. In like manner urban festivals (which may be regarded as integrative rituals — compare the miracle and passion plays) provide an abundant source for historico-cultural analysis; for instance, the marching order of the Corpus Christi procession in Madrid up until the nineteenth century neatly reproduced the current power hierarchy and social stratification. So, too, in Valencia today the fiesta of Las Fallas still faithfully manifests the division of the city into communities of barrios and, hence, the lack of neighborhood sentiment in the new high-rise areas.

Thus, before we turn to an analysis of anthropological fieldwork in Spain, we might emphasize our belief that we are merely continuing a tradition of study the bases for which were already laid by the Spaniards themselves, even though we might claim to be doing so in a more systematically anthropological way.

ANTHROPOLOGICAL FIELDWORK IN SPAIN

In this section, particularly, we are conscious that our review of research undertaken or underway may already be out of date by the time this book is published. Throughout the 1960s Kenny was able to keep an inventory of research in Spain by using a small but tight network of scholar-colleagues (Kenny 1971, 1972). By the 1970s this task was no longer practical for one person alone because of the boom in general professional activity in Spain — not only fieldwork — by both Spanish and foreign anthropologists.

One may cite an ethnological *tradition* in Spain dating from the early 1830s, later more institutionalized by the creation in 1865 of the first Spanish professional anthropological society (Sociedad Antropológica Española) and in 1975 of the first museum (Museo Antropológico). By 1862 scientific expeditions were being made to various parts of the world (Lisón Tolosana 1971), while inside Spain a revival of regionalism resulted in the flowering of regional folklore societies. Until the 1960s, when Claudio Esteva Fabregat founded the Escuela de Estudios Antropológicos (1966) as part of the Centro Iberoamericano de Antropología in Madrid, the discipline was deeply rooted in classical archeology, folklore, and Latin American studies. Julio Caro Baroja did much to change this focus, toward an institutionalization of Spanish ethnography as a discipline. With the establishment of the first chair in ethnology occupied by Esteva Fabregat in Barcelona, and later specialized programs within other schools in Madrid and Seville, the discipline of cultural anthropology steadily developed. Evidence of this growing professional activity can be seen in the creation of such journals as *Ethnica* (1971, published by the Centro de Etnología Peninsular in Barcelona, directed by Esteva Fabregat) and in the beginning of congresses and symposia (e.g., the first in Seville in 1972, others in Puertomarín [Lugo] in 1974, in Seville again in 1974, in Valle de los Caidos [Madrid] in 1975, in Tenerife and another in Barcelona in 1977), all of which united mainly Spanish anthropologists in an *esprit de corps* and sense of disciplinary purpose. Reflecting this new awareness and prolific research within the Iberian peninsula, publishing houses like Siglo XXI, Tecnos, Barral, and Akal began to devote more and more series to cultural anthropology (Prat 1977:133–34). In this steady growth of cultural anthropology as a separate discipline in Spain, a prominent role has been taken by Lisón Tolosana in Madrid both by his published research and the training of students.

Meanwhile foreign anthropologists had been exploring the Spanish countryside since the early 1950s and publishing in journals and with presses in, particularly, the United States and the United Kingdom. Even so, except for Kenny's pioneering study of a Madrid parish in the 1950s, most anthropologists — foreign and national — concentrated their efforts on examining rural life, following the peasant studies tradition in the decades of 1950 and 1960. Few observers would deny that these village studies served a most useful purpose as "salvage" anthropology (during a period of unusually rapid social change), as a data bank for future comparisons, and, moreover, as base-line data for the analysis of rural-urban links. Urban anthropology was as yet an unnamed stepchild of a cultural anthropology that was still enraptured by primitives and peasants. Thus there was little if any thought given to studying a town or city on its own merits. Even Kenny (1960a) seems to have split his *Spanish Tapestry* into two parts — one about a Castilian village — almost as if the latter urban section needed not only a contrast but also an endorsement by the village study.

Yet to speak of village versus town, as if they represented totally different worlds and lifestyles, is to miss the truth and embrace once again a dichotomizing folk-urban model now, happily, discarded. We cannot emphasize enough the "urban" quality of village life in Spain, indeed in the classical seat of urban civilization itself, the Mediterranean at large. In contrast to most other culture areas, "urbanicity" here is a major theme that reaches out to the smallest village. It can be argued, therefore, that the work in the 1950s and 1960s of such anthropologists as Pitt-Rivers, Kenny, Lisón Tolosana, Aceves, Hansen, Gregory, Luque, and Freeman, while focusing on the village, does in fact deal with the "urban," for the urban is written into the village system of values and institutions.

A finding common in many anthropological studies has been the yearning by villagers for city ways, the emulation of city institutions, and the aspiration — accelerated since the 1960s — to become a part of city life. In the analysis of village social systems one is inevitably examining the role of local elites, parish priests, civil guards, entrepreneurs, and the like, all of whom in some way are linked to the national system operative in regional and metropolitan capitals. Indeed some — like the police, mayor, and priest — may be actual representatives of a national system. In his analysis the anthropologist has most often been guilty of making the conceptual leap from village to nation-state, skipping in the process a variety of urban links along the way.

The consequence of such an emphasis on village studies has been a proliferation of conceptual models derived from a more homogeneous rural life that have been transferred inappropriately onto the urban and national scene. Some of these models influence the type of information gathered about sex roles and family relations, social class and social organization.

In any discussion of Spanish sex roles, both as an integral part of family systems and as an important individual personality component, the conceptual model of honor and shame has acquired an almost sacred explanatory function. This model was first developed by Pitt-Rivers in the 1950s in a rural setting in southern Spain where the precepts of honor and shame specifically relate to a man protecting his honor and a woman maintaining her shame *(vergüenza)*. [2]

With little or no empirical evidence this rural perspective on sex roles has been transposed onto urban residents. Indeed, during the early 1970s it became common to hear anthropologists at workshops and conferences, e.g., at the Valle de los Caidos (1975), use the honor and shame model whenever the discussion turned about male-female relationships, regardless of the social setting. This urban generalizing from a rural particular runs counter to at least one definition that links honor and shame to "individuals in small scale, exclusive societies where face to face personal, as opposed to anonymous, relations are of paramount importance and where the social personality of the actor is as significant as his office" (Peristiany 1966:11). It is probable that the unquestioning acceptance of this one conceptual model of sex roles inhibited many potential urban researchers from exploring this area of human relationships when studying cities and city people. Isidoro Moreno (1975) has criticized Spanish and foreign anthropologists alike for using a set of theories and models formulated from a strongly conservative perspective. Even so, some urban researchers working in southern Spain were led to re-examine issues that were significant for an understanding of the rural and regional context of the cities in which they worked.

Knipmeyer (1979) selected an agro-town of "gentry Spain" — Granada — for an investigation of the development of gender identity and sex-role learning among four- and five-year-old, working- and middle-class children. Although male and female socialization and enculturation practices vary by gender of the parent and of the child in question, and although significant sex-role differences among the children were found, little evidence emerged that would support or further document the honor and shame model.

In his study of another larger agro-town — Seville — Press (1979) uses

the concept of honor and shame as a tactical mode of exploring male and female values and sex-role behavior in the urban context; it is a starting point
rather than an end in itself. In contrast to the class-free generalizations
about Spanish men and women that were typical of the 1960s, Press carefully contrasts social class differences in sex-role behavior. What is controversial about his study is not so much the internal (within Seville) comparisons he makes but the comparisons with national values and mores that (he
contends) unite Spaniards across the country.

In discussing "the tyranny of sex-role" in Seville, Press implicitly uses
another standard rural model, i.e., the segregation of the sexes according to
"public" and "private" spheres of activity, as a starting point to explore its
modification in the urban context. Thus he finds that *pre*marital female employment is almost a necessity for couples who must save large sums for
downpayments and furnishings for their future home; that the woman without a mate or mother can live alone but the "autonomous" male cannot ("the
womanless male is simply allocated within his family to some other woman
who will perform household services for him"—Press 1979:123); and that it
is precisely in the city that extra precautions must be taken in maintaining a
reputation of honor because it is easier to *hide* dishonor in the city (the "urban
woman must restrict her behavior or allow it to be monitored. The urban
man must stay close to his home . . . and keep watch upon his women"—
Press 1979:137).

Others have pointed to the number of conceptual models of social dynamics that have been generated for Spanish pueblos on the basis of small-
unit research. Some paradigms have been proposed as valid interpretations
for social behavior in "population centers of all sizes throughout Spain"
(Freeman 1968:474). One of the central issues at stake revolves around the
question of size; since anthropologists have mainly concentrated their
studies in villages, the argument debates the issue whether larger rural communities are different in degree from smaller ones, and why. The argument
is pertinent to our urban focus, particularly as Gilmore (1976:90) aptly
points out that the small-village pattern is characteristic only of northern
Spain and of the economically marginal sierras; in the south and in the fertile plains regions the large agro-town is the rule and the small village the exception. Gilmore (1976:90–91) demonstrates the inadequacy of prevailing
analytical models by an examination of the alleged integrative functions of
three generalized constructs—patronage, religious-territorial "corporacy,"
and sociocentrism—and concludes that they fail to take into account the
variables of class consciousness and class conflict in the agro-towns and
larger cities.

Similarly, Corbin (1979:99), working in the small mountain city of
Ronda in Andalusia, extends the empirical range in his general support of
Gilmore's view that class is an important factor but suggests that its effects

are not independent of the operation of networks of personal relations, which include patron-clientage. Patronage, as a causal theme, was used by some anthropologists (e.g., Kenny 1960, 1968) to explain the reality of a parallel power structure in Spain. Moreover, patronage was thought to provide that very balance which regulated the interrelation between official and informal power structures. In like manner, patronage was posited as a significant mechanism operating the linkage between town and country via village elites. Yet useful though the concept of patronage may be for its potential to illustrate such structural mechanisms, the term has been generalized far too broadly with little regard to class differences.

Any analysis of anthropological work carried out in Spain must inevitably run into the difficulty of uncovering a pattern in the heterogeneity of research; anthropologists are notorious for being "lone wolves." Further problems arise in the selection of materials; not everyone who has carried out fieldwork or enthnohistorical research, or used anthropological models and techniques, has enjoyed formal anthropological training or manages to publish. It is quite impossible to be comprehensive. Finally, certain types of research defy a single classification such as "urban studies." Having undergone these difficulties ourselves, we recognize the valiant industry of those who have carried out similar analyses, e.g., Esteva Fabregat (1969), Lisón Tolosana (1971), Moreno (1975), and especially bibliographers such as Jimenez and Zamora (1975) and Prat (1977), from whom we have abstracted data relevant to our urban emphasis.

Of the 513 works cited by Prat (1977) he lists only 38 on "urban zones" (compare 397 on "rural"); of the 37 publications on marginal groups, he lists 23 in the "urban" category, a few of which are already included under the "urban zone" category above (Prat 1977:150). Compared to other countries in the Mediterranean, this is a relatively high proportion. A brief analysis of this useful bibliography already provides us with a glimmer of a pattern. With remarkably few earlier exceptions (e.g., Foster, Kenny, Whiteford, Nash), the boom in urban studies takes off in the 1970s. Moreover, conforming to the custom in other culture areas and in the Mediterranean at large, anthropologists in Spain have tended to study the urban exotica. The impact of the city itself was only of incidental concern, for anthropologists came on the urban scene accidentally, as it were, pursuing their interests in "marginal" peoples—Gypsies, Jews, the poor and abandoned, immigrants, practitioners of popular medicine, tourists, and even North American expatriates.[3] Very few published studies (e.g,. Schwartz 1972, for Trujillo in Extremadura; Press 1979, for Seville in Andalusia) have taken the town on its own merits with either an ethnographic or city-as-context approach; even Press dwells longer and more comfortably on a specific part of the city, a tenement housing complex *(corral)*. So, too, other urban fieldworkers have settled for a more customary (in size) unit of analysis such as the barrio in

Barcelona ("la Barceloneta" — see García 1977) or similar neighborhoods in Madrid (see Molina 1972; Kenny 1960, parish of "San Martin.")

A discussion here of the themes[4] treated by urban anthropologists will necessarily be arbitrary in its selection and occasionally leavened by references to other disciplines. It endeavors to touch on concerns of class, ethnic group, neighborhood and identity, the changing religiosity and influence of the Church, and the development of greater political and associational activity. At the same time we are conscious of the need to point to fruitful areas for future research.

While it cannot yet be maintained in Vance Packard's phrase that outright "prodigality is the spirit of the era," it is undeniable that in the 1970s Spaniards were better fed, clothed, and housed than ever before. By mid-1975 Spain's average per capita annual income was the equivalent of $2,075 (U.S.), higher than that of Greece or Portugal but lower than that of the rest of Western Europe (Keefe *et al.* 1976:83, 85). This is not to say that poverty was by any means eradicated, especially in the more agrarian provinces (Andalusia, Galicia, Extremadura), nor did it prevent the emergence of new pockets of paupers on the edges of expanding cities (Madrid, Barcelona, Bilbao, Seville, Valencia, Saragossa, Valladolid). These latter differ markedly from their rural counterparts in their high degree of transience, though not necessarily in experiencing an upward social mobility. It is a fallacy to assume that the poor and the working class are in some way automatically incorporated into a middle class merely by an increase of income or acquisition of consumer items, e.g., the vast new dispersion of *electrodomesticos* or household gadgets. Urban manual laborers in general enjoyed a higher average income (8,100 pesetas) than the agricultural middle class (6,900 pesetas) in 1969, but their lifestyle, values, and beliefs were not those of a bourgeois middle class (FOESSA 1970:534, 535).

Anthropologists have not studied the culture of poverty as such in Spain or, for that matter, the culture of wealth. Nor have they yet studied the gradual move from informal to formal patronage manifest in charity and social assistance for the poor. Spaniards still prefer individualized and personalized acts of charity; they would find a United Way Fund (such as that in the United States) far too impersonal an organism for distributing donations to the needy. Yet poverty is no longer (if it ever was) an individual problem but rather a social concern, much of whose alleviation now lies in the hands of CARITAS, an organization of the Spanish Roman Catholic church active in more than 30% of parishes throughout the country (FOESSA 1970:704). The gradual assumption by national agencies of (previously) kin or family responsibilities in welfare and health are fertile fields of study awaiting the urban anthropologist.

With few exceptions (Esteva Fabregat, Pi-Sunyer, Press) anthropologists have avoided the study of social and economic class in the city, preferring, at least in one case (Kenny 1961), to speak of social position and ideals. In part this may be explained by the seeming lack of class consciousness (though not class conflict) and the greater, current social mobility. Press (1979:176), speaking for Seville, puts it in these terms: "The lower [class] link themselves with the upper levels as sharing membership in a single socio-moral system . . . a matter of the equality of human potential for respect and honor. Wealth may qualify an individual for higher status, but only proper behavior can *validate* the position, and proper behavior is available to all." Rich and poor alike live in the same neighborhoods, attend the same churches. While a traditional stress upon land, title, family name, and manners may still serve to differentiate an elite stratum of ascribed membership in Seville beyond the aspirations of others, there are sufficient examples of mobility through luck, effort, marriage, and emigration to convince any Sevillano that most socioeconomic differences are achieved rather than ascribed. One marked difference between varieties of middle class is that of impermanence versus relative permanence; the former maintains his tenuous middle-class position only by dint of plural employment, combined family income, long hours, or overtime (Press 1979:158ff.).

Significant variation in class stratification can be found in cities that are not agro-towns, e.g., in Madrid where a new but growing proletariat is identified in the industrial complexes just outside the capital, and, of course, in the flocks of bureaucrats and military who make up a high proportion of the nonprofessional middle class in the capital. In contrast, middle-class Catalans have typically filled the liberal professions, industry, and commerce, spurning the state-related (Spanish) sectors. It is ". . . the Catalan bourgeoisie, and in particular the culturally conscious professional classes, [who] have traditionally acted as standard-bearers of Catalan nationalism and ethnic identity" (Pi-Sunyer and Pi-Sunyer 1975:291).

In most cities, nonetheless, certain ethnic groups have been maintained in a permanently marginal social (and sometimes physical) position such that certain neighborhoods or areas are associated with them: witness the Gypsies in the Sacro Monte caves in Granada, the troglodyte area in Guadix, the Pozo del Tio Raimundo and La Charca in Madrid, San Lucio in Barcelona, and similar areas in Saragossa, studied by anthropologists (see Quintana 1972, San Roman 1976, De la Peña 1970, Cazorla Pérez 1976, Kaprow 1978, Mulcahy 1976, McLane 1979). Kaprow claims that while larceny is commonly directed against non-Gypsies, murder and assault seem to be crimes carried out only against other Gypsies. Different symbols and occupational patterns ensure that Gypsies and "gentiles" maintain separate ecological niches. Urban middle classes, in particular, continue to view Gypsies as social pariahs. But while urban Gypsy emigrants in Guadix who returned from a migration tour in Germany soon spent their savings and re-entered the migratory cycle, their cave-dwelling compatriots who were agricultural laborers returned from emigration to Ibiza and bought up land for cultivation (McLane 1979:123) — a most unusual pattern for Gypsies anywhere.

Certain communities of Jews, generally of ancient residence in Mallorca (where they are known as *chuetas mallorquines*), still suffer some discrimination — despite their Catholic affiliation — by their neighbors and are associated with specific neighborhoods (see Moore 1977). Valuable ethnohistorical studies of Jews in Barcelona (Fernández 1978) and in Spain at large (Caro Baroja 1961) are also available. More comparative studies of these marginal ethnic groups and the networks by which they maintain their separate identity would be revealing, especially if these are carried out on a culture-area (Mediterranean) scale.

Anthropologists have yet to match the urban geographers' alliance with urban planners and architects. Today, in the complex process of urban planning and development — something more than architecture writ large — the voice of the people is in danger of being ignored. The development of Madrid was ". . . the result of decisions from above made in the interest of the ruling elite, not in furtherance of the common weal" (Gutkind 1969:409). Yet Spain is committed to comprehensive planning on a national scale and Madrid is the coordinating center. Anthropologists have much yet to offer in the planning of new barrios as well as in the conservation of old ones; here is where their predilection for the local and the "folk" can be put to good effect.[5] Foster (1960) and Kenny (1961), in earlier studies, both pointed to a vibrant sense of community still extant in cities and the need to study how identifying characteristics such as street names, or divisions of a parish, evoke this sense.

Every citizen lives by his own version of the city. Fieldwork using newer techniques such as social area analysis, cognitive mapping, network analysis, and projective tests can abstract the symbolic reference points (the "imageability" of Kevin Lynch 1960) by which established residents orient themselves, as well as the processes by which immigrants acquire these mental maps — the hidden "forms" in the vast sprawl of our cities. *Campanilismo* is, in effect, an urban concept. Those who never acquire it, perhaps because they live in an environmental bubble like many tourists and certain expatriate groups, may wallow in limbo, as did many North Americans in Barcelona and Madrid in the 1950s and 1960s (Nash 1970).

It should be clear that as the extraordinary pressures of urbanization have made themselves felt and the post-Franco political processes have evolved, a new associational activity is changing the *character* of urban life in Spain. This in turn has important implications for changes in values and mechanisms of social control, areas in which anthropologists have long specialized elsewhere. The growth of urban neighbors' associations (*Asocia-*

ciones de Vecinos) at the end of the 1960s and beginning of the 1970s is correlated with the swelling of larger cities with immigrants. The phenomenal
growth of population of great urban industrial centers, as well as less industrialized areas such as Murcia, Seville, and Mallorca, laid an intolerable
strain on existent urban services. Faced with the incapacity of local governments to provide these additional services, and spurred on by the political
transformation as Franco's regime came to an end, these popular associations flourished, albeit illegally,[6] in the 1970s. They provided a practical
training ground for political apprenticeship — organizations for free political
socializaion in a country that had denied such opportunities for nearly 40
years. Thus their activities declined as political parties were legalized, according to Bier (1979:182), who studied them in Alcalá de Henares
(Madrid) and Mataró (Barcelona). Yet their appeal and success suggest a
community consciousness among immigrants that runs counter to unpublished reports about the seeming lack of such consciousness in the new
barrios of Valencia. There the traditional Las Fallas fiesta — champion of
local solidarity — seems to have failed, but that may be because some of these
new neighborhoods are peopled by a prosperous middle class in little need of
additional urban services. Here is another fertile field of study for anthropologists.

Housing cooperative associations were also founded by returned
emigrants from northern Europe in desperation at the lack of accommodation and the inadequate governmental policy; see, for example, El Madroño
(formed by returnees from Madrid) and La Giralda (formed by returnees
from Seville) in the 1960s reported by an episcopal commission of the Catholic church (Kenny 1972a). The paradox of modern industrialization is that it
has made people prosperous but, often, only at the social cost of a devalued
environment. Experience in other European countries has shown that
cooperatives and similar housing organizations have an important role to
play in long-term planning as well as in providing medium-term guarantees
that the funds needed will flow regularly (Umrath 1968). Operating under
very diverse financial and administrative conditions, without central control
or organic framework, these cooperatives have undertaken a public role in
residential building in Italy (Conosciani 1969). Anthropologists would do
well to study their future in Spain.

There is no anthropological study wholly and directly focused on
religion in the city in Spain. Press (1979:180–88) allows the subject only
eight out of 287 pages in his book on Seville. In general, similarly cursory
treatment can be found in most rural studies by anthropologists; religion is
dealt with in passing or, at most, merits a chapter among others. Christian's
(1972) work in a peasant Santander valley area, which he extends to national
treatment of patrons and shrines, is an unusual and welcome exception.

Caro Baroja's (1961b) classical but historical work on witches and their world, especially the Basque provinces, and Lisón-Tolosana's (1979) and Henningsen's (1971) later work on more contemporary witchcraft in Galicia apply only indirectly to the urban scene.

Yet the changes in both beliefs and religiosity, and the Church's adaptive strategies in the city, are significant indicators of social change that anthropologists would do well to document. The disaffection of much of the working class, the indifference of the poor and the university students (in ideological conflict with the Church), were notably increasing well before the demise of Franco in 1975 despite active Church campaigns to play a greater role in the solution of social problems since the late 1940s (e.g., Catholic Action brotherhoods and youth groups among the workers, episcopal commissions to care for the migrants, CARITAS to succor the poor). These were almost entirely urban innovations that had little direct impact on rural populations or on traditional city or village parish organizations (e.g., confradías, sodalities). Diocesan clergy and members of religious orders are divided by a generational and ideological struggle within their own ranks. Many of the younger clergy see themselves as militant pioneers of change and were heavily fined or jailed for their "illegal" sermons or active support of revolutionary groups under the Franco regime. Despite a rise in recruitment of members of religious orders between 1915 and 1967 (Keefe et al. 1976:139), the ranks of the clergy in general are being thinned by drop-outs, and their efforts are being nullified by the increasing disproportion between them and the faithful they serve because of a population explosion (the ratio was 1:401 for the year 1859, compared to 1:1,228 for the year 1962 — see Duocastella et al. 1966:27–28). As the laity inevitably takes over some of the functions previously monopolized by the Church, so there will be a decisive change in the status and role of the secular priest, the monk, and the member of a religious community such as the Opus Dei, and their differential impact.[7]

Anthropologists can profit from the rich macrodata base supplied by sociologists and others (e.g., Keefe et al. 1976:127–44 and FOESSA 1970:433–70), e.g., typologies of religiosity by region (lowest in heavily industrialized zones, and in areas devitalized by migration). It may well be true that Spain is still the most avidly Roman Catholic country in Europe — a national Catholicism "more papist than the Pope" — but it should also be remembered that several hundred non-Catholic small sects and cults registered in response to the requirement of the 1967 law on religious freedom. Public expression of their faith was forbidden then; we can assume that since 1975 this prohibition has been removed but we know remarkably little of their activities or impact. Nor do we have in-depth studies of other religious minorities who cluster particularly in the larger cities and coastal ports; for instance, St. George's Anglican church was established as early as 1850 in Barcelona.

WHAT DOES THE FUTURE HOLD?

Anthropologists must plan to meet new challenges in the urban Spain of the 1980s. Foreign scholars will need to cooperate more actively with Spanish colleagues. Spanish anthropologists, now busily consolidating their own separate discipline, are heavily involved in more traditional studies but will, of necessity, turn increasingly to urban investigations. Both Spanish and foreign scholars will surely collaborate in team research as they put aside the lone-wolf tradition in order to carry out interregional urban studies within Spain and intercity comparative studies in the Mediterranean.

Anthropologists have much to offer in the understanding of how a changing urban environment affects traditional values and behavior. On the one hand, we need to study the "social coping" that ensues as a variety of new roles appears. An increasingly service-oriented, postindustrial labor force swollen by women; a proliferation of new political parties or factions; new clubs, syndicates, lobbying, and public interest groups—many of these are providing new roles and alternatives to more traditional family patterns or coalitions of patronage and "amigocracy." Returned migrants are populating the urban proletariats; managerial elites are changing the image and structure of the middle and upper classes. The city hums with the strain of coping with unaccustomed status.

On the other hand, future studies must take into account the "social articulation" by the urban resident with his cityscape environment. In turn, this articulation is dependent on a series of higher linkages—regional city with metropolis, megalopolis with external forces (tourism, Europeanization, cultural imperialism, standardization). If it is true that each urban resident has his own mental image of the city he lives in and articulates with, then the anthropologist should be concerned how these multiple images of various groups of citizens converge or merge with the symbolism by which a city is characterized, e.g., Barcelona as the convention center, Madrid as *castiza* ("pure and typical"—no longer true), Cadiz as "the silver cup" *(tacita de plata)*, San Sebastian as "the pearl of the Cantabrian," and so on.[8] The traditional anthropological concern with ecology can be well adapted to studying the influence on lifestyles, values, and interaction patterns in the hinterlands or exterlands of cities that are *centers* of some note, e.g., the *polos* of development. A focus on this articulatory dependence will constantly force the urban anthropologist to raise his sights to the analysis of different levels of urbanism in neighborhood, citywide, regional, national, and even international terms. This is a far cry from the comfortable little community study. It calls for a retooling of our methodology and a rethinking of our discipline. We cannot ignore the challenge.

NOTES

1. For this and several subsequent insights we recognize a debt to a variety of sources, in particular Violich (1962), Vicens Vives (1948), and Menendez Pidal (1966).
2. Discussions of the Spanish form of honor and shame can be found in Pitt-Rivers (1954) and Kenny (1960).
3. These groups are the ones largely reflected in the urban studies mentioned in Prat's bibliography (1977:141, 150).
4. Prat (1977:Appendix) makes a general analysis by theme of the 513 works he lists, the majority of which are rural in focus; 110 deal with "ideological aspects" (symbolism, values, cognition, health, fiestas), 67 with "social change" (depopulation, migration, technological change), 41 with "political aspects" (social and class structure), and the remainder with social, economic, ecological, demographic, and technological aspects.
5. Mulcahy (in press), in an ecological interpretation and recommendation, reports on a provisional school for Gypsy children ill-advisedly placed too close to "gentile" territory in Barcelona, which sparked off a bitter social conflict between city officials and local "gentiles."
6. *Governmentally supported* neighbors' associations came into being after the 1964 Law of Associations; they naturally represented the official policy under Franco.
7. We have little doubt that this will effect consequent changes in cultic behavior and beliefs. For example, despite the reputed significance of the Virgin Mary as a role model in young girls' sex-role development, there is little indication that the urban proletariat, at least in Granada, has incorporated this image in its childrearing practices (Knipmeyer 1979).
8. Such a study can well involve an analysis of urban sociocentrism, for which Caro Baroja (1966) has shown us the way. Foster (1960:36–37) has several opposite examples: "Quien sale de Valladolid a donde va a vivir?" ("He who leaves Valladolid, where will he go to live?"), or the more scornful (for one's neighbors) "Almazora La Vieja, montes sin leña, mar sin pescado, e hijos mal criados" ("Almazora the Old, woods without firewood, sea without fish, and inhabitants without manners").

REFERENCES

Bier, Alice Gail
    1979   "Vox Populi": El desarrollo de las asociaciones de vecinos en España. In *Papers, Revista de sociología*, no. 11 (Cambio Social en la Europa Mediterránea). Barcelona: Ediciones Peninsula, pp. 169–86.
Bosque Maurel, Joaquin
    1962   *Geografía urbana de Granada*. Saragossa: Departamento de Geografía Aplicada del Instituto Juan Sebastian Elcano, ser. 13, no. 31.
Caro Baroja, Julio
    1961a   *Los judios en la España moderna y contemporánea*. Madrid: Ediciones Arión.
    1961b   *Las brujas y su mundo*. Madrid: Revista de Occidente. *(The world of the witches*. London: Weidenfeld and Nicolson, 1964.)
    1966   *La ciudad y el campo*. Madrid: Alfaguara.

Cases Mendez, José Ignacio, and Octavio Cabezas Moro
1976   The relation between migration policy and economic development and the promotion of new employment possibilities for returnees (foreign investment and migrant remittance). *International Migration* 14, nos. 1-2:134-62.

Castells, Manuel
1974a   *La cuestión urbana.* Madrid: Siglo XXI.
1974b   *Movimientos sociales urbanas.* Madrid: Siglo XXI.

Cazorla Perez, José
1976   Minorías marginadas en España: El caso de los gitanos. *Revista española de la opinion pública* 45:25-36.

Christian, W. A.
1972   *Person and god in a Spanish valley.* New York: Seminar Press.

Chueca Goitia, Fernando
1951   El semblante de Madrid. *Revista de occidente* 19.

Conosciani, Luciano
1969   *Public organization and policy for low-rent housing in Italy* (L'organizzazione publica dell' edilizia). Milan.

Corbin, John
1979   Social class and patron-clientage in Andalusia: Some problems of comparing ethnographies. *Anthropological Quarterly* 52, no. 2:99-114.

Costa, Joaquin
1902   *Oligarquía y caciquismo como la forma actual de gobierno en España: Urgencia y modo de cambiarla.* Madrid: Ateneo.

De la Peña, Guillermo
1970   Settled Gypsies in Madrid. M.A. thesis, University of Manchester.

Díez Nicolás, Juan
1969   Determinación de la población urbana en España en 1960. In *La concentración urbana en España.* Madrid: Centro de Estudios Sociales.
1972   *Especialización funcional y dominación en la España urbana.* Madrid: Guadarrama.

Duocastella, Rogelio, *et al.*
1966   *Análisis sociológico del catolicismo español.* Barcelona: Nova Terra.

Esteva Fabregat, Claudio
1969   La etnología española y sus problemas. *Etnología y tradiciones populares* (Saragossa), pp. 1-40.

Fernández, Mercé
1978   *Estudio ethnohistórico de la comunidad judia de Barcelona.* Tésis de licenciatura, Universidad de Barcelona.

Fernandez Gutierrez, Fernando
1977   *Análisis geográfico-estructural de Granada y sus barrios.* Granada: Caja General de Ahorros y Monte de Granada Seminario de Estudios.

FOESSA, Fundación
1970   *Informe sociológico sobre la situación social de España.* Madrid: Editorial Euroamerica.

Foster, George M.
1960   *Culture and conquest: The American Spanish heritage.* New York: Viking Fund.

Fraga Iribarne, Manuel
1972   *El desarrollo político* (2nd ed.). Barcelona: Grijalbo.

Freeman, Susan Tax
1968   Corporate village organization in the Sierra Ministra: An Iberian structural type. *Man* (n.s.) 3:477-84.

García, María Soledad
   1977   Desarrollo social y formación social en un área de Barcelona. Tésis de
              licenciatura, Universidad de Barcelona.
Gaviría, Mario
   1968   Análisis sociourbanístico de un barrio nuevo español. *Arquitectura*, pp.
              113-14.
   1970   *Campo, urbe y espacio del ocio.* Madrid: Siglo XXI.
Gilmore, David
   1976   Class, culture and community size in Spain: The relevance of models.
              Anthropological Quarterly 49, no. 2:89-106.
Gutkind, E. A.
   1969   *Urban development in southern Europe: Spain and Portugal.* New York: Free
              Press.
Henningsen, G.
   1971   Tres años de investigaciones etnológicas en España. *Éthnica* 1:63-92.
Instituto Nacional de Estadística
   1972   *Anuario estadístico de España.* Madrid.
Jimenez, Alfredo, and Elias Zamora
   1975   *Primera reunión de antropólogos españoles.* Universidad de Sevilla.
Kaprow, Miriam Lee
   1978   Divided we stand: A study of discord among Gypsies in a Spanish city.
              Ph.D. dissertation, Columbia University.
Keefe, Eugene K., David P. Coffin, James M. Moore, Jr., Robert Rinehart, and
Susan H. Scurlock
   1976   *Area handbook for Spain.* Washington, D.C.: U.S. Government Printing
              Office.
Kenny, Michael
   1960a   *A Spanish tapestry: Town and country in Castile.* London: Cohen and West.
   1960b   Patterns of patronage in Spain. *Anthropological Quarterly* 33, no. 1:14-23.
   1968   Parallel power structures in Castile: The patron-client balance. In John
              G. Peristiany, ed., *Contributions to Mediterranean sociology.* The Hague:
              Mouton, pp. 155-66.
   1971   El rol de la antropología social dentro de las ciencias sociales en España.
              Éthnica 1:91-105.
   1972a   The return of the Spanish emigrant. *Nord Nytt* 2:119-29.
   1972b   The role of social anthropology in the social sciences in Spain. *Iberian
              Studies* 1, no. 1 (Spring):27-33; no. 2 (Fall):82.
Knipmeyer, Mary C.
   1979   Gender identity and sex-role preferences among Spanish pre-school chil-
              dren. Ph.D. dissertation, Catholic University of America.
Linz, Juan J., and Amando de Miguel
   1966   Within-nation differences and comparisons: The eight Spains. In Rich-
              ard L. Merritt and Stein Rokkan, eds., *Comparing nations: The use of quanti-
              tative data in cross-cultural research.* New Haven, Conn.: Yale University
              Press, pp. 267-319.
Lisón Tolosana, Carmelo
   1971   *Antropología social en España.* Madrid: Siglo XXI.
   1972   Sobre áreas culturales en España. In Manuel Fraga y Iribarne, Juan Ve-
              larde, and Salustiano del Campo, eds., *La España de los años 70: La socie-
              dad.* Madrid: Editorial Moneda y Credito, pp. 319-75.

1979   *Brujería en Galicia: Estructura social y simbolismo cultural.* Madrid: Akal Editor.

Lynch, Kevin
1960   *The image of the city.* Cambridge, Mass.: MIT Press.

Martinez-Mari, José María
1966   La inmigración en el área de Barcelona. *Estudios geográficos* 27:105.

McLane, Merrill F.
1979   Return migration of an ethnic minority: The Spanish Gypsy. In Robert E. Rhodes, ed., *Papers in anthropology* (special issue "The Anthropology of return migration"), vol. 20, no. 1. Norman: University of Oklahoma, Department of Anthropology.

Menendez Pidal, Ramón
1966   *The Spaniards in their history.* Trans. Walter Starkie. New York: W. W. Norton.

Miguel, Amando de, and Juan Salcedo
1972   *Dinámica del desarrollo industrial de las regiones en España.* Madrid: Tecnos.

Miguel, Jesus M. de, and Melissa G. Moyer
1979   Sociology in Spain. *Current Sociology* 27, no. 1 (Spring):1–299.

Ministerio de la Vivienda
1969   *Absorción del chabolismo: Teoría general y actuaciones españolas.* Madrid.

Molina, Esperanza
1972   Aportaciones para el mejor conocimiento de un área suburbana. *Revista Española de Antropología Americana* 7, no. 1:223–43.

Moore, Kenneth
1977   *Those of the street: The Catholic-Jews.* South Bend, Ind.: University of Notre Dame Press.

Moreno, Isidoro
1975   La investigación antropológica en España. In *Primera reunión de antropólogos españoles.* Seville: Editorial Jimenez, pp. 325–38.

Mulcahy, David
1976   Gitano sex role symbolism and behavior. *Anthropological Quarterly* 49: 135–45.
In press. Territorial difficulties in urban planning. In William Millsap, ed., *Anthropology for planners.* New York: Westview Press.

Mumford, Lewis
1938   *The culture of cities.* London: Harcourt.

Nash, Dennison
1970   *A community in limbo.* Bloomington: Indiana University Press.

Persistiany, John G., ed.
1966   *Honour and shame: The values of Mediterranean society.* London: Weidenfeld and Nicolson.

Perpiñá Grau, Román
1954   *Corología: Teoría estructural y estructurante de la población de España, 1900–1950.* Madrid: Consejo Superior de Investigaciones Científicas.

Pi-Sunyer, Oriol
1979   The politics of tourism in Catalonia. *Mediterranean Studies* 1, no. 2:47–69.

Pi-Sunyer, Oriol, and Mary Jane Pi-Sunyer
1975   Occupational groups and ethnicity: Some observations on the attitudes of middle-class Catalans. *Human Organization* 34:289–300.

Pitt-Rivers, Julian A.
1954   *The people of the sierra.* London: Weidenfeld and Nicolson.

Prat, Joan
    1977   Una aproximación a la bibliografía antropológica sobre España. *Éthnica*
            13: 131–71.
Press, Irwin
    1979   *The city as context: Urbanism and behavioral constraints in Seville.* Urbana: Uni-
            versity of Illinois Press.
Quintana, Bertha B.
    1972   *¡Que gitano! Gypsies of southern Spain.* New York: Holt, Rinehart and Win-
            ston.
Salcedo, Juan
    1977   Estudios regionales y urbanos en España. Unpublished ms. Lancaster.
San Roman, Teresa
    1976   *Vecinos gitanos.* Madrid: Akal.
Schwartz, Henry F.
    1972   *Trujillo: The ethnography of a pre-industrial city of western Spain.* Ann Arbor,
            Mich.: University Microfilms.
Stanislawski, Dan
    1946   Early Spanish town planning in the New World. *Geographical Review* 37:
            94–105.
Terán, Manuel de
    1961   El desarrollo espacial de Madrid a partir de 1868. *Estudios geográficos* 22.
    1964   Geografía humana y sociológica: Geografía social. *Estudios geográficos* 97.
Trías Beltran, Carlos
    1964a   La concentración urbana y la distribución de la aglomeración madrileña.
            In *Madrid 1964.* Madrid: Instituto de Estudios de Administración Local.
    1964b   *Area metropolitana de Madrid.* Madrid: Ministerio de la Vivienda.
Trías Fargas, Ramón
    1968   Algunos problemas de la infraestructura catalana. *Información comercial es-
            pañola* 417–418:95–104.
Umrath, Heinz
    1968   *Financing housing.* Brussels: International Congress of Free Trade Unions.
Vicens Vives, Jaime
    1948   *Geopolítica.* Barcelona: Vicens Vives.
Vila Valenti, Juan, and Horacio Capel
    1970   *Campo y ciudad en la geografía española.* Barcelona: Salvat.
Violich, Francis
    1962   Evolution of the Spanish city. *Journal of the American Institute of Planners,* pp.
            170–79.

Chapter 2

Urban Research in Italy

David I. Kertzer

Judging from the anthropological literature, one might well conclude that Italy is a nation of peasants living in remote and desolate villages (see Crump 1975; Saporiti 1978). Yet today most Italians live in urban areas, with close to 30% living in cities of over 100,000 inhabitants. In this chapter we will first briefly review Italian urban development and urban geography, and then some of the social research that has focused on city life in Italy will be considered, followed by a look at a number of sociocultural characteristics of Italian urban life. Finally, we will consider what contribution anthropology can make to Italian urban study.[1]

URBAN DEVELOPMENT IN ITALY

Italy has experienced steady urban growth over the past century, at the same time that rural areas throughout the country have been progressively depopulated. At the beginning of the nineteenth century only five cities had more than 100,000 inhabitants, accounting for just 6% of the country's population (Lucrezio 1970, Benini 1911:9). By 1977 there were 47 cities of this size, 11 of them having populations of more than 360,000 (United Nations 1978:271); over 16 million of Italy's 56 million population now live in these large cities. At the other end of the scale the proportion of Italians living in communities of under 3,000 shrank in the period 1881–1971 from 27.7% to 11.9% (Livi Bacci 1965:18, Golini 1974:87).

Although Italy has some very large cities, unlike other rapidly urbanizing nations, it has not been characterized by a single urban magnet, a primate city in which a large proportion of all urbanites live. Rather, most of the 94 provincial capitals have acted as poles of attraction for rural emigrants. No city counted more than a million inhabitants before the 1951 census, and there are still just four cities of this dimension.

When we look at greater metropolitan areas rather than at the urban *comuni* themselves, though, a somewhat different picture emerges, for while Rome, the largest city, has 3 million inhabitants, greater metropolitan Milan counts close to 6 million. In all, as of 1971, 32 metropolitan areas contained 43% of the Italian population. As shown in Figure 1, these highly

Figure 1. Metropolitan Urban Areas in Italy
From Golini 1974.

urbanized areas are not evenly spread throughout the peninsula; two-thirds of them are found in the northern part of the country, and all south of Florence are found on the coast. This uneven pattern of development reflects the uneven economic development of the nation, with industry largely concentrated in the north.

The cities of northern Italy include both industrial centers—particularly in the industrial triangle formed by Milan-Turin-Genoa—and market centers for some of the most fertile agricultural areas of Italy. Traces of the centuries-old walls that surrounded most of these cities can still be seen, though the expanding populations have long outgrown these barriers, which formerly separated each city from its surrounding hinterland.

Milan, the foremost city of northern Italy, had been a center for merchants, a point of communication and trade between Italy and the rest of Europe. It became one of the first industrialized cities of Italy in the mid-nineteenth century when the importation of heavy machinery resulted in the mushrooming of the textile industry. From 1861 to 1967 the proportion of Milan's population living in the old walled portion of the city shrank from 73% to just 8%. In the process, 127 neighboring *comuni* have been swallowed up into the sprawling Milanese metropolis (Boffi *et al.* 1972:49–67).

By contrast, the cities of the south are nonindustrially based and suffer from chronic unemployment, underemployment, and lack of social services. Southern Italian cities have not been efficient market centers, for their ties with their rural hinterland have been marred by weak communication and transportation systems and by poorly organized marketing mechanisms. Characteristic of the southern cities, but not only the cities, is the widespread struggle for a position on the public payroll. Though public administration has grown tremendously, this has not meant that adequate social services have been made available to the population. Public jobs are generally given out on a patronage basis by the ruling political parties (especially the Christian Democrats), and standards of performance (or even appearance) at work are on the whole minimal (Giantempo and Cammarota 1977).

Rome represents something of a special case, lying at the dividing line between north and south and, as the national capital, housing a vast national bureaucracy. Indeed, as Ferrarotti (1975:13) has written, "Apart from construction, which has unique characteristics of a post-agricultural and parain-dustrial activity, the bureaucracy remains the only true Roman industry." Of Rome's economically active population of 900,000, under 10% were employed in industry (outside of construction), while 270,000 held state-financed positions (1975:114).

Naples, with the second largest metropolitan population in Italy (over 3,600,000 in 1971), is the most industrialized city in the south, but its population is otherwise not atypical of other southern cities. Trade unionism is weak, as is formal associational life in general in comparison to the north.

Employment is for the most part insecure, with the exception of the large
public sector, and thousands of people engage in odd jobs, some illegal,
others semilegal, to make ends meet. Decades of misrule and lack of planning, together with rapid population growth, have resulted in a sanitation
system and other public infrastructure verging on catastrophe (Goddard
1977, Chubb 1979).

In Sicily the same pattern emerges. Of Messina's population, 14% live
in shanty towns and 40% in substandard housing. Parks and other green
space are almost wholly lacking, and the few social services are heavily concentrated in the bourgeois neighborhoods (Giantempo and Cammarota
1977). As in neighboring Catania, the largest employment sector outside of
the public payroll is provided by the construction industry. Thousands of
new buildings, the result both of public housing projects and private building speculation, have provided jobs, though on an impermanent and often
seasonal basis (Caciagli 1977).

In the south what industrial development exists is not confined to the
cities. Indeed, the massive government-financed development program for
the south was based on a decision to create industrial poles of development
in nonurban areas (though there are some exceptions such as Naples).
Hence in Sicily, for example, the large industrial plants are found not in or
around the largest cities but in or near smaller cities (such as Gela and Syra-
cuse-Augusta). The result is that the most highly industrialized localities are
not the largest cities (Catanzaro 1979:15, Collidà 1976).

ITALIAN URBAN STUDIES

Social scientific research in Italy, though blossoming in recent years,
was slow to develop. A variety of political and cultural explanations has been
offered to account for this fact, many focusing on the pre-eminent place of
idealist philosophy in Italian academia (Balbo, Chiaretti, and Massironi
1975; Garaguso 1976:94). This idealist tradition continues, with a large proportion of all scholarly writings by Italian social scientists stemming from
philosophical and political programmatic concerns, often with little attention to empirical, systematic data. This politicization of Italian social science
is reflected in the empirical work being done as well, with survey research
undertaken for such purposes as measuring the discontent of potentially politically sympathetic populations.

The empirical research conducted by urban sociologists in Italy[2] has relied heavily on survey techniques of formal interviewing. Typically, a variety of demographic and personal background questions is posed, followed
by a series of attitudinal questions, and the analysis is organized around a
series of tables that set forth the tabulated responses (e.g., Crespi and Martinelli 1968, Fasola-Bologna 1968). Similar survey research has been con-

ducted by American sociologists (Pearlin 1974) and political scientists (Evans 1967) as well.

Marxian perspectives guide many of the urban studies carried out in Italy in recent years,[3] as may be illustrated by the work of Vergati (1975–76) in Rome and Boffi *et al.* (1972) in Milan. Vergati, as part of a large-scale study by the Istituto di Sociologia of the University of Rome, has focused on the ghettoization of the city's poor and the way urban space is compartmentalized by class to serve the interests of the bourgeoisie. The city is seen, using a phrase that has gained a certain popularity, as a "social factory" in which forms of social life ultimately derive from the needs of the ruling class. Boffi *et al.* (1972:41) further detail this conception of the city by maintaining that, in the city, capital exercises its hold over the worker by "controlling him at the workplace, constraining his choices of consumption, obligating him to accept the bourgeois values of individualism, and even alienating him in his private, personal life." These studies, and many others like them (e.g., Conti 1974, Mingione 1977), have attempted to document this alienation of the working and lower classes in the city.

If many Italian urban studies have been primarily theoretical, there is one strand of more applied urban research that deserves mention here, that connected with urban planning (see Fried 1973). As is illustrated by the journal *Archivio di studi urbani e regionali,* one of the best publications in Italian urban social science, many urban planners have been collaborating with social scientists in seeking to determine the housing needs of urban Italy. Illustrative is the case of two anthropologists, Callari Galli and Harrison, who have collaborated with researchers at the Istituto di Architettura e Urbanistica of the University of Bologna in studying housing needs in the surrounding urban area. Over a thousand interviews were conducted in Bologna, Ferrara, and Modena, seeking to determine how families used the space available to them in their apartments. The anthropologists were especially interested in linking people's conceptions of their homes and of proper social life to their actual housing needs (Berardi *et al.* 1974, Callari Galli *et al.* 1974).

Certainly one of the best Italian urban studies yet published is Percy Allum's (1973) *Politics and Society in Post-war Naples,* a study of parliamentary electoral politics and clientelism in the capital of the Italian south. Allum identifies a central conflict between the "*Gesellschaft* norms of the state system and the predominantly *Gemeinschaft* values of local society" (1973:325). He details the way in which local patrons, tied into national centers of power, dispense favors in order to win electoral support and economic power. Methodologically eclectic, Allum's approach draws on interviews with the politically powerful, electoral data, secondary sources, various documentary evidence, and personal observation to produce a masterful analysis.

One final strand of urban research in Italy that should be noted is represented by industrial sociology. Research on factory organization and particularly on unions is now voluminous, with various journals publishing in this area and university professorships assigned to the subject. Given the geographical distribution of large industry in Italy, most of these studies focus on northern locales (see especially the five volumes edited by Pizzorno under the series title *Lotte operaie e sindacato in Italia (1968–1972)*; Regini and Reyneri 1971; Low-Beer 1978), but a few deal with the poles of industrial development in the south (Masi 1979).

ANTHROPOLOGICAL RESEARCH IN URBAN ITALY

Italy's tradition of philosophical idealism affected anthropology as much as any of the social sciences. Initially, in fact, anthropology was placed in the faculties of philosophy, occupying a painfully subservient position in the academic world (Garaguso 1976:96–97). Given the nature of fascism and the absence of a colonial empire to study, conditions were poor for the development of the discipline (Lanternari 1973:44–45).

Lacking an empiricist tradition, sociocultural anthropology emerged as an antiquarian, folkloristic, and historical pursuit, geographically concentrated in the most pristine areas of the nation, particularly the south. Indeed, a number of Italian anthropologists have cited the focus on research in the home country as one of the distinguishing characteristics of Italian anthropology (Bernardi 1973:103, Colajanni 1973:78). The foremost figure in this effort, and one who brought some methodological and conceptual rigor to southern Italian peasant village studies, was Ernesto De Martino (Lanternari 1977).

Though some urban anthropological research has been undertaken in recent years, Italian anthropologists have shared with their foreign colleagues a penchant for seeking out the fast-fading peasantry. Italian anthropologists have operated under an additional constraint as well as in their choice of research area, for the Italian university system does not normally allow faculty to take research leaves. This further militates toward domestic field study (Marazzi 1973:630–31). The rural bias of these studies is, paradoxically, apparent in the first urban anthropology text to be published in Italy (Stroppa 1978), for none of the 21 reprinted articles is by an Italian or based on Italian fieldwork.

Of the little urban research conducted by Italian anthropologists, two theoretical orientations stand out. One, which traces its inspiration to the legacy of American cultural anthropology, focuses on values; the other, flowing from a marxian perspective, focuses on class exploitation. Among the foremost exponents of the former approach are Tullio-Altan and Tentori. Tullio-Altan has been engaged in a large-scale, survey-based study of values among Italian youths from a variety of localities (Tullio-Altan and Marradi 1976, Tullio-Altan and Cartocci 1979). Tentori, who had done early work on the southern city of Matera (Tentori 1976), collaborated with a sociologist (Tentori and Guidicini 1972) to write the first book-length urban study by an anthropologist in Italy. Focusing on a neighborhood of Bologna, the study is a monument to traditionalism, seeking to recreate the *Gemeinschaft* community spirit which the authors feel characterized past life in the city. Elderly people, long resident in the area, were sought out for interviews and asked to provide their youthful recollections of the neighborhood. Two small samples of adults and youths were also interviewed to determine what changes had recently taken place in the locality. By taking this retrospective approach and by passing up the opportunity for participant observation, a limited and sentimental portrait of urban social history is provided.

Given the strength of marxism in Italian academia, it is hardly surprising that a good deal of Italian anthropology is informed by the marxist tradition. As was manifest in a recent national conference on anthropology and marxism (Remotti 1978), widespread efforts have been underway to make marxism the theoretical basis of a reconstituted anthropology (cf. Cirese 1973, Lombardi-Satriani 1976, Guarrasi 1978). Some of the implications of this for the development of urban studies in Italian anthropology can be gleaned from the recent call of Moluzzi and Bertolo (1977) for research focused on the mechanisms of class exploitation. Citing Antonio Gramsci, the foremost Italian marxist theoretician, as well as De Martino, who was himself influenced by Gramsci, they call for anthropological study of the relationship between "popular culture" and "hegemonic" or "official culture." In Gramscian terms, the exploitation of the masses is facilitated by the ability of the ruling class to get the members of the lower classes to embrace the world view and value system propagated by the ruling class. Yet the exploited masses have their own culture, deriving from their actual social and economic relations, which is in tension with the "official" culture (cf. Kertzer 1979). From this vantage point, urban life is of no less anthropological interest than rural life. The dynamics of social change, viewed as the product of this tension between the two cultures and the tension between the actual social/economic circumstances of the masses and the hegemonic culture which surrounds them, becomes the ultimate object of anthropological research.

Urban Italian research by non-Italian anthropologists has to date been rare. Researchers have converged on the small agricultural communities of the underdeveloped south, with some venturing to relatively isolated and small communities of the center and north. Yet the best of these studies have dealt with urban influence; none of these communities can be satisfactorily understood apart from the national political and economic system in which they find themselves. Examples of these attempts to document the rural-national ties are provided by Pitkin (1959), Silverman (1965), Davis (1975), Katz (1975), Blok (1974), and Schneider and Schneider (1976, 1980). Published work by non-Italian anthropologists based on urban Italian research is thus far limited to the writings of Belmonte and Goddard on Naples, Hilowitz on Syracuse, and Kertzer on Bologna.

CITY LIFE

Having sketched out the nature of urban development in Italy and having characterized social scientific approaches to urban Italian study, we turn now to an examination of some of the elements of urban life that bear further anthropological study. Five areas have been singled out and we will briefly discuss each in turn: family/kinship, sex roles, religion, associational activity, and neighborhood/community.

Family Relations and Kinship

Buonanno (1977) has recently published a review of the sociological literature on the family in Italy. In it she laments the dearth of empirical research, though she notes a burgeoning of family studies in the 1970s as a result of the growth of the women's movement. Many in the women's movement view the family as the social and physical location of women's exploitation and exclusion from wider social participation. Hence a number of sociologists, particularly women, have been launching investigations of family relations. Most of these have focused on relatively homogeneous, localized populations, with Balbo's (1976) comparative study of family life among the various classes in urban centers of the north being one of the rare exceptions. She concludes:

> . . . the man identifies principally with the world of the job, in a manner that is often passive and conflict ridden, but in any case with poor participation in family life. All the types one might find — the worker who accepts overtime to increase his wages, the type who sits down in front of the television after work, or the militant engaged in union or political activity — are equally marginal or excluded from any roles having to do with running the family. The consequence is that the role of managing family tasks falls entirely on the mother, and this role in its turn is also rigid. (Balbo and May 1975–76:94)

Despite the control exercised by the mother over the family, the ideology of male supremacy is still retained, though signs of its erosion have appeared. A survey of adolescents in Rome found that 57% of the males and 37% of the females agreed with the statement that it is the father who rules in the family. These figures are reversed for those who claim that both parents rule jointly in the family. Only a tiny minority felt that it was the mother who ruled. A direct relationship was found between the rural origin and low level of education of the father and the proportion of adolescents who felt that the father ruled alone in the family (Moluzzi and Bertolo 1977).

One of the crucial questions in understanding contemporary urban Italy is just how important family life is in providing people with their satisfactions and how this is changing with economic and social conditions. Pearlin (1974), in his study of family relations in Turin, sees the family as people's psychological refuge in a hostile world. Given the perceived unfriendliness and unpredictability of the world around them, according to Pearlin, parents are "fiercely protective" of their family and fearful that changing societal forces are threatening their one bastion of security (1974:36). This overwhelming importance of the family is seen as particularly pronounced among the working class, with the middle class being in a better position to benefit from nonfamilial institutions (1974:171).

Belmonte, who spent a year doing participant observation fieldwork in a lower-class *quartiere* of Naples, has presented a contrary view: "The facts of scarcity and the consequent failures of solidarity and trust, and the recurrent themes of suspicion, cruelty, and violence which stain the lives of the poor, do not stop at the barricades of the family but rather collect and fester at this critical node" (1979:53). In this perspective, individuals living in poverty become overly dependent on other family members, placing impossible demands on them that lead to turmoil rather than tranquillity. Guarrasi, conducting comparable research in a poor neighborhood of Palermo, finds both families that are tightly integrated and those that are coming apart; in the latter case the husband is usually unable to provide the requisite economic support. Strikingly, Guarrasi portrays a situation of polarization, in which families are characterized by one extreme or the other of cohesion and solidarity: "intermediate situations do not exist" (1978:147).

Relations between parents and children have been a subject of great popular interest in Italy, though oddly the social scientific literature on the question is sparse. A series of dramatic events, from the student rebellion of 1968 through the Red Brigades of a decade later, have put the issue of parent-child conflict in sharp public relief. While many adults lament the disintegration of what is nostalgically remembered as a secure, well-integrated family system, many young people have branded traditional norms governing family life as repressive. Balbo (1976) describes the tension between parental domination and the desire of young people (including unmarried youths in their twenties) for more autonomy as a key feature of Italian society.

The nature of relations with kinsmen outside the conjugal family has not been the subject of much research in Italy, and the scattered observations on the subject are contradictory. There is the controversial notion of Italians, particularly southern Italians, as confining their sphere of strong emotional ties and obligations to their own conjugal family.[4] Yet other accounts and observations of Italian life suggest that extended kinship ties are quite strong and important. Guarrasi, for example, argues that in industrial societies both the very rich and the very poor are heavily dependent on extended kinship ties. In the case of the Palermo poor he studied, he found that the extended family network was crucial to the survival of nuclear families experiencing unemployment (1978:150). More generally, the extended family among these people was found to provide one of the most important bases of social control: "The extended family exercises its control over individuals' behavior, especially when people patently stray from the group's own rules; it resolves disputes that arise within and sometimes even outside the family system; it influences its members' choices of a spouse, favoring certain kinds of marriages and blocking others" (1978:149).

These relationships and this mechanism of social control remain almost unchartered territory in empirical studies of Italian society. The importance of extended family relations in the urban north, though, has been argued by Bugarini and Vicarelli (1979) in a recent study of families in Bologna. They found dramatically high rates of newlyweds, at marriage, living with or very near their parents, and even as they moved out of the parental home, most people remained in the same neighborhood. Upon marriage, 51% of their working-class couples, 44% of the white-collar workers, and 24% of the professional couples co-resided with one set of parents. While these percentages dropped through the years of marriage, 15 years after marriage 65% either cohabited or lived in the same neighborhood as one set of parents. At this time, too, 76% of the couples in the survey visited the wife's parents at least once a week, while 65% visited the husband's parents with this frequency.

The extent to which elderly parents live with their married children is also an important issue, yet it too has received little empirical attention. In a study by Leonardi (1964) of factory workers in eastern Sicily, for example, 15% of the married workers were found to be living with their elderly parents. Given limited social security benefits and a tradition of elderly parents taking up residence with their married children (Kertzer 1977a, 1978, 1981; Douglass 1980), the extent and implications of extended family households are among the most urgent of topics in need of investigation.

Sex Roles

In addition to providing the material for countless films, sex roles in Italy provide fertile ground for social investigation. Again, regional variation is pronounced: in the south it often seems as though the better part of the adult female population wears the black garments of mourning, while unmarried but adult women are chaperoned by their mothers or their surrogates. In fact, a glance at the cars parked in the evening along the coast of Catania reveals more than one young adult couple whose conversation and activity are constrained by the presence of the woman's mother in the back seat. In the north young women are given more freedom, but it is still considered shocking by many for an unmarried woman in her twenties to live apart from her parents. One of the issues in need of empirical study is the nature of regional variations in sex roles: are the regional differences largely superficial, masking an essential similarity?

Central to understanding Italian sex roles is the fact that Italy has one of the lowest rates of female labor force participation of any European country. Moreover, female employment outside the home is largely limited to the years after school and before marriage or, at latest, until birth of the first child. This is related both to the nation's economic structure and to cultural norms regarding women's place. The fact that women are excluded from the official labor force does not mean, however, that they are not employed, for Italy has a huge illegal home industry occupying well over one million women. This system depends on work put out from factories through intermediaries who bring the work to the woman's home; the women do the work at home, often on machinery which they must provide themselves. The work is illegal because various legal guarantees are not met, including minimum wage, paid vacation, sick leave, maximum weekly hours, and safety precautions. In short, it is a way in which the factory owners can exploit the marginal situation in which women find themselves (Balbo and May 1975–76).

The pressures on women not to leave the home for employment are made evident in the study of Roman adolescents referred to earlier. Asked whether they were favorably disposed to having their mothers find jobs, only 26% of the girls and 8.5% of the boys responded yes. The reasons provided for this sentiment were that the mother's primary responsibility was to take care of the family and domestic duties, and that the children needed the presence of the mother at home (Moluzzi and Bertolo 1977:108).

Goddard's (1977) study of women in Naples provides further insight into this problem. Her qualitative study was designed to shed light on living conditions of working-class families in Naples in order to illuminate the factors lying behind the availability of cheap female labor. As she notes, the domestic industry of women working in the home is not new in Naples; many of the women now working for pay in the home have mothers and grandmothers who did the same.

These women are not working at home because of any objection to working in factories. They realize that factory work is better paid, with many other benefits as well, and many women said they would value the greater social contact work in a factory would bring. Indeed, many of the women had worked in factories before they were married, and some of them continued to work for the same factory at home, receiving substantially less pay. The reason they give for working at home is that they could not fulfill

their household duties and hold a factory job at the same time. Traditional
conceptions of the woman's role play a major part:

> . . . a considerable number of women gave up factory work after their
> engagement or their marriage even though it was not yet necessary for
> them to do so. This was due to their fiancés and husbands demanding
> that they leave the factory, because they were worried about the "bad
> influence" of other workers, and work at home with sisters or other
> kinswomen (his or hers). In some cases fathers forbade their daughters
> to work outside the home unless they worked with a kinsman or a per-
> son known and respected by the family. (1977:144)

The result of this is that the social life of women is much more circumscribed
than that of men, and much more tied to the kin network (see also Hilowitz
1976:143–45). It is noteworthy that, in general, the militant male cham-
pions of socialism share in the larger society's exploitation of women (Goddard
1977:148, Buonanno 1977:104, Grasso 1974, Kertzer 1982).

Religion and the Church

That the Roman Catholic church has played a major role in Italian
social life can hardly be disputed. There is some question, though, concerning the extent and meaning of the Church's influence in Italy today, particularly (but not only) in the nation's urban centers. Until national unification in the 1860s, a good part of the Italian peninsula was ruled by the
Vatican as papal states. From Rome to Bologna the clergy not only provided
the spiritual leadership but dominated the positions of political power as
well. Even in other parts of the peninsula the illiterate masses often turned to
the local priests for aid in a wide variety of contexts.

That while virtually all Italians are baptized, the extent to which they
identify with the Church and participate in it is highly variable by region,
locality, sex, and social class. The rates of participation have fallen dramatically over the past three decades, and in some cities, such as Bologna, less
than 5% of the working-class population attend Sunday mass. Just within
the past few years the proportion of civil weddings has grown astronomically
in the large cities. In Bologna, for example, civil weddings have risen in the
period 1968–77 from 3% to 28% of all those getting married for the first
time (Parisi and Senin-Artina 1979). Many of the disaffected are communists, and some of these choose alternative rites of passage offered by the
party (Kertzer 1975). But many others who are disaffected from the Church
to this extent are unsympathetic with the Communist party as well, not least
due to the party's conciliatory policy toward the Church.

Catholicism is far from a unitary phenomenon in urban Italy, and to
understand the nature of the Church's influence it is necessary to plot the diversity of the Church's incarnations. In addition to the traditional parish

church with its parish priest and assistant priests, there have been various forms of "progressive" church movements, some involving radical priests and some consisting of spontaneous groups organized without benefit of clergy (Kertzer 1980: chs. 8 and 9). These latter range from groups aimed at personal spiritual benefit to those with revolutionary political goals (Garelli 1977, Parisi 1978).

While religious activity can be studied without difficulty, the nature of people's religious conceptions presents considerable methodological problems. Italy is not lacking in surveys that call on people to state if they believe in the divinity of Jesus, but the superficiality of such impersonal interview data leads to grave doubts about their validity (Fasola-Bologna 1968). It has been claimed, for example, on the basis of interviews with poor people in Messina, that "religion . . . remains a superficial fact that is manifest in external rites: only two of the respondents were not married in the church and did not have their children baptized, but no one succeeded in articulating a motivation [for their religious behavior] that did not simply consist of a reference to a generic faith or conformity to what everyone else does" (Cammarota 1977:127–28). Along somewhat similar lines, Guarrasi (1978:141) has written that among the *Lumpenproletariat* of Palermo whom he studied, "witchcraft and other magical beliefs . . . are much more prevalent than is regular attendance of religious functions." The matter of gathering interview data on religious beliefs is complicated in the Italian case by the fact that social scientists and intellectuals in general are often perceived as left-wing and hence unsympathetic to the Church. People's difficulty in articulating the nature of their religious beliefs may be compounded by their reticence to appear devout in the presence of a skeptic.

Politics and Associational Life

The existence of and participation in formal associations of various kinds show a sharp cleavage between north and south. In the north, and particularly in the areas where the communists are strongest, there is a wealth of associations aimed at recreational, commercial, political, and special-interest (e.g., trade union, pensioners, veterans) activities. Local branches of these organizations are generally tied to regional or national organizations with close links to political parties. In the south fewer associations exist and a much smaller proportion of the population participates in them. Even where, in the case of political parties (especially the Christian Democrats), there is a large number of members, participation may be minimal. Indeed, numerous cases have been documented in Sicily of people annually having their Christian Democratic party dues paid without ever being aware of the fact that they were party members.

The two main fonts of associational life in Italy are the Church and the Communist party. In some areas of the country local associational life is dominated by one or the other through party sections and allied voluntary organizations. In other areas social life is fractured between the two spheres of organizational influence.

Hundreds of articles and scores of books have been published that examine political allegiances in various parts of the country. Most of these are based on interviews with political leaders, analysis of electoral results, and opinion polling. However, few studies focus on a single urban locality and detail the way in which the mass of people actually experience political activity and the social context in which they form their political allegiances.

Political participation among the unionized working-class population of Italy tends to be high and largely revolves around the Communist party. Participation among women and the workers holding more insecure employment is generally weak (Boffi *et al.* 1972). Cammarota's interview study of the poor in Messina found that while virtually all respondents felt that the society in which they lived was unjust and corrupt, "few think there is anything they can do to make it any better" (1977:120). Just 16% of those interviewed claimed to participate in any association at all, and most of these were drawn from the small number of unionized workers in the area.

Among the poor of Palermo, Guarrasi found much political interest, but this took personalistic and clientelistic rather than associational forms. When agitation for better housing and social services grew intense, the women of the *quartiere* demanded to speak with the mayor, for it was felt that only through his personal intervention could their grievances be addressed. The secretary of the local Communist party section characterized the people's attitude: "Institutions as such don't exist for them, only individuals. Political relations are relations between people, between people who are more or less powerful. The basic fact is this: the people don't understand what an institution is, what its function is, its significance . . . " (1978:152–53). The sociopolitical implications of this phenomenon are great. As people view politics in terms of the pursuit of personal advantage, the corrupt clientelistic broker is viewed more favorably than the sincere party activist. The activist, who claims to be motivated by ideology rather than personal interest, is viewed with suspicion, an attitude which has been particularly detrimental to the development of the Communist party in such areas.

Whether the poor of Italy question the legitimacy of the social, economic, and political system remains a lively issue. This topic has recently been raised in discussion of the class basis of the ultra-left terrorist groups. It is noteworthy that these groups have been organized in the northern cities rather than in the south, and that the leadership appears to be drawn from middle-class and stable working-class families. The only city of the south to see a large-scale organization of the poor has been Naples, where the League of the Unemployed was active in the mid-1970s. Of equal interest in Naples has been the political organization of the *contrabandisti,* the thousands of small peddlers of contraband, who have held demonstrations protesting attempted police crackdowns on their activities. Belmonte, in his study of a poor *quartiere* of Naples, stresses the absence of any communal political action by the poor, the emphasis on protecting one's own individual interests, and the lack of questioning of the legitimacy of the politico-economic system. These issues remain moot in the absence of more empirical work.

Studies dealing with the upper classes in urban Italy are few, and given the embattled situation in which the elite now find themselves, conditions for conducting research are not good. Only in the realm of political behavior have many studies been done. These have focused mainly on the ways in which the elite manipulate social ties and utilize political party connections to advance their careers (Allum 1973, Caciagli 1977).

Neighborhood and Social Identity

According to popular stereotype, Italian men gather at their neighborhood bar (café) each evening where they play cards, drink wine and coffee, and talk of soccer and politics. Women, on the other hand, gather on stoops in front of their homes where they gossip with neighbors, or stop to talk at the small neighborhood stores at which they shop. While, like all stereotypes, this one is guilty of overgeneralization, it does contain more than a small measure of truth. Yet one of the more important changes now occurring in the cities of Italy is the erosion of this sort of neighborhood activity and an increased privatization of social life.

A number of factors have been blamed for what is seen by most analysts as an undesirable trend in this direction. The separation of the workplace from the area in which the person lives leads to a fragmentation of social life. The recent nearly universal diffusion of television is often cited as keeping men at home in the evenings when they would otherwise have been socializing in the bars or participating in the activities of various voluntary associations. Changes in the physical structure of the city, too, have had their effect. With the recent advent of high-rise apartment construction, a kind of impersonalism has crept into urban neighborhood life (Crespi and Martinelli 1968:61–62). This has affected women as well as men. In fact, Hilowitz maintains that in the Syracuse area women are the greatest victims of this development, for they do not have the social outlet of the workplace, and many consequently suffer from intense loneliness (1976:150). Cammarota similarly found that 36% of the lower- and working-class respondents in her study claimed to have no friends at all, offering such justifications as "I'm a solitary type," "I don't have the time," and "True friends don't exist" (1977: 124–25).

Lest this portrait be misleading, it should be stressed that we are describing a trend. In general, particularly in the north, socializing outside the home appears to be much more common in Italy than in the United States. Conversely, the home is used much less often for entertaining friends and is often reserved for kinsmen.

Campanilismo, local chauvinism, is a fact of Italian life that has been little studied in the urban context, despite its important implications for urban social organization and culture. Just how strong such chauvinism based on one's hometown is, and what it means for associational patterns in cities having large populations of immigrants, remain to be determined. Such chauvinism works as well at the more local level, where people identify with particular neighborhoods. The best known and most dramatic case of this is found in Siena, in central Italy, where the symbolism of the Palio, highly developed ritualized identification with a city neighborhood associated with ritualized combat between neighborhoods, has provided a basic element of urban social organization (Dundes and Falassi 1975, Logan 1978, Silverman 1979).

People's sense of community and neighborhood identification in southern Italy is subject to conflicting forces. Chauvinism may seem particularly acute when one city's population appears to be losing some economic benefit to that of another city, as was violently displayed in the 1970 riots of the people of Reggio Calabria on hearing that Catanzaro was to be made the new regional capital (Cannizzaro *et al.* 1975).

Yet the economic precariousness of the poor in the south has had important implications for the sense of community and neighborhood expressed there (Catanzaro 1979). Guarrasi (1978:88) cautiously agrees with Oscar Lewis's characterization of the poor in the culture of poverty as having a minimum of organization beyond the nuclear family, but explains this in southern Italy as the result of the political subordination of the poor and the ideological control exerted by the ruling class. Yet while people may attempt to limit their social ties to their kinsmen, their *baracche* or slum neighborhood remains a significant basis of social identification. While some reciprocal assistance is available to them within their *baracche,* they face social ostracism if they venture forth into a *baracche* not their own (1978:86). Belmonte paints a similar picture of lack of community ties among the poor of Naples, though in even bleaker terms: "The experience of such doubts toward one's fellows, the uneasiness, and the fear of warranted or unwarranted reprisal is the kernel of social experience in lower-class Naples" (1979:47).

A LOOK AHEAD

Italy's rich urban texture provides fertile ground for anthropological study, ground that as yet has scarcely been plowed. With the changes that have taken place worldwide in anthropologists' conceptions of their role over the past decade or two, there are no longer any serious theoretical or methodological barriers to developing such research.

The contributions anthropologists are likely to make in Italian urban study flow from their use of participant observation methodology, along with a holistic comparative perspective, and from some of the more specialized areas of conceptual expertise developed in anthropology. Whether or not anthropologists collaborate in multidisciplinary research efforts, they must take advantage of the work done by sociologists, political scientists, historians, economists, psychologists, demographers, and others to maximize the value of their own work. Thus, for example, while political research in Italy is sorely lacking in systematic observational studies of local-level political activity among the masses, the value of any such anthropological case study would be greatly enhanced by relating it to the larger context already studied by other scholars. Indeed, anthropologists who undertake such research without careful study of the contribution of political scientists, sociologists, and historians to their problem would end up with a woefully inadequate product.

The almost total reliance by other scholars on survey interviewing as a method of grass-roots social study in urban Italy has produced questionable results. For example, the political attitudes and allegiances people express to a strange interviewer who appears at their door may have less to do with what they think and do than with how they want to manage the impressions the interviewer receives (Evans 1967, Visentini 1974). If we were to judge by interview studies of church attendance, for example, thousands of new churches should be built to accommodate the throngs of Italy's devout Catholics (Fasola-Bologna 1968:70).

The limitations of these studies are recognized by other scholars as well, and there has been a recent movement among sociologists (Marazziti 1977) and political scientists (Chubb 1977) to embrace participant observation as a key ingredient of urban social study. Nor have all works by anthropologists in this field been exemplars of methodological virtue. Hilowitz's (1976) study of the Syracuse area, one of the first book-length urban anthropological studies, barely discusses methodology but is apparently based on a few months of eclectic research. As Silverman (1978:823) points out, this is hardly an adequate time period for studying a province of 365,000 people in 20 communities, even if we knew more about what methods were used when and with whom.

As for the theoretical areas in which anthropologists can make important contributions to urban Italian study, two may be cited by way of example. Kinship is, of course, something of an anthropological trademark. As indicated in our earlier discussion, kinship in urban Italy remains a problematical subject. The importance of extended kin ties is in dispute, and the presumed regional and class variation in extended kin relations remains uncharted. The nature of kin ties is also changing and has been subject to changing social and economic conditions throughout history. Moreover, to understand rural-urban differences in Italy, more data on extended kin ties in both contexts are clearly needed.

Work on how urban Italians define their community and their social identity could also be profitably undertaken by anthropologists. Chauvinism in Italy has traditionally been based on very limited geographical areas, often reinforced by differences in dialects between neighboring areas. With an increase in interregional movement in the past decades, this is producing an urban social fabric replete with cross-cutting bases of social identity, with social class, political party, and Church allegiance tearing people in different directions (Kertzer 1977b). As old urban neighborhoods have been transformed through urban renewal and as previously rural communities on the periphery of cities have been progressively engulfed in expanding urban centers, people's definition of their community becomes a topic of great importance.

The time is ripe for a shift in the rural preoccupation of anthropological study in Italy to a more balanced approach. Italy is, after all, one of the world's leading industrial nations and, while anthropologists need not apologize for continuing to study the life of the small communities dotting the countryside, we can no longer justify this aversion to life in the cities. Indeed, if anthropologists do not shift their focus from peasants to urban dwellers, we will be in danger of becoming as marginal to the academic community as our traditional research subjects are becoming to Italian national society.

NOTES

1. I would like to thank Raimondo Catanzaro and Bernardo Bernardi for their help in the preparation of this chapter.
2. A recent annotated bibliographical compendium on urban research in Italy, containing works from a variety of disciplines, is provided by Ardigò (1977).
3. The importance of marxism for Italian anthropologists is evident in the large portion of all recent anthropological writings in Italy devoted to the explication of a marxist anthropology. For example, two special issues of the journal *Problemi del socialismo* (1979a, b) were devoted exclusively to this topic.
4. Banfield's concept of "amoral familism" and the literature it spawned provide an insight into this controversy.

REFERENCES

Allum, Percy A.
    1973   *Politics and society in post-war Naples.* Cambridge: Cambridge University Press.

Ardigò, Achille, ed.
  1977   *Borgo, città, quartiere: Rassegna bibliografica interdisciplinare sulle articolazioni minori della città nel contesto territoriale.* Milan: Franco Angeli.
Balbo, Laura
  1976   *Stato di famiglia.* Milan: Etas.
Balbo, Laura, and Marie P. May
  1975–76 Woman's condition: The case of postwar Italy. *International Journal of Sociology* 5:79–102.
Balbo, Laura, Giuliana Chiaretti, and Gianni Massironi
  1975   *L'Inferma scienza: Tre saggi sull'istituzionalizzazione della sociologia in Italia.* Bologna: Il Mulino.
Belmonte, Thomas
  1979   *The broken fountain.* New York: Columbia University Press.
Benini, Rodolfo
  1911   La demografia italiana nell'ultimo cinquantennio. In *Cinquant'anni di storia italiana,* vol. 1, bk, 3. Milan: Ulrico Hoepli.
Berardi, R., Matilde Callari Galli, E. G. Cuppini, and Gualtiero Harrison
  1974   Casa, dolce casa: Un dossier, un questionario tra Modena e Bologna. *Parametro* 31:22–30.
Bernardi, Bernardo
  1973   La situazione attuale degli studi etno-antropologici. *Rassegna italiana di sociologia* 14, no. 4:535–58.
Blok, Anton
  1974   *The Mafia of a Sicilian village 1860–1960.* New York: Harper and Row.
Boffi, M., S. Cofini, A. Giasanti, and E. Mingione
  1972   *Città e conflitto sociale: Inchiesta al Garibaldi-Isola e in altri quartieri periferici di Milano.* Milan: Feltrinelli.
Bugarini, Fabio, and Giovanna Vicarelli
  1979   Interazione e sostegno parentale in ambiente urbano. *Rassegna italiana di sociologia* 19:461–93.
Buonanno, Milly
  1977   Condizioni d'origine e orientamenti iniziali della sociologia della famiglia in Italia. *Rassegna italiana di sociologia* 18, no. 1:85–110.
Caciagli, Mario
  1977   *Democrazia Cristiana e potere nel mezzogiorno: Il sistema democristiano a Catania.* Florence: Guaraldi.
Callari Galli, Matilde, Gualtiero Harrison, and E. G. Cuppini
  1974   Ricerca sull'uso dell'abitazione in una fascia tipologica omogenea nell'area emiliana. *Costuire e abitare* 2:351–448.
Cammarota, Antonella
  1977   *Proletariato marginale e classe operaia.* Rome: Savelli.
Cannizzaro, Anna, Natale Jeracitano, and Giorgio Rossetti
  1975   Reggio Calabria: Un'inchiesta pre-elettorale. In Mario Caciagli and Alberto Spreafico, eds., *Un sistema politico alla prova.* Bologna: Il Mulino, pp. 253–316.
Catanzaro, Raimondo
  1979   Le cinque Sicilie: Disarticolazione sociale e struttura di classe in un'economia dipendente. *Rassegna italiana di sociologia* 20, no. 1:7–35.
Catanzaro, Raimondo, and Emilio Reyneri
  1978   Planning research into dual working in Catania. Paper presented to the Conference on the Design and Analysis of Current Social Science Research in the Central Mediterranean, University of Malta.

Chubb, Judith A.
1977   Schema riassuntivo della ricerca sui modi di utilizzo dell'emarginazione
        per rafforzare il sistema pollitico. *La Critica sociologica* 42:56–59.
1979   Naples under the left: The limits of local change. Unpublished ms.
Cirese, Alberto M.
1973   *Cultura egemonica e culture subalterne.* Palermo: Palumbo.
Colajanni, Antonino
1973   Comment on 'Le scienze umane oggi in Italia' by Vittorio Lanternari. In
        Bernardo Bernardi, ed., *Etnologia e antropologia culturale.* Milan: Franco
        Angeli, pp. 76–83.
Collidà, Ada Becchi
1976   La città meridionale. In F. Indovina, ed., *Mezzogiorno e crisi.* Milan:
        Franco Angeli.
Conti, Roberto
1974   Consenso e conflitto nella sociologia urbana in Italia. *Rivista di sociologia*
        12, no. 2:69–118.
Crespi, Franco, and Franco Martinelli
1968   La dinamica delle relazioni sociali nel contesto urbano. *Rivista di sociologia*
        6, no. 16:5–62.
Crump, Thomas
1975   The context of European anthropology: The lesson from Italy. In Jeremy
        Boissevain and John Friedl, eds., *Beyond the community: Social process in Eu-
        rope.* Amsterdam: Department of Educational Science of the Nether-
        lands, pp. 18–27.
Davis, John
1975   Beyond the hyphen: Some notes and documents on community-state
        relations in South Italy. In Jeremy Boissevain and John Friedl, eds., *Be-
        yond the community: Social process in Europe.* Amsterdam: Department of Ed-
        ucational Science of the Netherlands, pp. 49–55.
Douglass, William A.
1980   The South Italian family: A critique. *Journal of Family History* 5:338–59.
Dundes, Alan, and Alessandro Falassi
1975   *La terra in piazza: An interpretation of the Palio of Siena.* Berkeley and Los
        Angeles: University of California Press.
Evans, Robert H.
1967   *Coexistence: Communism and its practice in Bologna 1945–1965.* Notre Dame:
        University of Notre Dame Press.
Fasola-Bologna, Alfredo
1968   Il ruolo del sacerdote nelle aspettative della popolazione di una parroc-
        chia romana. *Rivista di sociologia* 6:69–88.
Ferrarotti, Franco
1975   *La città come fenomeno di classe.* Milan: Franco Angeli.
Fried, Robert C.
1973   *Planning the eternal city: Roman politics and planning since World War II.* New
        Haven, Conn.: Yale University Press.
Garaguso, Patrizia
1976   Problemi dell'insegnamento dell'antropolgia culturale in Italia: Didattica
        e ricerca. *La critica sociologica* 37:94–106.
Garelli, Franco
1977   Gruppi giovanili ecclesiali: Tra personale e politico, tra funzione educa-
        tiva e azione sociale. *Quaderni di sociologia* 26:275–320.

Giantempo, Nella, and Antonella Cammarota
   1977   Land and social conflict in the cities of southern Italy: An analysis of the
           housing question in Messina. In Michael Harloe, ed., *Captive cities.* New
           York: John Wiley, pp. 111–22.
Goddard, Victoria
   1977   Domestic industry in Naples. *Critique of Anthropology* 3:139–50.
Golini, Antonio
   1974   *Distribuzione della popolazione, migrazioni interne e urbanizzazione in Italia.*
           Rome: Istituto di Demografia dell'Università di Roma.
Grasso, L.
   1974   *Compagno padrone.* Florence: Guaraldi.
Guarrasi, Vincenzo
   1978   *La condizione marginale.* Palermo: Sellerio.
Hilowitz, Jane
   1976   *Economic development and social change in Sicily.* Cambridge: Schenkman.
Katz, Phillip
   1975   Village responses to national law: A case from the South Tyrol. In Jer-
           emy Boissevain and John Friedl, eds., *Beyond the Community: Social process
           in Europe.* Amsterdam: Department of Educational Science of the Nether-
           lands, pp. 56–64.
Kertzer, David I.
   1975   Italian communist participation in Catholic rituals: A case study. *Journal
           for the Scientific Study of Religion* 14, no. 1:1–11.
   1977a   European peasant household structure: Some implications from a nine-
           teenth century Italian community. *Journal of Family History* 2:333–49.
   1977b   Ethnic identity and political struggle in an Italian communist quartiere.
           In George L. Hicks and Philip E. Leis, eds., *Ethnic encounters.* North
           Scituate, Mass.: Duxbury Press, pp. 221–37.
   1977c   Anthropological research in urban Italy. *Comparative Urban Research* 4:
           92–100.
   1978   The impact of urbanization on household composition: Implications
           from an Italian parish (1880–1910). *Urban Anthropology* 6:1–23.
   1979   Ideological and social bases of Italian Church-communist struggle: A
           critique of Gramsci's concept of hegemony. *Dialectical Anthropology* 4:
           321–28.
   1980   *Comrades and Christians: Religion and political struggle in communist Italy.* New
           York: Cambridge University Press.
   1981   *Famiglia contadina e urbanizzazione.* Bologna: Il Mulino.
   1982   The liberation of Evelina Zaghi: The life of an Italian communist. *Signs,*
           in press.
Lanternari, Vittorio
   1973   Le nuove scienze umane oggi in Italia, nel contesto europeo-americano.
           In Bernardo Bernardi, ed., *Etnologia e antropologia culturale.* Milan: Franco
           Angeli.
   1977   Ernesto De Martino etnologo meridionalista: Vent'anni dopo. *L'Uomo* 1,
           no. 1:29–56.
Leonardi, Franco
   1964   *Operai nuovi: Studio sociologico sulle nuove forze del lavoro industriale nell'area sira-
           cusana.* Milan: Feltrinelli.
Livi Bacci, Massimo
   1965   *I fattori demografici dello sviluppo economico italiano.* Rome: Istituto di Statis-
           tica Economica dell'Università di Roma.

Logan, Alice Pomponio
1978   The Palio of Siena: Performance and process. *Urban Anthropology* 7:45–65.
Lombardi-Satriani, Luigi M.
1976   *Antropologia culturale e analisi della cultura subalterna.* 2d ed. Florence: Guaraldi.
Low-Beer, John R.
1978   *Protest and participation: The new working class in Italy.* Cambridge: Cambridge University Press.
Lucrezio, Giuseppe
1970   *Il fenomeno urbano.* Rome: An. Veritas Editrice.
Marazzi, Antonio
1973   La ricerca antropologica sul campo in Italia: Alcuni dati e alcune considerazioni. *Rassegna italiana di sociologia* 14, no. 4:625–42.
Marazziti, Mario
1977   Per una sociologia dei marginali nella città. *La critica sociologica* 41:48–63.
Masi, Anthony C.
1979   The labor force requirements of capital-intensive industrialization: Labor migration and labor absorption at Italisider's fourth integrated steel center, Taranto, Italy. Paper presented at the Conference of Europeanists, Washington, D.C.
Mingione, Enzo
1977   Sociological approach to regional and urban development: Some methodological and theoretical issues. *Comparative Urban Research* 4, nos. 2–3: 21–38.
Moluzzi, Luisa, and Giulia Bertolo
1977   Ruoli familiari e autorità in un gruppo di adolescenti in un quartiere di Roma. *La critica sociologica* 4:98–119.
Parisi, Arturo
1978   Tra ripresa ecclesiastica ed eclissi della secolarizzazione. *Città e regione* 4, no. 7:32–46.
Parisi, Arturo, and G. Senin-Artina
1979   *Matrimoni e secolarizzazione.* Florence: Istituto di Storia delle Istituzioni Religiose, Università di Firenze.
Pearlin, Leonard I.
1974   *Class context and family relations: A cross-national study.* Boston: Little, Brown.
Pitkin, Donald S.
1959   A consideration of asymmetry in the peasant-city relationship. *Anthropological Quarterly* 32:161–67.
Pizzorno, Alessandro, ed.
1975–79 *Lotte operaie e sindacato in Italia (1968–1972).* 5 vols. Bologna: Il Mulino.
Problemi del socialismo
1979a   *Orientamenti marxisti e studi anthropologici italiani — Problemi e dibattiti, I. Problemi del socialismo* 20, no. 15.
1979b   *Studi antropologici italiani e rapporti di classe — Dal positivismo al dibattito attuale, II. Problemi del socialismo* 20, no. 16.
Regini, Marino, and Emilio Reyneri
1971   *Lotte operaie e organizzazione del lavoro.* Padua: Marsilio.
Remotti, Francesco
1978   Tendenze autarchiche nell'antropologia culturale italiana. *Rassegna italiana di sociologia* 19, no. 2:185–226.

Saporiti, Angelo
  1978   Famiglia e studi di comunità in Italia. *Sociologia* 12, no. 1:13–48.
Schneider, Jane, and Peter Schneider
  1976   *Culture and political economy in western Sicily.* New York: Academic Press.
  1980   The dissolution of ruling elites in twentieth century Sicily. Paper presented to the annual meeting of the American Political Science Association, Washington, D.C.
Silverman, Sydel F.
  1965   Patronage and community-nation relationships in central Italy. *Ethnology* 4:172–89.
  1978   Review of *Economic development and social change in Sicily,* by Jane Hilowitz. *Economic Development and Cultural Change* 26, no. 4:821–27.
  1979   On the uses of history in anthropology: The *palio* of Siena. *American Ethnologist* 6, no. 3:413–36.
Stropppa, Claudio
  1978   *Antropologia urbana.* Brescia: Morcelliana.
Tentori, Tullio
  1976   Social classes and family in a southern Italian town: Matera. In John G. Peristiany, ed., *Mediterranean family structures.* Cambridge: Cambridge University Press, pp. 273–86.
Tentori, Tullio, and Paolo Guidicini
  1972   *Borgo, quartiere e città: Indagine socio-antropologica nel quartiere di S. Carlo nel Centro Storico di Bologna.* Milan: Franco Angeli.
Tullio-Altan, Carlo, and Roberto Cartocci
  1979   *Modi di produzione e lotta di classe in Italia.* Milan: Mondadori.
Tullio-Altan, Carlo, and Alberto Marradi
  1976   *Valori, classi sociali, scelte politiche.* Milan: Bompiani.
United Nations
  1978   *Demographic yearbook.* New York.
Vergati, Stefania
  1975–76 Il dibattito urbanistico e sociologico su Roma. *La critica sociologica* 36: 8–23.
Visentini, Giorgio
  1974   L'Image du parti comuniste. In Foundation Nationale des Sciences Politiques, ed., *Sociologie du comunisme.* Paris: Armand Colin, pp. 183–99.

Chapter **3**

Urban Research in Yugoslavia: Regional Variation in Urbanization

Michael Spangler

It is unfortunate that Bronislaw Malinowski, a Pole by birth, did not find South Slav urban life as fascinating as Trobriand Island society; I would then be able to quote his impressions, half literary and half anthropological, dutifully recorded as he visited the cities of Yugoslavia. Taking his *Argonauts of the Western Pacific* as a model, Malinowski would undoubtedly have supplied us with detailed descriptions of the physical types of the cities: walled, Renaissance Dubrovnik on the Adriatic coast; Sarajevo in the Balkan interior with its dozens of mosques, winding alleyways, and old marketplace; baroque Ljubljana nestled in a northwestern alpine valley; and the suburban apartment complexes of Novi Beograd on the Pannonian plain, blinking in the night sky like the data bank of a giant computer hurtling the postwar nation into an industrial age.

In place of a colorful and lively characterization of urban life, contemporary anthropological research in Yugoslavia presents us with a highly technical and well-advanced body of theory and data. The urban research is difficult to condense and, once condensed, obscures the almost bewildering diversity of urban settlements and urban life.

To complicate the situation further, the anthropological study of urban life in Yugoslavia is currently undergoing a major transformation in two ways. First, anthropologists are increasingly supplementing their own data with information from demography, economics, sociology, urban planning, and geography. Anthropological theory is consequently developing a wider data base and a greater interdisciplinary relevance than it would have in isolation. Foreign anthropologists especially have turned to other disciplines in conducting regional and national studies of aspects of Yugoslav urbanism and urbanization (e.g., Halpern 1964, Lockwood 1975, and Denich 1976). On the other hand, Yugoslav anthropologists, stimulated by the urban research of their fellow social scientists and foreign anthropologists, have only recently begun to consider the city as an ethnographic realm in its own right (cf. Barjaktarović 1962 and Knežević 1979).

Second, the anthropological study of Yugoslav urbanism is shifting its primary theoretical focus. Within the last three decades many Yugoslav cities have expanded rapidly because industrial and bureaucratic development has attracted large numbers of peasant migrants to the cities. Several anthropological studies of Yugoslav urbanization have been marked by the assumption of a smooth economic and cultural assimilation of the rural migrants into urban life (e.g., Denich 1970, 1976; Simić 1974). However, the homeostatic postulate of ongoing urban assimilation is now beginning to erode as the urban environment manifests serious social and economic problems (cf. Vrišer 1975).

These trends in anthropological research permit a critical appreciation of contemporary theory pertaining to Yugoslav urbanism. However, the present study will not merely examine contemporary theory in light of these trends but will also attempt to justify their significance. In relation to my critical stance the following discussion has three parts: (1) an analysis of the development of urban settlements in different regions of Yugoslavia and in the country as a whole; (2) a review of major anthropological and sociological investigations concerned with Yugoslav urbanism and urbanization after World War II; and (3) an examination of relatively recent developments in Yugoslav urban life as well as a prospectus for anthropological research based on them. In the conclusion of the chapter I shall return to a general consideration of the transformation of urban research in Yugoslavia.[1]

URBAN DEVELOPMENT AND REGIONAL VARIATION

A historical discussion of Yugoslav urbanization is particularly susceptible to problems of regional comparison. The country, a federation of six republics, contains significant geographical, economic, and social differences that have been reflected in equally diverse processes of urbanization. In addition, urbanization has been affected by historic events, notably changes in the political control of certain regions. All of the variables of urbanization mentioned above — political, economic, social, and geographical — have interacted in different ways, cutting across the generally accepted boundaries of regions. Despite such difficulties in regional comparison, I shall attempt to show that anthropological research is critically enlightened by the regional and national study of urban development.

Fisher (1966:35) has argued that there are five cultural regions in Yugoslavia. These regions are geographically demarcated by past political and cultural influences: the traditional spheres of foreign domination and the development of indigenous South Slav states. Fisher's regions, then, do not correspond to the standard culture areas of anthropological analysis; that is, it is not so much the distribution of cultural traits and subsistence modes (cf. Kroeber 1939:4–8) as it is former political boundaries that serve to define regions. As a result of Fisher's reliance on a political criterion, his regions, while a valuable historical starting point, require some modifications, as I shall demonstrate below.

The Austro-Hungarian region is in the northwestern part of Yugo-slavia, i.e., in central, western, and northern Croatia and in Slovenia and Vojvodina. Towns in the region were legally recognized in early medieval times, although these settlements remained small well into the nineteenth century because of warfare with the Ottoman Turks. Many of the towns, such as Karlovac, Nova Gradiška, and Novo Mesto, were originally mili-tary forts built against Ottoman invasions. It was only in the second half of the nineteenth century, with the consolidation of the Austro-Hungarian em-pire and concomitant social and economic improvements, that the towns en-tered into a period of significant growth.

Three qualifications should be placed on the historical generalizations offered above. First, Austrian and Hungarian economic policies were not always consonant after 1850. This conflict had a direct impact on the devel-opment of cities in the region, especially bureaucratic and industrial centers. For instance, Zagreb, the capital of Croatia, rapidly expanded into the low-land rather than the upland area in the late nineteenth century not only be-cause of the development of industry and rail transportation but also on ac-count of Hungarian conflict with Austrian policy. In fact, Zagreb prior to 1850 was confined to the hilly flanks above the Sava plain, and was the site of two independent centers: a Hungarian religious community and a Slavic civil community under royal charter (Fisher 1966:38).

Second, Slavonia in northeastern Croatia was resettled almost totally between the seventeenth and nineteenth centuries. After passing from Turk-ish rule to the Austro-Hungarian empire in the sixteenth century, Slavonia formed part of the "military border" *(vojna krajina),* defending against Otto-man attacks, with Serbs chiefly settling the previously depopulated region. Since there was little diversified economic development in the area, many of the settlements took the form of large agricultural communities (agro-towns). It is difficult to classify these settlements as cities or towns in terms of occupational diversity and specialization. Yet the settlements con-form to simple demographic definitions of a city. The same problem is even more significant in modern Vojvodina, whose resettlement was undertaken both in the nineteenth century and again after World War II.

Third, Slovenian and western Croatian urbanization established an even growth in both small and large urban settlements after World War II, which belies the nineteenth-century regional pattern of expansion in only the large communities. Slovenia also has significant agricultural set-tlements. I shall return to these considerations in the next section of the chapter.

The region of Italian influence is in the western part of Yugoslavia, in Dalmatia and Hrvatsko Primorje along the Adriatic coast. Several cities in the region can be traced back to Roman and Greek colonization periods (e.g., Split in the third century A.D. and Dubrovnik in the seventh century A.D.). During the Middle Ages Italian economic institutions, particularly Venetian trade monopolies, strengthened the earlier urban tradition based on sea trade. Cities of the region have generally been termed "Mediterranean" because of their littoral location and Italian cultural influences (Cvijić 1966:242, Halpern 1964:32). Indeed, Dubrovnik was the only city in the region to preserve its independent status during the Italian occupation from 1420 until 1797, when Austria occupied the region.

Beginning with the fourteenth century, several of the Adriatic coastal cities undertook large fortification programs, which enclosed parts of their expanding territories. For example, Split underwent two programs of fortification, the last in the seventeenth century (Fisher 1966:40). The resulting walled cities with relatively high dwellings and narrow streets became a distinctive urban plan that also penetrated into the interior to such cities as Postojna and Mostar (Kostić 1973:13). In the nineteenth century the economic importance of sea commerce gradually declined in the Mediterranean as a result of Western European industry and trade competition, and after the Austrian occupation Adriatic coastal cities conformed to the general pattern of urban and economic development in the greater Austro-Hungarian region.

The Byzantine-Ottoman region lies in Bosnia, Herzegovina, Kosovo, and Macedonia. Montenegro and Serbia were also strongly influenced by Byzantine power and Ottoman occupation up to the nineteenth century.

A succession of Byzantine, Bulgarian, Serbian, Venetian, and Hungarian states controlled urban settlements in the interior of the Balkan peninsula until the fourteenth century. At that time the Ottoman empire began to assert its power throughout the region by military conquest.[2] As the urban centers were brought under Ottoman control, the Eastern Orthodox Christian populations either converted to Islam or fled to rural areas. Some Christian populations were also deported by Ottoman rulers.[3] Nevertheless, cities and towns flourished along the trade routes of the feudalistic Ottoman empire until Turkish rule began to weaken in the eighteenth century.

While Ottoman rule inhibited the development of indigenous crafts and a non-Moslem Slavic urban class, it encouraged trade centers (*čaršija,* towns) tied into a complex social network. Social hierarchies of towns can be found in Ottoman economic and legal documents from the feudal era. For instance, towns were primarily classified into *varoš, kasaba, pazar,* and *sěhir* categories based on population size and the existence of mosques and marketplaces.[4] With the decline of Ottoman feudalism in the nineteenth century owing to growing Austrian and Serbian power, many towns and cities decreased in size. Some towns were totally abandoned for a period because the

Islamized population withdrew into Turkish territory with the vital trade centers and military garrisons necessary for sustaining the urban settlements.

Skopje, the modern capital of Macedonia, was under Ottoman control until 1912. As Fisher notes, the city was confined to the left bank of the Vardar River until the early twentieth century and was a major Yugoslav exemplar of the Levantine city, with its numerous mosques and minarets, Turkish baths and rest-houses, and narrow cobblestone streets (1966:40). With the 1963 earthquake and the subsequent reconstruction of Skopje, the old face of the city was partially transformed. Sarajevo, the capital of Bosnia-Herzegovina, has retained its Turkish appearance.

The Serbian region is within the present borders of the Serbian republic. The Serbian state emerged from Ottoman rule in the early nineteenth century. In 1830 Belgrade, the largest urban settlement in the region, was jointly ruled by Serbs and Turks. The city formally became the Serbian capital in 1841 under Prince Miloš Obrenović (the leader of the second Serbian insurrection), although the citadel, overlooking the confluence of the Danube and Sava rivers, remained in Turkish hands until 1867 (Milosavljević 1974:153). The development of a Serbian state in the nineteenth century led to a nearly total eradication of the previously pronounced Turkish appearance of Belgrade. The city not only contained the major Ottoman fortress in the region but many mosques as well, a fact that inflamed the Orthodox Christian sentiments of the Serbian revolutionaries.

The growth of Serbian towns and cities along with indigenous crafts and trade was strengthened beginning in the middle nineteenth century, although the policies of the fledgling state were very much under the control of more powerful European neighbors. Belgrade dominated the region politically and economically. Urban problems that Serbian city administrators faced in the nineteenth century were similar to those confronted by the modern Yugoslav government in Serbia and Vojvodina after World War II: the reconstruction and repopulation of towns and cities, the establishment of industry, and the colonization of outlying forest and agricultural areas. The nineteenth-century emergence and repopulation of urban settlements, principally in Moravian Serbia, north of Niš, led to towns of Cvijić's so-called patriarchal regime (Civjić 1966:247–48).[5]

The Montenegrin region is delineated approximately by the boundaries of the modern Montegnegrin republic. The monarchic state of Montenegro can be dated as far back as 1077, but was actually a theocratic princedom for most of its history, under foreign occupation several times, and not internationally recognized until 1878. Urban development in this region has constantly been plagued by a slow population growth and an underdeveloped economy. Coastal cities that fell within the Venetian sphere of influence for a period (e.g., Kotor) are exceptions to the above generalization. Interior urban settlements conformed to Cvijić's patriarchal type.

Cetinje, the capital of the Montenegrin monarchy, grew to prominence in the late nineteenth century, and several foreign embassies were established there. After World War II, however, the modern Yugoslav republic created a new capital on the site of the small prewar settlement of Podgorica and named it Titograd (Tito's City). The new capital is an industrial and bureaucratic center; it has better transportation connections with the other Yugoslav republics than has Cetinje, isolated in the rugged karst area of the republic. The growth of other towns and cities, such as Nikšić, can also be explained by industrial development in the post-World War II period.

Cities and towns in contemporary Yugoslav territory were very small up to 1750 and began to show significant increases in population size primarily after 1850. Zagreb, the capital of Croatia, had a population of less than 5,000 in 1787 but began to increase at an accelerated rate in the following century (Stoianovich 1967:166). Belgrade, on the other hand, had a population of almost 100,000 in the 1630s, only to dwindle to 15,000 in 1838 (Andrić *et al.* 1967:69). Belgrade and other Serbian, Bosnian, and Herzegovinian settlements reflect dramatic fluctuations in population size up to and during the nineteenth century. Military activity and the shifting political control of Ottoman regions account for this rise and fall of urban populations.

In general, urban development in Balkan territory has not involved large numbers of people until very recently. In 1550 only one city, Istanbul, exceeded 100,000 in size. Only in 1850 did Bucharest, the capital of present-day Romania, exceed this same limit. By 1920 the Yugoslav cities of Belgrade and Zagreb joined Istanbul, Bucharest, and five other cities as Balkan urban centers with a population of at least 100,000 (Stoianovich 1967:166–67). In Western Europe, on the other hand, London had already surpassed the million mark by 1800, with Paris following suit by 1850 and Berlin by 1875. Only in 1976 did a Yugoslav city, Belgrade, finally attain a population size of over one million (Zavod za Statistiku-Beograd 1977:49).

With the defeat of Austria in 1918, a Yugoslav national federation, the Kingdom of Serbs, Croats, and Slovenes, was formed under Serbian monarchical control. In 1929 the country was renamed the Kingdom of Yugoslavia, but it was abolished after World War II in favor of a socialist federation of six Yugoslav republics under the leadership of Josip Broz Tito. From 1918 to 1950 the political evolution of the Yugoslav state did not produce a single core area or primate city that politically and economically dominated the rest of the country. Instead, two major core areas emerged with their centers in Belgrade, the capital of Serbia, and Zagreb, the capital of Croatia. This represented the two major ethnic components of Yugoslavia and their history of conflict. Political authority became concentrated in Belgrade and wealth in Zagreb (Fisher 1966:42, 50–51). Figure 1 indicates by wider ar-

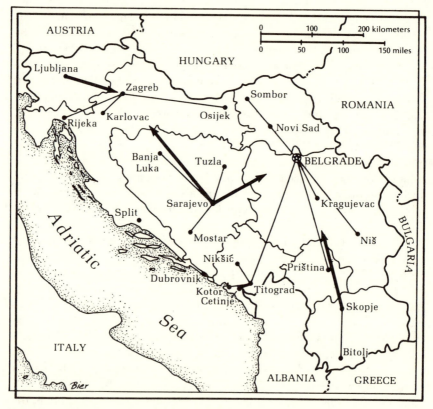

Figure 1. Socioeconomic Orientation of Major Yugoslav Cities
    From Fisher 1966, with modifications.

rows the socioeconomic orientation of large regional centers to Belgrade and Zagreb.

In 1960 Yugoslavia still had less than 20% of its population living in cities of over 20,000 people *(Popis stanovništva* 1961, 1965:xxii-xxiv), a relatively low percentage compared with Western European statistics such as 79.9% for England and Wales in 1960 (cf. United Nations 1971). Unsurprisingly, Yugoslavia ranked in the same year with Albania, Malta, and Portugal as the least urbanized countries in Europe. A table of urban population in Yugoslavia from 1921 to 1967 is given on p. 94.

In 1971, 35.3% of the total population of Yugoslavia lived in cities as opposed to 13.1% in 1921 (Ginić 1971:37). During the period from 1921 to 1971 the urban population quintupled in number, increasing rapidly especially in the middle 1950s and then more slowly accelerating in growth. The increase in urban population is directly correlated with industrialization and rural-urban migration. Hoffman and Neal have estimated migration to the cities as 380,000 annually just after World War II and 170,000 annually between 1953 and 1957 alone (1962:485). The shift away from agricultural labor is just as striking. In 1948, 79% of the labor force consisted of agricultural labor *(Popis stanovništva* 1948, 1954:xxx), and now the figure is less than 50%. Of course, industrial employment increased chiefly in the large cities of Yugoslavia during this same period.

Two main conclusions of anthropological significance can be derived from the regional and national comparisons we have made above. First, despite two primary patterns of contemporary urban development in Belgrade and Zagreb, a classification of urban industrial and commercial centers in advanced and underdeveloped regions of Yugoslavia conforms closely to the cultural regions we discussed earlier. More simply stated, the 1797 boundaries between the European powers of Venice and Austria-Hungary on the one hand, and the Ottoman empire on the other, coincide today with the borderline between Yugoslavia's advanced and underdeveloped provinces (Fisher 1966:3). Furthermore, with an older industrial tradition in the west and northwest, towns and cities in those regions may have been more adaptable to an expanding industry (Halpern 1964:37), thus bringing about a more balanced urban growth in both small and large urban centers during the last two decades.

Second, contemporary urbanization has been influenced in other ways by the traditional cultural regions considered above. In modern Serbia, a transitional but rapidly industrializing republic economically between the developed northwestern republics and the underdeveloped southeastern republics, urbanization has been characterized by the phrase *"peasantization of the cities"* (Kostić 1969). Modern peasantized cities in Serbia conform to Cvijić's nineteenth-century "patriarchal cities" in all but appearance (see n. 5). The anthropological concept of peasantization (cf. Kostić 1955, Halpern

1964, and Simić 1973a) is based only superficially on the rural origin and peasant culture of a large proportion of the urban population. An equally important and somewhat neglected factor in studies of peasantization is the degree of cultural discontinuity in urban/rural traditions, founded in a separation of urban and rural social roles and statuses and in their supposed lack of comparability. I shall examine the topic of peasantization in greater detail in the following section.

POSTWAR RESEARCH ON YUGOSLAV CITIES

In this section I shall review urban studies in anthropology and sociology as well as in other relevant disciplines. My treatment first considers national studies of urbanism and urbanization and then focuses on each Yugoslav republic.

General Studies

Joel M. Halpern has pioneered in the study of urbanization and peasant culture in Yugoslavia as a whole. His essay, *Peasant Culture and Urbanization in Yugoslavia* (1964), raises a number of issues that continue to be of central interest in anthropological theory. One of the most critical of these issues is his comparison of village organization in the developed northwest and the underdeveloped southeast of Yugoslavia. Halpern argues that non-kin-based organizations in the underdeveloped regions did not have a long history or a significant impact on peasant life. Thus in the underdeveloped regions village roles and statuses were at least at one time quite different from contemporaneous urban roles utilizing voluntary associations and formal statuses (1964:38). In the northwest, on the other hand, non-kin-based organization seems to have been common in villages as well as in cities (1964:26, 36). Halpern offers some supporting evidence, but his contention remains to be fully substantiated.[6]

Halpern's conclusions concerning urban/rural role differentiation in the southeast have largely been accepted in anthropological theory and form a conventional justification for the study of peasantized cities in Serbia and the southeastern republics. Rural migrants are assumed to have brought traditional values and kinship organization into the city not only because of the adaptive value of their rural roles but also because of the unfamiliarity of the migrants with urban roles and organizations (cf. Denich 1976). Another reason for the persistence of peasant culture in cities lies in the fact that economic and social opportunity in urban areas was severely limited for many rural migrants who could have easily responded to urban non-kin-based organization if it were economically practical and socially possible. Rural migrants who came to the cities between 1969 and 1979 are not as widely or gainfully employed as are earlier migrants because of a lower rate in industrial expansion (Hammel, personal communication). Recent migrant workers frequently return to their villages at harvest time not only to obtain foodstuffs but also to aid in the agricultural work, thus causing temporary labor shortages in urban enterprises (Z. Bogavac 1976). The tenacity of peasant culture may thus have a significant economic basis as well as effect.

Simić (1974) has also examined general urbanization processes in Yugoslavia and, more specifically, in Belgrade. He shares Halpern's approach to the peasantization of Serbian cities and concludes that peasant migrants have now been assimilated into urban life at all levels of economic and bureaucratic organization (1974:224). The contemporary urban culture of Belgrade contains both quintessential urban and rural elements. However, Simić also observes that inhabitants of Belgrade can be decidedly critical of what they consider to be the contemporary degeneration of earlier, somewhat idealized peasant customs and values (1974:220).

Simić's views require a stronger demonstration of the gainful employment of the majority of recent rural migrants to the city as well as of equal economic opportunity for the migrants. From 1958 to 1978 urban growth doubled the population of Belgrade, with lower income groups largely domiciled in company barracks and privately built homes in outlying boroughs of the city (e.g., Novi Beograd and Rakovica). Moreover, the cultural trend in both cities and rural areas toward recognizing a "degeneracy" in peasant culture may indicate a potentially radical disparity in urban and peasant roles or, more specifically, an invidious evaluation by longer-term urbanites of their own economic and social success as opposed to the relative deprivation of more recent migrants to the city. It is significant to note that Dvorniković, a Yugoslav anthropologist, documents the development of an invidious comparison of urban and rural cultures in Serbia during the interwar period. However, urban culture was "degenerate" at that time; that is, the urban bourgeoisie was judged to be parasitical and rapacious by a peasant class generally lacking the possibility of urban relocation as well as upward socioeconomic mobility (Dvorniković 1939:805–8). In the contemporary period peasant culture is viewed as "degenerate" partly because economic stratification in the city as well as urban population pressures place longer-term urbanites in a culturally ascendant and superior position.

Kostić, in his basic text for the sociology of the city in Yugoslav universities (1973), explores major problems in Yugoslav and world urbanization. Halpern has also written an excellent study of Balkan migration patterns that takes into consideration processes of urbanization (1975). However, because of the historical scope of his paper Halpern has not utilized many recent demographical studies (e.g., Rodić 1967; Ginić 1967; Ban 1970; Žuljić 1970, 1971; Vogelnik 1974). Vrišer's (1975) article on Yugoslav urbanization and Rogić's (1977) treatment of urban networks have been translated into English, and still remain the best summaries of modern demographic and socioeconomic trends. I will summarize Vrišer's demographic findings in the next section of the chapter.

Jack Fisher's *Yugoslavia — A Multinational State: Regional Difference and Administrative Response* (1966) is a classic study of postwar urban development from the point of view of a cultural geographer and urban planner. Essentially, Fisher's work deals with regional economic development and its relation to processes of urbanization. I have relied on Fisher's study in the first section of this study. City planning and historical materials are utilized in the book as well as extensive census data. Günther's *Die Verstädterung in Jugoslawien: Darstellung und Probleme* (1966) is similar to Fisher's work. Günther's study, unfortunately, has not enjoyed as wide a reception as Fisher's although it contains more detailed data on economic development in modern Yugoslavia. Rogić (1968) is also an important discussion of the geographical problems of Yugoslav urban-center networks in relation to contemporary development.

The Permanent Conference of Yugoslav Cities (Stalna Konferencija Gradova Jugoslavije) has produced two important statements (1964 and 1966) on problems of Yugoslav urbanization and urban planning. The Federal Legislature of Yugoslavia (Savezna Skupština Jugoslavije) has also made public recent political policies for urban planning (1969). The three documents deserve close study in relation to urban developments, which we shall consider later in the chapter. Piha (1964) has written a general introduction to Yugoslav economic and political policy pertaining to cities, while Djurić (1968), Stefanović (1965), and Prokić-Sulejmanović (1970) have considered the general socioeconomic bases of urbanization in Yugoslavia. Another important group of sociological studies — by Šuvar (1970, 1973), Milovančević (1961), and Simonović (1970, 1971) — concerns the complex relationship between the city and village in social and economic development.

Miloš Macura's (1954) short article, "Kriterium za razgraničenje gradskog i seoskog stanovništva" (A criterion for the delimitation of urban and village populations), is a crucial work for the understanding of Yugoslav administrative and census definitions of city and village. Macura's method of definition has been largely accepted throughout Yugoslavia since its publication. The procedure is based on two criteria: population size, and the ratio of nonagricultural population to total population in a settlement.

In using the above criteria, Macura found it necessary to establish a third category for "mixed settlements" since many communities were only marginally "urbanized," i.e., they were small in population in comparison to cities and yet with a greater percentage of nonagricultural workers than in villages.[7] Unfortunately, the categories obfuscate the urbanization patterns in Slovenia and Vojvodina, to name only two cases. In Slovenia many small settlements are almost all nonagricultural and yet are listed as mixed settelements because Macura has accepted a 2,000 limit on minimal town population. In Vojvodina many large towns are very close occupationally to mixed settlements, and thus the degree of urbanization for the area is illusory.

The final analysis of national urbanization to be reviewed here returns us to an anthropological study. Denich (1976) has considered women's roles in relation to urbanization in Yugoslavia. Denich essentially argues that village women have received greater economic autonomy in the city as industrial and bureaucratic workers. The women have concomitantly experienced greater political power in the household, since they contribute to the economic well-being and urban adaptation of the household. However, Yugoslav women have also witnessed a decline in political power in overall governmental positions from 15% in 1963 to 7% in 1969 (Burić 1972:67).

While Denich recognizes the decline in the public power of women, she does not adequately account for it because of limitations in data collection. Her explanation appears to lie in the reassertion of traditional male exclusivity in the domain of public authority (1976:14) and the practical limitations of women's roles in the household on their ability to perform in the public domain. In short, since women were traditionally oppressed, no new circumstance, short of legal provision, can be found to permit their liberation (1976:16). Denich quotes from Marx, "The traditions of all the dead generations weigh like a nightmare on the brain of the living" (1951:1). The appeal to tradition does not explain the significant decrease in the political power of women from 1963 to 1969. Is the statistical decline an artifact of the investigation, or were there more specific economic, political, and social changes during the period that account for the decline in the power of politically active women? It may be possible to relate the attenuation of women's political power to the postwar contraction of "exceptional" roles for women as established in the partisan resistance during World War II.

In general, anthropological studies of Yugoslav urbanization have concentrated to date on traditional culture and rural-urban migration. The above topics are undeniably important, since they represent widespread (and easily observable) phenomena in Yugoslav urban life. It is not surprising that little work has been done on urban/rural role and linguistic differentiation, since it has generally been assumed that the urban environment is adapting to the influx of peasants rather than the peasants to the city. Superficial changes in dress and speech do not prevent the anthropological or the longer-term urban community from identifying the recent migrants as peasants. Perhaps Nikolić's (1971) handbook for social investigations in urban areas indicates the initiation of new urban studies that will involve interdisciplinary cooperation and comparative data to a greater degree than the studies I have reviewed here.

When we turn to a review of urban studies by republic, a detailed picture emerges of urban research.

Slovenia

Melik (1964), Rusinow (1973), Kokole (1962, 1968, 1971), Vogelnik (1971), and Šifrer (1974) have presented economic, demographic, and housing studies of Slovenian towns and cities. It becomes apparent from their research that urbanization in Slovenia is sometimes divorced from industrialization because some of the settlements are agrarian. (Urbanization in Vojvodina is even more special in the same sense. Several towns in Vojvodina have a high proportion of agricultural workers, as I noted earlier.)

Rusinow (1973) has argued that general urban growth in Slovenia is more widespread with an even growth of middle-sized and small towns in relation to the large cities. The Slovenian pattern of urbanization is also common to western Croatia and the Adriatic coast (Vrišer 1975:335–36). Železnikar (1966, 1969) has compiled two bibliographies of Slovenian urban planning literature.

Irene Winner's (1971) anthropological study of a Slovenian village is currently available to scholars concerned with Slovenian settlements. More anthropological and sociological research is probably forthcoming, since the Yugoslav demographers and sociologists mentioned above have begun to generate scholarly interest in the even demographic growth of small and middle-sized towns in relation to the large cities.

Croatia

Modern Croatia evinces, as I have attempted to demonstate above, at least three distinct patterns of urbanization: (1) the Adriatic coastal and western Croatian pattern, exemplified by an even growth of small and large settlements; (2) the Slavonic pattern of large agricultural communities; (3) the primate city pattern of Zagreb in the center of the republic. Žuljić's (1960) demographic study of the urban population in Croatia partly masks the above variations. I shall concentrate on the third pattern here.

The modern development of Zagreb approximates that of Belgrade in Serbia. Population has increased dramatically in the last three decades because of labor migration. New settlements have sprung up around the city to become boroughs of the city rather than autonomous suburbs. Indeed, the new settlements, such as Novi Zagreb (New Zagreb), are dominated economically, socially, and politically by the older city partly because of urban planning. The new city boroughs do not have open-air markets or as many *kafane* (café-bars) as the city. Yugoslav social and economic life is difficult without such institutions and exacerbated by transportation problems.

Žuljić (1964) has considered contemporary problems of urban development in Zagreb. The Urban Bureau of Zagreb (Urbanistički Zavod Grada Zagreba) has also published a program (1963) for urban development.

Barić (1967a, b), Burić (1968, 1976), and Denich (1970) are relevant to the anthropological and sociological study of Croatian cities and towns. However, only Barić's investigations have actually been conducted in Croatia. All of the anthropological research cited above is principally concerned with kinship and migration and emphasizes the role of kinship as a communicative and economic link between rural and urban environments. The Belgrade studies discussed below are also relevant to Croatian cities. Since some recent political science studies have been conducted in economic firms in Croatian cities, the forthcoming publications may provide more information on urbanization and urban development.

Few anthropologists or sociologists, whether from Croatia or abroad, have selected Zagreb as a site of research. However, the Yugoslav *Review of Sociology (Revija za sociologiju)* devoted a special issue in 1975 to urban sociology. Five excellent studies are presented dealing with the rapid population growth of Zagreb and its environs. Cifrić's (1975) study of the attitudes of young migrants to Zagreb is especially recommended. The city of Zagreb has mostly attracted young migrants from the countryside within the last decade. Bene (1976) has also presented a study of the urbanization of villages in Slavonia and Vojvodina.

Bosnia-Herzegovina

Bosnia-Herzegovina is the least urbanized of the Yugoslav republics. I have argued above that nineteenth-century warfare and the slow economic development of the region inhibited urban development. Nonetheless, low urbanization statistics for modern Bosnia-Herzegovina may be deceptive, since large numbers of Bosnians are migrating to cities in Serbia, Croatia, and Western Europe. Many cities in Bosnia, such as Sarajevo and Tuzla, are growing as well. Božić (1967) is an interesting study of rural migrations into the urban region of Tuzla.

Bresloff (1967) and Lockwood (1975) are anthropological studies of Bosnian towns. Lockwood's study is extremely detailed, principally concerned with a market town (Bugojno) and the integration of a nearby village into wider society by economic and social transactions with the town. Lockwood's study is also important for its examination of ethnic groups, mainly Bosnian Moslems, who have been largely ignored in anthropological literature.

Montenegro

Very little anthropological and sociological research has been done in Montenegrin cities, perhaps because the rural population has been regarded as more interesting. Traditional Serbian social organization and values persist in Montenegrin village life. Indeed, in the nineteenth century the political and social life of the villages still reflected a segmentary patrilineage system involving tribes *(plemena)* at the highest level of lineage corporacy. Moreover, Montenegrin villages have been a classic subject of investigation since the founding of the ethnographic series of the Serbian Academy of Sciences and Arts.

If we exclude Bosnia-Herzegovina, Montenegro is the least urbanized republic in Yugoslavia. Geographic, demographic, and cultural causes can be assigned to the low urbanization of the republic. Most of Montenegro is made up of extremely rocky karst land, and population growth was small up to World War II because of a limited pastoralist and agricultural subsistence. Internecine feuds and warfare with the Ottoman Turks also retarded urban development in the nineteenth century and earlier. However, Titograd and Nikšić are growing quickly with postwar industrial development; and again, as in Bosnia-Herzegovina, there is extensive emigration to other Yugoslav cities. The coastal cities of the Adriatic, such as Kotor, are also growing. Building styles and plans vary widely in the small republic, reflecting many cultural traditions.

Macedonia

Within an economically underdeveloped region, Madeconia is the most urbanized republic in Yugoslavia (Vrišer 1975:336). It could easily be contrasted with industrialized Slovenia, which is clearly not as urbanized, or with economically underdeveloped Montenegro, where urbanization is very low (see Table 1). How do we explain the Macedonian discrepancy and the seemingly cross-cutting differences in economic and demographic patterns of urbanization?

Macedonia has an older urban tradition than does Montenegro, and industry in its large cities is expanding. Consequently, the large cities attract great numbers of labor migrants who remain unemployed or underemployed because of their sheer numbers. Birth rates in certain ethnic groups, such as the Albanian, also result in a very large increase in the urban population.

The urban development of Macedonia, as of Serbia and part of Croatia, is very uneven, with a tremendous expansion of only the large cities. In addition, emigration from the cities and rural areas to other Yugoslav cities probably leads to an underestimation of the already massive urban demographics of Macedonia. Studies have yet to be made of temporary peasant workers who either return to their villages or migrate to other regions.

Panov (1966) has written an excellent study of the functional development of Macedonian cities. Miščević (1965) and Galić (1968) consider urban plans for Skopje and are essential reading for scholars interested in administrative response to problems of urbanization and urban development.

Sociological and anthropological research in Macedonian cities is almost nonexistent. As in the case of Montenegro, Macedonian rural populations have traditionally been viewed by social scientists as more interesting.

Serbia

It is the urban development of the Serbian republic that has received the most attention by social scientists. It is not possible to mention all of the major works here.

Simić's *The Peasant Urbanites: A Study of Rural-Urban Mobility in Serbia* (1973a) is already a classic study for scholars interested in Belgrade. Even his footnotes continue to spin off research for younger scholars. The book is essentially concerned with the adaptive resources of peasant values and tradition as well as rural-urban social networks in integrating migrants into the city. The book remains a basic introduction not only to the general historical development of Belgrade but also to concepts of rural-urban migration and the peasantization of the city.

Marković (1966) and Mitrović (1970) provide good complements to Simić's urban study, since they have investigated the effect of urban immigration on agrarian structure and rural households respectively. Marković and Kostić (1964) is a shorter, more general study of social changes in the village as a result of postwar labor migration and other developments. Among these changes, one of the most significant is the increasing social isolation of the elderly in certain areas (Livada 1966). Simić (1978) has recently considered the elderly in Yugoslavia, although he does not explore urban/rural differences in a rigorous manner (cf. Erlich 1966, 1971).

Hammel's methodologically sophisticated study, *The Pink Yo-Yo: Occupational Mobility in Belgrade ca. 1915–1965* (1969a), is a critical work relevant to occupational heterogeneity in families and ethnic groups as well as to models of occupational prestige and mobility. In addition, Hammel (1970) has analyzed alternative models of occupational prestige in Belgrade. Denich (1969) has produced a doctoral dissertation relevant to Hammel's study, although her theoretical perspective emphasizes individuals more than the force of historical events. The dissertation is concerned with social mobility and industrialization in a Serbian town (Titovo Užice). Bićanić (1956) also considers occupational heterogeneity in peasant families.

Hammel (1957) has also published an analysis of Serbo-Croatian kinship terminology. The article presents a number of arguments concerned with rural/urban differences in vocabulary and kinship relations, many of which have not received wide attention. In particular, Hammel argues that certain changes in Serbian kinship terminology in urban areas may indicate the increasing role of the nuclear family (1957:65). Correspondingly, the patrilineage and extended family may be declining in relative importance in some urban populations. There are several other works that have contributed to our understanding of kinship relations in Serbia (Hammel 1969b; Hammel and Yarbrough 1973, 1974; Hammel 1977; and Simić 1973b, c). The works of Burić and Barić cited earlier are also relevant. Burić and Zečević (1969) have conducted a general sociological study of family life and social position in relation to urbanization. However, none of these authors has analyzed kinship terminology in relation to social structure as exhaustively as Hammel has done.

Perhaps the most recent study made of urban life in Serbia is Sharon Zukin's (1975) study of socialism and low-level decision making in economic firms. Her book presents data and interpretations on a wide range of topics beyond socialist theory and practice in the firms. In fact, the majority of economic and political studies pertaining to socialist enterprises in Yugoslavia has been urban-oriented (e.g., Kolaja 1966, Ward 1967, Milenkovitch 1971). The studies warrant a wider attention.

Serbian city demographics are best studied through the publications of the Federal Bureau of Statistics (Savezni Zavod za Statistiku), which has issued a series of almanacs. In addition to the general statistical almanacs, many Serbian cities also produce their own almanacs, as do other republics. Utilizing the above sources, Perišić (1970) has written an excellent overview of urbanization in Serbia.

Mitrović (1963), Djurić (1970), and Ilić (1970) are recent geographic and demographic studies of the functional classification of Serbian cities and their environs. As I noted above, the population growth of Belgrade is remarkable, having doubled in the last two decades. Many new municipal areas have been annexed to Belgrade because of their social and economic dependence on the city.

Meha (1971) has reviewed urban planning in Serbia from 1945 to 1970. Čirić (1967) has considered problems of economic development and urban dwellings in Aleksinac in eastern Serbia. Aleksić (1973) has published extensive data on daily activities and the budgeting of time for the population of Kragujevac (a major industrial city southeast of Belgrade). Time budget studies are very common in Serbian cities (e.g., Marković 1968, Aleksić and Petković 1967, Petković 1972, and Radunović 1969) because of two major factors. First, Yugoslavia shifted from a 48-hour to a 42-hour work week in the 1960s. Second, many Serbian workers are of recent peasant origin, and the time budget studies are essentially reports on ways of increasing industrial productivity and political consciousness among the workers. Yugoslav time studies require serious attention because (1) certain time concepts and attitudes are generally believed to be inherent in industrialization, and (2) Yugoslavia seems to be evolving quite different temporal attitudes from those assumed necessary for industrialization.

Spangler and Petrovich (1978) have published a short social psychological study of time perception among college students in Belgrade and Madison, Wisconsin. The study is concerned with modernization theories pertaining to future time perspective. Spangler (1979) has also written a doctoral dissertation on time concepts and attitudes and their relation to social and economic developments in Belgrade within the last hundred years.

The population increase in the capital city of Serbia is perhaps the dominant factor in the urban development of the republic. Besides conducting migration and time studies, sociologists have recently analyzed juvenile delinquency in Belgrade (e.g. Lazarević 1967, Zvonarević 1968, Todorović 1971). Unemployment and interethnic relations in Belgrade as well as in its counterpart, Zagreb, have been slighted, however.

The third volume of the monumental history of Belgrade, edited by Čubrilović (1974), is the most recent work to summarize a wide range of historical, economic, and demographic data on twentieth-century Belgrade as well as a few other Serbian urban settlements. It provides an excellent account of the postwar urban planning of Belgrade and of its proposed development to the year 2000. Unfortunately, the volume·has not been translated from Serbo-Croat.

Kosovo and Vojvodina are autonomous regions loosely federated with Serbia. They deserve special treatment because of the agricultural settlements of Vojvodina and the significant Albanian majority in Kosovo. Since there is little anthropological or sociological research now available for these areas, however, we will confine ourselves here to the citation of four important geographical studies. Veljković (1969) analyzes networks of cities in Serbia, Vojvodina, and Kosovo. Leši (1972) and Radovanović (1967) consider problems of the economic and geographic classification of settlements in Kosovo, as Bukurov (1973) has done for Vojvodina.

CONTEMPORARY YUGOSLAV URBANIZATION

As the previous sections have shown, regional variation in Yugoslavia has produced a number of distinct social and cultural processes of urbanization as well as differential patterns of population growth and dispersion. The ethnic, economic, and cultural diversity of Yugoslavia is a decisive factor in urbanism and urbanization.

Despite the many difficulties in generalization, I shall now attempt to draw some overall conclusions about Yugoslav urbanization, which suggest directions for future research. If for no other reason, such a programmatic exercise is simply customary, although it is perhaps more enlightening by what it omits than by what it states.

Vrišer (1975) has calculated the degree of urbanization in each Yugoslav republic from 1921 to 1967. His findings are presented in Table 1 below. Three generalizations emerge from Vrišer's table and other research:

(1) The degree of urbanization in Yugoslavia for 1961 is low (28.3%) compared to other European nations and remains low in 1971 (35.3%), but varies widely by republic.

(2) Urbanization was slow before the war and faster after the war as shown by the 1921 indices.

Finally, if we examine the number of settlements and their size,

(3) In 1967 a high percentage of the urban population lived in cities of over 50,000 (41.4%). Of the urban population, 31.7% lived in cities of over 100,000. By 1986 it is estimated that 42% of the urban population will live in cities of over 100,000 (Vrišer 1975:337).

"In spite of political decentralization and the planned development of underdeveloped areas, manufacturing industries, and consequent urbanization, continue to concentrate in larger towns and in more highly developed areas of the country" (Vrišer 1975:338). Hence the major problem of Yugoslav urbanization is "the spontaneous and uncoordinated development of the largest cities and the slower growth of medium sized and small towns" (Vrišer 1975:337).

Nowhere are problems of urban development more clearly manifested than in Belgrade and Zagreb. A chronic housing shortage (T. Bogavac 1976), inadequate public facilities, and older housing (cf. Kadić 1972) are only the obvious difficulties. Local transportation, distribution of goods and foodstuffs, and recreation centers have not kept pace with urban growth. Underemployment, unemployment (*Politika* 1976), and rising juvenile delinquency are social problems of a more serious nature. To borrow

Table 1. Degree of Urbanization in Yugoslavia, 1921–67

Year	Total Population (thousands)	Urban Population (thousands)	Percentage of Urban to Total Population	Index (1921 = 100)
1921	12,545	1,642	13.1	100
1931	14,534	2,194	15.1	133
1948	15,842	2,743	17.3	167
1953	16,999	3,688	21.7	225
1961	18,549	5,252	28.3	320
Macedonia	1,406	490	34.9	
Croatia	4,160	1,282	30.8	
Serbia	7,642	2,279	29.8	
Slovenia	1,592	461	28.9	
Montenegro	472	102	21.5	
Bosnia-Herzegovina	3,278	640	19.5	
1967	ca. 19,949	ca. 6,261	ca. 31.7	381

From Vrišer 1975, with slight modifications: "The figures for 1921, 1931, and 1948 refer to settlements of over 5,000 inhabitants and those for 1953 and 1961 are based on information computed by the Federal Statistical Office (using M. Macura's criteria). Figures for 1967 are estimates based on trends from the previous period."

Banfield's (1974) phrase, Yugoslavia has its "unheavenly cities." Yet it is important to note that Yugoslav cities are not as "unheavenly" as many American ones in which the inner city has deteriorated rapidly. Yugoslav cities do not have inferior housing in their centers and poverty is less evident.

Yugoslav administrators and urban planners are cognizant of the problems in their cities and environs. It is hoped that urban anthropologists and sociologists will also make a contribution to the solution of problems of Yugoslav urbanization. Simić's study in the present volume heralds a beginning in such work by focusing on some of the maladaptive results of Serbian rural-urban migration as well as of traditional social networks and values. Simić, however, is specifically concerned in his study with Serbian economic and bureaucratic organization and its functional relationship to personalistic social networks. I have attempted to bolster Simić's general position by focusing attention on what I believe is a relative deterioration of large urban centers over the last two decades in response to increased population pressure. Urban anthropology has yet to approach these problems from a theoretical or an applied standpoint.

Three general topics for future urban research may be recommended on the basis of the above trends in Yugoslav urbanization and their concomitant social dislocations: (1) more interrepublic comparisons of data, on a more interdisciplinary basis, since such comparisons are essential not only for understanding urban problems but also for cooperation in their solution; (2) investigations of the social, economic, and cultural factors beyond labor migration for the slow growth of middle-sized and small towns in the central and southeastern republics; and (3) applied studies of emergent urban problems. These topics will now be expanded and their relevance to anthropological concerns more precisely delineated.

In relation to the interrepublic comparison of data, the southeastern republics of Yugoslavia — Bosnia-Herzegovina, Montenegro, and Macedonia as well as the region of Kosovo-Metohija — provide a starting point for examination. Migrants, largely of Albanian, Serbian, Bosnian, and Macedonian descent, have created a demographic explosion in large regional centers such as Skopje. However, decreasing employment opportunities, particularly for the young, result in only transient settlement in the cities. Labor opportunities are believed to be more numerous in northwest Yugoslavia and in Western Europe. As a result, large cities in other regions of Yugoslavia, conventionally assumed to be ethnically homogeneous (cf. Simić 1974:216–17), are becoming increasingly ethnically heterogeneous. For example, in 1971 one out of five people in Belgrade was not Serbian (Bogavac 1974:665). However, 7 % of the population in Belgrade was made up of non-Serbian ethnic groups from the southeastern republics. We may assume that this percentage is low because many migrants identify themselves as "Serbian" although of other ethnic groups.[8] Of course, most migrations involve a series of movements over time and not a single interrepublic movement.

Interrepublic comparisons of economic development offer better knowledge of the migrations of people in Yugoslavia as well as permitting the reorientation of capital investment in relation to the human "capital" available.[9] Anthropological theory can contribute to migration research through studies of decision-making models of labor migrants in both underdeveloped and developed regions of Yugoslavia. Migration is more common in the developed rather than in the underdeveloped regions because of greater financial resources and better knowledge of conditions in other areas. The effect of labor migration to Western Europe and overseas must also be taken into account. The models of individual migrants can then be related to the more abstract models of economists, demographers, and politicians who are currently monitoring and governing the course of economic development.[10]

Anthropological research in urban settlements of Yugoslavia, then, must confront a perennial challenge to theory in urban anthropology: greater interdisciplinary relevance and the collection of more extensive and comparative data. Such topics as sex roles, kinship, and urban/rural social networks have not yet been investigated in many republics other than Serbia.

I have re-examined the process of peasantization in Serbia and southeastern Yugoslavia primarily from an economic standpoint. That is, peasant values and kinship organization persist in the city because they represent the most effective way for migrants to adapt and to live in the city. Previous definitions of peasantization, as I noted above, emphasized the unfamiliarity of peasants with urban organization in order to explain the maintenance of tradition. Clearly, a resolution of these two approaches to peasantization will lead to a finer discrimination of the economic, social, and cultural factors motivating rural and small-town migrants to come to only the large cities in the central and southeastern republics.

The second topic proposed for research is the slow growth of small and middle-sized towns in the central and southeastern republics of Yugoslavia. Are migrants aware of the risks in the contemporary situation in large cities and the decreasing employment opportunities in the cities and abroad? Are kinship networks and traditional migration patterns responsible for the continuing migration? Are small towns viewed as deficient in certain facilities and economic and social opportunities? The critical stance of the present study would suggest that economic and social opportunities are becoming increasingly restricted for lower strata (cf. Parkin 1976:33–36 as well as Hammel 1969a). An understanding of the motivations of the recent migrants to relocate only to large urban centers must be related to the perceived disadvantages of remaining in smaller urban centers as well as to the ongoing changes in large urban centers.

Yugoslav urbanization in central and southeastern republics may have begun to reach a point of urban saturation in the large settlements. And yet economies of scale, which are taken into account in assessing the future growth of settlements, may continue to delay the growth of smaller towns. The net result is the development of great metropolitan areas in which the surrounding suburbs are made up of increasingly deprived individuals as we move away from the urban center. This possible crisis in Yugoslav urban development must constitute at least one working hypothesis in future research. Moreover, Halpern's conclusions (1964:15) and those of Fisher (1962:259) concerning the conservative nature of Eastern European urban zoning would support the above view, as opposed to one in which new migrants are seen to be assimilated easily into all areas of the city and into all strata of Yugoslav urban society.

The final suggestions for urban research are not limited to applied anthropology but have implications for anthropological theory. The study of juvenile delinquency is one of the few cases of urban deterioration for which an extensive body of research now exists in Yugoslavia. Anthropologists have a special contribution to make to this subject, since they have a long-standing interest in family authority, sex roles, age groups, ethnic relations, and youth gangs (e.g., Keiser 1969). I have cited many of the principal works on Yugoslav juvenile delinquency under the Serbia heading in the second section of the chapter. The Yugoslav data are important because they allow us to compare both urban and rural environments. Juvenile delinquency is also a relatively new problem in Yugoslav cities.

Suburbanization provides another crucial topic for anthropological study, since this phenomenon seems to be occurring primarily in the economically developed regions of western Croatia, the Adriatic coast, and Slovenia, in addition to the two primate cities of Belgrade and Zagreb and other regional centers. The study of suburbs, some of which have less economic and social interaction with their large urban centers, should provide insights into the economic and social stratification of contemporary Yugoslav society. Some suburbs (e.g., Dedinje in Belgrade) exhibit considerable occupational and social class homogeneity. A careful analysis of suburban life should reveal a great diversity in "suburbs" from the satellite-like boroughs of Belgrade and Zagreb to the commuter settlements of Slovenia in which urban facilities are available to a greater degree.

Finally, relocation studies of industrial, medical, market, and recreational facilities are called for if urban development in the central and southeastern republics becomes more even in both small and large settlements. Social impact studies of economic development may soon be as numerous in

Yugoslavia as they are in comparable states in the United States. Departments of ethnology, notably the one in Belgrade, have already conducted major studies of building and road construction projects. Unfortunately, most of the studies are not only unpublished but also unfamiliar with inter-republic analyses of urban and economic development. Coordination in regional development thus remains a goal to be achieved.

CONCLUSION

Two significant social processes encourage a major transformation of anthropological research in Yugoslav cities. The integration of the social sciences concerned with the city underlies the trend toward increasing interdisciplinary cooperation and a more effective marshaling of data and theory in relation to urban problems. I hope that the present study has underscored the need for interdisciplinary relevance in anthropological theory, since the integration is going on with or without anthropologists. More important, data and theory exist in other disciplines for anthropological use, and, as I have suggested, anthropology has unique contributions to make in its own right. Nonetheless, if anthropologists are to make stronger contributions to urban studies, they may need to specialize in fields outside of traditional anthropological expertise, for few anthropological studies have taken a broader perspective in an attempt to characterize an entire city. Ironically, the interdisciplinary trend in urban studies could lead to the apparent "fragmentation" of anthropology. In essence, however, the specialization may only be an effort to reach a higher level of theoretical and empirical sufficiency as the discipline confronts what is still a relatively new research context.

The economic and social stratification of Yugoslav urban society underlies the research trend away from the conventional assumption of a smooth assimilation of rural migrants into urban life. Inherent in the recognition of economic and social stratification can be found historical and theoretical judgments. We can no longer assume, as several anthropological works have done up to now, that Yugoslav urbanization is a positive, egalitarian, and highly stable process. Certainly after World War II the socialist revolution eliminated the privileged interwar urban bourgeoisie, which had economically exploited the peasantry. However, new elites and socioeconomic strata have emerged in contemporary Yugoslav society (cf. Djilas 1957 and Barton *et al.* 1973), as they do in most societies. Moreover, increasing unemployment and underemployment in the present inflationary period have led to a greater range of relative social and economic deprivation in urban society (*Politika* 1977). Anthropological research must address itself to the implications of the process of economic and social stratification for contemporary urban life in Yugoslavia or else declare its theoretical disagreement.

NOTES

1. The views expressed in this chapter are those of the author and not necessarily those of the U.S. Department of State.

   Michael Harpke, John R. Lampe, Michael B. Petrovich, and Aidan Southall criticized a preliminary draft of the chapter. Constance Arzigian, Eugene A. Hammel, Andrei Simić, and Arnold Strickon reviewed a later draft and also improved the final manuscript. Robert Gakovich, Marija Kisovec, Olivera Petrovich, and Milan Radovich provided the author with bibliographic assistance.

   Peter Van Tuinen drew the map and devised the table.

   IREX and the Fulbright-Hays doctoral program supported library and field research by the author in Yugoslavia during 1976–77.

2. In addition to their organizational superiority, the Ottoman Turks had another military advantage in their relatively swift conquest of the Balkan interior. Few of the urban centers were compact settlements surrounded by walls.

3. After the Turks occupied Belgrade in 1521, almost all of the Serbian population was deported to Istanbul, where they were settled in a section of the city which became known as "Beligrad mahala" (Belgrade quarter).

4. The term *šehir* designated large strategic cities, *pazar* applied to smaller market towns, *kasaba* to Islamized towns without major markets, and *varoš* generally to predominantly Christian towns or suburbs tolerated at the fringes of *šehira*. All of the above terms are Turkish with the exception of *varoš*, which stems from the Hungarian language. Interestingly, *kasaba, varoš,* and the Italian word *palanka* are loans into the Serbian language and have the same contemporary meaning, "a small provincial town." Each state—Turkish, Hungarian, and Italian—bequeathed its linguistic terms for small towns to the indigenous Slavic populations of the Balkan interior.

5. The populations of the towns had previously lived in villages or rural areas and continued to maintain rural customs and traditional patrilineal authority. According to Cvijić, houses in nineteenth-century "patriarchal cities" were very small and each household had a large garden planted with corn, three pigs, and at least one cow (1966:248)! Towns of Cvijić's patriarchal regime were also found in Bulgaria, and a "mixed" type appeared in Herzegovina because of Turkish Islamic influences (1966:249). The term "patriarchal" is not Cvijić's usage but rather a native term typifying the authority structure and values of traditional peasant life.

6. Halpern's analysis of social organization in the Yugoslav southeast is similar in some respects to Banfield's discussion of southern Italian social organization (1958). Banfield's argument concerning the cultural resiliency of amoral familism and kin-based organization has also been queried on grounds similar to the ones raised here (see Briggs 1978, and Spangler and Ghitelman 1980).

7. The "mixed" category is not only relevant to settlements but is also used in classifying households in the national census. The category of "mixed settlement" is also employed in analyses of Italian, Spanish, and Latin American settlements.

8. Gypsies and Moslems migrating to Belgrade show a tendency to redefine their ethnic identities as Serbian for the official census. Some Montenegrins also oscillate between Serbian and Montenegrin ethnic designations, which are equally valid.

9. Labor migrations are not always adequately explained or predicted by economic indices. Demographic studies of contemporary migration within Serbia reveal

that some of the population movements are similar to those that took place over a hundred years ago in response to Turkish military movements (cf. Institut Društvenih Nauka 1971). The anthropological study of interregional migrations should demonstrate the importance of kinship networks and social tradition in defining certain migratory patterns, as it has already done for specific rural-urban migrations.

10. See Hammel and Šoć (1973) for a discussion of demographic models in relation to anthropological analysis.

REFERENCES

Aleksić, Predrag
    1973   *Budžet vremena gradskog stanovništva: Rezultati medjunarodnog ispitivanja u Kragujevcu* (The time budget of an urban population: Results of an international investigation in Kragujevac). Belgrade: Skupština Opštine Kragujevac.
Aleksić, Predrag, and V. Petković
    1967   Odnos radnog vremena, vremena obrazovanja, i političkog života (The relation of work time, education time and political life). *Zbornik radova sociološkog instituta* (Belgrade)1:73–94.
Andrić, N., R. Antić, R. Veselinović, and D. Burić-Zamolo
    1967   *Beograd u XIX veku* (Belgrade in the nineteenth century). Belgrade: Muzej Grada Beograda.
Andrić, D.
    1976   *Rečnik žargona* (Dictionary of slang). Belgrade: Beogradski Izdavačko-Grafički Zavod.
Ban, Milenko
    1970   *Naselja u Jugoslaviji i njihov razvoj u periodu 1948–61* (Settlements in Yugoslavia and their development in the period 1948–61). Belgrade: Centar za Demografska Istraživanja, Institut Društvenih Nauka.
Banfield, Edward C.
    1958   *The moral basis of a backward society.* New York: Free Press.
    1974   *The unheavenly city revisited: A revision of the unheavenly city.* Boston: Little, Brown.
Barić, Lorraine
    1967a   Levels of change in Yugoslav kinship. In M. Freedman, ed., *Social organization.* London: Cass, pp. 1–24.
    1967b   Traditional groups and new economic opportunities in rural Yugoslavia. In R. Firth, ed., *Themes in economic anthropology.* London: Association of Social Anthropologists of the Commonwealth, pp. 253–78.
Barjaktarović, Mirko R.
    1962   Promene u narodnom životu i mentalitetu naših ljudi za poslednjih dvadesetak godina (Changes in folk life and the mentality of Yugoslavs during the last twenty years). *Glasnik etnografskog muzeja na Cetinju* 2:207–16.
Barton, A. H., B. Denich, and C. Kadushin
    1973   *Opinion-making elites in Yugoslavia.* New York: Praeger.
Bene, M.
    1976   Procesi urbanizacije sela u Slavoniji i Vojvodini (Processes of the urbanization of villages in Slavonia and Vojvodina). *Sociologija sela* 14, nos. 1–2: 5–19.

Bićanić, R.
   1956   Occupational heterogeneity of peasant families in the period of acceler-
            ated industrialization. *Third World Congress of Sociology* 4, pt. 2:95.
Bogavac, Tomislav
   1974   Demografske promene u Beogradu 1941–1971 (Demographic changes in
            Belgrade 1941–1971). In Vasa Čubrilović, ed., *Istorija Beograda,* vol. 3.
            Belgrade: Prosveta, pp. 649–84.
   1976   *Stanovništvo Beograda, 1918–1971* (The population of Belgrade, 1918–
            1971). Belgrade: Muzej Grada Beograda.
Bogavac, Z.
   1976   Boli ih petak (Friday hurts them). *Zum* 41:12–3.
Božić, Lj.
   1967   *Društveno-ekonomska kretanja i promjena na selu u prigradskom području Tuzle*
            (Socioeconomic migrations and changes in the village in the region near
            Tuzla). Sarajevo: Akademija Nauka i Umjetnosti Bosne i Hercegovine.
Bresloff, L. M.
   1967   Economic adaptation and development of family types in a Bosnian
            town. In William G. Lockwood, ed., *Essays in Balkan ethnology.* Kroeber
            Anthropological Society, Special Publication no. 1. Berkeley: University
            of California, pp. 35–53.
Briggs, John W.
   1978   *An Italian passage: Immigrants to three American cities, 1890–1930.* New
            Haven, Conn.: Yale University Press.
Bukurov, B.
   1973   Klasifikacija vojvodinskih gradova (Classification of Vojvodina cities).
            Zbornik radova Prirodno-matematičkog fakulteta (Novi Sad, Serija za geogra-
            fiju) 3:253–81.
Burić, Olivera
   1968   Rural migrants in urban family life. Paper presented at the Second
            World Congress of Rural Sociology, Amsterdam.
   1972   Položaj žene u sistemu društvene moći u Jugoslaviji (The woman's posi-
            tion in the system of social power in Yugoslavia). *Sociologija* 4, 2:61–76.
   1976   The zadruga and the contemporary family in Yugoslavia. In Robert F.
            Byrnes, ed., *Communal families in the Balkans: The zadruga.* South Bend,
            Ind.: University of Notre Dame Press, pp. 117–38.
Burić, Olivera, and A. Zečević
   1969   *Porodični život i društveni položaj porodice* (Family life and social position).
            Belgrade: Institut Društvenih Nauka.
Cifrić, I.
   1975   Privlačnost Zagreba kao velikog grada (The attraction of Zagreb as a
            large city). *Revija za sociologiju* 5:82–92.
Cvijić, Jovan
   1966   *Balkansko poluostrvo i Južnoslovenske zemlje: Osnovi antropogeografije* (The Bal-
            kand peninsula and South Slav countries: Elements of anthropogeogra-
            phy). Belgrade: Zavod za Izdavanje udžbenika SRS.
Ćirić, J. V.
   1967   *Neki problemi razvoja i smeštaja Aleksinca u prostoru* (Some space problems of
            development and lodging in Aleksinac). Niš: Katedra za Geografiju Više
            Pedagoške Škole.
Čubrilović, Vasa, ed.
   1974   *Istorija Beograda* (History of Belgrade). 3 vols. Belgrade: Prosveta.

Denich, Bette S.
  1969   Social mobility and industrialization in a Yugoslav town. PhD. disserta-
          tion, University of California at Berkeley.
  1970   Migration and network manipulation in Yugoslavia. In R. F. Spencer,
          ed., *Migration and anthropology*. Proceedings of the 1970 annual spring
          meeting of the American Ethnological Society. Seattle: University of
          Washington.
  1976   Urbanization and women's roles in Yugoslavia. *Anthropological Quarterly*
          49:11-9.
Djilas, Milovan
  1957   *The new class: An analysis of the communist system*. New York: Praeger.
Djurić, V.
  1968   Ekonomsko-geografski položaj i funkcionalno diferenciranje jugoslov-
          enskih gradova (Economic-geographic position and functional differen-
          tiation of Yugoslav cities). *Zbornik na VIII kongres na geografite od SFRJ*.
          Skopje, pp. 227-35.
  1970   Opšti pristup funcionalnoj klasifikaciji gradskih naselja u SR Srbiji
          (General introduction to the functional classification of urban settlements
          in Serbia). *Geographical Papers* 1:83-94.
Dvorniković, Vladimir
  1939   *Karakterologija Jugoslovena* (Characterology of the Yugoslavs). Belgrade:
          Kosmos.
Erlich, V. Stein
  1966   *Family in transition*. Princeton, N.J., Princeton University Press.
  1971   Obespravljena generacija (The disenfranchised generation). *Sociologija* 3,
          8:489-98.
Fisher, Jack C.
  1962   Planning the city of socialist man. *Journal of the American Institude of Planners*
          28:4.
  1966   *Yugoslavia — a multinational state: Regional difference and administrative response*.
          San Francisco: Chandler.
Galić, R.
  1968   *Skopje: Urbanistički plan* (Skopje: An urban plan). Skopje: Nova Makedon-
          ija.
Ginić, Ivanka
  1967   *Dinamika i struktura gradskog stanovništva Jugoslavije: Demografski aspekt urban-
          izacije* (The dynamics and structure of the urban population in Yugoslav-
          ia: The demographic aspect of urbanization). Belgrade: Centar za
          Demografska Istraživanja.
  1971   Dinamika gradskog stanovništva Jugoslavije prema prvim rezultatima
          popisa od 1971 godine (The dynamics of the Yugoslav urban population
          according to the first results of the 1971 population census). *Stanovništvo*
          (Jan.-June):25-41.
Günther, Horst
  1966   *Die Verstädterung in Jugoslawien; Darstellung und Probleme*. Wiesbaden: Har-
          rassowitz.
Halpern, Joel M.
  1964   *Peasant culture and urbanization in Yugoslavia*. Waltham, Mass.: Department
          of Anthropology, Brandeis University.
  1975   Some perspectives on Balkan migration patterns (with particular refer-
          ence to Yugoslavia). In B. M. DuToit and H. I. Safa, ed., *Migration and*

urbanization: Models and adaptive strategies. The Hague: Mouton, pp. 77–115.

Hammel, Eugene A.
1957   Serbo-Croatian kinship terminology. *Papers of the Kroeber Anthropological Society* 16:45–75. Berkeley: University of California.
1969a   *The pink yo-yo: Occupational mobility in Belgrade ca. 1915–1965.* Berkeley: Institute of International Studies, University of California.
1969b   Economic change, social mobility, and kinship in Serbia. *Southwestern Journal of Anthropology* 25:188–97.
1970   The ethnographer's dilemma: Alternative models of occupational prestige in Belgrade. *Man* 5:652–70.
1977   The influence of social and geographical mobility on the stability of kinship systems: The Serbian case. In A. A. Brown and E. Neuberger, ed., *Internal migration: A comparative perspective.* New York: Academic Press, pp. 401–15.

Hammel, Eugene A., and Djordje Šoć
1973   The lineage cycle in southern and eastern Yugoslavia. *American Anthropologist* 75:802–14.

Hammel, Eugene A., and Charles Yarbrough
1973   Social mobility and the durability of family ties. *Journal of Anthropological Research* 29:145–63.
1974   Preference and recall in Serbian cousinship: Power and kinship ideology. *Journal of Anthropological Research* 30:95–115.

Hoffman, G. W., and F. W. Neal
1962   *Yugoslavia and the new communism.* New York: Twentieth Century Fund.

Ilić, J.
1970   Karakteristike funcionalnih odnosa izmedju grada i okoline sa posebnim osvrtom na SR Srbiju (Characteristics of functional relations between the city and its surroundings with special review of Serbia). *Stanovništvo* 13, nos. 3–4:167–89.

Institut Društvenih Nauka
1971   *Migracije stanovništva Jugoslavije* (Migrations of the population of Yugoslavia). Belgrade: Centar za Demografska Istraživanja, Institut Društvenih Nauka.

Kadić, M.
1972   Društveni uzroci i prostorni učinci bespravne stambene izgradnje (Social causes and space efficiency of illegal dwellings). *Odjek* (Sarajevo) 3.

Keiser, R. Lincoln
1969   *The vice lords: Warriors of the streets.* New York: Holt, Rinehart, and Winston.

Knežević, Srebrica
1979   The urbanized environment and the preservation of traditional folk medicine in Serbia. Paper presented at the Fifty-fifth Central States Anthropological Society meetings, Milwaukee, Wis.

Kokole, Vladimir
1962   Funkcije slovenskih mest (Functions of Slovenian cities). *Geografski vestnik* 34:21–60.
1968   *Sodobni trendi urbanizacije v Sloveniji* (Contemporary trends of urbanization in Slovenia). Ljubljana: Biro za Regionalno Prostorsko Planiranje.
1971   Centralni kraji v SR Sloveniji: Problemi njihovega omrežja in njihovih gravitacijskih območij (Central places in Slovenia: Problems of their network and their gravitational fields). *Geografski zbornik* 12:5–131.

Kolaja, Jiri T.
1966   *Workers' councils: The Yugoslav experience.* New York: Praeger.
Kostić, Cvetko
1955   *Seljaci industrijski radnici* (Peasants industrial workers). Belgrade: Rad.
1969   Poseljačenje naših gradova (Peasantization of our cities). *Politika,* Dec.
1973   *Sociologija grada* (The sociology of the city). Belgrade: Centar za Analizu i
        Projektovanje Prostornih Sistema—ISPU.
Kroeber, Alfred L.
1939   *Cultural and natural areas of native North America.* Berkeley: University of
        California Press.
Lazarević, D.
1967   Prevencija prestupničkog ponašanja maloletnika (Prevention of juvenile
        delinquency). In *Projekat: Položaj, mesto, i uloga omladine u našem društvu*
        (Project: Position, place, and role of youth in our society). Belgrade: In-
        stitut Društvenih Nauka, pp. 54–65.
Leši, Ć.
1972   Evoluiranje funkcija grada na primerima urbanih i urbaniziranih centara
        Kosova (The evolution of functions of the city in examples of urban and
        urbanized centers of Kosovo). *Zbornik F. F. u Prištini* 8.
Livada, S.
1966   Staračka poljoprivredna domaćinstva (Aged agricultural households). *So-
        ciologija sela* 13, no. 4:3–16. Zagreb: Agrarni Institut.
Lockwood, William G.
1975   *European Moslems: Economy and ethnicity in western Bosnia.* New York: Aca-
        demic Press.
Macura, Miloš
1954   Kriterium za razgraničenje gradskog i seoskog stanovništva (A criterion
        for the delimitation of urban and village populations). *Statistička revija* 4,
        nos. 3–4:371–77.
Marković, D. Ž.
1968   Determinante budžeta vremena i značaj njegovog sociološko-ekonom-
        skog proučavanja (Determinants of the time budget and the significance
        of its socioeconomic study). *Zbornik radova pravno-ekonomskog fakulteta* (Niž)
        7:163–76.
Marković, P. J.
1966   *Uticaj migracija poljoprivrednog stanovništva na promene agrarene strukture* (The
        influence of migrations of the agricultural population on changes in
        agrarian structure). Belgrade: Jugoslovenska Poljoprivredna Banka.
Marković, P., and D. Kostić
1964   Strukturalne promene na jugoslovenskom selu u posleratnom periodu
        1945–62 (Structural changes in the Yugoslav village in the postwar period
        1945–62). *Sociologija* 6, nos. 3–4:170–95.
Marx, Karl
1951   *The eighteenth brumaire of Louis Bonaparte.* New York: International Pub-
        lishers.
Meha, B.
1971   *Urbanističko i prostorno planiranje u SR Srbiji 1945–1970* (Urban and space
        planning in Serbia 1945–1970). Belgrade.
Melik, A.
1964   *Rast naših mest v novi dobi* (The growth of our cities in the new period).
        Ljubljana: Slovenska Akademija Znanosti in Umetnosti.

Milenkovitch, Deborah D.
1971   *Plan and market in Yugoslav economic thought.* New Haven, Conn.: Yale University Press.
Milosavljević, P.
1974   Druga vlada Miloša i Mihaila Obrenovića (1858–1967). (The second reign of Miloš and Mihailo Obrenović (1858–1967)). In Vasa Čubrilović, ed., *Istorija Beograda,* vol. 2. Belgrade: Prosveta, pp. 144–53.
Milovančević, Dj. B.
1961   *Selo i grad: Nastajanje, razvitak, i prevazilaženje suprotnosti* (Village and city: The origin, development, and synthesis of opposites). Belgrade: Zadružna Knjiga.
Miščević, R.
1965   *Skoplje — Centralno gradsko područje: Idejno urbanističko rješenje* (Skopje — The central city region: An urban plan). Zagreb: Urbanistički Institut SR Hrvatske.
Mitrović, L. R.
1970   *Ognjišta koja gasnu: Istraživanje o socijalnim problemima staračkih domaćinstava i društvenom položaju ostraralih na belopalanačkom selu* (Hearths which are going out: An investigation of the social problems of elderly households and of the social position of the elderly in a Belopalanka village). Belgrade: Ekonomska Politika.
Mitrović, M., ed.
1963   *Gradovi i naselja u Srbiji* (Cities and settlements in Serbia). Belgrade: Urbanistički Zavod NR Srbije.
Nikolić, P.
1971   *Priručnik za društveno istraživanje u urbanim područjima,* 1 i 2 deo (Handbook for social investigation in urban regions, 1 and 2). Belgrade: Jugoslovenski Institut za Urbanizam i Istraživanje.
Panov, M.
1966   Funkcionalni razvitak gradova u Nakedoniji u uslovima socialističke izgradnje (The functional development of cities in Macedonia under conditions of the building of socialism). *Glasnik Srpskog geografskog društva* 46, no. 2:169–78.
Parkin, Frank
1976   Market socialism and class structure: Some aspects of social stratification in Yugoslavia. In B. L. Faber, ed., *The social structure of Eastern Europe.* New York: Praeger, pp. 29–49.
Perišić, A.
1970   *Prikaz stanja urbanizacije u Srbiji* (Survey of the state of urbanization in Serbia). Belgrade: Urbanistički Savez Srbije.
Petković, V.
1972   *Društveno ekonomski problemi korišćenja vremena* (Socioeconomic problems of the use of time). Niš: Prosveta.
Piha, B.
1964   *Ekonomska politika i metodi usmeravanja razvoja gradova Jugoslavije* (Economic politics and methods of the direction of development of Yugoslav cities). Belgrade: Institut za Arhitekturu i Urbanizam.
Politika
1976   Nezaposleni se "podmladjuju" (The unemployed have reappeared). Oct. 23, p. 6.
1977   Životni stil radnika (The life style of the worker). Apr. 18, p. 7.

Popis stanovništva 1948
1954   Vol. 3: *Stanovništvo po zanimanju* (The population by occupation). Bel-
          grade: Savezni Zavod za Statistiku.
Popis stanovništva 1961
1965   Vol. 10: *Stanovništva i domačinstva u 1948, 1953, i 1961* (Populations and
          households in 1948, 1953, and 1961). Belgrade: Savezni Zavod za Statis-
          tiku.
Prokić-Sulejmanović, D.
1970   *Promene u društveno-ekonomskoj strukturi stanovništva prigradskih područja*
          (Changes in the socioeconomic structure of the population of regions
          nearby cities). Belgrade: Institut za Uporedno Pravo.
Radovanović, M.
1967   Prilog problemu ekonomsko-geografski klasifikacije naselja AP Kosovo i
          Metohija (A contribution to the problem of the economic-geographic
          classification of settlements in Kosovo and Metohija). *Zbornik radova
          Prirodno-matematičkog fakulteta univerziteta u Beogradu* (Geografski zavod)
          14:137–50.
Radunović, D.
1969   Društveno ekonomski aspekti prelaska na 42-časovnu radnu sedmicu
          (The socioeconomic aspects of the transition to the 42-hour work week).
          Produktivnost 11, no. 9:590–94.
Rodić, D.
1967   Dinamika i migracione karakteristike stanovništva večih naselja u SFRJ
          (The dynamics and migrational characteristics of the population of larger
          settlements in Yugoslavia). *Zbornik radova Prirodno-matematičkog fakulteta
          univerziteta u Beogradu* (Geografski zavod) 14:81–106.
Rogić, V.
1968   Historijsko-geografska problematika urbane mreže Jugoslavije u odnosu
          na osobine njenog savremenog razvoja (Historico-geographical problems
          of the Yugoslav urban network in relation to features of its modern devel-
          opement). In *Cvijićev zbornik,* pp. 357–72.
1977   The changing urban pattern in Yugoslavia. In F. W. Carter, ed., *An his-
          torical geography of the Balkans.* New York: Academic Press, pp. 409–36.
Rusinow, Dennison I.
1973   *Slovenia: Modernization without urbanization?* Hanover: American Univer-
          sity Field Staff.
Savezna Skupština
1969   *Osnovne politike urbanizacije i prostornog uredjenja: Teze za javnu diskusiju* (Basic
          politics of urbanization and space organization: Theses for public discus-
          sion). Belgrade: Prosveta.
Simić, Andrei
1973a   *The peasant urbanites: A study of rural-urban mobility in Serbia.* New York:
          Seminar Press.
1973b   Kinship reciprocity and rural-urban integration in Serbia. *Urban Anthro-
          pology* 2:205–13.
1973c   The best of two worlds: Serbian peasant in the city. In George M. Foster
          and Robert V. Kemper, eds., *Anthropologists in cities.* Boston: Little,
          Brown, pp. 179–200.
1974   Urbanization and cultural process in Yugoslavia. *Anthropological Quarterly*
          47:211–27.
1978   Winners and losers: Aging Yugoslavs in a changing world. In B. G.
          Myerhoff and A. Simić, eds., *Life's career — aging: Cultural variations in grow-
          ing old.* Beverly Hills, Calif.: Sage Publications, pp. 77–105.

Simonović, D. C.
1970   *Centri zajednica sela u Srbiji: Seoske varošice i seoske čaršije* (Centers of associations of villages in Serbia: Village towns and village markets). Belgrade.
1971   *Transfer Jugoslovenih seljaka u radnike: Posleratni ruralni eksodus* (The transfer of Yugoslav peasants into workers: The postwar rural exodus). Belgrade: Zadružna Knjiga.
Spangler, Michael
1979   Time and social change in a Yugoslav city. Ph.D. dissertation, University of Wisconsin.
Spangler, Michael, and S. Ghitelman
1980   The Italian-Albanians of Madison, Wisconsin: A group within a group. In F. Cordasco, Ed., *Festschrift in honor of Professor Peter Sammartino.* Forthcoming.
Spangler, Michael, and O. Petrovich
1978   Future time perspective and feeling tone: A study in the perception of the days by Yugoslav and American students. *Journal of Social Psychology* 105:189–93.
Stalna Konferencija Gradova Jugoslavije
1964   *Problemi urbanizacije u Jugoslaviji* (Problems of urbanization in Yugoslavia). Belgrade.
1966   *Društveno-ekonomski aspekti uredjivanja i korišćenja gradskog zemljišta* (Socioeconomic aspects of the organization and use of city land). Belgrade.
Stefanović, D.
1965   O dinamici urbanizacije u našoj zemlji (On the dynamics of urbanization in our country). *Ekonomski anali ekonomskog fakulteta u Beogradu* 16:3–28.
Stoianovich, Traian
1967   *A study in Balkan civilization.* New York: Alfred Knopf.
Šifrer, Žviko
1974   *Urbanizacija Slovenije* (The urbanization of Slovenia). Ljubljana.
Šuvar, Štipe
1970   *Sociološki presjek jugoslavenskog društva* (Sociological cross-section of Yugoslav society). Zagreb: Školska Knjiga.
1973   *Izmedju zaseoka i megalopolisa* (Between the small village and the megalopolis). Zagreb: Centar za Sociologiju Sela, Institut za Društvena Istraživanja Sveučilišta u Zagrebu.
Todorović, Aleksandar
1971   *Uslovi i uzroci maloletničkog prestupništva u urbanim i ruralnim sredinama* (The conditions and causes of juvenile delinquency in urban and rural environments). Belgrade: Institut za Kriminološka i Kriminalistička Ispitivanja Instituta Društvenih Nauka.
United Nations
1971   *Demographic yearbook 1970.* New York: Statistical Office of the United Nations.
Urbanistički Zavod Grada Zagreba
1963   *Urbanistički program grada Zagreba* (The urban program of the city of Zagreb). Zagreb.
Veljković, A.
1969   *Mreža gradova u užoj Srbiji, Vojvodini i Kosovu* (The network of cities in Serbia, Vojvodina, and Kosovo). Belgrade: Jugoslovenski Institut za Urbanizam i Stanovanje.
Vogelnik, D.
1971   *Projekcija prebivalište, delovne sile in mest SR Slovenija* (The projection of

homes and work force in cities of Slovenia). Ljubljana: Biro za Regionalno Prostorsko Planiranje.

1974 *Makrodemografski aspekti formiranja urbanih regija u Jugoslaviji* (Macrodemographic aspects of the formation of urban areas in Yugoslavia). I Slovenski Demografski Simpozijum, Ljubljana.

Vrišer, I.
1975 Yugoslavia. In R. Jones, ed., *Essays on world urbanization*. London: Philip and Son, pp. 331-40.

Ward, Benjamin N.
1967 *The socialist economy: A study of organizational alternatives*. New York: Random House.

Winner, Irene
1971 *A Slovenian village: Žerovnica*. Providence, R.I.: Brown University Press.

Zavod za Statistiku — Beograd
1977 *Statistički godišnjak Beograda* (Statistical almanac of Belgrade). Belgrade: Gradski Zavod za Statistiku.

Zukin, Sharon
1975 *Beyond Marx and Tito: Theory and practice in Yugoslav socialism*. New York: Cambridge University Press.

Zvonarević, M.
1968 Socijalno-psihološki faktori prestupništva (Social psychological factors of delinquency). In *Socijalna psihologija* (Social psychology). Belgrade, pp. 271-300.

Železnikar, Iva
1966 *Slovenska urbanistična bibliografija za leto 1965* (Slovenian urban bibliography for the summer of 1965). Ljubljana: Urbanistični Institut SR Slovenije.

1969 *Slovenska urbanistična bibliografija za leto 1966 in 1967* (Slovenian urban bibliography for the summer of 1966 and 1967). Ljubljana: Urbanistični Institut SR Slovenije.

Žuljić, Stanko
1960 Porast gradskog stanovništva NR Hrvatske (The growth of the urban population in Croatia). *Geografski glasnik* 22:31-42.

1964 Suvremeni problemi razvoja Zagreba (Modern problems in the development of Zagreb). In *Zbornik radova VII Kongresa geografa Jugoslavije*. Zagreb.

1970 *Proces urbanizacije na prostoru Jugoslavije: Značenje i predvidivi tok promjena do 1985 g.* (The process of urbanization on the area of Yugoslavia: Its meaning and predictable course of changes to the year 1985). Zagreb: Ekonomski Institut.

1971 *Pojava metropolskih regija i njihovo značenje za dalju urbanizaciju Jugoslavije* (The phenomenon of metropolitan areas and their meaning for the further urbanization of Yugoslavia). Zagreb.

Chapter 4

Urban Research in Greece

Hans Vermeulen

Although urban culture has played a prominent role in modern Greek history, and by 1971 more than 35% of the population lived in one of the three urban agglomerations of over 100,000 inhabitants, few anthropologists have chosen the city as their major research site. This neglect of urban areas by anthropologists thus confirms their well-known preference for the often smaller and more isolated villages of the Mediterranean (Davis 1977:8). Though interest in urban research is growing, up to now no published urban monograph exists on Greece and our knowledge of urban life remains fragmentary. Partly for this reason we will not restrict ourselves to a review of anthropological research only. First we will give a brief historical outline of Greek urbanization since the establishment of the modern Greek state.[1] This will provide a context of interpretation for the examination of urban research in the following sections.

URBANIZATION SINCE THE FORMATION OF THE GREEK STATE (1832)

Urbanization, the State, and the Greeks of the Diaspora (1832–1922)

When the Greek state was founded in 1832, it contained no large cities. At least 80% of the population lived in rural settlements of less than 2,000 inhabitants (Tsoucalas 1977:165). By the beginning of the twentieth century the urban population had increased substantially: roughly one out of four Greeks lived in population centers of more than 5,000 inhabitants. The pace and degree of urbanization were much higher than they were in the neighboring Slav countries. Though there was some development of industry during the late nineteenth century, the expansion of the urban population was not primarily due to industrialization. As a result, the percentage of the urban population employed in industry remained low. A further characteristic of Greek urbanization is its high degree of concentration on the capital, especially after 1880. Athens, a small provincial town after the struggle for independence, soon became the largest city of Greece and in 1907 had—together with nearby Piraeus—a population of 250,000, almost 10% of the total population.[2]

During the first decade after independence regional fragmentation remained pronounced, as a result of both the resistance of regional powerholders to centralizing tendencies of the new state and the lack of communications and internal trade. Most cities continued to function as regional centers of trade, export, and production for their own hinterlands, and the balance between Athens and the other urban centers was not yet disturbed to the disadvantage of the latter (Burgel 1976:176–84). Only the harbors of the Aegean islands — except Syros — suffered an early decline. The regional powerholders soon discovered that it was more profitable to exploit the state apparatus from within than to combat it. In this way they became brokers between the state and their regional constituencies; by providing jobs in the state bureaucracy for their clients, they contributed both to the expansion of the state apparatus and to the integration of city and countryside. The increasing commercialization of agriculture after the mid-nineteenth century, the growth of the population as a result of decreasing mortality, and the improvement of communications accelerated rural-urban migration. From about 1880, migration was increasingly directed at the capital, which more and more came to dominate the national economy (Burgel 1976:173–76, Tsoucalas 1977:164–8). From 1889 to 1920 the population of Athens increased by more than 200%, while during the same period the next 22 largest cities grew by only 30% (based on Tsoucalas 1977:167–70). As a result of this unequal growth the total population of these cities in 1920 amounted to about 75% of the population of the capital. Urban decline was total on the Cyclades and the Ionian islands. In the newly acquired territories of Thessaly and Arta the urban centers were much more able to hold up against Athenian competition. Thessaly's major urban center, the industrial port of Volos, was the only city whose demographic growth during this period (170%) was close to that of Athens. In the rest of Greece the situation was intermediate. Here Patras, the second largest city of Greece, was one of the fastest growing cities (67%). Both from a demographic and from an economic point of view it remained, however, far behind both Athens and Volos in its growth.

Already shortly before the struggle for independence (1821–29) the incipient industrialization of the Greek regions of the Ottoman empire (shipbuilding, textiles) had suffered a severe setback as a result of the influence of the English industrial revolution (Kremmydas 1976:146). The breakdown of industry continued after independence (Mouzelis 1978:15). Greeks who disposed of capital avoided investment in industry, and the productive sector of the urban economy was relatively unimportant. According to Tsoucalas (1977:191, 199–200), at least 60% of the urban population consisted, during all of the nineteenth century, of people not directly involved in productive activities, and the tertiary sector was more extensive than in any

other European country. Besides those working in commerce or transportation, civil servants, servants, professionals — mainly lawyers, teachers, and
physicians — and rentiers constituted a large part of this nonproductive
population. Nothwithstanding a certain degree of industrialization after
1870–80, the industrial proletariat remained relatively insignificant: indeed, in certain working occupations foreigners were heavily represented,
e.g., Bulgarians in the building trade. Neither was there a large marginal
population of unemployed labor. The unproductive character of the urban
population was particularly pronounced in Athens, where many were
directly and indirectly dependent upon the state bureaucracy.

The extent and nature of Greek urbanization — the large state bureaucracy, the vast expansion of the tertiary sector, and the rapid growth of the
capital at the cost of other cities — cannot be understood without paying attention to the role played by the Greek diaspora. From the seventeenth century onward the exports of the Ottoman empire increased as a result of rising demand in Western Europe. Greek merchants came to play an active
role in the expanding commercial activities, and Greek expatriate communities were established in Central and Western Europe. During the second half of the eighteenth century — partly as a result of the French-British
wars during which both the English and the French merchant marine suffered great losses (Kremmydas 1976:118) — Greek commerce experienced
an unprecedented growth. The leading role of the Greek bourgeoisie during
and after the struggle for independence "explains to a great extent why the
merchant class became the value originator and the standard setter of Greek
life" (Mouzelis and Attalides 1971:169). From the beginning of the nineteenth century Greeks oriented themselves increasingly toward the Near
East, where they became important intermediaries between the industrial
states of Western Europe and the peripheral regional economies. The Greek
diaspora communities, of which those of Asia Minor, Romania, south
Russia, and Egypt were the most important, expanded rapidly after 1840.
Though old Greek communities existed notably in Asia Minor and the
southern part of Russia, this expansion was mainly due to emigration from
Greece. After independence, conditions in Greece became worse than they
had been under Turkish rule. The country was devastated as a result of ten
years of war; taxation had increased and banditry was common in the countryside. Many Greeks left their country for Turkey and relatively few followed the opposite route (Woodhouse 1977:161). Tsoucalas (1977:107)
estimates that between 1834 and 1846, 60,000 Greeks — at least 7 to 8% of
the total population — left Greece to settle in Turkey. The emigration toward
Turkey and other parts of the eastern Mediterranean continued throughout
the nineteenth century. To this overflow must be added the overseas emigration, mainly to the United States, which took on massive dimensions

during the first decades of the twentieth century. Even before the emigration to the United States, however, more Greek villagers established themselves abroad than in the urban centers of their own country.

The large majority of the Greek population of Asia Minor, Romania, Russia, and Egypt was urban. Around the middle of the century the Greek population of Constantinople numbered 120,000 and that of Smyrna 60,000, while Athens, already the largest city of Greece, had only 36,000 inhabitants. Moreover, even the nonurban Greek population of the diaspora was often not involved in agriculture. Many, following the construction of railways, had established themselves as small entrepreneurs, often as *bakalides* (grocers),[3] in the small interior villages. Though detailed and reliable data on the urban Greek population of the diaspora are not available, it is clear that this urban population increased much faster and outnumbered the total urban population of Greece during the whole period (Tsoucalas 1977:298–99). Many diaspora Greeks owned shops or other small businesses and often acted as local moneylenders. Greeks were, however, also well represented among the professionals (e.g., physicians, dentists, pharmacists). A much smaller but rich and influential section of the Greek communities abroad consisted of merchants, shipowners, and bankers. Though a Greek proletariat developed to some degree in Asia Minor after 1870, Greek workers usually aspired to petit bourgeois status and identified with their richer compatriots (Tsoucalas 1977:345).

Greek emigrants usually came from the same regions as those who migrated to the capital. These were regions characterized by a smallholding peasantry (e.g., Peloponnesus, Cyclades, the southern Ionian islands — see Burgel 1976:375, Tsoucalas 1977:112–23). Most male migrants left their families behind, at least temporarily (Burgel 1976:385, Tsoucalas 1977:145). They usually kept in touch with the family and village of origin, which could support them in case of failure or provide them with personnel or a partner in business in case of success. Even in the smaller villages of the emigration regions opportunities for education were relatively good. Many peasant families would send one or more sons to school as a preparation for an urban career in the capital or abroad. Typically, out-migration involved not proletarization but a transition to petit bourgeois status. This resulted in a petit bourgeois ideology even among the peasants of these regions and reduced the potential for conflict between city and countryside (Tsoucalas 1977:132). Family and patronage relations formed the main links between the rural and the urban world.

Many richer Greeks established themselves in Athens, where they conducted their businesses. Others returned to Greece to live as rentiers. Those who remained abroad regularly sent money to their families in Greece. Up to 1880 the money which was sent or brought to Greece in these ways was mainly spent on consumption. These remittances not only covered the considerable deficit in the balance of payments but also indirectly contributed to state income. Tsoucalas estimates that 5 to 10% of state income resulted from import duties owing to increased consumption (1977:243). Moreover, the Greeks of the diaspora reduced state expenditure by taking over some of the tasks of the state. The contribution of private capital to the cost of education, for example, was much more important than that of the state. After 1880 the rich bourgeoisie of the diaspora started to invest in Greece, especially in mining, banking, and communication. This was the result of emergent nationalism, particularly in Romania and Russia, as well as of changes in the world capitalist system. Many of these activities, such as those in banking, required large concentrations of population; as a result, it was mainly Athens that profited.

Urbanization, the Settlement of Refugees, and Industrialization (the post-1922 period)

In 1922 the Turks under Kemal Ataturk defeated the Greek army in Asia Minor. This meant a definitive blow to Greek irredentist claims and resulted in the arrival of more than a million Greek refugees from Asia Minor. By now the bulk of the diaspora, with as major exception the Greeks of Egypt, had arrived in Greece. The relation between Greece and the diaspora, which had such a formative influence on urbanization up to 1922, now lost its significance.

According to the population census of 1928 the refugees constituted almost 20% of the total population. Larger cities received more than their share of the burden. According to the same census, 32% of the population of cities of over 20,000 inhabitants consisted of refugees. Though some of the smaller cities of Macedonia had the highest proportion of refugees—e.g., Drama (70%) and Kavalla (57%)—Athens received the bulk of the refugees settled in cities (Kayser 1964:31–34, Pentzopoulos 1962:111–15). The rapid urbanization during the twenties owing to refugee settlement and internal migration was followed by a period of relative stability. Though during World War II and the civil war many people fled the insecurity of the countryside, internal migration took on massive proportions only after the civil war. While from 1928 to 1951 the urban population increased from 31% to 38%, by 1971 more than half the Greek population was urban (53%). During this whole period Greece remained much more urbanized than the neighboring Slav countries.[4]

The influx of refugees not only accelerated the process of urbanization but also gave a big push to economic development, in agriculture as well as in industry (Pentzopoulos 1962:143–67, Vergopoulos 1978:40–44). The presence of refugees as well as the annexation of new territories (part of Epirus, Macedonia, and Thrace) had considerably enlarged the internal market. Moreover, urban refugees constituted a cheap and relatively skilled urban labor force, and a number of refugees disposed of both entrepreneurial skills and capital. The import of foreign capital, primarily in the form of public loans and aid to refugees, also contributed to industrial development.

This process of industrialization was interrupted by World War II, but a new wave of industrialization started in the sixties.[5] It differs in several respects from the industrialization of the interwar period. First of all, while industrialization during the interwar period was partly the result of the interruption of Greece's relation with the international market during World War I and the economic crisis of 1929-32 (Vergopoulos 1978:73–77), recent industrialization is related to the country's further integration into the world economy. Second, postwar industrialization is no longer directed at import substitution. The export of industrial products is becoming more and more important and by 1972 surpassed agricultural exports in value. Furthermore, for the first time foreign capital came into the country on a large scale in the form of direct investments in industry. This was partly the result of favorable conditions offered to foreign capital by postwar Greek governments. A last point to be noted is the shift from the light consumer goods industry to the production of capital goods. Some characteristics of Greek industrialization during earlier phases, however, remain important even today. Greek industry continues to be characterized by a very large number of small family businesses. In 1930, 93% of manufacturing establishments employed fewer than five persons and the figure was still as high as 88% in 1963. In 1973 there were 121,357 manufacturing establishments employing 604,042 persons, i.e., almost five persons per establishment.

This enormous fragmentation of Greek industry has major consequences for urban life. For example, it has been one of the major obstacles for the organization of labor. The large firms that do exist usually belong to the foreign-dominated sectors of the economy. Notwithstanding the expansion of industry, the Greek economy still shows characteristics of underdevelopment. Even during the postwar period Greek capital avoided investment in industry, preferring quick profits in shipping or tourism. When investment in industry occurs, it is directed toward the traditional branches such as textiles and food, leaving the most crucial sectors of the modern economy to foreign capital. The country remains heavily dependent on migration, shipping, and tourism to purchase its basic necessities, and the tertiary sector retains its inflated character.

The development of an urban proletariat constituted the most important change in the urban stratification system during the interwar period. Class-based organizations and forms of social action became more prominent and Greek politics assumed a more pronounced class character. The size of the proletariat remained limited, however, and patronage continued to play a central role, though it took on a more party-political character. Postwar rural-urban migration and industrialization did not fundamentally change the urban stratification system (see Campbell and Sherrard 1968:

370, Mouzelis and Attalides 1971:183–85, Nikolinakos 1974:147–64). The capital-intensive nature of the new large firms and the continuing reliance on family labor of the small enterprises restricted the growth of the proletariat. Many of those who left the countryside found work in the tertiary sector of the cities or migrated abroad. The middle classes of professionals, small entrepreneurs in commerce and industry, and civil servants continued to form the majority of the urban population. Though industrial interests played a more prominent role in the upper levels of the urban stratification system than before, bankers, shipowners, and merchants maintained their leading position.

The process of concentration of the urban population in Athens and the related decline of rural regions and their urban centers, which had become a main feature of urban development during the late nineteenth century, slowed down after the annexation of new territories and the arrival of refugees. In particular Thessaly, Macedonia, and Thrace experienced an important population growth and their active industrial and commercial urban centers expanded. In Old Greece, however, demographic and economic decline or stagnation remained the general picture. Only a few cities and their surrounding regions escaped this fate, the main example being Patras. From the early 1960s onward a massive rural exodus—to a large extent directed toward the cities of Western Europe—brought demographic decline also to the north. Many urban centers in these regions, such as Drama, Edessa, and Serres, lost their demographic and economic vigor. Burgel concludes that "there is an order in the zones which Athens destroys: the Peloponnesus follows the islands and Northern Greece follows the Peloponnesus" (1976:159).

During the postwar period only Salonika showed a rate of growth comparable to that of Athens (see Table 1). Other cities around or in between these two urban agglomerations profited from their development (e.g., Larissa, Lamia, Chalkis). Thus it became customary to refer to the core region of Greek economic development as "the Athens-Salonika axis." It should be realized, however, that the growth of Salonika and other urban centers that can be considered to belong to this axis absorb only a small part

Table 1. Postwar Growth of Cities with Population of More Than 100,000 in 1971

| | Population in | | | Population 1971 |
	1951	1961	1971	Population 1951
Greater Athens	1,378,586	1,852,709	2,540,241	1.84
Greater Salonika	302,124	380,654	557,360	1.84
Greater Patras	86,267	103,941	120,847	1.39

From Nicolacopoulos and Tsouyopoulos 1976.

of total urban growth in comparison to Athens. From 1961 to 1971, 72% of total urban growth was due to the growth of Athens and 15% to that of Salonika, leaving only 13% for all other cities combined (Burgel 1976:26). Also, economically speaking, Athens's leading role has been strengthened. Because it has the largest port (Piraeus), it is the main center of distribution. Industrial development outside the capital is to a large extent subject to Athenian initiative and control. As far as origin of its inhabitants is concerned, however, Athens remains primarily a city of southern Greece. Only relatively recently has immigration from other regions become more important.

Athens is first of all a center of distribution, consumption, and administration. Roughly two-thirds of its population are employed in the tertiary sector, which amounts to 44% of the total Greek population working in this sector. In certain areas this concentration is even higher: wholesale trade (58%), banks (58%), transportation (64%), and insurance (83%) (Burgel 1976:86). Notwithstanding the importance of the tertiary sector, Athens is also the most important industrial center, producing 48% of the industrial output in 1969 (Burgel 1976:68).

THE STATE OF URBAN RESEARCH

Since Papanastasiou founded the first Association for Social and Political Sciences in 1910, the social sciences in Greece have made little progress. The general political and intellectual climate during the postwar years, when interest in the social sciences was often equated with socialist or communist sympathy, was the main impediment to its growth. Though there are a few social science chairs, up to the present it is impossible to obtain a degree in such disciplines as sociology or anthropology. As a result Greek students interested in the social sciences have to study abroad, and most Greek academic social scientists are to be found outside the country (e.g., Damianakos, Mouzelis, Tsoucalas, Savramis). Social scientific research in Greece, including urban research, is mainly carried out by a few research centers outside the universities. The National Center of Social Research, now headed by Vasilis Filias, was founded in 1960 by the Greek government in cooperation with UNESCO. It publishes the quarterly *Greek Review of Social Research*, the only social scientific journal of Greece, as well as a series of empirical studies (e.g., Sandis 1973). Some Greek social scientists now working abroad (e.g., Damianakos, Tsoucalas) as well as a number of foreigners have been affiliated with the center for some time. John Peristiany, the first director of the center, did much to stimulate the development of the social sciences in Greece. The Athenian Institute of Anthropos, founded in 1962 by private initiative by Vassiliou, carries out research in the areas of social psychology and social psychiatry. Research on urban planning and housing is carried out by the Athens Center of Ekistics and by a group of architects at the University of Salonika (e.g., Fatouros, Papadopoulos, and Tentokali). The center (founded by Doxiades, the city planner), publishes the internationally well-known journal *Ekistics,* which is also of interest to social scientists. Considerable attention is paid in Greece to the study of folklore (*laografia*), but students of folklore have — almost by definition[6] — paid little or no attention to the city. The only exception is the autodidact Elias Petropoulos, who has been called "the folklorist of the modern urban environment" (see Chiliotis 1980). Petropoulos has published a number of photographic essays (1976a, b, and c) as well as studies on urban popular art (1968, 1978) and prison life (1975). Petropoulos's work on the *rebetika* songs has contributed very much to a broad interest in this popular music among the general public, as well as to the scientific study of it.

Given the underdevelopment of the social sciences, it is not surprising that the output of social research in Greece is very limited. Moreover, since Greek social scientists received their training in different foreign countries — mainly the United States, France, England, and Germany — there is no national tradition. There is, however, at the moment a fairly strong marxist orientation among the younger generation of Greek social scientists, at home and abroad.

Two groups of foreign social scientists have been particularly active in studying Greek society: French geographers and Anglo-Saxon anthropologists. Much of the work of the French geographers provides useful information on urbanization at the national level (Kayser 1964, Kayser *et al.* 1971), while other studies concentrate on particular regions, including their urban centers (e.g., islands, Kolodny 1974, and Thessaly, Sivignon 1975). The most important contribution to urban research is Burgel's (1976) detailed study of the capital, which concentrates on the mechanisms of its growth through time in relation to the development and decline of other urban centers and the development of the national economy.

Foreign anthropologists — like their colleagues elsewhere in the Mediterranean — have till recently avoided the cities. Most have preferred small rural communities. In many of these studies, however, attention has been paid to rural-urban links, especially in the discussions on patronage (e.g., Campbell 1964, Siegel 1973) and out-migration (e.g., Dubisch 1977). Some found their way to the city by following the migrants (Friedl 1976, Kenna 1977). Only four anthropologists have reported on research that took the city as the sole or primary locus of study, mainly in the form of theses: Gutenschwager (1971), Hirschon (1976), Sutton (1978), and Vermeulen (1970). All worked in Athens.

DIMENSIONS OF URBAN LIFE

Taking as a guide what research has taught us about life in Greek cities, we now turn to a discussion of some of the topics and issues that are important for the study of urban life in Greece and that will indicate some of the needs for future research. We will do so under six broad headings: immigrants in the city, family and kinship, sex roles, religion and the church, politics and associational life, and social identity.

Immigrants in the City

As a result of the massive rural-urban migration of the postwar years, the majority of the population of the big cities still consists of recent immigrants. From this point of view Athens is largely a city of peasants, a huge provincial town (Burgel 1976:13–14). It is remarkable, however, that the level of unemployment among the immigrants does not differ much from that of the rest of the urban population (Kayser 1964:96). Moreover, though immigrants are relatively strongly represented in some sectors of the urban economy—building and the tertiary sector, except for commerce (Kayser 1964:113, Tsoucalas 1969:128)—their occupational level is not lower than that of the nonmigrants. A study of 400 randomly selected migrants to Athens and a control group of nonmigrants, carried out by Gioka for the National Center of Social Research, even suggests that migrants have higher occupational levels than nonmigrants (see Friedl 1976). This seems related to the higher participation of children from peasant background in institutions of higher education as compared to those from the urban working class (Lambiri-Dimaki 1976). This successful adaptation of migrants in the city is in a sense a continuation of the already noted pattern of the nineteenth century. Patronage and familial links as well as the importance attached to education by many villagers have long contributed to the migrant's capacity to compete for the resources of the city (Friedl 1976, Tsoucalas 1977). The successful adaptation of migrants during the postwar period is also related, however, to recent national and international developments, such as the availability of emigration as an option for those leaving the countryside and the consequent shortages on the labor market since the late sixties (Nikolinakos 1973).[7]

Family and Kinship

Arranged marriage and the dowry have received attention in several urban studies. While arranged marriage is less frequent in the city than in the countryside, existing research suggests that it is still common among the working class, but it also invites some questions. In Yerania (Piraeus), a working-class neighborhood of refugees with a long urban tradition, marriages are said to be arranged with few exceptions (Hirschon 1976:86). In Nea Aeolia (Athens), a very similar neighborhood, "marriages are by and large arranged by the parents" (Gutenschwager 1971:85). Both authors seem to imply that arranged marriages do not decrease. This contrasts with the results and conclusion of Nicolaïdou's research in Megara, a small agricultural town (1975). She found arranged marriage much more frequent among the older factory women she interviewed (21 out of 24 cases) than among the younger (five out of 18 cases). How are these differences to be explained? Are they the result of differences in research techniques or in the concept of arranged marriage? If not, how is it to be explained that the institution of arranged marriage is losing its strength in a provincial town where many families live mainly from agriculture whlie this is not the case among the urban working class in the capital? Only further research can answer such questions.

Like arranged marriage, the dowry is less common in the city than in the countryside. Especially among the well-educated part of the urban middle class, the daughter often does not receive a dowry (Lambiri-Dimaki 1972). The provision of a dowry remains, however, a daily concern for most urban families with daughters. In contrast to the countryside, where in most regions the dowry is variably composed of the trousseau, furniture, money, and land, the most crucial component of the urban dowry is a house or apartment. This has important consequences for both inheritance and residence patterns. The provision of the dowry may require so much of the family's resources that it represents much more than the daughter's share in the inheritance. Gutenschwager remarks that in Nea Aeolia "patrimony by custom is not always divided equally among siblings. Sons do not necessarily expect to inherit anything from their parents, and actually on occasion they too have to work for their sister's dowry" (1971:89).

A second important effect is the tendency toward matrilocal residence (see, e.g., Hirschon's contribution to this volume). The inclusion of a "house" in the dowry as well as the maintenance of the dowry even among the most urbanized sections of the population indicate that the dowry cannot be understood as a mere rural survival, but must be interpreted as an adaptation to the pressures of urban living in a state that intervenes little in the area of housing. Sutton suggests a relation between the dowry and the low participation of women in the work force after marriage: "The wife no longer contributed economically to the family after marriage, so she could bring a large nest egg to it" (1978:134). Little is known as yet, however, about adherence to and functioning of the dowry among the various social classes and sections of the urban population.

A global characterization of the urban Greek family would include many features — e.g., the strong loyalty of its members, the high degree of differentiation and complementarity of the roles of husband and wife, and the control of female sexuality — that remind one of the descriptions of the rural family. It is this continuity between the rural and the urban worlds that is particularly stressed in the case studies of Hirschon (1976) and — to a somewhat lesser degree — Gutenschwager (1971).[8] This may be related to a mode of description that pays little attention to variation within the community studied. Continuity between city and countryside itself requires an explanation not merely limited to stressing the "tenacity of traditional culture" (Gutenschwager 1971:157).

Safilios-Rothschild (1967, 1976) and Vermeulen (1970) have stressed variation and change rather than continuity in their studies of the urban family. Vermeulen's research concentrates on the interrelations among the family's position in the urban environment, family structure, and socialization. Data were obtained from 258 children in the fifth grade of elementary school and from interviews with both their parents. Some of the results regarding the relation between urbanization and family structure may be briefly summarized. In families with little experience in the urban environment, husband and wife are relatively isolated and, as a result, have to rely on each other in decision making as well as for emotional support. Among the more urbanized lower-class families living in older and more stable neighborhoods, role differentiation is more pronounced and women tend to have a relatively prominent role. Among the urbanized families of the higher social strata, role differentiation is less pronounced. The more educated husbands and wives often discuss and act together, though it is usually the men who have the final say in family decision making.

The tendency toward matrilocality noted earlier also has consequences for relations with kinsmen outside the nuclear family. Women often live close to their mothers and sisters after marriage, and the relation between the men who have married sisters, the *badzanakides,* is usually intimate (Hirschon 1976:154–75). In the urban situation spiritual kinship is a relation between social equals — friends, relatives, or neighbors — rather than part of a system of patronage (Hirschon 1976:221, Sutton 1978:135). There is still much to be learned about urban kinship, however, and anthropologists are undoubtedly the most qualified to contribute to our understanding in this area.

Sex Roles

On the basis of research by the Athenian Institute of Anthropos the following description has been given of the male role:

> The man is supposed to have more freedom of movement and to be less restricted than the woman. He has implicit permission to "trespass" certain social barriers. Moreover, he is expected to be highly competitive and upwardly mobile, asserting himself in any situation. Typically, he has been persuaded to pursue the goals that he shares with his family and mostly with his mother. In this effort he counts on his ingroup — those people who show concern for him, who are for the most part members of his family, who are his friends. . . . Within this group he is supposed to be loyal, trustworthy, and sincere, responding to the generosity of his friends with even greater generosity. In short, his be-

haviour toward the ingroup is expected to accord with the highest value of the milieu, the *philotimo.* He must respect, obey, and follow authority. Outside his ingroup, however, he is expected to be competitive, to outmaneuver his rivals, cheating them if necessary, and to defy any "stranger" authority. (Spinellis *et al.* 1970:311–12)

The feminine role is described in the following way:

> From antiquity to the present, the woman has played a rather secluded social role. Early in life her behaviour is restricted and she is required to follow the prevailing moral code much more closely than is the case of the average boy of her age. In fact, Greek women, according to the traditional patterns, are not expected to become involved in socioeconomic activities. . . . Woman's increased participation in industry has . . . failed to elevate her position sufficiently to shape her for a new role similar to that of the male. (Spinellis *et al.* 1970:312)

The research carried out by the Athenian Institute of Anthropos gives no attention to variation in role conceptions according to sex, region, social class, or other criteria.[9] In her study of a working-class neighborhood Hirschon stressed the similarity in sex roles between city and countryside:

> . . . the sexual dichotomy and the separation of roles which are noted aspects of life in rural Greece have not been shaken in the context of urban life. . . . This division of activity at the ideal level is a fundamental tenet of family life in the heart of the city as well as in the village. It is a value which has withstood the pressures of economic need and many actual divergences in practice. In fact, the separation is even clearer here, since in village life women are inevitably drawn into the many tasks surrounding agriculture or shepherding. (Hirschon 1978:72, 73)

Spinellis *et al.* suggest that such divergences between the ideal and the actual as Hirschon refers to lead to role strains, especially for the woman, and that she needs a "new pattern, more syntonic with the requirements of her present milieu" (1970:316); Vermeulen's research suggests that pressures for change come primarily from women, mainly the more educated ones (1970:92).

Research on female employment is particularly important in understanding sex roles. According to the census of 1971, three out of ten people who are actively employed are females. At least among the working class, however, women often work only before marriage, and control over women by members of the family during absence from home is maintained as much as possible. Women often work at home — e.g., as hairdressers — or in the same factory as a male member of the family. In 1959 Lambiri carried out research among female workers of a cotton factory in Megara, a country town on the road from Athens to Corinth (1965). Almost all of the female workers were unmarried. These girls entered industrial employment mainly in order to contribute to the dowry and alleviate the economic need of the family. Though factory work for girls had lost its negative moral connotations since the establishment of the factory in 1950 and though the factory girls had gained some economic independence, factory work had freed them little from family supervision. In 1974 Nikolaïdou did a restudy among the female workers of this same factory (1975). Almost no change could be discovered in the attitude toward female employment during the 15 years since Lambiri did her research, and few other changes could be noticed regarding female roles. Hirschon's research in an Athenian neighborhood, where female employment existed for decades, leads to very similar conclusions (1976:251–59).

No research has been done on female employment among the urban middle and upper classes. In a comparative article on modernization in Greece and the United States, Safilios-Rothschild (1969) makes, however, some interesting remarks regarding employment of female university graduates. After having concluded that the percentage of females who were employed full time around 1960 was roughly equal in both countries, she notes that while in the United States 55% of the women with a university degree take on some form of employment, in Greece the percentage is closer to 90%. Moreover, Greek women more often aspire to a career than American women do. The difference is largely explained, according to Safilios-Rothschild, by the availability of people who can look after the children, such as grandparents or servants, and by the fact that in Greece to leave the child to be cared for by others is not considered to be negative. She concludes: "Thus, in Greece, the professional role seems to us to be often compatible with the maternal role, while this is rarely the case in the United States" (Safilios-Rothschild 1969:33, translated from French). This contrast between Safilios-Rothschild's comments on female university graduates and the earlier mentioned research on female employment among the working class clearly points to the need for future research in this area and illustrates the importance of class variation.

Religion and the Church

Though there is no lack of historical and theological literature on the Greek Orthodox Catholic religion and church, there is hardly any empirical research on the meaning of orthodoxy in the daily life of rural and urban Greeks. Only one article by an anthropologist is concerned with religion in an urban context (Kenna 1977). There are also a detailed ethnographic account of religious beliefs and observances in Hirschon's thesis (1976:268–319) and a brief discussion of the role of the church in contemporary Greek society in Gutenschwager's (1971:127–30). Greek social scientists have devoted very little attention to the role of religion and the church in contemporary Greek society, and there is virtually no Greek sociology of religion.[10]

At first glance religion seems to play a minor role in the life of Greeks. Not more than 2% of the population is said to attend church regularly (Campbell and Sherrard 1968:212) and it may even be lower among the urban population. The church is mainly the domain of older women. Proscriptions regarding fasting are still followed by a few. In the city the priest seldom acts as an important community leader. Anticlericalism exists and a critical attitude toward the priest and the church is the rule. The influence of the church on specific issues such as birth control is restricted, since most people seem to consider that their private business (Gutenschwager 1971: 130). Though there is little doubt that the role of the church in the life of the people is decreasing and that there is "a loss of spiritual consciousness" (Campbell and Sherrard 1968:208-9, 212), the above-mentioned facts should not too quickly be considered as indicators of a process of dechristianization. Even those Greeks who hardly enter the church usually react with abhorrence at the slightest suggestion of atheism. This may perhaps be partly explained by the strong association between the church and the Greek nation, and by the fact that orthodoxy is a state religion in Greece, which makes open dissociation from the church almost equal to national treason. This implies, for example, that even an atheist has to marry in church. To stress this too much would, however, neglect the very real expressions of belief in the life of many Greeks, also in the city. One occasion when religious notions and values are expressed is during life crises, such as illness, when pilgrimages may be made to saints to ask for help (Hirschon 1976:309-16, Kenna 1977). Religion also plays an important role in daily life. Even in left-wing working-class neighborhoods each house has its own sacred place, the *iconostasis,* and is in a sense its own church (Hirschon 1976:275). Gutenschwager writes of the neighborhood she studied: "What strikes an outside observer most is the 'individualistic' concept of religion. People prefer to communicate with the supernatural alone in their homes with their families and to have the feeling that somehow they are able to establish a 'personal' relationship with a Saint, who will apparently respond more readily to the prayers of specific individuals than to the prayers of an amorphous congregation" (1971:129-30). To conclude from this that religion in the city is more a private affair is, however, dangerous; differences in this respect between the city and the countryside may be less significant than one might expect.

The political role of the church in Greece has been largely conservative (Savramis 1969). Progressive church movements such as characterize many Catholic countries nowadays are largely absent. Anthropologists can contribute significantly to our understanding of the political role of the church, the nature and extent of anticlericalism, and the meaning of religion in everyday life by studying such topics and their interrelations in particular neighborhoods and among specific sections of the urban population.

Since about 97% of the population belongs to the Greek Orthodox church, religious minorities such as Catholics, Armenian Christians, Protestants, and Moslems have played a minor role in Greek life. As a result these tiny minorities have been little studied. Though research on all of these minorities would be useful, a study of the Jehovah's Witnesses would probably be most relevant to the urban situation. The Jehovah's Witnesses seem to have found a willing ear among some members of the urban lower classes, notwithstanding strong condemnation and even persecution by the Orthodox church and the state.

Politics and Associational Life

There is an abundant literature on political developments in postwar Greece, but not even one study on politics in a particular urban locality. The period of the dictatorship (1967–74), which stimulated interest in the prevailing political situation and its origins, was itself one of the obstacles to the study of local politics (see Hirschon 1976: preface).

Though Greek political parties evolved from loose associations of localized patronage networks to more centralized organizations, personalistic ties continued to characterize the major political parties of the postwar period. The Communist party was for a long time the only nonclientelistic party. Recently the PASOK—a left-wing part of the post-junta period—also managed to build up a national organization with many local branches. This and the success of the PASOK at the general elections of 1977 indicates a decline—perhaps temporary—of clientelism (Mouzelis 1978b).

Greek political development is characterized by a high degree of instability, which results in what Mouzelis refers to as an alternation between dependent integration and dictatorial exclusion of the masses from the political process (1978a). Comninos's (1978) article on Kavalla, an industrial town in northern Greece, is particularly relevant in this respect.[11] Kavalla had one of the strongest working-class movements in Greece during the prewar period and the Communist party was particularly strong. After the civil war and the defeat of the left, the repressive mechanism of the state prevented the reactivation of the labor movement, aided by the economic decline of the town. The repression had an individualizing effect on the voters and resulted in the resurgence of clientelism. These and later developments in Kavalla (Comninos 1978) indicate that clientelism cannot be understood simply as a remnant of rural political attitudes or as a mere expression of the basic values of Greek culture. Clientelism and the pursuit of restricted individual or familiar interests have to be understood in relation to possibilities for class-based modes of political organization such as those that result, for example, from the scale of industrial and commercial establishments and the degree and nature of political repression. This implies that the study of clientelism and formal political associations should be placed in the context of Greece's national development and its semiperipheral position within the world economy. Sutton's research on an Athenian association of migrants may be seen as an attempt in this direction.

Sutton considers the Aiyiali Union, one of the three regional associations from the Cycladic island Amorgos, as fairly typical of the roughly 500 regional associations that existed, according to her estimate, in 1975 in Athens. She analyzes the development of the Aiyiali Union against the background of Greek national development, paying special attention to the relation between Amorgos and the capital. Regional associations were established in a relatively late phase of migration to the capital at a time of economic decline of the region. Those who became active in the Aiyiali Union came from families which were relatively well established in the city. These and other findings lead Sutton to conclude that the union did not play an important role in the adaption of recent immigrants to the city. According to her, the primary and explicit function of the regional association was to help the region of origin. Lobbying with the government was one of the main ways in which the union tried to reach its goals.

Sutton's analysis constitutes an important and stimulating contribution to the understanding of the role of regional allegiances in city politics and the nature of political links between city and countryside. It is a pity that, though the analysis is placed against the background of national development, the connection between migrants and their region of origin through the union is little related to other rural-urban links such as patronage and party politics. There may possibly be a different interpretation. Though the main and explicit goal of the union was the promotion of economic development of the region of origin, the main effect of its activities — partly as the result of its very limited success — may have been dependent integration, i.e., the maintenance of inequality, the diffusion of discontent, and the creation of allegiance to the governing establishment. Such an interpretation seems in keeping with Tsoucalas's (1977) analysis of the relation between city and countryside during the nineteenth century. The nature of rural-urban relations and consequently the incidence and role of regional associations may well vary from region to region, depending, for example, on length of integration within the nation-state and degree of access to the state apparatus. Future research should also devote attention to the possible relation between regional associations and class-based modes of organization. It would be interesting to know, for example, how membership in trade unions and membership in regional associations relate to each other.

Social Identity

The large number of regional associations as well as the relative concentration of people from the same village or region in one or more neighborhoods and/or occupations (see Sutton's contribution to this volume) indicate the strength of regionalism, or the Greek version of *campanilismo*.

Among refugees, identities based on common origin—e.g., Pontic and Minor Asiatic identity—and past experience as refugees continue to play some role, especially among the older population. Hirschon (1976:27–55) relates how a number of factors—e.g., common experiences before arrival, the original physical distance between the refugee settlement and the rest of the urban population, and continuing grievances and a sense of neglect by the Greek state—fostered the development and continuation of a sense of separate identity. These different ethnic identities[12] exist, however, within a context of common religion and language and an overarching Greek identity. As a result, there are now few barriers to intermarriage between people from different regions and origin (Gutenschwager 1971:86, Sutton 1978:135, 180). For an increasing part of the urban population such separate identities are becoming less meaningful.

In the urban working-class neighborhoods of long standing—such as in the Athenian refugee neighborhoods (Gutenschwager 1971:130–40, Hirschon 1976:176–225, Sandis 1973:127–47)—neighborhood life is often intense. When weather permits, people leave their crowded houses and sit in the courtyard or in front of their houses facing the street talking to neighbors, who may also be friends or kinsmen. While women's contacts are usually confined to a fairly small area around the house, men will spend part of their time in one of the neighborhood coffeeshops and their network may cover a somewhat larger area. In neighborhoods where recent immigrants predominate, neighborhood attachment is less intense (Sandis 1973:127–29), and in some older inner-city neighborhoods where old houses are destroyed and new apartment buildings erected the pre-existing social fabric seems to break down and lose its community character. Little is yet known, however, about variations in the significance of neighborhood ties for its inhabitants. The few studies that have been made pertain only to more stable working-class neighborhoods.

A third type of social identity is that based on one's position within the urban economy, which includes occupational identities as well as the problem of class consciousness (see previous section). Here we will briefly discuss the research of Damianakos, which is most directly relevant and concerns the relations between popular art and social identity. Damianakos (1974, 1976) made a study of *rebetika* songs, based mainly on the analysis of some 500 songs from the different historical periods in the development of the *rebetika*. According to Damianakos, the *rebetika* constitute an urban folklore that thrived during the period between the decline of peasant folklore, which accompanied the dissolution of traditional society, and the emergence of modern mass culture. The author describes how these songs developed from songs of the marginal urban population of the big cities of the Aegean—e.g., Smyrna, Syros, and Piraeus—revolving around themes like the jail, hashish, and violence, to songs referring increasingly to emigration and social injustice in the period 1940–55. This evolution was, however, interrupted by the increasing commercialization of these songs and their acceptance by the bourgeoisie. As a result they lost their character of expressing a collective identity. It is a pity that this interesting study is almost exlusively based on the analysis of the songs themselves and devotes so little attention to the development of the urban economy and class structure. It nevertheless points to an interesting field of study that is perhaps too much neglected by anthropologists.

The Anthropologist as Immigrant:
Adaptation to the City

Anthropologists seem to have approached the city in two main ways. The first might be called the migrant or ethnic approach. It begins by viewing people in terms of their rural and ethnic origin. It includes research that is an extension of village-based research, as well as research that takes the city itself as point of departure. Both variants are interested in similar questions such as rural-urban relations, adaptation of migrants to the city, and migrant associations. With the second, or community, approach, the anthropologist does not enter the city by way of the village (as in a sense he did in the first approach) but looks for the village in the city. Thus he selects for research those localities in the city which show a high degree of community life; these tend to be stable working-class neighborhoods. Both approaches are not so much theoretical approaches as strategies for entering the complexity of urban life. These strategies are the result of the anthropologist's previous rural experience. So the anthropologist reacts to the city as any immigrant does: by trying to cope with urban complexity in terms of his own previous experience.

The few anthropologists who have done urban research in Greece have, almost without exception, followed one of the two above approaches. These strategies have given us insights in areas too often neglected by other disciplines and have corrected older views that often suggested too simplified a picture of city and countryside. Moreover, this is a type of research for which anthropologists are most qualified, and further research in Greece along these lines is badly needed. However, by sticking too closely to what past training has taught him (or her) to handle, the anthropologist's view of the city is bound to remain partial. In the urban anthropological research on Greece there is, for example, little that offers an insight into class relations, class differences in family and kinship, bureaucratic and formal organizations, and the urban economy. To amplify and correct their view of the city, anthropologists should take cognizance of the work done by other disciplines. Multidisciplinary research, though easier preached than practiced, may be a useful outcome of such interdisciplinary contacts. Anthropologists are, however, most likely to contribute to an understanding of the city if they, as recent immigrants, are able to open up new areas of research. They may be forced to do so when they discover that the research done by scientists from other disciplines, however useful and stimulating, does not provide them with detailed answers to the questions they want to pose. In Greece, for example, the study of small-scale industry, which continues to play an important role in the economy (see, e.g., Mouzelis 1978:37–41), might be one of these areas.

NOTES

1. This section relies heavily on Burgel (1976) and Tsoucalas (1977).
2. In 1907 Athens and Piraeus did not yet form part of one continuous urban agglomeration. The development of Piraeus was, however, very much dependent upon that of Athens; to a lesser degree, the reverse also held. Wherever Athens is mentioned, reference is made to greater Athens, i.e., the urban agglomeration as a whole.
3. Ancel (1923:10, translated from French) remarks: "The Greek seems so much a townsman to the people of the Balkans that for a long time the most typical merchant, the *bakal* (grocer), was generally called 'Greek,' whatever language he spoke."
4. The categories rural, semiurban, and urban refer to the population living in settlements of respectively less than 2,000 inhabitants, 2,000 to 10,000 inhabitants, and more than 10,000 inhabitants. In 1961, 42% of the Greek population was urban while in Yugoslavia only 24% was urban. In Bulgaria the urban population reached 29% in 1956.
5. More detailed discussions of postwar industrialization and economic development can be found in Campbell and Sherrard (1968:299–321), Evangelinides (1979), Nikolinakos (1970, 1973:106–64), and Pangalos (1975).
6. "In Greece, as well as elsewhere, the scholarship of folklore was founded upon the distinction between two levels of culture within one and the same people (*populus;* in Greek, *laos*). This caused the meaning of the term *laos* to narrow down to *folk,* denoting especially the rural, as distinguished from the urban part of the population." (Kyriakidou-Nestoros 1971:487).
7. The shortages in some sectors of the labor market have led to the immigration of foreigners (Pakistanis, Egyptians, Sudanese, and others). The Greek merchant marine has become heavily dependent on foreign labor, and its threatening "dehellenization" was recently a topic of discussion in parliament.
8. The continuity of culture between the rural world and the urban refugee neighborhoods noted by Gutenschwager and Hirschon is the more striking because most of the refugees had an urban background when they settled in Athens (see first section of this chapter and Sandis 1973:72–77). Gutenschwager's opinion that the mass of refugees in Athens were peasants (1971:44) and her reference to this supposed background in explaining features of urban behavior (e.g., 1971:93, 99) must be considered mistaken.
9. The aticle from which we quoted is based on a number of studies conducted by the Athenian Institute of Anthropos during the sixties. These studies made use of several research methods, such as the role differential and projective techniques. Some of the studies were carried out in Athens while others made use of representative national samples. The purpose of the research was partly to compare Greek role conceptions with American ones (Triandis *et al.* 1968).

10. One of the few Greek sociologists doing research on religion is Savramis, who teaches at the University of Cologne.
11. We have not been able to consult Maria Comninos's recent dissertation, "The Development of the Patronage System in Aitolo-Akharnania and Kavala" (London School of Economics, date unknown).
12. We use the term "ethnic identity" here in the sense of a past-oriented form of identity (see DeVos and Romanucci-Ross 1975).

REFERENCES

Ancel, Jacques
    1923   *Manuel historique de la question d'orient (1792–1923).* Paris: Librairie Dela-
            grave.
Burgel, Guy
    1976   *Athens: The development of a Mediterranean capital* (In Greek), Athens: Exan-
            tas.
Campbell, John
    1964   *Honour, family and patronage: A study of institutions and moral values in a Greek
            mountain community.* Oxford: Clarendon Press.
Campbell, John, and Philip Sherrard
    1968   *Modern Greece.* New York: Praeger.
Chiliotis, Thanasis
    1980   Folklore of marginal types (In Greek). *Antí* 7, no. 147:10–11.
Cole, J. W.
    1977   Anthropology comes part-way home: Community studies in Europe. *An-
            nual Review of Anthropology* 6:349–78.
Comninos, Maria
    1978   The formation of the political identity of Kavala (In Greek). *Antí* 5, no.
            113:34–38.
Damianakos, Stathis
    1974   Culture populaire et groupes marginaux: A propos de rébétika grecs. *Les
            temps modernes* 29:1447–60.
    1976   *Sociology of the rebetika* (In Greek). Athens: Ermias.
Davis, John
    1977   *People of the Mediterranean: An essay in comparative social anthropology.* London:
            Routledge and Kegan Paul.
DeVos, George, and Lola Romanucci-Ross
    1975   Ethnicity: Vessel of meaning and emblem of contrast. In George DeVos
            and Lola Romanucci-Ross, eds., *Ethnic identity: Cultural continuities and
            change.* Palo Alto, Calif.: Mayfield, pp. 363–90.
Dubisch, Jill
    1977   The city as resource: Migration from a Greek island village. *Urban Anthro-
            pology* 6:65–81.
Evangelinides, Mary
    1979   Core-periphery problems in the Greek case. In Dudley Seers, Bernard
            Schaffer, and Marja-Liisa Kiljunen, eds., *Underdeveloped Europe.* Sussex:
            Harvester, pp. 177–95.
Fatouros, D. A., L. Papadopoulos, and V. Tentokali
    1979   *Studies on habitation* (In Greek). Athens: Paratiritis.
Friedl, Ernestine
    1976   Kin, class and selective migration. In John G. Peristiany, ed., *Mediterra-*

nean family structure. Cambridge: Cambridge University Press, pp. 363–87.

Gutenschwager, Mary C.
1971   Nea Aeolia: Persistence and tradition in an urban Greek community. Ph.D. thesis, University of North Carolina at Chapel Hill.

Hirschon, Renée B.
1976   The social institutions of an urban locality of refugee origin in Piraeus. Ph.D. thesis, Oxford University.
1978   Open body/closed space: The transformation of female sexuality. In Shirley Ardener, ed., *Defining females: The nature of women in society.* London: Croom Helm, pp. 66–88.

Kayser, Bernard
1964   *Géographie humaine de la Grèce.* Athens: Centre des Sciences Sociales.

Kayser, Bernard, Pierre-Yves Pechoux, and Michel Sivignon
1971   *Exode rural et attraction urbaine en Grèce.* Athens: Centre National de Recherches Sociales.

Kenna, Margaret
1977   Greek urban migrants and their rural patron saint. *Ethnic Studies* 1:14–23.

Kolodny, Emile Y.
1974   *La population des Îles de la Grèce: Essay de géographie insulaire en Mediterranée orientale.* Aix-en-Provence: Edisud.

Kremmydas, Vasilis
1976   *Introduction to the history of new-Greek society* (In Greek). Athens: Exantas.

Kyriakidou-Nestoros, Alke
1971   The theory of folklore in Greece: *Laographia* in its contemporary perspective. *East European Quarterly* 5:487–504.

Lambiri, Ioanna
1965   *Social change in a Greek town: The impact of factory work on the position of women.* Athens: Center of Planning and Economic Research.
1972   (pub. under name Lambiri-Dimaki, Jane)
        Dowry in modern Greece: An institution at the crossroads between persistence and decline. In Constantina Safilios-Rothschild, ed., *Toward a sociology of women.* Lexington, Mass.: Xerox, pp. 73–85.
1976   (pub. under name Lambiri-Dimaki, Jane)
        Regional, sex and class distribution among Greek students: Some aspects of inequality of educational opportunities. In Muriel Dimen and Ernestine Friedl, eds., *Regional variation in modern Greece and Cyprus.* New York: New York Academy of Sciences, pp. 385–94.

Mouzelis, Nicos
1978   *Modern Greece: Facets of underdevelopment.* London: MacMillan.
1978a   Class and clientelistic politics: The case of Greece. *Sociological Review* 26:471–97.
1978b   On the Greek elections. *New Left Review,* no. 108:59–74.

Mouzelis, Nicos, and Michael Attalides
1971   Greece. In M. Scotford Archer and S. Giner, eds., *Contemporary Europe: Class, status and power.* London: Weidenfeld and Nicolson, pp. 162–97.

Nicolacopoulos, I., and G. S. Tsouyopoulos
1976   Structural aspects of the network of Greek cities (In Greek). *Greek Review of Social Research* 7:54–64.

Nikolaïdou, Magda
1975   The working woman in Greece (In Greek). *Greek Review of Social Research* 6:470–506.

Nikolinakos, Marios
  1970   Materialien zur kapitalistischen Entwicklung in Griechenland *Das Argument* 12:164-215, 340-74.
  1973   The contradictions of capitalist development in Greece: Labor shortages and emigration. *Studi Emigrazione,* no. 30:3-16.
  1974   *Widerstand und Opposition in Griechenland.* Darmstadt und Neuwied: Luchterhand.
Pangalos, Theodor
  1975   Die Grenzen des Ausschlusscharakters der abhängigen kapitalistichen Entwicklung: Der Fall Griechenlands. In Claus Leggewie und Marios Nikolinakos, eds., *Europäische Peripherie.* Meisenheim am Glan: Verlag Anton Hain, pp. 186-95.
Pentzopoulos, Dimitri
  1962   *The Balkan exchange of minorities and its impact upon Greece.* Paris: Mouton.
Petropoulos, Elias
  1968   *Rebetika songs: Folkloristic study* (In Greek). Athens.
  1975   *From the jails* (In Greek with summary in English). Athens.
  1976a   *La voiture Grecque.* Paris: Editions Moments.
  1976b   *Cages à oiseaux en Grèce.* Paris: Editions Moments.
  1976c   *La kiosque Grecque.* Paris: Editions Moments.
  1978   *Underworld and Karangiozis* (In Greek). Athens: Grammata.
Safilios-Rothschild, Constantina
  1967   A comparison of power structure and marital satisfaction in urban Greek and French families. *Journal of Marriage and the Family* 29:345-52.
  1969   Quelques aspects de la modernisation sociale aux États-Unis et en Grèce, *Sociologie et sociétés* 1:23-37.
  1976   The family in Athens: Regional varaition. In Muriel Dimen and Ernestine Friedl, eds., *Regional variation in modern Greece and Cyprus.* New York: New York Academy of Sciences, pp. 410-18.
Sandis, Eva E.
  1973   *Refugees and economic migrants in greater Athens.* Athens: National Center of Social Research.
Savramis, Demosthenes
  1969   Die religiösen Grundlagen der neugriechischen Gesellschaft. In Marios Nikolinakou and Kostas Nikolaou, eds., *Die verhinderte Demokratie: Modell Griechenland.* Frankfurt am Main: Suhrkamp Verlag, pp. 64-87.
Siegel, Bernard J.
  1973   Cultural mediation in Greece. In Kurt Weibust, ed., *Kulturvariation I Sydeuropa.* Copenhagen: NEFA Forlag, pp. 35-48.
Sivignon, Michel
  1975   *La Thessalie: Analyse géographique d'une provence Grecque.* Institut des Etudes Rhodaniennes des Universités de Lyon.
Spinellis, D. C., Vasso Vassiliou, and George Vassiliou
  1970   Milieu development and male-female roles in contemporary Greece. In George H. Seward and Robert C. Williamson, eds., *Sex roles in changing society.* New York: Random House, pp. 308-17.
Sutton, Susan Buck
  1978   Migrant regional associations: An Athenian example and its implications. Ph.D. thesis, University of North Carolina at Chapel Hill.
Triandis, Harry C., Vasso Vassiliou, and Maria Nassiakou
  1968   Three cross-cultural studies of subjective culture. *Journal of Personality and Social Psychology* 8, no. 4:1-42. Monograph Supplement.

Tsoucalas, Constantine
   1969   *The Greek tragedy.* Harmondsworth: Penguin Books.
   1977   *Dependence and reproduction: The social role of educational mechanism in Greece
            (1830–1922)* (In Greek). Athens: Themelio.
Vergopoulos, Kostas
   1978   *Nationalism and economic development* (In Greek). Athens: Exantas.
Vermeulen, Cornelis J. J.
   1970   Families in urban Greece. Ph.D. thesis, Cornell University.
Woodhouse, C. M.
   1977   *Modern Greece: A short history.* London: Faber and Faber.

PART TWO: RURAL-URBAN MIGRATION

Chapter **5**

Spanish Urbanization from a
Grass-roots Perspective

Hans Buechler

Since World War II Spain has experienced an extremely rapid rate of urban growth. In this chapter we shall deal with the processes of rural-urban migration and migrants' adaptation to the urban conditions that accompanied this growth. We will view these processes of urbanization in relation to economic and political structures and governmental policies that affect the nation as a whole, rather than analyze them as independent phenomena with dynamics of their own. The uneven growth of Spanish cities was but one of the effects of these policies. Other effects included both the neglect of agricultural development and the systematic exploitation of many areas of Spain, accompanied by a massive labor migration to other European countries and overseas. In southern Spain large property owners controlled most of the land but invested little to enhance its productivity, leading to large-scale unemployment. In northern Spain farmers were (and still are) subject to high taxes and stringent price controls that favor the urbanite at their expense.

For many peasants the only choices left were either to migrate to a large city in Spain or to emigrate abroad. These choices, in turn, influenced one another and affected the processes of urban growth. Remittances sent home from abroad by migrants there have benefited the industrialized regions in Spain more than the rural areas of origin of these migrants. For their part returnees from abroad have often preferred to settle in cities to avoid the risk of rural poverty again. Thus a study of adaptation to urban settings must always keep these wider contexts in mind.

In our analysis we shall emphasize the concrete actions and interactions of individuals. In an urban environment where the interests of industrialists and private urban developers are paramount, adaptation by migrants has been possible only through elaborate support networks of interpersonal ties and, ultimately, the creation of voluntary associations to defend their interests. Social networks underlie the phenomenon called chain migration, whereby migrants follow the path of previous migrants, leading to concentrations in the city of migrants from the same place of origin. Such networks facilitate the initial move to the city as well as the procurement of lodgings and employment. Generally they make life under adverse conditions in the city more bearable, not least by providing the basis for continued contact with the place of origin. Finally, they often provide the impetus for the creation of voluntary associations. These associations have experienced a phenomenal growth since the last years of the Franco regime and may well become a major force in shaping Spanish cities.

Thus, with the adaptation of the individual firmly in focus, our presentation here will cover, first, urban growth in general and then the migration *process*. There follows a consideration of the housing problem (so important a factor in the adaptation of the migrant) and an analysis of the struggle for urban amenities and education. Such an analysis logically leads to an assessment of the associations that migrants join, or form, and their collective action. To remind the reader that the migrant does not disassociate himself from his rural origin, we shall then discuss kin ties and rural-urban linkages. These latter inevitably involve some commuting between new urban settlement and rural community of origin. Concomitant with this development is the growth of small towns, which merits special treatment in our final section.

URBAN GROWTH

Let us begin our analysis with a general discussion of the growth of Spanish cities. Urbanization that results more from incoming migrants than from the natural growth of cities may be stimulated by inter-, rather than intraregional factors. Thus, while the growth of urban centers in a given region is to be expected because of the attraction of a part of the rural population from their rural hinterlands, in-migrants often originate from rural communities well beyond regional boundaries. Recent trends in Spain are a prime example of this process, which has led to the depopulation of a large part of the country and the explosive expansion of a small number of urban centers, most of which are concentrated in a single quadrant of the nation.

In the past, urban growth in Spain was more evenly distributed. To be sure, Gallego stone masons, servants, and night watchmen have been a familiar part of life in Madrid for many centuries. But provincial cities grew too. Thus during the period 1910-30 there occurred a rapid growth in provincial capitals throughout the country as well as in the "agro-towns" of southern Spain, which house large numbers of landless wage laborers employed on a temporary basis in the vast latifundia that characterize the region (Miguel and Salcedo 1972:103). In fact, in this period the rate of urban growth — 414 per thousand — exceeded that of the subsequent period (1931-60), which was only 361 per thousand (Barbancho 1967: Table A32). Urbanization during the early period 1910–30 was of a very different nature from that of recent years, and was stimulated largely by an expansion of the service sector owing to a rapidly expanding state bureaucracy.

In the following decades urban growth was spurred by Spain's rapid industrial development. This time the expansion of three cities — Madrid, Barcelona, Bilbao, and their suburbs — far outpaced that of other urban centers. In fact, the only other areas experiencing any significant growth at all were Valencia and Navarra; the latter province has the distinction of being the only area that grew as a result of *agricultural* development.

A graphic idea of the magnitude of this growth can be gleaned from the fact that between 1962 and 1968 the region of Madrid grew by three-quarters of a million inhabitants, that is, by about the same amount as Paris, a city twice its size (Miguel and Salcedo 1972:60). Barcelona and its suburbs have undergone a similar growth. The province of Barcelona had an average growth of 212,000 per decade in the first three decades of this century, 480,000 in the 1950s, and 650,000 in the 1960s (Barbancho 1975: Table A2). The expansion of Bilbao was even more spectacular; while the city's average growth in the first three decades was only 24,000, it jumped to 108,000 in the 1950s and 141,000 in the 1960s. In fact, in the decade 1960–70 Madrid, Barcelona, and the Basque provinces received 57% of all migrants in the nation. In contrast, the rates of growth elsewhere in Spain slowed down considerably in the last four decades. Thus, while between 1911 and 1920 only two out of the 50 provincial capitals lost more population through emigration than they gained, in the 1950s this figure jumped to 16 out of 50, decreasing again to nine out of 50 in the following decade (Barbancho 1967: Table A10; 1975: Table A7).

This lopsided population distribution shows some signs of change. The region of Valencia grew three times faster in the 1960s than it had in the 1950s, faster than all three other growth regions; there is also a tendency for cities in the axes between Barcelona-Madrid and Madrid-Bilbao (e.g. Vitoria, Burgos, Saragossa) to absorb some of the growth.

The foregoing trends indicate that urbanization in Spain in the last 30 years is not merely the result of increasing industrialization in the cities and the concomitant mechanization of agriculture that releases men from the land. Rather, it is largely the product of the development of areas characterized both by a long history of industrial and mercantile development and by close proximity to markets elsewhere in Europe. In addition, in the case of Madrid, urban expansion is the result not only of administrative centralization but also of metropolitan access to the rapidly developing coastal regions; this makes it possible for Madrid to act as a marketing center for the entire nation (cf. Perpiñá Grau 1954). Finally, urban infrastructures supporting tourist, recreation, and retirement settlements have all sprung up since the 1950s along the Costa Dorada on the eastern seaboard.

The imbalance between what Beiras (1972) has called the "industrial triangle" (Madrid, Barcelona, and the Basque provinces) and the rest of Spain is aggravated by governmental policies that stifle attempts at development in less developed areas. Thus banking policies make it difficult even for rural savings banks to invest more than a small percentage of their assets locally. As a result, a large part of the savings of Spanish migrants remitted from northern European countries benefit industries in the industrial triangle rather than those in the areas of origin of the migrants. Let us see how this development affects the migration process.

THE MIGRATION PROCESS

The principal regions of origin of the rural-urban migrants are characterized by either (1) latifundios, (2) excessive minifundio, or (3) particularly problematic agricultural conditions. Thus, between 1960 and 1965, some 51% of the migrants to Barcelona came from Andalusia, 19% came from the Castiles and León, and 11% came from Extremadura (Esteva Fabregat 1973:148). Madrid has a somewhat narrower field of attraction than Barcelona; most of its in-migrants come from the surrounding provinces, from the south-central provinces, and from Extremadura. It must be noted, however, that one emigration area, Galicia, has a relatively low emigration rate to these Spanish cities, relying instead on migration to other European countries (and, previously, to overseas destinations). The pattern for these smallholders in Galicia is to earn as much as possible abroad and then to return, purchase a house plot or perhaps even some land, build a modern house, and in some instances open a tavern or other small business in their place of origin or in a nearby town or city.[1]

Research by sociologists and accounts by novelists in the 1950s attest to the abysmal conditions that rural-urban migrants were escaping from in the regions of emigration. Seasonal employment aggravated by incipient mechanization in the southern latifundia induced many to migrate to Madrid. Siguán (1959) gives particularly poignant examples from this period when rural conditions were particularly bad. Thus Jesús, one of the 57 agricultural laborers in a sample of 100 migrants to the nation's capital, had been earning only 25 pesetas a day back home including his wife's income from the same activity.[2] When there was no work, they made charcoal, which requires very heavy physical labor. Sometimes Jesús had to poach in order to have enough to eat. The couple lived in a hut in the middle of a field. They finally decided to move to Madrid when the employment situation became even worse. Some of Siguán's informants were itinerant workers and had worked in the rice harvest in Valencia. Three, including Pablo from the province of Salamanca and Manuel from Badajoz, were sharecroppers who were displaced when the owner decided to raise cattle on the land they had been cultivating. Manuel had done reasonably well on land ceded to him by landowners who had been glad that he had succeeded in making it productive again after a period when it had gone to weeds. "But all of a sudden they converted all the properties to grasslands. As a result work became scarce. I had to herd cattle and with that kind of job one doesn't even earn enough to eat" (Siguán 1959:67–68).

The hardship and uncertainties of agricultural wage labor and minifundio were also major contributing factors inducing migration to Barcelona. The novelist Francisco Candel (1965:125ff.), who came from the province of Valencia, recounts that his father used to work in the wheat harvest with a group of farm workers who traveled in a wide area of Aragon. In addition, he worked some land of his own, although it was far too little and of poor quality. His uncle joined his brother-in-law in Barcelona upon his marriage in 1924 after unsuccessfully trying his luck in France and various shorter trips to the Catalonian metropolis. There they worked in a stone quarry. Other members of the family, including Candel's father, followed suit, taking up jobs that their siblings had found for them.

Similarly, for poor, single, rural Galician women, including girls as young as 11 or 12, employment in a city was one of the only ways to escape the hard life of an indentured farmhand or of a day laborer earning barely enough to survive. A good example of this is Hortensia, who worked in La Coruña as a servant for some 50 years (Buechler and Buechler 1981: ch. 4). Her father died when she was still a child. When her mother got sick and could not pay the rent on the land, the eight siblings went to live in the homes of various relatives. Later Hortensia found a job as a servant in La Coruña; in turn, she helped her 11-year-old niece Carmen find a job in the same city, thereby sparing her the even harder labor of an indentured agricultural worker.

Other peasants migrated to the cities because of family difficulties, for example, because they could not get along with their parents-in-law with whom they were living, a reason particularly common among the 16 farmers in Siguán's sample. Similarly, in La Coruña (Galicia) some young women took jobs as servants after they had become pregnant and their boyfriends had refused to marry them, supposedly because they came from poor families. Some informants in Siguán's sample left their villages because a family member required medical attention that could not be obtained there; others (11%) left because they wished to leave dangerous jobs. Still others migrated simply because a close relative living in Madrid suggested the move or because a well-placed acquaintance (e.g., the village doctor or the landlord of the estate on which they had worked) had arranged a job for them in Madrid. In Siguán's study 7% of his informants mentioned such patronage ties as contributing decisively to their choice to migrate.

The mechanism whereby such contacts are established may be complicated indeed. Thus Jesús, a blacksmith from Santa Maria in the province of La Coruña, and his wife became the superintendents of an apartment building in the provincial capital as a result of the mediation of a government official. He had lost one lung to tuberculosis and could no longer work on his land in the hamlet. He and his wife subsequently opened a bakery and distributed bread in Santa Maria, but the wife was frequently ill and thus the family led a precarious existence. Jesús's father had become acquainted with a veterinarian from Madrid in a nearby town when he brought his bull to him for treatment, a contact that had led to the hiring of Jesús's daughter in the veterinarian's household in La Coruña. Later another sister was hired by a La Coruña family. When she had a child, she returned to the hamlet until she was ready to work again. At this point her former employer landed her a job with the government official, who later not only found a superintendent job for her sister-in-law but a job as an electrician for Jesús as well.

More unusual circumstances surrounding the decision to migrate included business failures (e.g., of stores and taverns), the obsolescence of traditional crafts such as those involved in manufacturing agricultural implements, and, conversely, the chance to employ one's skills more profitably in the city. Two individuals in Siguán's sample even left because they had attracted the ire of their neighbors as a result of some moral scandal.

Today the proportion of those who migrate out of dire necessity has decreased greatly, but the differential between rural and urban incomes and the more comfortable existence possible in the city are still the principal motives for migration. Thus, "when Faustino Pradera moved to Madrid (from Beceda, a village in southwestern Castille in 1969) he found work as a part-time garage attendant at 12,000 pesetas (about $170) per month. By comparison his village income would not have exceeded 60,000 pesetas for the entire year" (Brandes 1975:57).

Returned migrants from Latin America and, later, from Europe provided a strong impulse for rural-urban migration within Spain. Thus, when contracts in Germany could no longer be secured, most young migrants from Andalusia, both single and married, on their return from Germany, moved to urban industrial centers, provincial capitals, and coastal cities rather than return permanently to their rural villages (Rhoades 1978:139).

Similarly, in Galicia many migrants do not expect a return to their places of origin. Thus Josefa and her husband, who come from a rural parish in Lugo, moved to La Coruña in 1962. Previously they had migrated to Argentina, where he had worked for eight years in a shoe factory. They returned to Spain because of the political and economic crises in Argentina. Ironically, her husband is working as an electrician in the construction of an aluminum factory, a job which he not only considers dangerous but which, according to critics, will have severe environmental effects on the couple's place of origin.

Maria runs a small pension in a rented flat in the center of La Coruña. She moved to the city from her native Santa Maria, a hamlet located some 30 miles away, after having worked in Geneva, Switzerland, for nine months, where her husband continues to work. She prefers the city to the country: "Life is very different here," she claims. "One has to work too, but the work is more pleasant *(más llevadero).*"

José, who comes from the same parish as Maria, opened a tavern near the stadium of Riazor in La Coruña after long peregrinations abroad. First he worked in France for three years. Then he moved to Switzerland to work in a factory. When he thought he had saved enough money, he decided to return to Spain permanently. However, after two months as a construction worker the low pay made him change his mind. Swiss migration laws prevented him from returning to his former job in Switzerland, so he took a job in Germany. There the high salary deductions for social security, etc., made him try for a Swiss job once more. This time he stayed only for a few months and then joined his wife Jesusa and their small daughter in the apartment that they had bought some time earlier in La Coruña, where he opened the tavern. Jesusa had emigrated too. They had been working in France together but she decided to return to Spain a year after her daughter was born. As José says, "It is inconvenient to travel all over the world with a child. A man can cope better by himself." For José, and indeed for most Spanish migrants, coping means living in simple or even primitive conditions in order to be able to save as much as possible. "One has to live through a thousand calamities and deprive oneself of everything. In Switzerland one earns good money but if one wants to save, one has to live very simply. You know well that if a man spends a moment in a bar and drinks a little cognac, money soon vanishes. And of course since we don't speak the language, one doesn't feel at home in those places." The decision to settle in La Coruña may have been facilitated by the fact that Jesusa's uncle had established himself there earlier. He also runs a tavern combined with a small restaurant and speculates in real estate in and around the city.

Originally, José had planned to go back to his native Santa Maria, where his brothers still live. He built a house there and had already inherited some land from his mother, who had died nine years earlier. He finally sold all his property to his brother. "Here in the city life is difficult enough," he explains, "but in the country it's even worse. One has to work a great deal for nothing. It's not like in Switzerland, Germany or France and places like that where a farmer has his car and agricultural machinery. Here it is impossible to reach the point where one can mechanize, because the intermediary and not the farmer takes the largest share. . . . So I thought to myself: I am spending eight to ten years abroad at considerable sacrifice. Now if I return home and buy land, all that will happen is that I will work like crazy without gaining anything at all."

José went on to praise emigration, which at least makes it possible to improve one's situation somewhat, and to criticize Spain: "With the money of the Gallegos they build industries in Cataluña, Barcelona and other industrial places and this produces a lot of money, but not here. I don't know why. Here, for every hundred openings in a small industry there are fifty thousand applicants, so no one wants to come to La Coruña but has to pick up his suitcase and go off to Switzerland or Germany." Then he added, presumably referring to the Franco regime: "Where the captain commands some go hungry and others go to the trough." Even at this stage he was not certain whether or not he might have to entrust the tavern to his wife and emigrate once more.

Moving to the city upon one's return from a stint abroad is not always an appealing solution. Sometimes it means working in jobs that not only pay less, a factor the migrant has been able to prepare himself for to some extent by accumulating savings, but also provide less satisfaction. Thus Rodrigo was particularly distraught when we interviewed him and his wife in La Coruña. He had been working for 16 years as a foreman in a plastics factory near Geneva, Switzerland. After living there for five years, he and his wife Adela at last brought over their daughter, who had been living with her grandmother and later with an aunt. In addition, life in Switzerland was made more pleasant because Adela's brother and sister were living in the same locality. The family returned to Spain a year before we interviewed them at the insistence of Adela, who was tired of working in a noodle factory and taking care of an elderly lady in her spare time. Rodrigo took a job as a building superintendent and they bought a nice sunny apartment in the city on the same floor as that of one of her sisters. Adela has stopped working and is enjoying every minute of her new freedom arranging the apartment and visiting with her sisters. In contrast, her husband appears to loathe living in La Coruña.

The couple has one more year to decide whether they want to return to Switzerland before they lose the rights acquired through their long residence there. It was immediately apparent that there was considerable disagreement between them about what choice to make. Pacing nervously around the room, Rodrigo paused long enough to say: "I compare (my wife) with a bird who spent its life in a cage and when the owner forgets to close the door one day, the bird goes out but then goes back in again and does not seek its freedom. According to my wife this is our country even though we live badly here. But a man has the entire world as his country. I am leaving you now, because I don't like to talk about these matters."

Situations such as Rodrigo's are more likely to arise in the urban centers in less industrialized areas than in Bilbao, Madrid, or Barcelona. In Barcelona a sociological study of workers in large metallurgical factories (considered to be an elite occupation among the workers) who had returned from Germany showed that a significant number had improved their occupational standing compared with their situation before they had left Spain. Almost all of those who had improved their standing during their stay in Germany were able to preserve their goals upon their return to Spain (Pascual 1970:201–2). However, even in this relatively privileged sample of 90 workers, 10 planned to emigrate again and an additional 11 considered it as a possible option (Pascual 1970:184). Not least among their reasons for wanting to re-emigrate was difficulty in obtaining suitable housing.

THE HOUSING PROBLEM

Particularly in the past, once an individual found employment in the city, the major difficulty was to find adequate lodging. This problem was especially severe in the 1950s and early 1960s, when migration to cities like Barcelona and Madrid took on the proportions of an avalanche.

A migrant's first abode in the city was usually either with kin who had migrated earlier or in a sublet room. The housing shortage was so acute that an unwary migrant could sometimes be persuaded to sign a fake lease upon his arrival at the train station and be swindled out of the little money he had been able to bring along (Matas Pericé 1970:88).

Conditions in lodgings were often hair-raising. Large families, already overcrowded in their dwellings, would sublet a room or a bed or even the use of a bed for considerable sums during either night or day. In this way they could more readily afford their own payments for their apartment, although not without some risk, since such practices were often officially prohibited.

In the early 1960s payments or rent for a three-room apartment amounted to some 1,000 pesetas a month. Two rooms might be sublet to four men and each charged 400 to 600 pesetas for lodgings and laundry but excluding cooking rights. As Candel puts it: "Such (landlords) have a strange concept of living well. They live with all the accoutrements: luxurious dining room furniture, a refrigerator full of food, a television set and four, five, or six men sleeping in the apartment. Some even make a business out of subletting by purchasing a second apartment and subletting it to men or to two families. Some subdivide their already tiny rooms into cubicles just large enough for a bed."

Few landlords were willing to sublet to couples or families, even if they had resigned themselves to living under such conditions, so a man who lived under such an arrangement had to wait until he found more suitable lodgings before he could bring his family. Thus Aquilino rented a room with cooking rights in Madrid and then brought his family without telling the owner that he had four children. When the landlord refused to grant them entry, the neighbors rose in protest and they were allowed to remain for two weeks until they could construct a shack in the distant suburb called Pozo del Tio Raimundo (Siguán 1959).

A more common short-term solution was for the arriving migrant to stay with a relative or acquaintance. An analysis of the 100 cases gathered by Siguán shows that 44 either stayed with relatives or (in four cases) obtained temporary or permanent lodgings through their mediation. More than half of these kin were members of the migrants' immediate family, with the kin of both spouses equally represented. In an additional 14 cases mere acquaintances provided assistance. However, in only half of these cases did assistance take the form of providing lodgings.

The foregoing aspect of chain migration becomes even more apparent when one analyzes the origin of migrant families in specific suburbs. Thus Castro (1961:512) notes that 97 (10%) of the families living in Pozo del Tio Raimundo came from one locality in Andalusia. Presumably they had all obtained housing through direct or indirect contact with one of the original settlers of the Pozo who came from that locality.[3]

With the exception of those rare instances where kin or acquaintances had ample room to share or where two families built houses on a jointly purchased plot of land, co-residence with kin rarely lasted very long. Often, the newly arrived migrant had to find other lodgings within a few days or a few months at the most. Similarly, families who lived in sublet rooms sought to leave such expensive and inadequate housing as soon as they possibly could. Given the housing scarcity of that period, families of recent immigrants were forced to live in one- to three-room shacks or even in caves carved out of mountain slopes. In 1957, out of 177,000 persons living in the suburbs of Barcelona, " . . . 66,000 lived in 12,494 barracks and shacks and 46,298 in isolated housing blocks with 6,477 apartments. The rest lived in more or less urbanized areas" (Candel 1965:181–82).

Sometimes the shacks were set up illegally on private or public land. More frequently, however, the owners of the land or speculators sold plots for considerable sums. A good example is the slum area known as Pozo del Tio Raimundo, on the outskirts of Madrid (Castro 1961:505–17). After three migrants established their "houses" on this site some time between 1925 and 1927, no further construction took place until 1940. But between 1940 and 1952 some 61 more families were settled, originating mostly from the town of one of the founders; by 1956 there were 1,775 families established there. Concomitantly, the price of a square foot of land in this area rose from 0.15 pesetas in 1925 to 0.50 pesetas in 1940 and 8–9 pesetas in 1956. The landowners agreed among themselves to parcel the land into plots of equal size, leaving space for streets. Their idea was to facilitate eventual legalization of the settlement, for which there were already some precedents in other barrios. In the meantime, however, since no urban plan had been approved, all building activity in the area was in effect illegal. Frequently a group of men would get together and roof a hut overnight, for once a house had a roof on it the authorities would generally not level it.

Achieving final ownership of one's home was thus often an uphill struggle. Until the authorities had actually nailed metal housenumbers on one's house, one could never be secure from demolition. An illustrative case is that of a widow from Galicia who came to Madrid to work as a domestic because she could not take care of her rural homestead alone; she lost her shack in Madrid twice to the demolitioners. "With part of my savings I bought a building lot and erected a shack with the help of two men, but soon they demolished it, following municipal orders. So I bought another plot of land and built once more only to have it demolished again. The third time I had become wiser and first made sure it wouldn't happen again and this time they let it stand. I am well aware that I can't live here all my life, but when I do have to go then they will have to give me some compensation and other lodgings" (Siguán 1959:188).

The policy of demolition (which was actually haphazard rather than systematic) may have been related in part to attempts at restricting immigration into crowded cities. When migration to Barcelona took major proportions again in the 1940s after a lull during the Civil War (1936–39) and its aftermath, there were official steps taken to prevent the arrival of migrants. Train travelers who *looked* like migrants were arrested by the police and sent back to their places of origin; migrants — on request — could obtain tickets to return back home at half fare. Such draconian measures were not effective. In fact, they were taken advantage of by migrants who wished to spend a vacation at home (Candel 1965:121–22).

Migrants' shacks were also removed by officials either to put the land to other uses, such as building factories, or simply to eliminate what the upper strata considered an eyesore. Thus, when Barcelona landowners first found squatters on their land, they took advantage of the situation and charged them rent. Later, with the increase of industry and the consequent rise in land values, they attempted, sometimes successfully, sometimes not, to get rid of the shacks (Candel 1965:201–2).

The migrants often built their dwellings according to the styles of their areas of origin. In the Pozo del Tio Raimundo the architecture of the houses was similar to that of Andalusian villages: whitewashed facades, small windows against the sun, and in some instances even the same type of construction material of poured mud mixed with straw (*tapia*). Nevertheless, the speed with which clandestine houses had to be built led to a preference for brick construction. Even with the lack of space, most families still left an open area beside their house. In the countryside this corresponded to the corral, but in the new surroundings it had no function except where it had been used to dig a well or, in a few instances, to keep chickens. Inside, the houses also had a rural appearance with their low chairs, wine casks, photographs of deceased family members, weddings, and men in uniform, and religious images. Owing to the crowded living conditions, daily life spilled over into the streets, where groups of neighbors sang, played cards, and chatted (Castro 1961:522–24).

The most ardent desire of the shack dwellers was to obtain government-subsidized apartments. The first step beyond shacks were wooden barracks constructed in the mid-fifties by the municipal government as a stop-gap measure. Alarmed by the potential for political unrest that the policies of rapid industrialization of the dominant Opus Dei technocrats had brought with them, as well as by the erosion of their own power in the government, the falangist bloc pushed for short-term measures to stem the discontent and at the same time gain political capital for themselves (Castells 1977:52–53). So these "temporary" structures were still standing in the mid-seventies.

After the barracks came more permanent government-subsidized but privately built housing, still of extremely low quality.[4] Concomitantly, urban development came to be regarded as a lucrative enterprise, furthering land speculation and initiating a construction boom. A good example is El Besós, a government-sponsored housing project near Barcelona, initiated in 1960. For the first 1,100 apartments there were 18,000 applicants, even though the space allocated per person was little more than half of the absolute minimum (20 square meters) suggested by the International Architects Union (Matas Pericé 1970:35–36).

Considerable red tape was involved in obtaining subsidized housing. Thus in Seville poor families were only eligible for such housing if their *corrales,* low structures whose entrances faced a common patio with shared toilets, had been condemned by the city. In this case they would be moved into temporary shacks[5] and placed at the bottom of a waiting list for an apartment sometimes located far from the city center. The cost of such housing was low, around 15,000 pesetas down (about two months' wages) in the early 1970s, with some 600 to 800 pesetas monthly for the next 50 years. Even this small downpayment was difficult to accumulate for the very poor (Press 1979:199–201). Such apartments could be obtained by purchase only. With spiraling housing costs, those who were able to purchase an apartment early were at a considerable advantage over those who came later. The same is true for the few rented apartments; these are so strictly controlled in Spain that tenants who moved into their apartments in the fifties or early sixties pay ridiculously low rents today while owners of new apartments or apartment buildings charge exorbitant prices in order to protect themselves from future inflation.[6]

Today the problem is no longer the availability of apartments but the ability to afford one. Mortgages are difficult to obtain; they have short terms (five to ten years) and offer only a small fraction of the cost that can be financed in this manner. In Galicia one of the most frequent solutions for accumulating the necessary capital for the downpayment is to emigrate abroad. Similarly Sevillanos migrate to France, Germany, and Switzerland, where a worker can earn up to four times as much as in Seville (Press 1979: 222-24).

In many instances where migration does not play a direct role in the purchase of an apartment, it nevertheless plays an indirect role. For example, when the Ramirez family acquired an apartment in 1973 in La Coruña after 16 years in a tiny uncomfortable garret in a house where Mrs. Ramirez was working as a servant, they financed it with the help of a loan from a relative: "We thought we would never finish paying for it," Mrs. Ramirez said when we interviewed her in 1978.

> We bought a used one, but we had to borrow money left and right. The price was 350,000 ptas. We borrowed 50,000 ptas. from a brother-in-law who migrated to Holland and another 50,000 from his brother who was also working there. We ourselves had 50,000 of our own and with this we were able to obtain a loan from the savings bank at a very high interest rate. When we obtained the loan, I began to work again. I had worked at cleaning houses before but had stopped. In one, I work every morning and in the other only on Monday and Wednesday afternoon. Now I am going to stop because I will have a grandson and I will stay at home and take care of him so that my daughter can continue to work. Now we have almost finished paying for the apartment. There are only two or three months' payments to be made. It helped most when my daughter finished C.O.U. (pre-university year) and then when she finished her training as a secretary she began to work. Until she married, she helped us a lot. That's when we were able to pay off most of what we owed. Before that, we thought that we would never get out of debt.

In another case in the same city the husband went to sea in order to be able to afford an apartment, and in still another the couple sold land they still owned in their community of origin. Our assistant, who studies at the University of Santiago with this couple's daughter and knows her weakness for the country, asked the mother who would eventually use the apartment if her daughter did not want to live in the city. "Yes," she answered, "she likes the country because she doesn't know what country life is really like. Watching someone else working in the fields is fine, but if she had to live in the country like a poor slave she wouldn't want to either. She just likes to go there for fun, like a little bird."

Another option is to hold more than one job. Thus in Seville Hernán works mornings as a messenger for city hall and afternoons for a tile company, laying flooring and carpeting. In this way he averages some 25,000 pesetas, "most of which I'm saving for a *piso* (apartment) and for furniture. I could easily afford a car. Hell, I'd have it paid off in no time. But I'll hold off on this." Once their goals were achieved, Press's informants looked for one full-time job and stopped working in two jobs (Press 1979:224–25).

THE STRUGGLE FOR URBAN AMENITIES AND EDUCATION

One of the major problems in the early suburbs was the lack of urban amenities. Water often had to be purchased from trucks or even from vendors who brought it in on muleback, or fetched from the neighborhood's sole water fountain. Few dwellings had electricity, and it was often very complicated to get to one's place of work. These conditions have changed only very slowly. The government-sponsored apartments constructed in the 1960s had electric light and running water, but many of the streets remained unpaved and unlit.

In the province of Madrid housing projects were usually built next to towns on the periphery of the capital city with infrastructures designed only for 5,000 inhabitants: almost overnight these had to serve populations of more than 10,000 (Castells 1977:63). Public transportation was often deficient or lacking altogether, and access roads became so congested during peak hours that traffic often became totally paralyzed. Residents of the lower-class suburbs of Barcelona faced similar problems. Thus, in spite of constant promises of magnificent schools in the suburb of Besós, none at all were built during the first six years and then only a few provisional wood barracks were erected. The barracks were the last straw for the distraught residents, who sought every opportunity to destroy them. Two of the promised schools were finally built two years later, in 1968, when the population of the suburb had grown to 83,000 inhabitants, but work on the third had still not begun by 1970. Those who could afford it sent their children to private "academies" installed by enterprising individuals in any nook or cranny they could find. Even so, a survey undertaken in 1968 found no day-care centers for infants, only 1,700 places for 7,000 two- to five-year-olds,[7] and 8,500 places for 16,000 children between six and 17 years of age (Matas Pericé 1970:69–74).[8]

In the 1970s the Spanish government undertook an ambitious school building program to remedy the poor schooling situation in the cities as well as in rural areas. However, by 1974, although education was in principle obligatory, only 63% of primary school age children (enseñanza general básica) and 38% of high school age children (enseñanza media) went to school in Madrid as a whole, while in some of the peripheral townships only 51% went to primary school. Most went to private schools conceived as money-making enterprises rather than as a means of providing an adequate education (Castells 1977:41, 85, 143).

In spite of the abysmal educational situation in the poor suburbs of large cities, rural migrants have long looked to the city as an arena for the educational advancement of their children. In 1966 Douglass (1975:115, 190) counted 44 students who had moved to a city to study beyond the village level in Murélaga, a Basque village of a little over 1,000 inhabitants; in 1974 this figure had risen to 64. Similarly, in Galicia some rural families have attempted to place their children in urban boarding schools. Thus Isabel, a widowed farmer and tavern owner in Santa María (a parish in the province of La Coruña), succeeded through subterfuge and kin connections with a nun in placing two of her children in parochial boarding schools for the urban poor. The eldest daughter stayed for 17 months, learned how to type, and passed the entry examination for a school of commerce. However, at this point her mother was forced to take her home to help out. Isabel then brought her two eldest sons to a school for delinquents in La Coruña for lack of better opportunities. Finally, she managed to relocate them into a better school and one of them eventually became a priest; later he formally left the Church, then married and emigrated to France.

In the next generation one of her sons, who had been working in Switzerland for many years, sent his two daughters to boarding school in La Coruña, much to the distress of Isabel, who took care of them earlier and had a particularly close relationship with the younger one. This is a frequent practice, perhaps not least because children are thus raised together with children of higher social strata, which might assist social advancement.

Some migrants whom we interviewed in La Coruña mentioned the education of their children as their principal reason for migrating. Thus Mercedes, a seamstress who sews fur coats, and her husband moved to La Coruña when her father, with whom they had been living, died. "There we couldn't give them a education," she said. "Apart from the fact that we didn't have the money, everything was so far away. Here with the children living at home, a secondary education did not cost us anything. So my husband took a job here and I started to work sewing fur coats, and now I employ a number of women to assist me." Similarly Brandes (1975:57), speaking of migration from Castilian villages to Madrid in the early 1970s, remarks: "Ex-villagers who are now engaged in urban unskilled labor expect their children to become skilled workers, or even professionals. For, all that is needed in their view, is that educational institutions and employment opportunities are available. . . ."

Our interviews with students of migrant origin at the University of Santiago de Compostela in 1978 revealed a considerable range of backgrounds, although most came from families who had already enjoyed a higher than average standard of living in their communities of origin.[9] Some, like Josefa, came from an educated background. Her father was a poor peasant, who at the tender age of 16 was forced to sleep on park benches in Bilbao where he had gone in search of work. But her mother was a

school teacher who had already studied in Santiago. She came from a well-
to-do background and her father worked in Argentina in 1915. The father
was always the first in the community to make innovations such as purchasing farm machinery, and he was delighted when women began to wear
pants. Upon Josefa's marriage the parents had moved to La Coruña, where
the father had started a business transporting fish to Madrid, an activity he
had pursued during military service in the city. The mother continued
teaching school until her child was three years old. But then she gave it up.
"The other day my daughter asked me if I would live at home if I was twenty.
I answered her that I would but that I would never abandon my career. My
husband didn't force me to. But what was I to do? I could have requested a
permanent teaching position, but they would have sent me into some mountain hamlet where one is cut off all winter from the world. That's what they
do with women who become teachers. Today, I am sorry I gave up teaching
because I am all alone. My husband comes home only every two days."
Other parents are small-scale merchants or skilled workers in small provincial towns, and still others already have a family history of urban employment as rural-urban commuters.

The chances for successful completion of one's studies are inferior to
those of students from more privileged backgrounds, for poorer students
must rely on scholarships, which carry the stipulation that they pass all ex-
ams during their tenure. Furthermore, family illness or other misfortune is
more likely to force them to interrupt their studies and seek employment.
Once they complete their studies, students are highly dependent upon personal recommendations to find a job, and here again these migrants are at a
disadvantage.

ASSOCIATIONS AND COLLECTIVE ACTION

Although most of the new urban residents' efforts at gaining access to
scarce services are geared toward cutting through bureaucratic red tape by
the judicial use of patronage ties, they are also increasingly resorting to collective action. Neighborhood associations were already founded in the early
1960s. One such organization in the barrio of Besós in Barcelona had little
difficulty in obtaining official recognition. The leaders were falangistas and
therefore politically acceptable. However, for years the organization did little else than write polite letters to government officials and self-con-
gratulatory reports in its newsletter. Finally, in 1967 it managed to organize
a center where older men could gather and play cards, and a school for sub-
normal children. However, as late as 1970 the school was on the verge of
closing because of a lack of external financial support. Similarly, a youth
group was formed in the barrio to organize recreational activities ranging
from sports to dancing. Previously, young barrio members were forced to go

to the center of Barcelona to dance or watch a movie. They went in age-segregated groups and found it difficult to meet young people of the opposite sex. Catalán neighborhoods in this period also frequently organized small fairs with games for both children and adults during the fiesta of their patron saint, and this, too, contributed a modicum of community spirit.[10]

In the final years of the Franco regime the neighborhood association movement began to gain in importance and effectiveness. In Madrid a wide spectrum of neighborhoods of shacks, "provisional" housing estates built in the mid-1950s, company housing estates, state-subsidized and privately financed suburban apartment blocks, inner-city neighborhoods threatened by urban renewal, and even middle-class suburbs formed associations to improve conditions in their neighborhoods and fend off development projects by unscrupulous builders and real estate speculators inimical to their interests. As we have already seen, the first such organizations were formed in the poorer neighborhoods to request minimal services and organize recreational activities and centers. Later these functions were expanded to include the right to make home improvements in houses previously slated for demolition. Finally, from 1974 on they became more and more successful in requiring that development projects serve the needs of the original inhabitants of a neighborhood rather than the interests of the middle class and/or purely commercial interests. They were finally able to influence even the actual design of new housing and urban services (Castells 1977:77–78, Rebollo *et al.* 1977, CIDUR 1977, Borja 1975). These movements are linked in varying degrees to political parties. The communist Comisiones Obreras have been particularly active in supporting the associations. Conversely, the associations are involved in specific worker union actions as well as in more generalized political mobilization.

Politicization has sometimes led to internal squabbles between members who view the associations as means to achieve specific goals and those who use them as forums for class struggle in a wider sense. Nevertheless, faced with an imminent threat, splinter groups with different political ideologies often join forces. Supralocal support can also come from other citywide organziations. An example was the struggle against the construction of a large shopping center in La Vaguada in Madrid that not only would have removed the last open space available for park and recreational facilities but threatened the existence of the 1,500 small businesses established in the area. In this case the retail stores in the neighborhood were able to gain the support of the Association of Independent Retailers, which decided to carry out a citywide closing and thereby forced reconsideration of the project (Castells 1977:148–54).

Associations representing divergent social strata sometimes collaborate to achieve shared goals as well. In Madrid and Barcelona they have even formed citywide federations (Rebollo *et al.* 1977:36, CIDUR 1977:

39–40). A good example of the evolution of a neighborhood organization is the association of the residents of Pozo del Tio Raimundo, whose
beginnings we described earlier (Castells 1977:114–18). In 1956 the expropriation of the land where the barrio was built had brought construction to a
standstill. Compensation had been paid to the original owners of the land
rather than to the shack owners to whom they had sold it, but the *guardia civil*
had stifled all protest. About a third of the inhabitants later obtained apartments, but since land in the area was still plentiful, developers exerted little
pressure to remove the remaining residents and nothing more happened for
almost two decades. Then, in 1964, an association was founded to demand
running water and a sewage system, a goal which was finally achieved. This
success spurred the members to request the right to make improvements on
their properties, a right they had lost as a result of the expropriation, and
finally to secure adequate housing.

In the late 1960s the association was plagued by the same paternalism
and power concentration in the hands of single leaders characteristic of the
Franco regime in general. The president dealt with urban authorities directly, allowing little input from other members. At the same time the association became highly politicized. However, in 1971 a change in the board of
directors led to dropping purely ideological agitation and curtailing the
direct use of the association to further illegal political campaigns, permitting
collaboration with political groups only to further specific common goals.
Thus the association joined with the Comisiones Obreras to organize a
union school and an employment bureau for unemployed workers in the
neighborhood but refused the use of the association headquarters for
meetings of an extreme left group.

Political moderation contributed to the association's growth and made
it a more difficult target for official repression. Successful ventures multiplied. The association succeeded in having water and an electric transformer
installed and the streets paved. Then, in order to force an improvement in
the service, the members refused to pay taxes for electricity. The major battle, however, came when the city and private interests planned to build a
shopping center whose access ramps threatened to destroy part of the neighborhood. The association met to discuss their own plans for the neighborhood's future, inviting representatives of various government agencies. The
latter all refused to participate, disclaiming any responsibility. When the
members left the assembly, the police charged, leading to a serious confrontation. However, this only served to alert the press. The association
launched a campaign to mobilize support among other associations, and a
week later the plans for the access ramps were altered and a plan for new
housing announced.

However, the new housing still did not materialize. In 1975 a plan was
discovered that reserved most of the land for private developers while con-

centrating the residents in a small area next to the throughway. After re-newed protests the neighborhood finally succeeded in having a joint com-mission established to which the association and its hired experts would have their own input, and by 1977 construction began following the jointly elaborated plans.

In many instances the associations have also had a direct effect on the social life of the neighborhood. Under Franco, festive gatherings had long been among the few permitted forms of congregation.[11] At that time fiestas were often organized and controlled by the municipality. But even then they sometimes became a means of mobilization as well as an end in themselves. Thus neighborhoods began to organize their own fiestas. For instance, the neighborhood association of the Madrid barrio of Orcasitas wrested control over the barrio fiesta from the local *caciques* and brought the image of a saint from a nearby hermitage (Castells 1977:112). After Franco's death this trend accelerated, and barrio after barrio from Palmas de Gran Canaria in the Canary Isles to Logroño in northern Spain became involved in the organization not only of traditional fiestas but of new festivals and fairs as well. In Caliu in the province of Valencia neighbors demanded that the fiestas change their elite character and become more popular, while in some Madrid neighborhoods the associations organized parallel festivities to those organized by city officials, thereby protesting the lack of involvement of the neighbors in their planning and execution (CIDUR 1977:308).

A barrio could also make an effective political statement by refusing to hold a scheduled fiesta in a given year. Thus in Vitoria (Old Castile), where five persons were killed in labor strikes in 1976, all barrios agreed to boycott all fiestas. In one barrio the protest ended in a popular demonstration that was dispersed by the police (CIDUR 1977:151).

New festivals, too, were introduced all over Spain. Sometimes these festivals serve to underline regional or ethnic identity. Thus in Vitoria associations not only introduced typically Basque customs in the traditional fiestas but organized new Basque song festivals. Often, however, the festi-vals were specifically designed to generate support for a new association or for specific demands. In Barcelona one association organized a rock version of Don Juan in an old market to gain support for the plans to convert it into a public theater (CIDUR 1977:27). Similarly, in 1977 a middle-class suburb organized a song festival with Basque songs to celebrate Santa Agüeda as well as a funerary mass for a young girl from the barrio killed by the police during a political demonstration earlier that year (CIDUR 1977:159–60).[12]

Some groups have been organized on a citywide basis. In 1978 a group of handicapped individuals launched a campaign in La Coruña to make the city more livable for the handicapped. A photographic exhibition with cap-tions in Gallego illustrated the plight of the handicapped, and militant leaflets and posters demanded immediate corrective action. Voluntary associations on both the neighborhood and the city levels may thus become an important cornerstone of the democratization process in Spain.

KIN TIES AND RURAL-URBAN LINKAGES

Voluntary associations cannot be considered as an urban substitute for kinship ties. Both rural and urban Spaniards are highly dependent upon such ties, whose importance seems to be quite independent of the length of urban residence. Thus Press (1979:90–95) shows how Sevillanos create dense network clusters by interweaving friendships and matings: close friends often date siblings, creating complex interdependencies. Furthermore, women maintain strong links with their mothers even after marriage; uxorilocal residence or at least residence near the wife's family is common. Visiting is frequent, and in the case of the upper classes "daily phone calls — often *many* daily phone calls — are mandatory" (Press 1979:127). Similarly, the rural-urban migrants we interviewed in the city of La Coruña maintained close ties with their urban kin. Thus Rogelio's father-in-law has given his apartment to his single children, a daughter and two sons. Two other daughters who married on the same day share an apartment furnished with furniture given to them by Rogelio. Rogelio, who is the captain of a fishing vessel, also brings fish to both his sisters and parents-in-law (Buechler and Buechler 1981:159).

Recent migrants differ from more established urbanites in the extent of their ties in their communities of origin. Indeed, the creation of new forms of rural-urban linkages is a major concomitant of massive rural-urban migration. As we have seen, these linkages, through letters, visits of migrants to their places of origin and vice versa, catalyze and channel migration flows, leading to chain migration.

Keeping a house in one's village of origin enables urban residents to escape into the countryside for vacations or whenever they can. A leisure home has become much in vogue in cities like Madrid, where thousands flee to their country houses on weekends and vacations. Similarly, in La Coruña wealthier city dwellers build cottages along the ocean in nearby bays. A second house in one's place of origin fulfills the same purpose and also makes it possible for a migrant to tend to whatever economic interests he still maintains at home. Thus in Becedas, which is only three and a half hours from Madrid by car or taxi, households receive at least one set if not a continuous string of visitors from Madrid during the hot summer months. Many also stay in their own houses because some 27% of the houses in Becedas are owned by ex-villagers; of these, one-third are used as summer homes, for which they are often remodeled. People from Becedas also visit kinsmen in Madrid. Widows and widowers in particular spend as much as half of the year — the harsh winter — with various children in the city and the other half in the village. Relatives also make shorter visits or stay at their kinsmen's homes when they require specialized medical attention (Brandes 1975: 123–25). Similarly, school children from La Coruña frequently spend their summer vacations on their grandparents' farms in rural hamlets.

Many Galician migrants, particularly more recent ones, continue to have economic interests in the home community. Thus José, who formerly used to commute to work from a nearby hamlet, presently still spends most of his weekends there. He buys the seed and his father plants it. Then he and his wife help in the fields throughout the season. The couple also helps the wife's siblings in a somewhat more distant community when they have time during periods of intense agricultural activity. Josefa spends most weekends in the home community, an hour and a half away by car. She has a considerable amount of land there, which her sister and brother-in-law cultivate by tractor. Their children have left the hamlet as well. Josefa stays at her parental home even though she also has a house of her own there: "In August some thirty relatives get together. We are a very united family."

Finally, Ramón continues to cultive some land near Ferrol, an hour or so away by car. "We harvest almost everything we need to live on: beans, tomatoes, onions, leeks, peppers, potatoes, strawberries, chickens and rabbits." He goes there twice a week and leaves the animals alone in between times.

Even those who do not own land often gain access to country produce by helping their kin or simply by receiving produce, particularly potatoes, as a gift. Thus one of our assistants in Santa Maria regularly provides the families of her two children who live in La Coruña with potatoes. Even we were given potatoes (for which any form of payment was refused) because our assistant could not bear to see us buy potatoes at market prices, and inferior ones to her own to boot!

In time, urban residents may reduce their visits to the country. As we have already noted, the proceeds from the sale of land or one's country house may serve as a downpayment for an apartment. With less at stake at home, the visits may be confined to fiestas when a sumptuous meal awaits the visitor from the city.[13]

COMMUTING

Another form of rural-urban contact occurs through commuting. Both men and women may continue to live in their rural hamlet and commute to work by bus. Some commuters have less than half an hour to travel, but many commute for an hour and a half or more each way. The advantage of commuting is access to cheaper accommodations in the country and, more important, the possibility for women to continue in agriculture. With relatively few well-paying jobs for women, this alternative is particularly attractive. As a result, many migrants have chosen to build a house in their hamlet rather than in a town or city, giving rise to increasingly modern and expensive homes being built in the rural hamlets. We even met families who had already established themselves in a town and then decided to move back to the hamlet.

A dual economy based on agriculture and urban employment is a prevalent feature of the highly industrialized Basque provinces. Thus Douglass (1975:191) writes that life in Echelar and Murélaga "encapsulated a unique blend of part-time agriculture, commuter industrial employment, occasional emigration and tourism." Similarly, in the Basque provinces, according to Greenwood (1975:50–51), one-third of the active population of Fuenterrabia is employed outside agriculture, yet lives on the farm. The commuters include heirs whose farms are too small to provide for subsistence, bachelors who are allowed to remain on the family farm, and adolescents and young adults who commute before leaving the farm permanently and settling in the city.

A good example of a hamlet with a large percentage of commuters is the Galician hamlet of Chamín. When we lived there in 1972–73, few of the people worked elsewhere, and those were mainly in construction. By 1978 the number of commuters had increased considerably, for a new industrial complex had been built in Sabón, only 15 minutes away. Cars have proliferated in the parish, making the trip to Sabón and La Coruña even easier. An economic life-style based on a combination of agriculture and wage labor has made it possible for individuals from extremely poor families of day laborers to catch up with their farmer neighbors in terms of standard of living. Indeed, they may have somewhat more leisure time than the farmers who can no longer rely on wage labor to help them (cf. Buechler and Buechler 1981: ch. 7). Carmela, for example, decided to work in La Coruña when she returned from Geneva, Switzerland, where she and her husband had been working. Her husband is still there, but she felt she could not leave her children at home with her mother any longer and, like most migrants, did not want to have her children in Switzerland where they would receive a French education, which would make readaptation to Spain difficult.

Carmela found employment through a friend and neighbor who also works in La Coruña. She leaves home at 6:45 A.M. by bus and rarely is back in Chamín before 8:30 or 9:00 P.M. She works very hard loading boxes weighing 50 to 80 kilograms on trucks by hand from a wet hall where she is forced to wear rubber boots and gloves constantly. The fish would spoil if they were not dispatched on the same day, so she must often stay as late as 10:00 P.M.[14] Then her boss pays for a taxi to take her and her neighbor home. For all this she earns 4,500 pesetas a week plus insurance and four weeks extra pay per year. "I could work cleaning houses where one doesn't work as hard and the work is clean, but it's difficult to earn even 3000 ptas. a week and that . . . usually without insurance. With the bus trip costing 100 ptas. a day not much is left." Carmela's mother prepares lunch for the children so she need not worry about them. Since the family has no cattle, the children need only feed the rabbits and do some chores around the house when they return from school. However, they have rented some land to cultivate potatoes, which Carmela does on weekends. Carmela's husband had worked in La Coruña too before he emigrated to Switzerland, but he could not resist the higher pay in Switzerland, which has permitted the couple to buy a house plot and build their home in Chamín. They hope to be reunited some time either in Switzerland or in Spain, but it is not easy. Carmela's mother is 80 years old and, being the only daughter, Carmela feels an obligation to take care of her. It would be next to impossible to move her to Switzerland for both legal and practical reasons, and the problem of the children's education would remain. It would be equally difficult for Carmela's husband to return to Spain permanently.

Carmela has a deep distrust of the construction industry where her husband would most likely have to work. First, such work is often impermanent. With the construction of a nearby industrial complex there is plenty of work at the moment, but builders are wary of giving long-term contracts: "When a man goes to a construction company they give him a contract for three months and after that they throw him out. . . . They do this so that the worker won't accumulate rights. When they want to fire a man or woman who has worked for a company for 10 to 12 years they can't do it because they would have to pay him or her a considerable sum." Second, good jobs are difficult to come by, especially if one wants to work in the area rather than travel to distant sites. "Often a person who has a good job has to pay more to get it than he will earn while someone who can't pay is thrown out." Finally, Carmela's husand was ill and, following his doctor's recommendation, had to switch from construction to a lighter job in a hotel in Switzerland. Such work would be even more difficult to find and in any case would pay very little.

Maria, who is 17 and also from Chamín, works in a new clothing factory in the industrial complex of Sabón. She had been working in a hotel since she was 14 but found this more taxing and is quite pleased with her new employment. She praises the company's modern dining hall where workers can eat for 70 ptas. ($0.90) — about half of what a restaurant charges. Her work day begins at 8 A.M. and ends at 5 P.M. Previously she worked one hour less but had to work until noon on Saturday mornings. Maria earns 13,500 pesetas a month and has a one-month vacation in summer when the entire factory closes. During the previous summer she had continued to work in a restaurant on weekends, and after work she still found time and energy to go out to dance with her boyfriend. Needless to say, she was exhausted and planned to get more rest on weekends. If Maria marries her boyfriend, she plans either to continue working in the factory and have her mother take care of her children, or to migrate to Switzerland with her husband. She wants to save for a house and live in the hamlet rather than move into an apartment in the city. What she is earning now goes toward her clothing and a few things now and then for the household. The rest she is saving.

THE GROWTH OF SMALL TOWNS

A description of rural-urban migration in Spain would not be complete without mentioning the growth of small towns in areas like Galicia where in the past towns were often little more than sites for a weekly market, centers for minimal services, and, in the larger centers, perhaps the location of two or three small factories. Many such towns have experienced a spectacular growth in recent years owing mainly to the increased demand for agricultural machinery and consumer goods in the surrounding rural areas, which in turn was fueled by revenues from migration to other European countries. A good example is the town of Carballo in the province of La Coruña. Carballo had (with a little bit of fudging according to one census taker) 10,000 inhabitants in 1970. The town's growth rate can be seen from the tax lists, which record the establishment of 16 new businesses in 1966, 64 in 1971, and 144 in 1976.[15] Between 1973 and 1977 the income from municipal taxes almost quadrupled. The rate of housing starts (for which there are no adequate records, since most construction, including high-rises, is done without official permits pending the completion of an urbanization plan) is even more spectacular, for migrants have been investing in building lots and apartments at an accelerating rate. In 1978 we estimated that there were around 500 apartments under construction. Real estate speculation was rampant, with lots and finished buildings rapidly changing hands in the process. As a bank manager told us, an individual might buy on one day and sell on the next without even having taken a careful look at the property because he already had a client lined up willing to pay 500,000 pesetas more. By the summer of 1978 a crisis was brewing, and many a speculator who had overextended himself was in danger of bankruptcy. Apartments were selling for the same price as three years earlier, which, given the high rate of inflation, must have amounted to at least 50% less than the speculators had anticipated. Among the reasons for the sudden downturn is the fact that many migrants are choosing to build houses in their hamlets instead, which give them more room and, as indicated earlier, the possibility to supplement wage employment with agriculture. Also, the future of a town like Carballo is far from assured, for its principal source of wealth is construction. In 1978 the town had only one major factory, a recently modernized fish canning industry employing 300 workers. It seemed doubtful whether the prospective inhabitants could all find employment in Carballo if they were all to return from abroad.

In conclusion, the breath-taking pace of industrialization in the past two decades combined with the centralist policies of the Franco dictatorship have led to spectacular growth of Spain's major metropolitan centers. The uneven geographical distribution of this development has led to migration over long distances and concomitant depopulation of many agricultural areas. The excesses of a laissez-faire economy directed by the regime's Opus Dei technocrats, and the repression of all protest until the last years of the Franco regime against policies designed for the benefit of the wealthy developers at the cost of the poor, aggravated the problems of rapid urban growth. The progressive democratization of the nation's institutions has already given some hope for improvements in urban living conditions. However, a more even development of the various regions of Spain and an end to the continued exodus from predominantly rural areas and the heavy reliance on international migration still remain elusive goals.

NOTES

1. See Buechler and Buechler (1975, 1981). We carried out research on migration to La Coruña and to Carballo, in connection with a larger study on migration to Switzerland, in 1972–73 and in the summers of 1974 and 1978.
2. The day laborers may be slightly overrepresented because migrants from Jaén were overrepresented in Siguán's sample, compared to the migrant population as a whole.
3. Esteva Fabregat (1973:163) also underlines the importance of kin in finding lodgings in Barcelona.
4. In 1961, the first year of the National Housing Plan, 135,400 housing units were built. In its last year (1975) this figure had increased to 374,300. However, the proportion built with government subsidies decreased from 90% to 53% during this period.
5. By 1974 the refuges were no longer necessary.
6. Controls only affect leases already in effect. New leases depend on market forces alone. See Press (1979:190–92) for some examples of the unintended effects of these laws.
7. This in spite of the fact that an estimated 22% of the women worked outside their homes and 50% did remunerated work at home (Matas Pericé 1970:97).
8. This situation contrasts sharply with illiteracy in Barcelona as a whole, which was 5.82% of the population above ten years of age in 1950 (Ivern 1958:152). The total incapacity of the state schools to handle increasing numbers of migrants and the private attempts to remedy the situation are shown in earlier figures from another suburb of Barcelona, San Sebastián. In 1959, out of a school age population of 4,533, only 1,929 went to school. Two years earlier the figures were 3,844 and 300 respectively. The improvement in those two years was due mostly to the increase of private schools (Candel 1965:273–74). Interestingly, the religious orders did not initiate any of these schools. It must be

added that education in public schools was not entirely free. The parents were forced to supplement the low salaries of the teachers with contributions of their own (Candel 1965:276).

9. Between 1969–70 and 1974–75 the number of students at Spanish universities increased from 150,094 to 275,300.

10. Kenny (1972:110, n. 3) mentions another form of joint endeavor in this period, namely housing cooperatives in Madrid and Seville, formed on the initiative of returned migrants from other European countries.

11. Although even they required official permission.

12. Festivals have also become a major means of political mobilization for the Communist party in Portugal. Political parties employ the medium of fiestas and fairs in Spain as well. Thus many political parties obtained pavilion space at the April *feria* (agricultural fair) in Seville, a privilege open only to the wealthy in Franco's day. In 1978 "flamenco-garbed members and guests in the Communist Party *caseta* clapped and stomped their way through traditional Sevillana dances, distinguishable from others only in the substitution of politically appropriate lyrics for the standard chauvinistic tributes to the city. 'Viva la Revolución' replaced 'Viva Sevilla'" (Press 1979:286–87).

13. Sometimes the participation of migrants in cities and abroad takes on a more active character. Thus Kenny (1969:112) indicates that bachelors from the village of Ramosierra living in Madrid contributed significantly to keeping the fiesta of San Roque alive, and expatriate emigrants maintain their hand in the affairs of their home village by letting their visits coincide with key periods such as fiestas (Kenny 1972:105). Similarly Gallego emigrants to Switzerland and Germany often sponsor masses (even if sometimes only *in absentia*) at fiestas in and around their home communities.

14. The Spanish workday includes a two-hour lunch break.

15. These figures are for the municipality as a whole but, except for bars, taverns-cum-grocery-stores, and builders, most of the growth corresponds to the town itself.

REFERENCES

Barbancho, Alfonso G.
    1967   *Las migraciones interiores españoles*. Madrid: Instituto de Desarrollo Económico.
    1975   *Las migraciones interiores españoles en 1961–70*. Madrid: Instituto de Estudios Económicos.
Bier, Alice Gail
    1979   "Vox Populi": El desarrollo de las asociaciones de vecinos en España. *Papers, Revista de sociología, no. 11*. Barcelona: Ediciones Peninsula, pp.169–83.
Beiras, Xosé Manuel
    1972   *O atraso economico de Galicia*. Vigo: Galaxia.
Borja, J.
    1975   *Movimientos sociales urbanos*. Buenos Aires: Ediciones S.I.A.P.
Brandes, Stanley H.
    1975   *Migration, kinship and community: Tradition and transition in a Spanish village*. New York: Academic Press.
Buechler, Hans, and J-M.
    1975   Los Suizos: Galician migration to Switzerland. In H. I. Safa and B. M.

DuToit, eds., *Migration and development: Implications for ethnic identity and political conflict.* The Hague: Mouton, pp. 17–31.
1981   *Carmen: The autobiography of a Spanish Galician woman.* Cambridge: Schenkman.
Candel, Francisco
    1965   *Los otros catalanes.* Madrid: Penísula.
    1972   *Inmigrantes y trabajadores.* Barcelona: Planeta.
Castells, Manuel
    1977   *Ciudad, democracia y socialismo: La experiencia de las asociaciones de vecinos en Madrid.* Madrid: Siglo XXI.
Castro, Constancio de
    1961   El Pozo del Tio Raimundo. *Estudios geográficos* (Aug.-Nov.:501–21.
CIDUR
    1976   *Vallecas: Las razones de una lucha popular.* Madrid: Ediciones Mañana.
    1977   *Las asociaciones de vecinos en la encrucijada: El movimiento cuidadano en 1976–77.* Madrid: Ediciones de La Torre.
Douglass, William A.
    1975   *Echelar and Murélaga: Opportunity and rural exodus in two Spanish Basque villages.* New York: St. Martin's Press.
Esteva Fabregat, Claudio
    1973   Aculturación y urbanización de inmigrados en Barcelona: Cuestión de etnia o cuestión de clase? *Éthnica* 5:137–89.
Garcí Fernandez, Javier, and María Gonzalez Ruiz
    1976   *Presente y futuro de las asociaciones de vecinos.* Madrid: Ediciones Pecosa.
Greenwood, Davyyd
    1976   *Unrewarding wealth: The commercialization and collapse of agriculture in a Spanish Basque town.* Cambridge: Cambridge University Press.
Ivern, Francisco
    1958   *Hospitalet de Llobregat, cuadernos de información.* Barcelona: Cuadernos de Información Económica y Sociológica.
Kenny, Michael
    1969   *A Spanish tapestry: Town and country in Castile.* Gloucester, Mass.: Peter Smith.
    1972   The return of the Spanish emigrant. *Nord Nytt* 2:101–29.
Matas Pericé, Alfred
    1970   *Al sud-oest del riu Besós: Deu anys de la vida d'un barri barceloní.* Barcelona: GP.
Miguel, Amando de, and Juan Salcedo
    1972   *Dinámica del desarrollo industrial de las regiones en España.* Madrid: Tecnos.
Pascual, A.
    1970   *El retorno del emigrante.* Barcelona: Nova Terra.
Perpiñá Grau, Román
    1954   *Corología: Teoría estructural y estructurante de la población de España, 1900–1950.* Madrid: Consejo Superior de Investigaciones Científicas.
Press, Irwin
    1979   *The City as context: Urbanism and behavioral constraints in Seville.* Urbana: University of Illinois Press.
Rebollo, Rodriguez y Sotos
    1977   *El movimiento ciudadano ante la democracia.* Madrid: Editorial Cenit.
Rhoades, Robert E.
    1978   Intra-European return migration and rural development: Lessons from the Spanish case. *Human Organization* 37:136–47.
Siguán, Miguel
    1959   *Del campo al suburbio: Un estudio sobre la immigración interior en España.* Madrid: Consejo Superior de Investigaciones Científicas.

Chapter **6**

Migration in Italy

William A. Douglass

MIGRATION STRATEGIES IN PERSPECTIVE

There was a time when social anthropology was virtually defined by its subject matter as the study of the world's isolates—the relatively self-contained tribal, island, or peasant village societies. The anthropologist's reliance upon participant observation limited the manageable unit of analysis to the "little community," which, for heuristic purposes, was often treated as a closed universe. Evidence of external influences and internal social change was either ignored or held constant so as not to contaminate the attempt to capture/reconstruct a particular culture's ethnographic present. As a technique for documenting the spectrum of human ingenuity, the approach yielded important results; as a vehicle for conveying time-specific social reality, it was flawed, and has been so critiqued (Boissevain and Friedl 1975).

The intellectual issues posed by the discipline's methodology aside, anthropology's traditional approach was challenged directly by twentieth-century developments. Two world wars, the communications explosion, and an accelerating technological revolution have all served to reduce every society's isolation. From the perspective of the village community this frequently translates into a rural exodus. The lure of city life (or at least the attraction of urban employment) has proven to be the single most powerful factor in the twentieth-century decline, if not demise, of the world's tribal and peasant cultures.

Not surprisingly, then, today's anthropological study is likely to focus, at least partly, upon some aspect of rural-urban interaction. Increasingly, there are treatises on the tribalization or peasantization of the urban milieu (e.g., Mangin 1970), while investigators focusing upon rural communities document the feedback from the cities of resources and ideas.

These new approaches have not, however, been without their own intellectual lacunae; too frequently there is a tendency to treat rural-urban migration as an essentially modern and self-contained phenomenon. There is much in the process that is unique to the twentieth century, but there is also a sense in which such a reduced time frame violates the history of many parts of the world. To treat rural-urban migration as a category *per se* is to ignore the fact that movement to the cities is only one of several migration ploys available to the rural actors, notable alternatives being foreign emigration and cyclical seasonal labor movements (a point that is clearly recognized and developed by Alberoni 1970 for Italy). Furthermore, there is too great a tendency to treat migration to the cities (or emigration abroad) as a unidirectional process. In point of fact, oftentimes the migrant is more a sojourner than a permanent departee (though his/her absence may be measured in years). Finally, there is the fact that for many actors migration becomes an intrinsic part of the life process rather than a simple event. That is, the individual may combine several migration strategies and/or engage in the same ones at more than one point in time. Thus the intervening period between a person's birth in a rural community and burial in an urban cemetery may well encompass several sojourns abroad, residence in a number of different cities, stays in a variety of rural communities, and periodic returns to the natal village (e.g., Lauriente 1953, Schreiber 1973).

These generalizations are applicable to most of Europe, which is one of the world's longstanding and major staging areas of both internal migration and transoceanic emigration. However, for the continent the specifics vary considerably from country to country, as well as regionally within nations. It is against the backdrop of the foregoing caveats that we examine migration strategies in Italy.

SOME RELEVANT HISTORY AND GEOGRAPHY

Extending for almost a thousand miles from the southern reaches of western Europe into the heart of the Mediterranean, the Italian peninsula embraces a variety of ecological zones, and the contrasts are heightened by a broken topography. Subtropical conditions sometimes obtain within a few kilometers of alpine environments. Excepting a few regions, like the Po Valley and the Apulian plain, it is a harsh land — noteworthy more for the fecundity of its population than the fertility of its soil.

In ancient times foreign powers and a number of indigenous tribes contested control of the peninsula. The Greeks established enclaves on the southern littoral (which to this day lend ethnic distinctiveness to parts of the south). Etruscans, Samnites, and Latins struggled for hegemony of the area. The ascendency of the Latins, and the attendant emergence of a potent political force in the western Mediterranean, prompted the Carthaginians to launch their famed, if ill-fated, invasion of the peninsula. As the seat of one of history's mightiest and most durable empires, Rome became the most important urban center of the ancient world, both exporting a part of its own population and attracting "migrants" from throughout the Mediterranean basin and beyond. In the process many areas of southern Europe were latinized, while for the first time western Asia, northern Africa, and western and northern Europe were articulated through the vehicle of a single cosmopolitan metropolis.

The collapse of the Roman empire in the fifth century A.D. itself triggered new movements into the peninsula, invasions by barbarian tribes from the north. During the Middle Ages parts of southern Italy were alternately controlled by the Moors, the Turks, the Normans, the Swabians, the Angevins, and the Aragonese. Mercenaries serving in the armies of both the invaders and the defenders of particular areas were drawn from throughout Europe. Many stayed, adding to local ethnic diversity. The Albanian enclaves of the Italian south, which still retain their identity, are a case in point.

By the mid-fourteenth century political fragmentation of the peninsula was pronounced. Sicily and Naples each constituted a separate kingdom. Central Italy was under papal control. Venice was an independent city-state and a Mediterranean imperial power in its own right. Sardinia pertained to the kingdom of Aragon. North Italy contained a plethora of independent duchies and republics loosely federated under the Holy Roman Empire, with its political axis in Central Europe.

More recently parts of Italy have been dominated periodically by Spain, Austria, and France, becoming pawns in the power struggle between the imperial giants. All contributed to Italian life in a cultural, as well as a genetic, sense.

For more than a millennium after the collapse of the Roman empire, then, the peninsula lacked any kind of meaningful political, economic, or social unity. It was not until Garibaldi's incursion into Sicily little more than a century ago that events were set in motion which culminated in the creation of the modern Italian state. In many respects Garibaldi's campaign was more the conquest of the south by the north, and a battlefield confrontation between liberalism and the old order, than a popular expression of spontaneous nationalism. Thus, if the Italian peninsula is the locus of one of the Western world's oldest cultural traditions, it also hosts one of its younger nations. Indeed, the process of nation building, as measured by success in infusing the entire populace with a sense of common purpose, remains incomplete to this day.

From both a temporal and a cultural viewpoint, then, it is illusory to speak of "Italy," for there are indeed many Italys and each differs from the others, at least in part, precisely because of its unique history of migration factors — as receiving area for new settlers, crossroads of human activities and ideas, and seedbed of wayfarers.

There is the island world, dominated by the two Mediterranean behemoths of Sicily and Sardinia, which at times shared in the political, economic, and social arrangements of adjacent mainland areas but at other times diverged from them. Strategically located astride the trade routes, Sicily served as the universal joint in the political and economic machinery of the Mediterranean. It was there that Byzantium, North Africa, and Western Europe periodically contested hegemony of the basin.

The *mezzogiorno,* or the Italian south, is stereotypically the most backward and poverty-stricken area of the nation. Long dominated by out-siders and politically one of the most reactionary regions in Europe, the south evokes visions of oppression, overpopulation, famine, disease, illitera-cy, and natural disasters. It is an area of enormous landed estates and tiny, fragmented peasant holdings. The South Italian peasant is frequently de-picted as a walking symbol of social injustice. He is the *cafone*—the brutish, frequently landless migrant worker or sharecropper who scratches a meager existence out of a hostile social and natural environment (Friedmann 1962).

Central Italy, on the other hand, is a gentler land of appreciable wealth and culture. There city-states such as Siena and Florence emerged as cradles of the Renaissance and hence the torchbearers of Western civilization. Simi-larly, the social and economic organization of the rural ambiance was and is considerably more equitable, though far from egalitarian. Farm units are larger and more consolidated than in the south, and provide the producer with a higher standard of living. The basic social unit is the patrilineally ex-tended joint family, which enjoys considerable continuity on the land both from year to year and from generation to generation (Silverman 1975).

North Italy embraces both the Tyrol and the Po Valley, which are high-ly contrastive milieus. The northern lowlands have long been Italy's most fertile region, an area of irrigated agricultural estates employing considera-ble labor forces. During the late Middle Ages, as population pressure on the adjacent plains became excessive, agriculture was extended into the Tyrols. However, it was the small, self-contained farmstead worked by a stem family that emerged as the basic social and economic unit (Cole 1971). Such an arrangement seems to correlate with agricultural colonization of frontier areas on the one hand (Wolf 1970) and alpine ecologies on the other (Burns 1963). The Tyrol also became an area of considerable permanent culture contact, a zone where the frontiers of Italian, French, and German culture coincided and, in some cases, interpenetrated. The Germanic flavor of the area was enhanced during the late Middle Ages by the arrival of thou-sands of Bavarian miners, many of whom settled permanently (Cole and Wolf 1974:38–39). Despite its mountainous terrain, the Tyrol has served more as a facilitator than a barrier to the movement of people and ideas. The pilgrim routes to Rome utilized by the devout from throughout Europe passed through the Alps. Furthermore, the Brenner and Reschen passes were the main links between transalpine and cisalpine Europe, the vital land corridors through which, prior to the Atlantic voyages of discovery, trade goods from the Orient reached western and northern markets. More recent-ly, northern Italy has emerged as the peninsula's industrial zone. Today the "industrial triangle" of Genoa, Milan, and Turin constitutes one of Europe's major manufacturing zones.

There is a maritime Italy, epitomized by Venice to the east and Genoa to the west. Historically more oriented to international commerce than to their immediate hinterlands, the maritime city-states developed their own characteristic societies. Bitter rivals and, at times, battlefield adversaries, Venice and Genoa served as Western Europe's pre-Columbian window on the world — the conduit to North Africa, Byzantium, and beyond.

Finally, there is Rome. As the focal point of the ancient world, the fount of Latin culture, and the womb of Christendom, the eternal city was historically both a cosmopolitan hybrid on the Italian scene and the seat of a theocracy that at times dominated parts of the peninsula.

Prior to the discovery of the Americas and the opening of sea routes to the Far East, parts of the peninsula dominated Europe's intercontinental trade. It was in central and northern Italy that modern mercantilism was born. The newly emergent money economy in turn provided the financial underpinning of the cultural climax known as the Renaissance. Italian interests were also important in the development of other Western European economies during the late Middle Ages, exercising considerable influence in places as distant as England (Postan 1951) and Spain (Melis 1976). However, once the continent's energies shifted from the Mediterranean basin to the Atlantic and beyond, Italy was essentially bypassed.

Politically fragmented and physically removed from the new trade routes, the peninsula as a region did not participate (until quite recently and then in only perfunctory fashion) in European colonial expansion. This is not to say, however, that Italians as individuals, as well as Italian commercial interests, were excluded entirely. Men like Columbus and Amerigo Vespucci played key roles in the voyages of discovery. Italian banking firms and commercial houses helped to underwrite the imperial ventures of other nations. One need only cite the activities of the Genoese in Seville (Pike 1966) and the sixteenth-century Italian influence in French financial circles (Wallenstein 1974:263) as cases in point.

The illustrious successes of a few Italians as handmaidens of foreign colonial enterprises notwithstanding, Italy's lack of an overseas empire was to color its subsequent migration history. Unlike the Spanish, Portuguese, French, Dutch, and English, the Italians had no dominions to administer, no distant dependencies in which to invest national energies. There were two immediate consequences. First, unlike many of their neighbors, Italians were largely precluded from developing a pronounced and longstanding emigratory tradition. Second, when, beginning in the mid-seventeenth century, all of Western Europe experienced a population explosion (McNeill 1963:627), Italy lacked the option of transferring abroad its excess numbers as colonists. If for many European countries population increase fueled and strengthened the colonial effort, in Italy it translated into progressive deterioration of the standard of living.

While Italians were largely excluded from colonial enterprises, they participated with a vengeance in the late nineteenth- and early twentieth-century transatlantic migration of the "huddled masses." By the mid-nineteenth century the United States was no longer under British control, much of Hispanic America was the master of its own destiny, and Brazil was an independent nation. The former slave traffic had been largely abolished and the indigenous population of many New World areas all but exterminated. With few people relative to their vast areas, several of the New World nations subscribed to the Argentine social critic Alberdi's dictum, "to govern is to populate" (Cuccorese and Panettieri 1971:395). Consequently the United States and the southern South American countries in particular liberalized their immigration laws and even actively competed for newcomers by dispatching recruiting agents to Europe, instituting assisted passage plans, establishing receiving centers, etc.

By the turn of the century Australia and Canada had entered the picture as well. While still incorporated into the British empire, both nations were increasingly in control of their own immigration policies and shared the view that national development was equated with population increase. There was yet a further source of competition for cheap laborers. European countries undergoing rapid industrialization welcomed the sojourner (though not encouraging permanent settlement). France, Switzerland, and Germany thereby became the destinations of thousands of Italian migrants.

Statistics on the magnitude of the emigratory movement are flawed in many respects, and are most certainly understated, particularly for the early years when there was little control. However, even the official Italian count, running into the tens of millions, is impressive. During the peak period of 1906 to 1910 an average of 651,288 Italians emigrated abroad annually. Of this total 40% selected a European destination, while the remainder crossed the Atlantic (Ratti 1934:257).

Emigration was not distributed evenly within Italy. It began in the north and moved progressively southward. During the period from 1876 to 1880 there was an annual average of 108,797 emigrants. Venetium had 33,204, the Piedmont 27,544, Lombardy 18,040, and Liguria 4,428. Thus the four northern regions in combination supplied over three-quarters of all emigrants. The entire south, including Sicily and Sardinia, averaged but 13,992 departures annually (Ratti 1934:256). By the end of the century (1896–1900) the northern totals averaged 153,095 emigrants annually, while the south had 111,540. Furthermore, by this time the majority of northern Italian emigrants (76.5%) were departing for another European country, while fully 91.5% of the southerners were crossing the Atlantic. In the year 1913, 872,598 Italians emigrated, 313,032 to European destinations and 559,566 overseas. Of the former total 209,217 (66.8%) were from the extreme north, while of the latter sum 388,613 (69.5%) were from the south. Sicily alone provided 141,880 transoceanic emigrants (Ratti 1934:256).

World War I disrupted transatlantic emigration considerably, and Mussolini's rise to power in the 1920s culminated in anti-emigration legislation as he steeled the nation for its ill-starred drive for national glory. Beginning with the Abyssinian campaign and the Spanish Civil War, many Italians left the country to serve as soldiers. A large number were killed in such distant places as North Africa, Greece, Germany, and the Russian steppes.

During the post–World War II era, excepting Australia, the former major overseas receiving areas of Italian emigration have pursued more restrictive immigration policies. Latin America, in particular, has attracted few Italians in recent years (Lucrezio M. and Favero 1972). For the period 1946–70, 1,619,000 Italians emigrated permanently to an overseas destination. Canada and the United States continued to be favored countries, suggesting that many of the emigrants were effecting family reunions.

Of particular note during this period, however, had been the emergence of a pronounced pattern of intra-European Italian migration. Switzerland's expanding economy encouraged the temporary labor migrant, while creation of the European Economic Community provided laborers with access to employment in France, West Germany, and the Benelux countries. Italians joined the wave of Spaniards, Portuguese, Yugoslavs, Greeks, Turks, and North Africans that flocked to the nerve centers of the burgeoning Western European economies.

Their living and working circumstances were not always favorable, and the migrants were frequently the objects of overt anti-Mediterranean discrimination (Blumer 1970, Favero and Rosoli 1975). They were welcomed only insofar as the host country required a source of relatively inexpensive, largely unskilled labor that could be discharged readily in the event of a downturn in the economy. Switzerland, in particular, discouraged permanent immigration by issuing one-year work permits (Kuhn 1978:210–14). The migrant was, then, a *Gästarbeiter* ("guest worker") in every sense of the word, a sojourner rather than a potential citizen of the host country. In the case of Italians, for example, between 1946 and 1970, 4,534,000 persons departed for another European country, but 3,011,000 returned to Italy (Lucrezio M. and Favero 1972:6).

In sum, over the past century the Italian emigratory movement has been massive but far from unidirectional. For example, during the 1921–30 period departures averaged 255,064 persons annually, but there were fully 137,814 repatriations each year (Istituto Centrale de Statistica 1968:28). Of the approximately 26 million Italian emigrants during the 1871–1971 period, slightly more than half have returned to Italy (Rosoli 1977:235).

For more than a century, then, emigration policy has been a dominant theme in Italian life. The sheer magnitude of the movement means that few Italians have been unaffected by it. Indeed, the configuration of modern Italy is inextricably intertwined with the feedback of men, money, and ideas from abroad. Any consideration of internal migration patterns within the nation that failed to take the emigration alternative into account would be deficient.

THE COUNTRYSIDE AND THE CITY

In light of the foregoing review of migration history, one might easily, yet erroneously, conclude that there is a cosmopolitan air to Italian life, even in the countryside. In point of fact, the cultural climaxes and crossroads to which we have referred are relatively remote in time. The emigratory movement of the past century has clearly had an impact on the rural psyche, society, and economy but in many respects remains circumscribed and individualized. Indeed, to this day Italy harbors one of Europe's most traditional peasantries as well as one of its most impoverished and downtrodden rural proletariats. At times, but not always, the two categories overlap.

Until recently, to a great extent the world of the *contadino*, or peasant, was both unknown and ignored. To be sure, there was a plethora of travel accounts like Amy Atkinson's *In the Abruzzi* (1908) and Norman Douglas's *Old Calabria* (1915) that gave some insight into an isolated and closed universe that seemed almost as exotic as any encountered by Marco Polo or Columbus. Occasionally there were parliamentary inquiries into the plight of the peasantry (Jarach 1909), and political activists such as Antonio Gramsci (1970, first published in 1926) sought to galvanize the situation into a political issue. Novels such as Ignacio Silone's *Fontamara* (1930) and *Pane e vino* (1937) and Francesco Jovine's *Le terre del sacramento* (1950) shed further light upon the *contadini*. Above all Carlo Levi's classic, and controversial, work *Cristo si é fermato a Eboli* (1946), with its vivid description of life in a remote village of Lucania, brought the Italian peasant to the awareness of the nation and, in translation *(Christ Stopped at Eboli)*, the world at large.

Social scientific studies employing a community perspective have further underscored the relatively closed universe of the *contadini*, particularly in the south. Without attempting to be exhaustive, one could cite Banfield (1958), Maraspini (1968), Brögger (1971), Galtung (1971), and Chapman (1971). To be sure, some accounts, such as Friedmann (1960), Lopreato (1967), Davis (1973), Gross (1973), Cole and Wolf (1974), and Silverman (1975) do address the question of social change and outside influences, but on balance the emphasis remains upon the closed and backward nature of rural Italian society and the recency of change within it.

Much of the above cited work focuses upon geographically remote areas, even by Italian reckoning,[1] with the implication that there is concordance between physical and social isolation. However, others have eschewed the community perspective (*e.g.* Scotellaro 1972, Dolci 1970, Istituto per lo Sviluppo dell'Edilizia Sociale (1965) and treated the *contadini* as a ubiquitous rural proletariat. The picture that emerges is again one of a closed society. In this case, however, closure is effected more by perfidious social and economic arrangements, ignorance, and poverty than by geographical circumstance *per se.*

Given the foregoing discussion of the images of the countryside, it may seem anomalous to note that Italy (possibly excepting the Tyrol) is pervaded with an urban mentality. Pitkin finds that the Mediterranean culture area may in part be defined by a predilection for urban life, a tendency most notable in Italy (1963:121). A propensity toward nucleated settlement, while most apparent in the south, characterizes the peninsula.

The spectacle of Italian towns and cities perched on rocky precipices and promontories has elicited numerous attempts to "explain" the pattern. Defensive strategies, a need to reside above malarially infested lowlands, and an unwillingness to use valuable arable land for human habitation have all, singly and in combination, been suggested as possible explanations.

If the arguments regarding the origins of the nucleated settlement pattern deal in the plausible rather than the demonstrable, its historical and contemporary ubiquity may not be refuted. Furthermore, there is a concomitant urban world view. Silverman (1975) and Davis (1969) have both noted the extent to which, in small-scale, seemingly rural contexts, *civiltà* ("civility") is equated with life in a nucleated setting. So pronounced is the preference for town residence that many small Italian cities (i.e., in the 30,000-40,000 inhabitants range) are actually dormitory towns peopled by peasants who daily travel considerable distances to cultivate their fields (Pitkin 1959:164). Conversely, in parts of the Abruzzi and Molise peasants who reside on disseminated farmsteads also maintain a town residence (Douglass n.d).

The fact that there is a discernible urban mentality in Italian society and culture, including its rural sector, is itself an important datum when considering the migration history of the peninsula. While it is possible to depict urban Italy and rural Italy as worlds apart, there is also a sense in which the Italian peasant is possibly less awestruck at the prospect of moving to a city than his counterpart in other peasant societies. Furthermore, his propensity for "life with people" may also facilitate his adjustment to the urban milieu. One need only deal with the street-wise Roman taxi driver, who is more likely to have been born in a village of the Abruzzi-Molise than in Rome, to appreciate the nature and extent of this adaptability.

THE DEMOGRAPHIC PROFILE

Table 1 employs official statistics in order to analyze population movement within Italy from the first post-unification census in 1871 to the most recent census in 1971, a time span of one century. Figures for the years 1931 and 1951 are included as well, in order to provide internal brackets that correspond to significant benchmarks in Italian migration history. Thus the period 1871–1931 was that of major transoceanic and intra-European emigration. The 1931–51 period encompasses the two decades during which both external and internal migration were severely limited. Its beginning coincides approximately with the time when Mussolini prohibited emigration. Furthermore, as the Duce prepared Italy for World War II, emphasis was placed upon early marriage, fecundity, and self-sufficiency for the nation. Since Italy was traditionally a major importer of foodstuffs, the fascist government proclaimed "the grain battle," in which even the most marginal land was to be brought under cultivation. Part of the strategy was to lock the peasantry in place. Hence in 1938 severe restrictions upon internal migration, and particularly rural-urban change of residence, were mandated.

World War II limited both external and internal movements of Italians except as a part of military operations. In the immediate aftermath of the war most of the former receiving countries of transoceanic Italian emigration tightened their immigration policies. The surrounding European countries were economically prostrate and unable to absorb sojourning Italian workers. The Italian economy was itself so disrupted that the fascist government's regulations regarding internal migration were left in effect. Consequently, despite its war casualties, during the period 1931–51 Italy's population increased by a hefty 16.2%. The increase was registered broadly across the spectrum of Italian society. The only negative indicator in Table 1 is the 0.75% decline in rural Piedmont.

The period 1951–71 embraces the years of recovery, both in Italy and in neighboring countries. The former translated into what has been labeled the "economic miracle," during which northern Italy emerged as one of Europe's major industrial centers. Developments in the industrial triangle cities of Milan, Turin, and Genoa provided Italy with one of the highest economic growth rates in the world (Hildebrand 1965:vii). Between 1954 and 1961 real gross national product rose by no less than 7.9% annually and inflation was modest (Hildebrand 1965:12).

In 1958 Italy entered the Common Market, which facilitated export of Italian goods as well as excess Italian labor. At the same time overseas emigration again became possible, particularly for those with kinsmen abroad who could expedite arrangements. The combined effects of Common Market and overseas alternatives did not, however, impede noticeable national population growth; between 1951 and 1971 Italy's populace increased by

Table 1. Population Profile of the Regions, Major Cities, and Rural Districts of Italy, 1871–1971

I. Northern Italy

Place	1871	1931	% of Change	1951	% of Change	1971	% of Change	% of Change 1871–1971
PIEDMONT	2,817,430	3,413,677	+ 21.16	3,544,636	+ 3.84	4,461,527	+ 25.87	+ 58.35
Turin	213,414	597,260	+179.86	721,795	+ 20.85	1,187,832	+ 64.57	+456.59
The region excepting provincial capitals	2,432,348	2,545,881	+ 4.67	2,526,671	– .75	2,871,419	+ 13.64	+ 18.05
LIGURIA	851,532	1,436,708	+ 68.72	1,573,790	+ 9.54	1,868,630	+ 18.73	+119.44
Genoa	259,969	608,096	+133.91	687,480	+ 13.05	821,851	+ 19.55	+216.13
The region excepting provincial capitals	518,718	631,306	+ 21.71	674,168	+ 6.79	796,051	+ 18.08	+ 53.47
LOMBARDY	3,442,772	5,546,649	+ 61.11	6,518,421	+ 17.52	8,504,061	+ 30.46	+147.01
Milan	291,424	990,887	+240.02	1,276,521	+ 28.83	1,724,819	+ 35.12	+491.86
The region excepting provincial capitals	2,883,189	4,073,844	+ 41.30	4,652,820	+ 14.21	5,984,051	+ 28.61	+107.55
TRENTINO-ALTO ADIGE	532,174	658,795	+ 23.79	739,394	+ 12.23	845,111	+ 14.30	+ 58.80
Trent	32,547	56,760	+ 74.39	65,375	+ 15.18	94,869	+ 45.12	+191.48
The region excepting provincial capitals	484,686	561,276	+ 15.80	601,728	+ 7.21	645,041	+ 7.20	+ 33.08
VAL D'AOSTA	81,760	80,260	– 1.83	95,924	+ 19.52	111,239	+ 15.97	+ 36.06
Valle D'Aosta	7,669	13,935	+ 81.71	24,839	+ 78.25	39,299	+ 58.21	+412.44
All other communities in the valley	74,091	66,325	– 10.48	71,085	+ 7.18	71,940	+ 1.20	– 2.90
VENETO	2,168,155	3,405,022	+ 57.05	3,834,857	+ 12.62	4,122,697	+ 7.51	+ 90.15
Venice	164,748	260,247	+ 57.97	322,457	+ 23.90	377,587	+ 17.10	+129.19
The region excepting provincial capitals	1,744,724	2,683,681	+ 53.82	2,928,870	+ 9.14	2,940,178	+ .39	+ 68.52

Place	1871	1931	% of Change	1951	% of Change	1971	% of Change	% of Change 1871-1971
FRIULI-VENEZIA-GIULIA	710,912	1,106,149	+ 55.60	1,197,133	+ 8.23	1,244,347	+ 3.94	+ 75.04
Trieste	123,063	249,503	+ 102.74	270,164	+ 8.28	273,928	+ 1.39	+ 122.59
The region excepting provincial capitals	536,759	749,537	+ 39.64	802,257	+ 7.03	765,277	− 4.61	+ 42.57

II. Central Italy

Place	1871	1931	% of Change	1951	% of Change	1971	% of Change	% of Change 1871-1971
EMILIA-ROMAGNA	2,171,558	3,218,270	+ 48.20	3,519,580	+ 9.36	3,853,434	+ 9.49	+ 77.45
Bologna	120,690	256,200	+ 112.28	350,676	+ 36.88	502,421	+ 43.27	+ 316.29
The region excepting provincial capitals	1,669,354	2,356,285	+ 41.15	2,448,989	+ 3.93	2,366,844	− 3.35	+ 41.78
MARCHE	915,419	1,217,746	+ 33.03	1,348,812	+ 10.76	1,350,879	+ .15	+ 47.57
Ancona	47,856	75,372	+ 57.50	86,013	+ 14.12	112,881	+ 31.24	+ 135.88
The region excepting provincial capitals	797,979	1,036,438	+ 29.88	1,129,625	+ 8.99	1,052,639	− 6.82	+ 31.91
TUSCANY	2,089,954	2,895,791	+ 38.56	3,165,016	+ 9.30	3,501,568	+ 10.63	+ 67.54
Florence	197,029	314,998	+ 59.87	390,769	+ 24.05	482,268	+ 23.42	+ 144.77
The region excepting provincial capitals	1,528,301	2,062,667	+ 34.96	2,164,118	+ 4.92	2,261,166	+ 4.48	+ 47.95
UMBRIA	469,050	690,829	+ 47.28	803,762	+ 16.35	779,926	− 2.97	+ 66.28
Perugia	49,503	79,270	+ 60.13	97,265	+ 22.70	131,843	+ 35.55	+ 166.33
The region excepting provincial capitals	397,012	553,116	+ 39.32	622,614	+ 12.56	542,138	− 12.93	+ 36.55
LATIUM*	1,211,371	2,393,229	+ 97.56	3,383,883	+ 41.39	4,754,484	+ 40.50	+292.49
Rome	242,937	1,000,371	+ 311.78	1,701,913	+ 70.13	2,842,616	+ 67.02	+1070.10
The region excepting provincial capitals	911,648	1,310,782	+ 43.78	1,542,221	+ 17.66	1,695,843	+ 9.96	+ 86.02

*Northern Latium is sometimes regarded as part of central Italy and southern Latium a part of the south. However, in order to avoid unnecessary statistical refinements, I have included all of the region within the former.

Table 1 (continued).

III. Southern-Insular Italy

Place	1871	% of Change	1931	% of Change	1951	% of Change	1971	% of Change	% of Change 1871–1971
CAMPANIA	2,492,780	+ 40.08	3,491,978	+ 23.47	4,311,398	+ 15.91	4,997,401	+ 15.91	+ 100.48
Naples	494,252	+ 69.83	839,390	+ 22.06	1,024,543	+ 22.86	1,258,721	+ 22.86	+ 154.67
The region excepting provincial capitals	1,897,078	+ 30.95	2,484,285	+ 23.04	3,056,726	+ 11.19	3,398,715	+ 11.19	+ 79.16
ABRUZZI-MOLISE	1,234,440	+ 20.58	1,488,453	+ 8.85	1,620,112	– 11.63	1,431,636	– 11.63	+ 15.97
Pescara	11,535	+ 229.40	37,996	+ 69.65	64,460	+ 89.34	122,048	+ 89.34	+ 958.07
The region excepting provincial capitals	1,130,067	+ 16.43	1,315,778	+ 5.81	1,392,218	– 22.05	1,085,173	– 22.05	– 3.97
APULIA	1,440,276	+ 72.97	2,491,270	+ 28.17	3,193,164	+ 9.40	3,493,265	+ 9.40	+ 142.54
Bari	61,574	+ 182.60	174,010	+ 57.35	273,801	+ 33.25	364,852	+ 33.25	+ 492.54
The region excepting provincial capitals	1,278,673	+ 61.70	2,067,651	+ 21.92	2,520,954	+ 2.48	2,583,446	+ 2.48	+ 102.04
BASILICATA	510,543	– .55	507,750	+ 21.32	616,009	– 8.24	565,252	– 8.24	+ 10.72
Potenza	18,513	+ 23.17	22,803	+ 44.94	33,050	+ 76.26	58,253	+ 76.26	+ 214.66
The region excepting provincial capitals	477,718	– 2.72	464,704	+ 18.88	552,448	– 16.29	462,465	– 16.29	– 3.18
CALABRIA	1,206,302	+ 38.35	1,668,954	+ 18.79	1,982,473	– 6.35	1,856,586	– 6.35	+ 53.91
Reggio di Calabria	62,021	+ 74.87	108,459	+ 28.58	139,459	+ 16.49	162,450	+ 16.49	+ 161.93
The region excepting provincial capitals	1,102,387	+ 34.48	1,482,494	+ 16.30	1,724,076	– 12.71	1,504,990	– 12.71	+ 36.52
SICILY	2,584,099	+ 50.80	3,896,866	+ 13.96	4,440,936	+ 3.19	4,582,541	+ 3.19	+ 77.34
Palermo	222,156	+ 75.42	389,699	+ 29.11	503,137	+ 30.65	657,326	+ 30.65	+ 195.88
The island excepting provincial capitals	2,018,403	+ 40.69	2,839,647	+ 8.80	3,089,611	– 6.58	2,886,192	– 6.58	+ 42.99

	1871	1931	% of Change	1951	% of Change	1971	% of Change	% of Change 1871–1971
SARDINIA	636,660	973,125	+ 52.85	1,269,438	+ 30.45	1,445,787	+ 13.89	+ 127.09
Cagliari	40,349	98,992	+ 145.34	142,744	+ 44.20	231,670	+ 62.30	+ 474.17
The island excepting provincial capitals	557,898	811,266	+ 45.41	1,037,162	+ 27.84	1,073,830	+ 3.54	+ 92.48

IV. Summaries

Place	1871	1931	% of Change	1951	% of Change	1971	% of Change	% of Change 1871–1971
Northern Italy	10,604,735	15,647,260	+ 47.55	17,504,155	+ 11.87	21,157,612	+ 20.87	+ 99.51
Central Italy	6,857,352	10,325,865	+ 50.58	12,221,053	+ 18.35	14,240,291	+ 16.52	+ 107.66
Southern-Insular Italy	10,105,100	14,518,396	+ 43.67	17,433,530	+ 20.08	18,372,468	+ 5.39	+ 81.81
All Italy	27,567,187	40,581,521	+ 47.21	47,158,738	+ 16.21	53,770,371	+ 14.02	+ 95.05

From Istituto Centrale di Statistica, 1967, 1972.

14%. During the same period internal migration, largely of a rural-urban nature, emerged as the country's most important demographic issue.

Table 1 arranges the statistics by regions within the broad designations of northern, cental and southern-insular Italy. Figures[2] are given for each region as a whole (but not individual provinces within it), its major city, and all communities excepting provincial capitals. This last category designates an essentially rural milieu, since in Italy virtually every city of any consequence is also a provincial capital.

There are many demographic trends discernible over the past century of Italian population history. Of paramount interest is the fact that despite a net loss of several million emigrants, Italy's populace more than doubled (from 26,567,000 in 1871 to 53,770,000 in 1971). However, the gains were not distributed evenly across the various regions and sectors of Italian society. To the extent that some areas registered population gains in excess of natural increase while others failed to attain expected levels, we are dealing with internal migration patterns. While they are often treated under the general rubrics of "rural exodus" and "rural-urban migration," there are actually several processes at work. First, there is depopulation of mountainous habitats apparent throughout Italy. Second, there is intraprovincial and intraregional rural-urban displacement. Third, there is movement from throughout Italy to certain urban megalopolises.[3] Each may be treated in turn.

Depopulation of the Highlands

The major cities in Italy are located at or slightly above sea level, so that statistically any treatment of rural-urban migration would presumably reflect a degree of depopulation of mountainous zones. However, it is also clear that within the rural sector of Italian society the magnitude of population decline generally correlates with elevation; i.e., the greater the elevation the greater the decline. For Italy as a whole the percentage of the populace living below 100 meters above sea level increased from 36.5% in 1886 to 43.3% in 1951. Conversely, during the same period the numbers of persons residing over 600 meters above sea level declined from 12.1% to 8.5% of the national population (Tagliacarne 1966:6). This population shift represents more than simple within-Italy rural-urban transfer. Rather, the higher mountainous regions are major staging areas of both emigration and internal rural-rural migration. In the latter instance the movement is from the harsher high mountain climes to agricultural districts of the foothills and the plains. (While the generalization is essentially true for the nation, there are exceptions. Between 1951 and 1961, for example, the Venetian plain registered a net decline of – 2.07% in its population, concentrated, however, mainly in the Po delta (Rovigo – 22.4%), which is an inhospitable agricultural environment (Gasparini 1966:152).)

Table 2 profiles the trends between 1871 and 1961 in the provinces of

Turin, Modena, Foggia, and Palermo, samples from northern, central, southern, and insular Italy. Without contending that the process is ubiquitous throughout the nation (contrary cases could be cited), the examples suggest that it is not limited to any particular region within it.

Thus we find that over the 90-year period the mountainous districts of both Turin and Foggia actually registered notable population decline, whereas in Palermo and Modena the gains were considerably below what might have been expected from natural increase. The plains districts of all four provinces, which contain the major urban centers, all experienced sharp increases, ranging from 86.08% in Modena to 206.47% in Turin. At the same time the populace of the foothills districts, basically an agrarian zone, registered respectable gains in all four provinces, clustering in the plus-20 percentile range in Turin, Foggia, and Palermo and showing a startling increase of 123.05% in Modena. Indeed, for the latter the growth rate actually outstripped that of the plains, although in terms of actual numbers of persons it was more modest.

Two patterns of rural-rural migration are discernible within recent Italian history. On the one hand there is intraprovincial and intraregional (or between contiguous regions) movement of agriculturalists from the highlands to more productive lowland climes (Barberis 1966b:50–54). At the same time there has been a degree of "southernization" of North Italian agriculture. Barberis notes that during the decade 1950–60 approximately one-tenth of South Italian migrants to North Italy remained in agricultural pursuits (1966a:29), as either salaried fieldhands or, in some cases, new proprietors of smallholdings. The defection from agriculture is more noticeable

Table 2. Population Distribution by Altimetric Zones within Italy, 1871–1961

Province	Classification of Terrain	Population in 1871	Population in 1961	% of Change
Turin	Mountainous	194,855	140,959	− 27.66
	Foothills	227,323	283,079	+ 24.54
	Plains	468,895	1,437,031	+ 206.47
Modena	Mountainous	51,545	55,751	+ 8.16
	Foothills	37,354	83,318	+ 123.05
	Plains	196,663	365,954	+ 86.08
Foggia	Mountainous	28,942	23,626	− 18.37
	Foothills	150,556	188,819	+ 25.41
	Plains	162,644	420,447	+ 158.51
Palermo	Mountainous	121,991	125,049	+ 2.51
	Foothills	243,765	327,580	+ 34.38
	Plains	255,771	649,672	+ 154.01

From Istituto Centrale di Statistica, 1967.

among northern Italian women than men, so another development is for northern males to marry southern women willing to remain on a farm (Saunders 1980:828).

From this brief review, then, several caveats emerge that must be taken into account when evaluating rural-urban migration in Italy. First, the "rural crisis" is more pronounced in the mountainous districts. Second, many of Italy's agricultural areas have actually registered substantial population increases over the last century. Third, in some cases such increase is not due solely to natural increment of the local populace but, rather, reflects a degree of rural-rural migration. The magnitude of the latter for a particular period is greater than the simple formula: rate of rural-rural migration (RRM) equals actual population (AP) minus prior local base population (LBR) plus natural increase (NI), or,

$$RRM = AP - LBP + NI$$

Rather, in many relatively favored agricultural districts there is a rate of out-migration from the local population that is more than compensated for by the in-migration of persons from more marginal agricultural zones. Thus the appropriate equation is: rate of rural-rural migration (RRM) equals actual population (AP) minus prior local base population (LBP) plus natural increase (NI) minute local outmigration (LO), or,

$$RRM = AP - LBP + NI - LO$$

Intraprovincial and Intraregional Rural-Urban Migration

Without exception every provincial capital in Italy has experienced considerable population increase, both prior to and during the time period under consideration. In part this is a simple reflection of the progressive bureaucratization of Italian life, paralleled by a strong tendency to centralize industry by siting it in capital cities.

The pattern of rural-urban migration between hinterland and provincial capitals is longstanding. To cite an example from the remote past, much of the sharp increment in the populations of the city-republics of northern and central Italy during the twelfth and thirteenth centuries has been attributed to locally circumscribed rural-urban movement (Waley 1969:34–38). In fact, the tendency was so pronounced that a number of republics, fearing a food shortage, promulgated laws forbidding agriculturalists to relocate in the city (p. 38). Such measures notwithstanding, every Italian city has an active history of two-directional interaction with its immediate rural hinterland. Today it is a rare rural family that lacks relatives in the nearby provincial capital, as well as one or two kinsmen in the region's major city. For the student of migration there are considerable social and economic implications in such arrangements.

Prior to World War II rural-urban migration within Italy entailed three probable destinations (in descending order of preference): (1) from a

Table 3. Population Growth of the Major City and the Remaining Provincial Capitals of the Regions of Piedmont, Emilia-Romagna, Apulia, and Sicily, 1871–1971

Place	Population in 1871	Population in 1971	% of Change
PIEDMONT			
Turin	213,414	1,187,832	+ 456.59
All other provincial capitals	171,668	402,276	+ 134.38
EMILIA–ROMAGNA			
Bologna	120,690	502,421	+ 316.29
All other provincial capitals	381,514	984,169	+ 157.96
APULIA			
Bari	61,574	364,852	+ 492.54
All other provincial capitals	100,029	544,967	+ 444.81
SICILY			
Palermo	222,156	657,326	+ 195.88
All other provincial capitals	343,540	1,039,023	+ 202.45

From Istituto Centrale di Statistica 1967, 1972.

particular rural hinterland to its provincial capital; (2) from a particular rural hinterland to the region's major city; and (3) from the countryside and smaller urban centers to Rome.

The last pattern will be treated in the next section; the first and second trends are best examined in tandem. Table 3 profiles examples of the major city and the remaining provincial capitals in the regions of Piedmont, Emilia-Romagna, Apulia, and Sicily (the same regions from which the examples in Table 2 are drawn).

In the cases of the Piedmont and Emilia-Romagna the growth rate of the major city is much greater than that of the provincial capitals. In Apulia the major city has grown somewhat more rapidly than the provincial capitals, while in Sicily the latter have increased at a slightly greater rate than Palermo. These trends would support the generalization that in parts of northern and central Italy the major city has far outstripped the remaining provincial capitals, whereas in southern Italy (excepting Rome) the rate of growth of the regional center and the remaining provincial capitals is more equivalent.

The pronounced increase of certain cities such as Turin, Genoa, Milan, Florence, and Bologna will be examined in the next section. At this juncture, however, a distinction between growth rate and population numbers should be made. In the case of many provincial capitals the initial base population from which the subsequent growth rate is derived numbers in the tens of thousands. A prime example in Table 1 is Pescara, which during the period under consideration increased by 958%. However, its 1971 population was only 122,048 inhabitants, up from 11, 535 residents a century earlier. If the statistics for Sicily are refined accordingly, between 1871 and 1971 Palermo alone grew by 435,170 persons, accounting for fully 38.5% of the total increase in the population of the island's nine provincial capitals.

The impressive growth of each region's major city is due to compounding of the factors underlying the urban development of the provincial capitals. In addition to serving as the capital for its own province, the major city is usually the seat of the regional government as well. Again an exception is Pescara, which, however, nicely illustrates the argument, since in the early 1970s the city was the scene of bloody rioting as residents protested the smaller L'Aquila's right to house regional governmental services. Similarly, the tendency to site industry in capital cities is even more pronounced in the case of regional governmental centers. Finally, geographical factors can contribute to the importance of the regional center. Both Bari and Palermo are major seaports.

Movement to Certain Urban Megalopolises

Rome was mentioned as a possible destination of migrants from throughout the nation. Over the past century no Italian city has grown at a faster rate — from 242,937 inhabitants in the first census after unification (1871) to 2,842,616 persons in the last national census (1971), or an increase on the order of plus 1070%. The city's impressive growth is both unique and somewhat "artificial," deriving almost exclusively from its function as the national capital rather than from the emergence of autochthonous industry. Rome therefore epitomizes the service-based economy, attracting migrants from every corner of the nation and every walk of life — from the elected representative, attorney, and university professor to the bootblack.

Another focus of pronounced growth, dependent in part upon interregional population transfers, is found in central Italy. Both Bologna and Florence have emerged as major centers, drawing substantial numbers of migrants from the rural districts of the Marches (Centro Nazionale di Prevenzione e Difesa Sociale 1966:206).

Of greatest importance with respect to both sheer magnitude and overall impact within the national economy, however, are the developments within the industrial triangle. The cities of Milan, Turin, and Genoa have experienced spectacular growth since unification. It was during the first two decades of Italian nationhood that many of the country's major industries were founded, and the majority were sited within the industrial triangle (Jucker 1970:28–29). Between 1871 and 1901 the combined populations of

Genoa, Turin, and Milan increased by slightly more than half a million persons (Istituto Centrale di Statistica 1967:3, 5).

In large measure this initial industrialization and attendant urbanization of the triangle cities was a localized North Italian phenomenon. Most of the population growth was registered at the expense of impoverished rural districts throughout North Italy. We earlier noted the extent to which the region of the Veneto was affected by transoceanic and intra-European emigration during the latter part of the nineteenth century; internal migration from the region to the triangle cities was also prevalent. As a consequence, between 1871 and 1901 the population of the region's major city, Venice, increased by only 23,551 persons (Istituto Centrale di Statistica 1967:5).

The period of truly spectacular growth in the industrial triangle cities is the post–World War II era. In considering this trend, magnitude of increase as measured in population numbers is more significant than growth rate *per se.* Thus between 1951 and 1971, for example, the Valle d'Aosta experienced a growth rate of 58% while acquiring only 14,460 new residents. Conversely, the rate of increase in Milan was only 35%, which, however, supposed a net gain of 453,238 residents over a 20-year period. Nor may the recent increment in the industrial triangle be computed solely in terms of population movement to the three major cities. Rather, each has now developed its satellites of smaller manufacturing towns. Industry in the area is no longer as centralized as it once was (Mannucci 1970:257). Consequently, the net population gain within Liguria, Piedmont, and Lombardy between 1945 and 1970 has been more on the order of 6 million persons (Pellicciari 1970)!

RURAL MIGRANTS IN URBAN CONTEXTS

The literature on rural migrant adaptation to city life is both extensive and limited. It is extensive in the sense that the post–World War II developments discussed above have brought rural-urban migration squarely to the attention of Italian and non-Italian journalists, anthropologists, political scientists, economists, sociologists, and social historians alike. It is limited in both a chronological and geographical sense, since the large majority of studies deal with post–World War II patterns in the urban megalopolises of the industrial triangle[4] (as well as Rome and Naples to a lesser degree). The following discussion, then, is drawn primarily from studies of post–World War II rural migrant adaptation to the industrial milieu of North Italy. It is also limited largely to the years of the first wave of migration, which coincided with the economic boom of the late 1950s and early 1960s. Subsequent developments will be considered in the conclusion.

Who Are the Migrants?

The industrial triangle has attracted professionals and skilled workers

from throughout the nation. However, most of the area's population increase is represented by unskilled rural migrant labor. Initially, or during
the early 1950s, the majority were drawn from poor agricultural districts
within the industrial triangle regions themselves (Villani 1966:97). Increasingly, however, the migrants derived from two extraregional sources, Veneto and the south. With respect to the former, between 1951 and 1961, of the
240,000 persons who abandoned agriculture, fully 190,000 left the region,
relocating primarily in Piedmont (Gasparini 1966:152). Of greater significance, however, is the fact that between 1955 and 1970 an average of 84,000
South Italians annually migrated to the industrial triangle (Golini 1978:
402).[5] Of the 4.5 million persons who left South Italy between 1951
and 1975, 58% were internal migrants, 90% of whom resettled in the north
(Malfatti 1976:151–52).

Why this should be the case is reflected in a few stark statistics. South
Italy is heavily populated (17,433,530 inhabitants in 1951) yet has little industry, an underdeveloped commercial infrastructure, an arid climate, and
an adverse topography (two-thirds of the area is mountainous versus one-
third of North Italy) (Cafiero and De' Rossi 1966:79). Natural increment in
South Italy's population is among the highest in Europe, and more than
twice that of the natural growth rate in North Italy (Vicinelli 1966:133).
Despite this disparity the population of the south increased less than that of
the north over the past century (18.8% versus 99.5%), due in part to a high
rate of out-migration. Throughout the period economic growth and expansion of the labor market have transpired mainly in the north. By 1970, 90%
of all Italian industry and 91% of all firms employing more than 50 workers
were located in central and northern Italy (Sacchetti 1971:144).[6]

The resulting population transfer from the south to the north, with its
attendant problems, have made the "southernization" *(meridionalizzazione)* of
Italian life a hotly debated national issue (Centro Nazionale di Prevenzione
e Difessa Sociale 1966:208). The contrasting values, lifestyle, and even
physical appearance of North and South Italians provide ethnocentric overtones to the debate. For the biased North Italian the southerner is a *terrone*
(earth grubber) or *marocchino* (Moroccan).[7] He is a little, dark, uncouth man
who is loud of speech, hot-headed and volatile, dangerous when crossed,
prone to criminality (e.g., a possible *mafioso*), given to fathering broods
of children, and unconcerned with personal hygiene. For the biased
southerner the North Italian is a *polentone* (one who eats *polenta,* a kind of ce-
real pudding that is particularly offensive to the southern palate). He is a
cold, reserved, and aloof man embued with a sense of his own superiority.

Students of migrant adaptation in the industrial triangle are often at
pains to demonstrate that the "invasion" from the south is overstated (e.g.,
Mannucci 1970:258 notes that in the upper Milanese area less than 30% of
the migrants are from the south),[8] as is the reputed unwillingness of south-

erners to adapt to northern conditions. (Fofi 1970:282–84 underscores the fact that southerners participated fully with their Piedmontese counterparts in the first major strike against Fiat as evidence of southerner assimilation). However, that such arguments are felt to be necessary at all itself under-scores the pervasiveness of antisoutherner bias and the fragility of northern-er-southerner social relations. In point of fact, it is apparent that southerners are frequently denied housing and job mobility and are unduly subjected to official surveillance and even harassment (Baglivo and Pellicciari 1973).[9]

In evaluating rural migrant adaptation in Italy, then, we are not mere-ly faced with a situation of urbanite snobbery vis-à-vis country bumpkinism. Rather, there is the further element of overt discrimination that assumes racist overtones. That such is the case is underscored by job and housing ad-vertisements in northern newspapers that state "No southerner need apply" and "We do not rent to southerners" (Schreiber 1973:127). It is also seen in the relative lack of interaction between southerners and northerners in the recreational and associational spheres. Southerners frequent their own bars and restaurants (Majorino 1970:307–8), whose clientele is likely drawn from a highly circumscribed southern locality, possibly a single community (Siegel n.d.:8). To the extent that they articulate with northerners, the con-text tends to be lower-class establishments (which scarcely gives the south-erner a comprehensive view of North Italian life) (Majorino 1970:313). While some southerners manage to establish ties with northerners,[10] it is usually on an individual basis, and also partly predicated upon the person's ability to "desouthernize" himself (p. 312). Conversely, as a group, south-erners participate minimally in the voluntary associations of the wider com-munity. Such is even the case with respect to the Church, which southerners find to be "foreign" in its North Italian form (Monelli and Pellicciari 1970:334, 336; Kertzer 1977:226–28).

Finally, relations between the sexes are an arena in which interaction can reach the flash point. The two groups have differing value systems re-garding the relationship between feminine chastity and family honor. Vio-lence may ensue when the males of a southern family mistrust the advances of a northerner toward their sister/daughter (Schreiber 1973:118) or young northern males object to the overtures of "latin lovers" to local girls (Major-ino 1970:313). Not surprisingly, the intermarriage rates between the two groups remain low (Moretti 1970:57).

The Migration Process

As a potential rural migrant contemplates his options, the industrial tri-angle presents certain advantages and disadvantages over Common Market and transoceanic destinations. Chief among the former is the informational factor. During the postwar period public educational programs and the mass media have expanded considerably the mental horizons of the peasantry.

One doubts that there is a single *contadino* left who has not heard of Turin or Milan and lacks at least some preconception of life there. Furthermore, with each passing year movement to the industrial triangle gains a momentum of its own, as the bases for continued chain migration become more firmly established.[11] Thus the potential migrant is likely to have kinsmen or at least acquaintances in the city who have preceded him and who are potential sources of assistance. Former migrants who resettle in the village are founts of information.[12] Similarly, there is considerable feedback to the villages as migrants return on holiday. The veritable glut of automobiles with northern license plates found throughout South Italy in the vacation month of August and during the Christmas season itself has a "demonstration" effect that success may be achieved in the city. Finally, while there are apparent dialectical and cultural differences between the north and the south, the potential migrant knows that in the industrial triangle he would have at least some working familiarity with the language and way of life.

On the negative side[13] the internal migrant can expect little in the way of governmental assistance. If he opts for a Common Market destination, there is a defined support network of assured jobs, travel assistance, receiving centers, and even temporary subsidies for his family back in Italy.[14] In Milan or Turin, however, the most he can expect is job and housing advice provided by an informational office in the train station (Melilli 1966:193–94), and over time the effectiveness of even these minimal services has declined (Baglivo and Pellicciari 1973:75–76). Relatively perfunctory assistance is rendered to the more critical cases by religious charitable organizations (Fofi 1970:279).

Migrant Adaptation in the Urban Milieu:
The Initial Period

Given the sheer magnitude of rural-urban migration, the cultural distinctions between urbanites and peasants, and the general antisoutherner sentiment in North Italy, we might expect that the recent history of peasant adaptation to urban life would be problematic at best. To this sad litany, however, may be added the fact that the migrants were, until the mid-1960s, technically outlaws. Fascist legislation from the 1930s designed to keep the peasantry on the land was not repealed during the first two decades of the postwar period.

The rural migrant therefore faced a classic Catch-22 situation. The law stated that he could not apply for employment without having an established residence in the city, and he could not rent or purchase a residence without demonstrating that he had a job (Capo 1966:124, Mannucci 1970:263). While the national legislation was clear, in practice it came to be ignored by the local authorities in places like Milan and Turin, where, during the years of industrial expansion, there was only one local candidate for each new job that was created (Cafiero and De' Rossi 1966:86). Migrants were accorded "provisional residence" (Fofi 1970:276). However, while providing them with a foothold in the city, the fiction also placed them beyond the pale of statutory protection in both housing and job markets, making them easy prey for the unscrupulous.

In the area of housing there were essentially two approaches. The first pattern is described vividly by Fofi for Turin and may be labeled the "downtown solution." On the one hand, enterprising locals purchased the dilapidated garrets in Old Turin and rented them to migrants. The rents were exorbitant and there was therefore a tendency for several persons to share quarters, thereby overcrowding already inadequate facilities. Similarly, locals put six or eight cots into an extra room in their own apartments and paid their whole rent by gouging the migrants (Fofi 1970:274–76). Over time some of the properties were acquired by migrants themselves who were not always above profiting from the defenselessness of their fellows. In this fashion the most dilapidated neighborhoods came to be dominated by migrants, characterized by high population concentrations and deteriorating living conditions and public services.

The other alternative, described by Villani (1966) for Milan and Capo (1966) for Rome, might be labeled the "outskirts solution." Reference is to the creation of the slum or *corea*[15] at or beyond the fringe of the city. Villani notes that as all urban center property increased in value to the point where commercial, industrial, or modern expensive housing were the only rational uses, the dilapidated dwellings disappeared. At the same time farmers with land two or three kilometers beyond the city limits found themselves squeezed by a rural labor shortage, poor farm prices, and soaring taxes owing to increasing value of their plots for nonagricultural uses. They were therefore receptive to middlemen, frequently entrepreneurial migrants themselves, who purchased or took on consignment blocks of land which they subdivided into house sites (frequently as small as 100 square meters in size) for sale to desperate, displaced migrant families. In some cases more than one family had to pool its resources to erect a veritable shanty on the tiny parcel. The new owners then scrounged for building materials, provided the labor themselves, and often occupied the dwelling before the walls were even completed.

The typical *corea* was devoid of virtually every service. Lacking sewers, one family's well was another's cesspool. Electricity and inside plumbing were unattainable luxuries. When it came to paved streets and public lighting, not to mention such amenities as parks and schools, local officials largely ignored the "phantom" settlements. Even the parish priest might be little concerned with his new parishioners (Villani 1966:98–100). If the migrant had established a tenuous physical presence in the city, he remained in social and spiritual limbo.[16]

There are ways, however, in which the migrant urban ghetto and fringe slum impacted inevitably (and negatively) upon the wider society. Adjacent neighborhoods and communities were the ones to feel the immediate brunt. Two areas of particular concern were schooling and medical care. Lacking their own facilities, the migrants used the schools and clinics of contiguous areas that had nominal jurisdiction over, and hence responsibility for, the migrant district. Mannucci cites a case in the upper Milanese area in which 2,000 children were crowded into 29 classrooms, forcing the authorities to go to split sessions and reduced hours of instruction for each student (1970:259).[17] Similarly, municipalities were responsible for underwriting hospital care, for which they were normally subsequently reimbursed through insurance plans. However, since in about 70% of the cases migrants lacked coverage, enormous uncollectable obligations were rapidly incurred (Mannucci 1970:259). Villani (1966) provides a laundry list of such problems, which have brought community after community in the greater Milan area, as well as the city itself, to the brink of bankruptcy.

Life in the dilapidated inner city or the fringe *corea* was the residential purgatory borne by the majority of migrants in the industrial triangle. However, to speak of purgatory supposes the existence of hell. For the truly unfortunate even the slum dwelling was unattainable and home was a stable, a tool shed, a wine cellar, or a hillside cave. Then there was the extreme case in Turin of a Sardinian family with seven children living in the subterranean labyrinth of the city's sewer, using a manhole cover as their front door (Albertelli and Ziliani 1970:288)!

The migrants' circumstance in the job market was no better. In retrospect, it seems clear that many small- and large-scale industrialists depended upon the migrants as both a source of cheap labor and a scab alternative that inhibited the capacity of the local labor force to strike. Migrant laborers were organized by middlemen (frequently earlier, experienced migrants themselves) into illegal labor cooperatives. The middlemen contracted with the owners on a piece-work basis. Most of the unskilled jobs were covered in this fashion, but in some cases members of such cooperatives worked on the assembly lines alongside regularly salaried employees. The difference was that the migrant was paid two-thirds or even half the going rate for the same work. Nor did he qualify for regular insurance and benefit programs, a considerable additional payroll savings for the employer. The earnings of its members were paid directly to the cooperative in a lump sum, from which its organizers then deducted a fee that could amount to as much as half of the member's earnings (Fofi 1970:272).

Recruitment of workers for the cooperatives was well organized. Recruiters traveled throughout the south looking for potential migrants, making exaggerated promises, and contracting for their services (Baglivo and Pellicciari 1973:62–63). Similarly, they worked the migrant trains, searching out individuals without a prior job offer (p. 68). The train stations in places like Milan have been called "slave markets," where recruiters vied for control of the migrant's destiny (pp. 69–83). This whole system of recruitment and delivery of labor to industry through the cooperatives was reputed to be controlled by the Mafia (pp. 104–21).

Paralleling the system of labor cooperatives was that of the small gang (five-ten men) specializing in the building trades. These usually consisted of persons who were related and/or who were from the same rural area. Their success depended upon the shrewdness of their leader, who contracted their services on a piece-work basis. Such groups demonstrated remarkable ingenuity in a generally hostile and alien environment, and usually secured more equitable recompense for their members. They remained, however, bereft of work benefits such as health and unemployment insurance, and thereby placed their members at considerable personal risk (Fofi 1970:273).

Fofi notes that the migrant's dream was to enter the regular industrial labor force. In the case of Turin a job at Fiat was equated with attainment of earthly paradise. The harsher reality, however, was that the factory owners issued short-term contracts of three months' duration to the migrant laborers. Faced with such tenuous employment, the migrant was unlikely to protest dangerous working conditions or unrecompensed overtime. Furthermore, he bore the immediate brunt of any short-range downturn in the fortunes of the enterprise. His was the classic case of "last hired, first fired" (Fofi 1970:273–74).

One can distinguish an industrial career trajectory that, if not typical for every migrant, characterized the job mobility of many. On first arriving in the city he was essentially unskilled and unconversant with urban life. During his initial adaptive stage he was likely to be underemployed in menial tasks secured through personal ties within a labor cooperative or a labor gang. Construction work represented somewhat of an advance and minimal preparation for a factory job.

Success or failure was predicated more than simply upon the acquisition of job skills, however. Rather, the rural migrant had to make the mental transition from the rhythm of his life in agriculture to the hectic and demanding schedule of industrial employment. Seemingly minor discrepancies could lead to major misunderstandings, as reflected in the example of migrants losing their jobs because they failed to show up on rainy days, applying a rural assumption regarding the relationship between weather and work (Capo 1966:130).

While the literature on migrant employment focuses upon the industrial sector, another syndrome is apparent in Rome, if not in the industrial triangle. Rome is a service center *par excellence,* and one can discern migrants clustered in certain occupational sectors. Mention was made of the high proportion of Molisani employed as taxi drivers in the city. There is also a contingent from the region owning restaurants in Rome. Here, again, we are dealing with a career trajectory. Entry into the latter category requires capital and working familarity with urban life, both of which can be acquired while driving a taxi (the former occupation of the majority of restaurant owners). At times, however, the occupational niche is considerably more circumscribed in that persons from a single village or district may monopolize it and remain therein. For example, many chestnut vendors in Rome are from Schiavi d'Abruzzo, and most migrants to the city from Schiavi sell chestnuts.

In sum, in the city the rural migrant encounters prejudice, discrimination, lack of services, poor housing, and job insecurity. The statistical litany underscores many of the problems and their consequences. Between 1959 and 1970 fewer than 10% of the migrants to Milan were able to obtain public housing (Baglivo and Pellicciari 1973:84–85). Only 5% of the migrant labor force found employment through official (and thereby protected) channels (p. 99). Ninety percent of the city's unemployed were southerners (p. 92). More than 90% of inmates of one prison were southerners (p. 174).

Why, then, did they come? Need we look much beyond the simple fact that in 1957 per capita income in the north was three times that of the south and was still twice as much ten years later (Moretti 1970:158–59)?

THOSE WHO REMAIN

At the outset we noted that rural-urban migration patterns can only be properly understood within the broader context of overall migration opportunities and strategies. Similarly, it is myopic to restrict the analysis to developments within the receiving areas. Migration as a social phenomenon is more than a concatenation of isolated events (i.e., the decisions of individual actors to leave their natal community). Rather, it is a process that creates an ongoing dialectic between host and donor societies. Each migrant becomes a possible source of feedback in many forms (information and resources). He constitutes an element in the anticipatory socialization of his fellow villagers as they evaluate in personal terms the merits of remaining or leaving. His departure impacts upon his home community in a variety of ways, affecting former social, economic, and political arrangements as well as the equation between population and natural resources. A family has lost a member, an employer an employee, a field one of its tillers, a patron one of his clients, and a priest one of his parishioners. There is a sense in which no two migrants ever leave precisely the same ambiance, even if their birth certificates state that they are from the same village.

What, then, have been the consequences of migration for the structure of rural Italian society? While there is a literature regarding nineteenth- and early twentieth-century trends (largely in response to overseas emigration), the following treatment is limited to post–World War II patterns.

In recent years both the percentage of the Italian work force active in agriculture and the actual numbers of agriculturalists have declined dramatically. In 1951, 8,261,000 persons (42% of the work force) engaged in farming. A decade later the respective figures were 5,657,000 persons and 29% (Barberis 1966a:25). The figures provide a stark statistical profile of what is labeled the "rural exodus," the contraction of rural Italian society owing to migration in all its forms.

Several selective factors are evident in the postwar rural exodus. The typical candidate is the young male. Consequently there is progressive aging and feminization of the rural sector of Italian society (Barberis 1963). If in 1931 34.8% of the active agricultural work force was under 25 years of age, by 1961 the figure stood at only 19.2%. The percentage of agriculturalists over 45 years of age has increased from 33.3% to 42.6% (Barberis 1966a:31). During the same period the percentage of women in the agricultural work force grew from 19% to 26.6% (p. 33). With respect to the latter trend it is the *vedova bianca,* or "white widow," who is becoming more common. Reference is to the wife of a migrant sojourning in a Common Market country or the industrial triangle who remains behind to manage the family's landholdings.

Not surprisingly, the sharpest declines in the agricultural work force have been registered in the ranks of salaried permanent farm laborers and seasonal migrant farm workers. In 1951 there were 1,837,000 of the former in the nation, a figure which had been reduced to 589,000 by 1964 (Barberis 1996a:36). The seasonal migrant farm worker has all but disappeared (from 560,000 in 1910 to 135,000 in 1961) (p. 27).

Contraction of the rural populace is not, however, limited to the loss of individual males. During the postwar period it has become increasingly common for whole farming families to abandon agriculture (Baglioni 1966:19).

The foregoing would suggest that the rural sector of Italian society has undergone profound debilitation within a highly circumscribed time frame. Furthermore, there are ominous signs of further contractions. In 1963 the average size of the agricultural family in the plains and foothill districts was 3.44 persons, while in the mountainous areas it was only 2.98 members (Barberis 1966a:36). Consequently many farming domestic groups now consist of a solitary middle-aged couple all of whose offspring have migrated elsewhere. Such units are clearly incapable of reproducing themselves on the land in the next generation. The fact that young peasant women are now little disposed to marry a man who intends to remain in agriculture (Alberoni 1970:311) scarcely bodes well for the future of the rural lifestyle.

Migration also tends to be selective from an educational standpoint. While, as we have seen, the literature on urban adaptation of rural migrants underscores their low level of formal schooling and job training, viewed in rural context the picture shifts. Rather, it is the better educated, the functionally literate individual who is most likely to leave (Barberis 1966a:30).[18] This means that on the one hand there is a "brain drain" from the countryside; on the other, and despite the recent democratization and expansion of the Italian school system, rural illiteracy rates remain stubbornly high. For example, in the Veneto 67.7% of all agriculturalists were illiterate as recently as the mid-1960s (Gasparini 1966:164). For Italy as a whole, between 1951 and 1963, the percentage of male agriculturalists without any kind of school degree actually rose from 36.4% to 48.6% (Barberis 1966a:32).

Finally, it should be noted that within the rural community migration is not limited to the peasant sector. Indeed, in the south the migration rate is higher among artisans and merchants (De Luca 1966:76). Consequently the typical rural community is not only losing its cultivators but its entire infrastructure is contracting. Those who decide to remain are therefore faced with the prospect of declining services in many areas of life.

The picture is not, however, uniformly gloomy. There has been some decentralization of industry within postwar Italy, so that in some selected areas the rural resident actually enjoys a greater *in situ* range of economic opportunity than was formerly the case. In the foothill regions of the Veneto this process is so advanced that one can distinguish a kind of part-time–farmer/commuter–factory-worker syndrome. By the mid-1960s, in 43% of the area's families censused as "agriculturalist," one or more active adults had a nonagricultural profession (Gasparini 1966:168). It is this agricultural/industrial zone that has manifested the greatest demographic stability for the region during the postwar period.

On balance, all of the foregoing developments could scarcely help but have profound implications for the structure of the rural family and the peasant community. Regarding the former it is clear that the traditional patriarchal system in which fathers controlled the destinies of their sons is largely shattered. The migration alternative provides young male dependents with newfound leverage (Douglass n.d.). To a lesser degree, the same is true regarding female dependence/independence within the rural family (Barberis 1966a:37).

In several respects migration can entail profound human costs for the children of migrant families. At times both parents leave for an extended period of time, entrusting their offspring to relatives or placing them in boarding schools. In some cases the reasoning is economic while in others it is cultural; i.e., the parents feel that the children are better off in the home region rather than in the migrant ghettoes of urban Italy or in foreign lands. In either case the children are subjected to painful separation, possibly even losing contact with their siblings when brothers and sisters are boarded in different institutions. In the bargain they may develop lifelong resentment with respect to their parents. The psychological effects upon children raised without an immediate adult role model have yet to be delineated fully (Schreiber 1973:176–92).

With respect to the peasant community, it is evident that the general aging of the population poses formidable problems of a social welfare nature. The proportion of persons requiring charity, pensions, and medical services has clearly converted rural Italy into an enormous burden upon the gross national product (Barberis 1966a:40). Yet Clark believes that without such postwar social security benefits Italy's rural exodus would have been much greater (1977). There is a sense, then, in which the rural sector has become the residual category of twentieth-century Italian life.

Economic transformation of the countryside has assumed many forms. Field and farm abandonment are two obvious consequences of the rural labor crisis. This is particularly evident in the mountainous districts, where, with the encouragement and active subsidization of government planners, former grainfields are converted to either silviculture or pasture (Melilli 1966:182, Vicinelli 1966:140). However, it should be noted that the decline of agricultural activity is not limited to the marginal districts alone but is evident even in areas amenable to mechanization and modernization (Melilli 1966:187).

Among the remaining agriculturalists there has been the restructuring of land tenancy arrangements. Particularly notable is the increase in the percentage of owner-cultivator enterprises (from 53% of all holdings in 1948 to 70% in 1961) and the attendant decline in renters (25% to 14%) and sharecroppers (22% to 16%) (Barberis 1966b:44).[19]

Migration has played a major, and often ironic, role in the emergence of the peasant-owner syndrome. On the one hand, migrant or emigrant remittances (or the savings of the returnee migrants disposed to invest in land) have provided the peasants with the wherewithal to purchase property or clear up mortgages against their holdings. The fact that the migration alternative dried up the rural labor force itself created a market in rural real estate as larger absentee landlords found it increasingly difficult to operate their estates profitably. Ultimately they simply sold the parcels to their former workers and sharecropping tenants. The pent-up desires of a land-oriented, land-starved peasantry frequently bid up the values to unrealistic levels (De Luca 1966:73).[20] Many a migrant paid a premium price for his dream of ownership, only to see it evaporate. The peasant-migrant failed to realize that in the long run his twin goals of land ownership and education for his children were incompatible. The peasant's son, with his *laurea* or diploma in hand, is little reconciled to an agricultural system becoming increasingly anachronistic in a modernizing world. Common, then, is the aging returned migrant/peasant and spouse living alone and embittered, forced to curtail their agricultural activity with each passing year. Similarly, there is the peasant/migrant who re-emigrates, abandoning the holdings that he purchased so enthusiastically upon his first return to the village (Douglass n.d.).

Another complicating factor is the proclivity for migrants with dwellings and landholdings in the countryside to retain them indefinitely. Psychologically, for the urban migrant such ownership can become both an umbilical cord and a lifeline — a means of sustaining an important aspect of self-identity while hedging against the precarious nature of city life. Disadvantaged in so many other respects vis-à-vis his urban counterpart, the rural migrant who still owns land in his natal village has a hole card to fall back upon in the event of either personal failure in the city or general collapse of the urban economy. The reluctance of the migrant to sever his ties is seen in the 504 "abandoned" dwellings in the small Molise town of Agnone that are neither for sale nor for rent but are retained by their migrant owners for the occasional visit home (Douglass n.d.). Schreiber sums up the situation by stating, "To understand the drama of today's migration, it is important to realize that many of those who are emigrating are the ones most bound to the land, to the home village, and to tradition. Even though they may be away for extended periods of time, they still keep their homes in the village, and if possible, use their migration earnings to construct a new modern home . . . but they may never be able to live in it, for when they finally return, many find themselves no longer able to fit back into the old way" (1973:61).

The migrant's fields are another matter as they suffer from disuse and lack of care, ultimately reverting to second growth. Consequently a new kind of land rental system has emerged in which the transactions are primarily between kinsmen (Barberis 1966b:47). It is a custodial arrangement in which the fields are "lent" to a relative remaining active in agriculture and may be reclaimed from him at any time. The custodian then farms the land and in return pays the taxes on it (p. 46).

Finally, a word should be said about the impact of migration upon rural Italy's rather notorious patron-client political system. It has been contended that migration undermines the power and authority of the traditional elite (Vicinelli 1966:137, Cafiero and De' Rossi 1966:88–89). Migration supposes a decline in the sheer numbers of clients that a patron can command. At the same time the migration alternative itself serves to loosen the patron's grip over the destinies of his clientele.

While there are elements of the foregoing, the reality tends to be a bit more complex. In point of fact, the kinds of transformations of rural society considered above have actually enhanced the power of the elite in certain critical respects. Government has emerged as by far the largest single employer in rural Italy. In many parts of the south the combination of migrant remittances, public administration, and public assistance account for more than 50% of the local economy (Vicinelli 1966:136, Reyneri 1978:33-34).[21] Access to posts and, at times, to social benefits that are theoretically one's right as a citizen in fact require the infamous *raccomandazione* (recommendation) from a well-placed patron. Whether the individual seeks a scarce student slot in an Italian university, a job in a nearby factory, or the post of janitor in the town hall, he knows that it is futile to simply fill out the application and await his turn. Public positions can be politicized to an astounding extent, fractionated and then dispensed as "favors" by patrons to their clients. In a town of the Molise with slightly over 6,000 inhabitants, for example, in the early 1970s there were no fewer than 148 "school teachers," most of whom were employed an hour or two daily (Douglass n.d.). Chronic underemployment coupled with a surplus of local *laureati* made even the leftist-leaning *maestro/a* beholden to the DC-dominated political machine for such token favors. There are those, then, who have been adept at exploiting the crisis in rural Italy to consolidate their own position as the new elite. Today's patron may no longer be the baron or bishop of former times, but he is no less patronizing in his outlook.

CONCLUSION

The foregoing discussion concerns developments in Italy from the end of World War II until the late 1960s. In terms of migration history the period was characterized by (1) a decline in transoceanic emigration, (2) considerable movement of sojourning Italian workers to Switzerland and the Common Market countries, and (3) massive internal rural-urban migration. Whether his destination was Milan or Munich, Genoa or Geneva, the migrant encountered considerable discrimination and difficulty, particularly regarding housing and employment. That the human costs were enormous may not be disputed; that they were sustained at all underscores the magnitude of the economic differences between traditional rural Italy and the urban-industrial sectors of the modern world.

An observer of the scene in the late 1960s might have forecast that the migratory trends, with all their problems, would continue unabated for the foreseeable future — and he would have been wrong. If the actual decision to migrate is frequently under the control of the individual, the factors that enter into it rarely are. In point of fact, the past decade of Western European economic history has been characterized by setbacks and uncertainty. The postwar recovery has long since played out, and the twin evils of inflation and unemployment now plague the weaker economies and prompt extreme conservatism in stabler countries such as Germany and Switzerland. In 1974 the tenuous position of the *Gästarbeiter* was underscored by the joint decision of Switzerland and Italy's Common Market partners to close their frontiers to new immigrants. In 1975, 55,000 Italian workers were repatriated from Switzerland alone (Rosoli 1977:236).

What of internal migration patterns within the nation? By the late 1960s there were signs that the industrial triangle had reached the saturation point with respect to its capacity to absorb new migrants. Rather, the former receiving areas of Genoa, Turin, and Milan were themselves becoming the staging areas of emigration — both to their immediate hinterlands (as industry was decentralized) and abroad (as rural migrants gained some skills in one of the cities and then "traded up" by applying them in a neighboring country) (*La Redazione* 1969:241–44).

The typical new arrival was no longer the head of a household seeking to establish a new life for his family in the urban milieu. Rather, he/she was young, single, and willing to take a chance in the city. Much less was at risk for the individual in what has been labeled the "second wave" of postwar rural-urban migration. The young migrant had few responsibilities and could count on a degree of assistance from established kinsmen and friends — veterans of the first wave. The fact that the northern cities had undergone a degree of southernization meant that the new arrival encountered a somewhat less hostile and unfamiliar environment than did his predecessors. He was likely more educated and in possession of a marketable skill (*La Redazione* 1969:246). Some were returnees from a Common Market country, anxious to re-establish themselves in Italy but unattracted to the countryside (p. 246). furthermore, many of the inequities of the earlier years in housing and employment had ameliorated at least somewhat (p. 247).

Such was the situation in the early 1970s when the Italian economy entered the same period of uncertainty characteristic of Western Europe as a whole. Indeed, within Italy the crises was exacerbated by one of the continent's highest rates of inflation, a paucity of natural resources, overpopulation, and regional underdevelopment. Furthermore, as neighboring countries expelled the *Gästarbeiters,* Italy was faced with reabsorbing thousands of its workers into an already faltering economy.

For all of the foregoing reasons there is noticeable suspension of migration in all its forms in contemporary Italy. Between 1972 and 1975, and for the first time in the past century, more Italians actually returned from abroad than emigrated (Malfatti 1976:154). Interregional migration is down noticeably. The average annual south-north population transfer between 1971 and 1975 declined 21% with respect to the 1955–70 period (Golini 1978:402). Intraregionally, migration to provincial capitals has declined as well (p. 401). Of particular significance is the fact that the urban megalopolis seems to be losing its attraction. Between 1972 and 1976 Italy's 11 largest cities actually registered a net loss of 164,000 inhabitants (p. 402).

That the outer limits of the urban center's capacity to provide a tolerable human environment may have been reached prompted at least one observer to conclude that "the myth of Milan . . . is finished!" (p. 402).

Whether recent trends represent a plateau or a pause in Italian migration history is a question of profound social and economic policy implication for the nation as a whole.

NOTES

1. Crump (1975) upbraids his fellow anthropologists for purposely seeking out backwoods bastions of traditional exotica rather than more "representative" Italian agricultural communities.
2. The following analysis details the population actually present at the time of the census *(popolazione presente)*. The Italian census also distinguishes population of legal residence *(popolazione residente)*. For instance, in 1901 Turin had a present population of 335,656 while the number of persons with legal residence in the city was only 329,691. Conversely, in Agnone, a regional center in the Molise, there were 10,189 legal residents but only 9,793 persons present at the time of the census (Istituto Central di Statistica 1967:2, 3, 290, 291). Such discrepancies themselves reflect migration patterns, suggesting that Turin was receiving migrants while Agnone was producing them. However, such refinement of the statistics will not be attempted, since, for present purposes, it would complicate the argument unduly.
3. Again the validity of the statistics must be qualified. On the one hand, there is a strong tendency for the migrant who views his absence as a temporary sojourn to retain his official residence in his hometown. On the other, local officials sometimes encourage such behavior, since a community's claim upon government subsidies is partly predicated upon its population size. Hence official statistics grossly understate the extent of the rural-urban population transfer.
4. A partial list of monograph-length treatments includes Compagna (1959), Barberis (1960), Diena (1963), Cavalli (1964), Fofi (1964), Pellicciari (1970), and Baglivo and Pellicciari (1973). Also, for a general bibliographic overview, see Liguori (1979). The literature on developments outside the main urban centers of northern and central Italy is much sparser. Masi (1979), however, does provide an analysis of the impact of siting a state-sponsored steel plant in Taranto.
5. In one small town of the Molise fully 81% of the inhabitants had migrated at one time or another within Italy, many to Milan and Turin (Schreiber 1973:72).
6. It should be noted that the foregoing economic and demographic rationale, while predominant in the literature, is not accepted uncritically by all investigators. Macdonald contends that migration rates are more likely to co-vary with social structural factors than income levels. Specifically, he notes that areas characterized by the socially atomistic nuclear family and an absence of voluntary associations (i.e., the "typical" south) were prone to emigration. Conversely, in areas with traditions of greater associational activity the peasantry was more likely to direct its desire for economic betterment into a concerted class struggle (Macdonald 1956).

7. Schreiber notes that when she divulged to an informant that she planned to conduct a study in the province of Campobasso, she was told the acronym for the area (CB) stood for *Congo Belga,* or the Belgian Congo (1973:47)!

8. Conversely, in the year 1961 about one-half of all migrants to Turin were southerners (Fofi 1970:270).

9. Throughout South Italy one finds the disillusioned returned migrant who abandoned Milan or Turin because economic security was not worth the affront to personal dignity. In one survey 49% of the southerners in a northern city expressed the desire to return home (Moretti 1970:57). Conversely, there is the southern migrant who engages in the personally demeaning behavior of trying to "pass" as a northerner (Schreiber 1973:109).

10. Seventy percent of southern respondents in a social survey stated that they had at least one North Italian friend (Moretti 1970:57).

11. For example, there are presently thousands of migrants from the town of Pietraperzia (Sicily) in the town of Pioltello (province of Milan) (Baglivo and Pellicciari 1973:146).

12. Schreiber found that 34% of the postwar migrants from a Molise community had returned (1973:79).

13. Lest the case be overstated, there are counterexamples. When in 1968 a large area of Sicily was devastated by an earthquake, the municipal authorities and charitable entities of Turin assisted 775 families (3,000 persons) to resettle in the city, underwriting their initial period of adjustment (Documentazioni 1969).

14. Reliance upon such assistance, however, subjects persons to considerable frustration in dealing with the bureaucracy. Schreiber notes that few migrants from the Molise find the benefits worth the hassle (1973:60).

15. Named for the country Korea, the slum dwellings of which were brought to Italian awareness by the Korean War.

16. Diena (1963) describes the circumstance of migrants in a *corea* near Milan as one of almost complete social and cultural isolation vis-à-vis the indigenous population.

17. The cultural deprivation of the migrant children, and particularly their lack of familiarity with standard Italian, has a further negative effect upon their classroom performance (Siegel n.d.:11).

18. This is not to say, however, that he/she is likely to arrive in the urban megalopolis. Rather, the best educated rural migrants tend to resettle intraregionally in a nearby city. It is the unskilled and unlettered who are more prone to brave the industrial triangle (Moretti 1970:151).

19. The owner-cultivator category masks both the large capitalistic agricultural venture with a crew of salaried employees and the peasant who owns and personally tills his land.

20. In one study of Sicilian emigrants 45% of those interviewed invested their savings in the purchase of land and/or a house (Reyneri *et al.* 1976:44).

21. A study in 1975 of a large sample of Sicilian households with emigrant members found that 71% were receiving remittances and nearly 60% depended upon an old-age pension or other public subsidy (Reyneri *et al.* 1976:36).

REFERENCES

Alberoni, Francesco
    1964   Integrazione dell'immigrato e integrazione sociale. *Studi di sociologia*
            2:347-70.

1970   Aspects of internal migration related to other types of Italian migration. In Clifford J. Jansen, ed., *Readings in the sociology of migration.* Oxford: Pergamon Press, pp. 285–316.

Albertelli, Gianfranco, and Giuliana Ziliani
1970   Le condizioni alloggiative della popolazione immigrata. In Giovanni Pellicciari, ed., *L'immigrazione nel triangolo industriale.* Milan: Franco Angeli, pp. 283–303.

Atkinson, Amy
1908   *In the Abruzzi.* London: Chatto and Windus.

Baglioni, Guido
1966   Le motivazioni degli emigrati italiani interni. In Commissione Nazionale Italiana UNESCO, *L'esodo rurale e lo spopolamento della montagna nella società contemporanea.* Milan: Società Editrice Vita e Pensiero, pp. 41–69.

Baglivo, Adriano
1970   Caratteristiche e funzioni delle associazioni che operano nel settore dell' immigrazione." In Giovanni Pellicciari, ed., *L'immigrazione nel triangolo industriale.* Milan: Franco Angeli, pp. 516–31.

Baglivo, Adriano, and Giovanni Pellicciari
1973   *La tratta dei meridionali.* Milan: Sapere Edizioni.

Banfield, Edward C.
1958   *The moral basis of a backward society.* New York: Free Press.

Barberis, Corrado
1960   *Le migrazioni rurali in Italia.* Milan: Feltrinelli.
1963   La femme dans l'agriculture italienne. *Etudes rurales* 10:50–67.
1966a   L'esodo: Conseguenze demografiche e sociali. In Commissione Nazionale Italiana UNESCO, *L'esodo rurale e lo spopolamento della montagna nella società contemporanea.* Milan: Società Editrice Vita e Pensiero, pp. 24–40.
1966b   Esodo agricolo e strutture fondiarie: Con particolare riferimento ai comprensori montani. In Commissione Nazionale Italiana UNESCO, *L'esodo rurale e lo spopolamento della montagna nella società contemporanea.* Milan: Società Editrice Vita e Pensiero, pp. 41–69.

Barbero, G.
1961   *Land reform in Italy: Achievements and perspectives.* FAO Agricultural Studies, no. 53. Rome: Food and Agriculture Organization of the United Nations.

Blumer, Giovanni
1970   *L'emigrazione italiana in Europa.* Milan: Feltrinelli.

Boissevain, Jeremy, and John Friedl, eds.
1975   *Beyond the community: Social process in Europe.* The Hague: Mouton.

Brögger, Jan
1971   *Montevarese: A study of peasant society and culture in southern Italy.* Bergen, Oslo, Tromsö: Universitetsforlaget.

Burns, Robert K.
1963   The circum-alpine culture area: A preliminary view. *Anthropological Quarterly* 36, no. 3:130–55.

Cafiero, Salvatore, and Guido De' Rossi
1966   Lo spopolamento della montagna meridionale. In Commissione Nazionale Italiana UNESCO, *L'esodo rurale e lo spopolamento della montagna nella società contemporanea.* Milan: Società Editrice Vita e Pensiero, pp. 79–92.

Capo, Enrico
1966   I problemi economici e socio-culturali delle zone di destinazione dell' esodo rurale. In Commissione Nazionale Italiana UNESCO, *L'esodo*

rurale e lo spopolamento della montagna nella società contemporanea. Milan: Società Editrice Vita e Pensiero, pp. 121-31.

Cavalli, L.
1964   *Gli immigrati meridionali e la società ligure.* Milan: Franco Angeli.

Centro Nazionale di Prevenzione e Difesa Sociale
1966   Introduzione alla tematica dell'esodo rurale. In Commissione Nazionale Italiana UNESCO, *L'esodo rurale e lo spopolamento della montagna nella società contemporanea.* Milan: Società Editrice Vita e Pensiero, pp. 195-259.

Chapman, Charlotte Gower
1971   *Milocca: A Sicilian village.* Cambridge, Mass.: Schenkman.

Clark, M. Gardner
1977   *Agricultural social security and rural exodus in Italy.* Western Societies Program, Occasional Paper no. 7. Ithaca, N.Y.: Cornell University.

Cole, John W.
1971   *Estate inheritance in the Italian Alps.* Research Reports no. 10. Department of Anthropology, University of Massachusetts, Amherst.

Cole, John W., and Eric R. Wolf
1974   *The hidden frontier: Ecology and ethnicity in an Alpine valley.* New York and London: Academic Press.

Compagna, Francesco
1959   *I terroni in città.* Bari: Laterza.

Crump, Thomas
1975   The context of European anthropology: The lesson from Italy. In Jeremy Boissevain and John Friedl, eds., *Beyond the community: Social process in Europe.* The Hague: Mouton, pp. 18-27.

Cuccorese, Horacio Juan, and José Panettieri
1971   *Argentina: Manual de historia económica y social.* Buenos Aires: Ediciones Macchi.

Davis, John
1973   *Land and family in Pisticci.* London: Athlone Press.

Davis, John H. R.
1969   Town and country. *Anthropological Quarterly* 42, no. 3: 171-85.

De Luca, Mario
1966   Le conseguenze economiche sui luoghi di provenienza. In Commissione Nazionale Italiana UNESCO, *L'esodo rurale e lo spopolamento della montagna nella società contemporanea.* Milan: Società Editrice Vita e Pensiero, pp. 70-78.

Diena, L.
1963   *Borgata milanese.* Milan: Franco Angeli.

Documentazioni
1969   Recenti immigrati a Torino: Un indagine sui terremotati. *Studi emigrazione* 15:204-18.

Dolci, Danilo
1970   *Report from Palermo.* New York: Viking Press (reprint of 1959 ed.).

Douglas, Norman
1915   *Old Calabria.* London: M. Secker.

Douglass, William A.
n.d.   Emigration and urban decline in a South Italian hill town: An anthropological history. In press.

Favero, Luigi, and Gianfausto Rosoli
1975   I lavoratori emarginati. *Studi emigrazione* 38-39:155-329.

Fofi, G.
  1962   *Immigrazione e industria.* Milan: Edizioni di Comunità.
  1964   *Immigrazione meridionale a Torino.* Milan: Feltrinelli.
  1970   Immigrants to Turin. In Clifford J. Jansen, ed., *Readings in the sociology of migration.* Oxford: Pergamon Press, pp. 269–84.
Friedmann, Frederick G.
  1960   *The hoe and the book: An Italian experiment in community development.* Ithaca, N.Y.: Cornell University Press.
  1962   The world of *La Miseria. Community Development Review* 7:91–100.
Galtung, Johan
  1971   *Members of two worlds: A development study of three villages in western Sicily.* New York and London: Columbia University Press.
Gasparini, Innocenzo
  1966   Tratti socio-economici dell'emigrazione dalla montagna e dalla collina del Veneto. In Commissione Nazionale Italiana UNESCO, *L'esodo rurale e lo spopolamente della montagna nella società contemporanea.* Milan: Società Editrice Vita e Pensiero,, pp. 150–76.
Golini, Antonio
  1978   Le tendenze recenti nelle migrazioni interne. *Studi emigrazione* 15, no. 51:401–3.
Gramsci, Antonio
  1970   *La questione meridionale.* Rome: Editori Riuniti.
Gross, Feliks
  1973   *Il paese: Values and social change in an Italian village.* New York: New York University Press.
Hildebrand, George H.
  1965   *Growth and structure in the economy of modern Italy.* Cambridge, Mass.: Harvard University Press.
Istituto Centrale di Statistica
  1967   *Popolazione residente e presente dei comuni ai censimenti dal 1861 al 1961.* Rome.
  1968   *Sommario di statistiche storiche dell'Italia. 1861–1965.* Rome.
  1972   *11° censimento generale della popolazione. Primi risultati provinciali e comunali sulla popolazione e sulle abitazioni. Dati provvisori,* vol. 1. Rome.
Istituto per lo Sviluppo dell'Edilizia Sociale
  1965   *Il comprensorio di soverato.* Florence: La Nuova Italia Editrice.
Jarach, Cesare
  1909   *Inchiesta parlamentare sulle condizione dei contadini nelle provincie meridionali e nelle sicilie.* Rome.
Jucker, Ninetta
  1970   *Italy.* London: Thames and Hudson.
Kertzer, David I.
  1977   Ethnic identity and political struggle in an Italian communist quartiere. In George L. Hicks and Philip E. Leis, eds., *Ethnic encounters.* North Scituate, Mass.: Duxbury Press, pp. 221–37.
Kuhn, W. E.
  1978   Guest workers as an automatic stabilizer of cyclical unemployment in Switzerland and Germany. *International Migration Review* 12, no. 2:210–24.
Lauriente, Camille
  1953   *The chronicles of Camille.* New York: Pageant Press.
Liguori, Maria
  1979   Fenomeni migratori e sociologia: La letteratura sociologica sulle migra-

zioni interne nel triangolo industriale (1958–1968). *Rassegna italiana di sociologia* 20, no. 1:109–46.

Livolsi, Mariano
1966   Integrazione dell'immigrato e integrazione comunitaria. *Studi emigrazione* 5:124–51.

Lopreato, Joseph
1967   *Peasants no more: Social class and social change in an underdeveloped society.* San Francisco: Chandler Publishing Co.

Lucrezio M., Giuseppe, and Luigi Favero
1972   Un quarto di secolo di emigrazione italiana. *Studi emigrazione* 25–26:5–91.

Majorino, Giorgio
1970   Il tempo libero e gli immigrati: I rapporti tra i vari gruppi. In Giovanni Pellicciari, ed., *L'immigrazione nel triangolo industriale.* Milan: Franco Angeli, pp. 304–23.

Malfatti, Eugenia
1976   Le migrazioni meridionali alla luce delle fonti statistiche ufficiali (1951–1975). *Studi emigrazione* 42:148–58.

Mangin, William, ed.
1970   *Peasants in cities: Readings in the anthropology of urbanization.* Boston: Houghton Mifflin.

Mannucci, C.
1970   Emigrants in the upper Milanese area. In Clifford J. Jansen, ed., *Readings in the sociology of migration.* Oxford: Pergamon Press, pp. 257–67.

Maraspini, A. L.
1968   *The study of an Italian village.* Paris: Mouton.

Masi, Anthony C.
1979   The labor force requirements of capital-intensive industrialization: Labor migration and labor absorption at Italsider's fourth integrated steel center, Taranto (Puglia), Italy. Paper given at the conference of the council of European Studies, Washington, D.C.

Macdonald, J. S.
1956   Italy's rural social structure and emigration. *Occidente* 12, no. 5:437–56.

McNeill, W. H.
1963   *The rise of the West.* Chicago: University of Chicago Press.

Melilli, Giovanni
1966   Assistenza, previdenza e sicurezza sociale di fronte all'esodo rurale e allo spopolamento montano. In Commissione Nazionale Italiana UNESCO, *L'esodo rurale e lo spopolamento della montagna nella società contemporanea.* Milan: Società Editrice Vita e Pensiero, pp. 185–94.

Melis, Federigo
1976   *Mercaderes italianos en España: Siglos XIV–XVI.* Seville: Universidad de Sevilla.

Monelli, Adriana, and Giovanni Pellicciari
1970   Comportamento di voto e pratica religiosa. In Giovanni Pellicciari, ed., *L'immigrazione nel triangolo industriale.* Milan: Franco Angeli, pp. 324–38.

Moretti, Giancarlo
1970   Nord-sud: Squilibri che tendono a persistere. In Giovanni Pellicciari, ed., *L'immigrazione nel triangolo industriale.* Milan: Franco Angeli, pp. 49–184.

Moscati, Roberto
  1967   Considerazioni sul comportamento politico-elettorale degli immigrati nel
          triangolo industriale. *Studi emigrazione* 8:123–46.
Pellicciari, Giovanni, ed.
  1970   *L'immigrazione nel triangolo industriale.* Milan: Franco Angeli.
Pike, Ruth
  1966   *Enterprise and adventure: The Genoese in Seville and the opening of the New World.*
          Ithaca, N.Y.: Cornell University Press.
Pitkin, Donald S.
  1959   A consideration of asymmetry in the peasant-city relationship. *Anthropo-
          logical Quarterly* 32, no. 4:161–67.
  1963   Mediterranean Europe. *Anthropological Quarterly* 36, no. 3: 120–29.
Postan, M. M.
  1951   Italy and the economic development of England in the Middle Ages. *Jour-
          nal of Economic History* 11, no. 4: 339–46.
Ratti, Anna Maria
  1934   Migratorie correnti. *Enciclopedia italiana* 23:250–59.
La Redazione
  1969   Le migrazioni interne italiane oggi. *Studi emigrazione* 6, no. 16:225–72.
Reyneri, Emilio
  1978   Emigration and sending area: The case of Sicily. Paper presented to the
          Conference on the Design and Analysis of Current Social Science Re-
          search in the Central Mediterranean, University of Malta.
Reyneri, Emilio, *et al.*
  1976   *L'emigrazione meridionale nelle zone d'esodo.* Vol. 3: *Sintesi e conclusioni operative.*
          Catania: Facoltà di Scienze Politiche dell'Università di Catania.
Rosoli, Gianfausto
  1977   L'emigrazione di ritorno: Alla ricerca di una impostazione. *Studi emigra-
          zione* 47:235–44.
Sacchetti, G. B.
  1971   Regioni e migrazioni. *Studi emigrazione* 22:143–57.
Saunders, George R.
  1980   Peasant Life in Piedmont. *Current Anthropology* 21, no. 3: 827–28.
Schreiber, Janet Mogg
  1973   To eat the bread of others: The decision to migrate in a province of south-
          ern Italy. Ph.D. dissertation, University of California at Berkeley.
Scotellaro, Rocco
  1972   *L'uva puttanella: Contadini del sud.* 2d ed. Bari: Editori Laterza.
Siegel, Bernard J.
  n.d.   Tensions between ethnic and class identity among Italian migrants to
          Milan. Unpublished ms.
Silverman, Sydel F.
  1975   *Three bells of civilization: The life of an Italian hill town.* New York and Lon-
          don: Columbia University Press.
Tagliacarne, Guglielmo
  1966   Spopolamento montano ed esodo rurale, misura e prospettive. In Com-
          missione Nazionale Italiana UNESCO, *L'esodo rurale e lo spopolamento della
          montagna nella società contemporanea.* Milan: Società Editrice Vita e Pen-
          siero, pp. 3–14.

Vicinelli, Paolo
    1966   Esodo rurale e programmi di sviluppo del mezzogiorno italiano. In Commissione Nazionale Italiana UNESCO, *L'esodo rurale e lo spopolamento della montagna nella società contemporanea.* Milan: Società Editrice Vita e Pensiero, pp. 132–49.
Villani, Andrea
    1966   Analisi delle conseguenze economiche e finanziarie delle migrazioni interne sulle zone di destinazione. In Commissione Nazionale Italiana UNESCO, *L'esodo rurale e lo spopolamento della montagna nella società contemporanea.* Milan: Società Editrice Vita e Pensiero, pp. 93–120.
Waley, Daniel
    1969   *The Italian city-republics.* London: Weidenfeld and Nicolson.
Wallerstein, Immanuel
    1974   *The modern world-system: Capitalist agriculture and the origins of the European world-economy in the sixteenth century.* New York and London: Academic Press.
Wolf, Eric R.
    1970   The inheritance of land among Bavarian and Tyrolese peasants. *Anthropologica* (n.s.) 12:99–114.

Chapter 7

Urbanization and Modernization in Yugoslavia: Adaptive and Maladaptive Aspects of Traditional Culture

Andrei Simić

It is an accurate though hackneyed observation that Yugoslavia is a land of contrasts. Such has been the historic legacy of the meeting of East and West in the Balkans, and, later in modern times, the product of the confrontation between traditional and contemporary culture. Even the casual visitor to southeastern Europe cannot fail to note the omnipresent and seemingly incongruous juxtapositions. This is perhaps most true in the cities, where ancient and sometimes crumbling monuments of the past vie with the stark symbols of the new socialist order; where peasants in rustic dress rub shoulders at teeming outdoor marketplaces with chic urbanites; and where preindustrial craftsmen linger on, plying their trades in the very shadow of the most advanced factory complexes. However, there is another, less obvious level of opposition, one rooted in the very nature of the South Slav mentality and social structure. Not only has this traditional world view demonstrated surprising vigor in the face of change, but it has also acted as a double-edged sword in the Yugoslav modernization process. Thus, paradoxically, the very same ethos can account for both the Yugoslav success in urbanization, as reflected by the smooth integration of millions of former peasants into city life, and the failure of the society to develop large-scale institutions based on a predominantly "rational" or modern model.

Anthropological studies of urbanization and modernization in Yugoslavia have focused to date almost exclusively on the adaptive aspects of traditional culture (see Halpern 1963, 1965; Simić 1974), and in particular have underscored the salient role of kinship as an integrative mechanism both on the personal level and as a link joining rural and urban sectors of the society (see Barić 1967a, b; Denich 1969; Hammel 1969a, b; Hammel and Yarbrough 1973; Simić 1973a, b, 1974, 1977). While such assertions are undeniably rooted in widespread and readily visible phenomena, these conclusions are also in part the result of selective observations probably related to a quasi-ideological stance in reaction to the negative stereotypes of urbanization and urbanism that had previously typified the social sciences. Phrased in another way, there has been a tendency to overcompensate for earlier conceptual errors with the result that particular values and modes of behavior have been singled out and accentuated at the expense of others. Thus there has been a tendency to interpret the persistence of traditional norms and customs in relation to urbanization solely with reference to their contributions to the cultural and social integration of new migrants into city life.

In contrast, little or no attention has been directed to the negative and maladaptive aspects of Yugoslav culture in respect to other kinds of social goals such as those associated with ideas about the nature of "modernity," "progress," and "rationality" in the Weberian sense. For example, many Yugoslavs, especially those concerned with economic planning and social engineering, have voiced dissatisfaction and even acute disappointment in their country's failure to develop a "thoroughly contemporary mentality" after more than 30 years of accelerated industrial and urban growth under a socialist system. More often than not, and with some justification, these "shortcomings" have been attributed to the weight of history and its concomitant legacy of traditional social structures and values. It is seemingly contradictory that in the case of Yugoslavia the very forces and sentiments that have provided stability in change are at the same time inhibiting the attainment of many of the goals perceived by the political leadership and intellectual elite as central to the modernization process.

Clearly, the South Slav case adds further weight to Oscar Lewis's contention that urbanization is a process that assumes "different forms and meanings, depending upon the prevailing historic, economic, social, and historical conditions" (1952:40). Moreover, if modernization is conceptualized as a multifaceted process involving not only the expansion of city life and an increase in the scale, complexity, and efficiency of technology and production but also a deep alteration in the various aspects of social structure, culture, and particularly world view, then it is evident that change may occur at a different rate (or not at all) in each of these areas. Thus the possibility of paradoxical contrast and conflict is ever present in developing societies, and modernization will not only show considerable cross-cultural variation, but, indeed, may never be realized fully in respect to any given ideal model.

Yugoslavia provides a complex case in which modernization has exerted differential influences in various arenas of life, proceeding at a vastly faster pace in some than in others. For instance, the tempo of urbanization would suggest a very rapid rate of change if considered in isolation; however, a very different impression is gained from the analysis of the underlying assumptions that govern the conduct of social relations even within the newly created institutions of the ostensibly modern state. It is this inconsistency and disparity in the Yugoslav modernization process that provides a central focus for this chapter, which will examine the situation from several perspectives. First, the broader historical and cultural context in which industrialization and urbanization have taken place will be considered, focusing particularly on Serbia, where the majority of contemporary anthropological studies have been carried out. Second, traditional social structures and their associated values will be related to the smooth integration of millions of peasant migrants into contemporary urban life. Finally, these same values and structures will be analyzed with regard to certain ideas associated with modernity, particularly as they appear to be maladaptive in light of its goals.

THE HISTORICAL AND CULTURAL CONTEXT OF YUGOSLAV URBANIZATION

A little over a hundred years ago the last official vestige of Ottoman rule came to an end in the Serbian capital of Belgrade. The preceding half-millennium had been largely dominated by the Turkish presence in the Balkans, and even today Yugoslavs have a tendency to rationalize all inefficiencies, backwardness, and primitivism as the inevitable fruits of "benighted" Moslem rule. In fact, almost every failure is explained by a shrug of the shoulders and the explicative "five hundred years under the Turks" *(petsto godina pod turcima)*. While there is clearly some injustice and inaccuracy in this evaluation, nonetheless the centuries of foreign rule have without doubt molded many aspects of contemporary South Slav life.

The appearance of the Ottomans during the fourteenth century in southeastern Europe set into motion mass migrations of indigenous populations: northward across the Danube and Sava rivers into Christian Hungarian lands, and westward up into the barren and infertile ramparts of the Dinaric Mountains high above the Adriatic. The result was that for centuries the rich rural heartland of the Balkans remained only sparsely populated, and the urban vacuum created by the retreating Slavs was filled by a heterogeneous, mostly alien population of Turks, Greeks, Albanians, Sephardim, Gypsies, islamized Slavs, and others from the far-flung reaches of the Ottoman empire. In this way city life quickly assumed a Middle Eastern aura with urbanites cultivating a sophisticated Moslem and Levantine tradition, a tradition contrasting sharply with the rustic and archaic life style of the Christian Slavic countryside. The old aristocracy was either displaced or retained its privileges through conversion to Islam or cultural and political accommodation to Turkish norms. While urban life persisted, and even flourished under the centuries of Islamic domination, it did so as foreign islands in an indigenous sea. For example, in Serbia, as was the case in much of the

Balkans, native culture largely died out in the towns but persisted as a folk tradition among the peasantry and mountain tribalists and as a limited "Great Tradition" within the Eastern Orthodox church.

It was only in the nineteenth century, after several hundred years of gradual decline, that Ottoman hegemony came to an end in southeastern Europe. With the expulsion of the Turks, native populations began to return from the desolate mountains to the fertile lowlands, where pastoral tribalism was relinquished in favor of village life or settlement in towns.

With the revival of a South Slav urban tradition there emerged a new bourgeoisie and elite drawn largely from the native peasantry. Owing not only to the rural backgrounds of these new urbanites but also to the influence of European romanticism and nationalism, the indigenous folk tradition was able to play a significant role in the building of city life. However, at the same time the South Slavs were militant in the mimicking of European styles as part of their obsession to obliterate every remnant of the Islamic past. Thus, though a superficially contemporary facade was imposed, westernization remained an essentially symbolic act rather than a deep-rooted, substantive metamorphosis. By European standards most of the Balkans remained a semi-Oriental, economically backward agrarian frontier.

Descriptions of urban life in Serbia during the last century closely approximate Sjoberg's (1960) characterization of the "preindustrial city." Social relations were highly personalistic, family groups comprised most economic units, universalistic standards were lacking, mass production for the market was generally absent, technology remained at a low level, and the work ethic was poorly developed. Moreover, throughout the Balkans, towns and cities most often resembled large villages rather than urban centers. For example, in 1867 the population of Belgrade, Serbia's capital and largest city, barely exceeded 24,000 people (Andrić et al. 1967:69).

Following World War I, the creation of the Yugoslav state (the fulfillment of a nineteenth-century nationalist dream) failed to bring about either significant economic betterment or ethnic solidarity among the diverse groups that populated this part of the Balkans, Rather, the interwar period was characterized by the exacerbation of ethnoreligious rivalries, economic stagnation, political instability, and the eventual collapse of parliamentary government.

As elsewhere in the so-called underdeveloped world, World War II heralded deep and fundamental changes in the structure of Yugoslav life. After a prolonged and bitter struggle against Axis domination and a bloody civil war stemming from both political and ethnic oppositions, a new society emerged. With the fall of the Karadjordjević monarchy, the prewar elite, standing in sharp contrast to the masses of poverty-stricken peasants and the small urban working class, was displaced. The emergence of Tito's marxist-dominated partisan movement as the masters of Yugoslavia following the close of hostilities determined that the course of South Slav history would now be in the direction of socialism, economic and social reform, and industrial urbanism.

The task undertaken by the new leadership was an enormous one. In 1948 the Yugoslavs were among the four least urbanized peoples in Europe, with only 12.5% of the population living in communities of over 20,000 people and with only two cities exceeding 100,000. However, the rapid transformation that was to occur is evidenced by the fact that in 1961 there were already seven urban centers with over 100,000 people, and almost 19% of Yugoslavs lived in towns larger than 20,000 inhabitants (Socijalistička Federativna Republika Jugoslavija 1965:xxii–xxiv). Probably nowhere was the metamorphosis more evident than in Belgrade. At the outbreak of World War II its population numbered under 400,000, while today the city with its suburbs has passed the million mark. What is most notable is that this transformation, accomplished through the migration of masses of villagers, has been wrought without major cultural dislocations or social pathologies, characteristics so often attributed to urbanism and urbanization. In other words, the negative indicators so painfully obvious in many other parts of the world are, for the most part, lacking. For instance, there are no vast squatter settlements, no armies of the unemployed or marginally employed, nor have rural migrants persisted as an inferior and easily distinguishable social category. While it is true that housing in urban centers is in short supply, that many live under what would be regarded as primitive overcrowded conditions by American standards, that there has been a dramatic increase in unemployment in recent times, and that urbanites frequently make fun of the rustic ways of newly urbanized peasants, these manifestations are relatively mild when held up against the yardstick of urban problems in such areas as Latin America, the Middle East, or India.

Clearly, if the standard of the integration of new, mainly rural populations is applied to the evaluation of Yugoslav urbanization, it must be judged as an almost unqualified success. To the foreign observer the most notable aspect of South Slav modernization is the rapidity with which rural migrants have literally disappeared into the urban mainstreams of national life. This phenomenon can be explained with reference to a number of specific historical and cultural conditions coalescing in a unique constellation:

(1) The destruction of the existing class system twice during approximately the last century resulted in a relatively unstratified social system at the close of World War II when massive industrialization and urbanization commenced.

(2) Following the liberation from the Turks in the nineteenth century and the defeat of the Germans in the twentieth, cities grew almost exclusively through rural migration, bringing about the peasantization of urban centers.

(3) Rapid economic growth immediately following World War II permitted the expansion of employment opportunities to keep pace with the influx of rural migrants.

(4) The major period of Yugoslav urban growth has taken place during the last three decades, a time in which communications throughout the country have increased greatly in efficiency and scope. As a result, innovations occurring in one sector of the society have tended to diffuse very rapidly to others, thus diminishing the cultural distance between village and city.

(5) Rural-urban migration has largely followed internal ethnic boundaries, and in so doing has lessened the tendency for rural migrants to form ethnically distinct and inferior categories in the cities (though there are some exceptions such as Gypsies and Albanian-speaking Moslems).

(6) The tenacity of traditional values with respect to social relationships, particularly those associated with kinship, has assured, for the most part, that personal mobility has not been of an atomistic nature but, rather, has remained rooted in an ideological system stressing familial corporacy. Thus the relationships between kin, and by extension between rural and urban segments of kinship groups, have not been significantly disrupted by urbanization and economic modernization.

In many respects Yugoslav urbanization has paralleled that in other parts of the world. As elsewhere, peasants have abandoned their native villages in favor of city life motivated by the familiar "push-pull" stimuli. In other words, migration represents a reaction to what are perceived as unfavorable village conditions combined with optimistic urban images. These images include not only considerations of economic gain and social mobility but also less tangible advantages such as the greater stimulation, anonymity, and individualism offered by the city. However, while Yugoslavia resembles the general world pattern in terms of rural-urban migration, it appears to be rather unique in respect to the manner in which migrants have been incorporated and routinized into the urban sociocultural milieu. Not only have millions of peasants settled in urban centers with little indication of social pathology, but traditional norms and values have contributed significantly to the molding of the new large-scale institutions associated with the modernization of the Yugoslav state.

KINSHIP AND RURAL-URBAN INTEGRATION

Of all the traditional elements affecting the ubanization and modernization processes in Yugoslavia, kinship is surely the most salient and visible. While the positive ramifications of tight-knit family relationships based on ideas of corporacy are undeniable, the negative aspects of these ties are also inescapable. For instance, the Yugoslavs themselves frequently claim that "kinship constitutes a kind of national vice." Among others, family sociologist Olivera Burić (1976:117–18) has commented that the traditional values associated with kinship are regarded by many Yugoslav scholars as a significant impediment to national development.

To understand the manner in which kinship and its concomitant social values (as well as the models derived from them) function both as channels and impediments to modernization, a grasp of their historic and modern forms is imperative. This is a central issue not only because archaic forms of household organization have persisted in many rural areas, but also because even in the largest urban centers an ideology rooted in kinship solidarity and multistranded reciprocity has survived virtually intact, and has been projected into non-kinship social arenas as well.

At the turn of the century the dominant form of the South Slav family was still the patriarchal, patrilocally extended household, the *zadruga,* a corporate entity holding land, livestock, agricultural equipment, and other material and ritual property in common. These kinship groups acted as the basic units of production and consumption, and in many cases were large enough so that a high level of self-sufficiency was achieved through internal occupational and craft specialization. While the *zadruga* predominated in the fertile heartlands of the Balkans (in Serbia, Macedonia, Bulgaria, and in parts of Bosnia-Herzegovina and Croatia), a closely related and perhaps more ancient form of social organization occurred among the Slavic and Albanian speakers of the Dinaric highlands, where pastoralism provided the economic basis of an essentially tribal society. Here relatively small, economically independent households were organized into patrilineal clans, which provided the dominant loci of personal and family identity and acted as the organs of political articulation through the medium of the blood feud and related institutions (see Hammel 1968:23–25, Simić 1967). Both variants of Balkan kinship organization were characterized by cyclical periods of growth and dissolution with periodic redistribution of wealth and the realignment of power resulting from demographic pressures and internal structural and psychological stresses. Nevertheless, even fission or the sloughing off of excess personnel did not necessarily result in the total abandonment of reciprocity between former household or clan members or in the erosion of kinship ideology.

Since the beginning of the twentieth century the influence of a cash economy, the expansion of occupational opportunities in the nonagricultural sector, emigration abroad, and internal migration to the cities have resulted in a marked decline in both the size and the significance of rural, extended family corporations. However, the change has been less one of function than of form, with a tendency toward lineal rather than lateral extension (Halpern and Anderson 1970) or the splitting up of family corporate groups between several loci of residence without a significant diminution of internal reciprocity (Simić 1973:112–25). Moreover, even in contemporary

Yugoslavia there are frequént reports of exeedingly large rural households, sometimes consisting of more than 100 co-resident members, though surely such cases are rare.[1]

Dinaric tribal society has experienced a fate similar to that of the *zadruga*. Of particular significance is the fact that the increasing power of the central government over the last century has gradually usurped and made unnecessary the political and quasi-military functions of highland lineages. However, this too has been accomplished without the destruction of the concomitant ideology, and as Hammel (1969a:196) has observed, "The maps in peoples' heads are the last thing to go."

The tenacity of traditional norms in Yugoslavia in the face of momentous socioeconomic change points emphatically to the fact that, in spite of their functonal interrelationship, social and cultural processes may exhibit developmental histories that are analytically separable (see Simić 1973a:207). This is perhaps most evident in the way that rules governing kinship relationships have adapted to the exigencies of urbanization and social mobility. For example, of more than 200 individuals from all walks of life interviewed by the author during fieldwork conducted in Belgrade on five occasions between 1966 and 1978, only one belonged to a family that did not maintain some form of ongoing material and ritual reciprocity with village kin.[2] In this regard Yugoslavia contrasts markedly with other areas of the Mediterranean such as Spain or Italy, where families have traditionally exhibited a high level of internal socioeconomic homogeneity, a feature tending to solidify and maintain class boundaries over a number of generations. Thus, in Yugoslavia the traditional concept of kinship corporacy, together with the emergence of a new, relatively unstratified society, has counteracted the centrifugal and fragmenting forces of individual spatial and socioeconomic mobility.

As might be anticipated, rural-urban migration is rarely an entirely individual matter, and the first family member to arrive in a city such as Belgrade is unlikely to be the last. In almost every case history collected by the author, each migrant in turn aided some other kinsman to follow in his footsteps. Significantly, these reciprocal responsibilities do not end with the migrating generation but also fall to those subsequently born and reared in the city. In this way, rural-urban mobility is actually encouraged and nurtured by the division of families and larger kinship groups between village and city households.

Rural-urban reciprocity phrased in the idiom of kinship and moral obligation is not limited to simply facilitating migration but in most instances comprises a multistranded exchange of an economic, symbolic, and affectual nature. Thus, family members, regardless of where they may reside (even abroad in such distant places as the United States or Australia), remain tied together in the normal course of events by a constant flow of favors, material goods, visits, and participation in crisis rites. In fact, urbanization appears to have actually broadened the opportunities for the exploitation and cultivation of kinship ties. For instance, Barić (1967a) has observed that, with the decline of the *zadruga,* the substratum of kinship organization that encompasses not only agnatic links but also matrilateral and affinal ties has emerged as a significant systemic feature. In other words, levels which were previously passive have now been activated according to the same rules that formerly governed only agnatic relationships.

Briefly, the characteristics of the contemporary Yugoslav family, whether urban or rural, can be summarized as follows. Though smaller than its earlier counterpart, the household has essentially incorporated and nourished the same principles that once regulated behavior within the *zadruga* and clan. By extension these same rules are extended to incorporate more distant relatives, though frequently in a more idiosyncratic and attenuated manner with somewhat greater stress being placed on achievement than was the case in the past. Nevertheless, in spite of these changes, the common American middle-class ideal of family life with its stress on individualism, personal independence, self-determination, and privacy even within the household remains rather alien to the South Slav model (see Simić 1977).

Roles within the contemporary Yugoslav family tend to be symbiotic and mutually reinforcing. For example, while the talents of individual members are encouraged, they are done so not in the interest of personal gratification so much as for their potential contribution to the total well-being and reputation of the family group. Similarly, children are less oriented toward their peers than they are to other members of their own households. In the same vein, economic behavior reflects the corporate ideal, and close kin, whether or not co-resident, are expected to share their good fortune with those who have less. Though this phenomenon generates tension and even conflict, it nevertheless functions under the aura of moral compunction and provides an impetus for intense engagement and interaction. In fact, the evidence suggests that dissatisfaction is at least one of the dynamics underlying the functioning of the system. In succinct terms, those with more material and social resources feel that they contribute a somewhat unjust and excessive share, though they continue to do so under normal circumstances; at the same time those who have less suspect that they are not receiving "their fair share."

Other familial characteristics are essentially correlates to the central ideology of corporacy. Among others, one might mention that both rural and urban families often span a number of generations without total cleavages in household composition such as those that occur in highly industrialized and urbanized countries like the United States. For example, premarital neolocality so common and idealized in America is almost totally lacking,

and postmarital neolocality is severely restricted by both custom and economics. Similarly, ties of affect and authority in the Yugoslav household
tend to bind together those of different generations, while the communicative aspects of the marital bond are de-emphasized in favor of ex-
ceedingly close ties between parents and children. This does not tend to
diminish the importance of marriage but simply points to its particular functions in Yugoslav society, one of the most important of which is the linking
of unrelated kinship groups. Similarly, the husband-wife relationship is the
medium by which children are tied to two separate lineages, each with the
potential for rewarding reciprocity.

In summary, traditional Yugoslav culture, particularly as related to
family and kinship, has provided the individual with a sense of vital participation in continuing sets of intimate and predictable relationships at a time
when rapid demographic and economic change might otherwise subject him
to severe stress and alienation. However, these positive contributions are
not without their price, a price that is exacted in the larger social arena.

MODERNIZATION AND
TRADITIONAL CULTURE IN YUGOSLAVIA

To adequately evaluate Yugoslav ubanization as part of a larger and
more abstract process of modernization, some general, working definition
of this phenomenon must first be established. In this respect it should be recognized that modernization represents a more profound change than simply
the expansion of city life and the emergence of an industrial economy. Unfortunately, though numerous attempts have been made to define this concept (for instance, see, among others, Eisenstadt 1968), agreement regarding its exact content and meaning still remains tenuous. Nevertheless, the
contrast between so-called simple and complex societies has captivated
man's imagination since at least the period of classic Mediterranean civilization, when the opposition was conceptualized in terms of the morally salu-
brious countryside and the degenerative city (see Caro Baroja 1963). This
same viewpoint has a long and venerable history in the social sciences,
where it has assumed a variety of related forms. For example, from a
plethora of similar theoretical statements can be cited such basic ideas as
Durkheim's concept of mechanical and organic solidarity (1933), Tönnies's
Gemeinschaft and *Gesellschaft* (1957), Sapir's genuine and spurious culture
(1964:78–119), and Redfield's model of the folk-urban continuum (1941)
and the moral and technical order (1953).

Another familiar interpretation of the modernization process, one that
can contribute to our understanding of the Yugoslav case, has emerged from
Max Weber's famous study, *The Protestant Ethic and the Spirit of Capitalism*
(1930). A dominant theme in this analysis of the relationship between reli-

gious ideology and economic behavior in capitalist, industrial Western European society is the idea of rationalism. Perhaps one of the clearest and most succinct summaries of Weber's concept is that of Peter L. Berger (1976:330):

> Modernity may be defined as a complex of social patterns based on the application of thoroughly rational methods to the solution of human problems. Max Weber, the classical German sociologist, has called "rationalization" the prime moving force of the recent era in world history. Its pervasive spirit marks all the new social constructions of this period, especially the major ones—the capitalist economy, the bureaucratic state, and the system of industrial production. Each of these represents a revolutionary "rationalization" in its particular sphere of influence. Each has brought forth types of men—entrepreneurs, administrators, engineers—who share an ethos of emphatic rationality. The application of this rationality to every conceivable area of human concern largely accounts, no doubt, for the historically unprecedented success of modern institutions in transforming the world.

For the purposes of this essay I would like to redefine and interpret "rationalism," in a particular limited and contextual sense, *as an instrumentality directed toward the achievement of certain ends in the most direct and efficient way possible without reference to unrelated goals or extraneous purposes and relationships.* In today's world such objectives are commonly subsumed under the rubric of "progress," as defined in terms of industrial or other types of economic development whose final end is not only the most efficient and copious possible productivity but also the equitable distribution of its concomitant bounty. Moreover, such an equitable distribution is frequently seen as a prerequisite for the attainment of "social justice." However, economic rationalism is inseparably associated with administrative and bureaucratic rationalism, since planning and coordination are viewed, especially in most marxist societies, as central to the entire process. Moreover, rationalism has been associated with the emergence of the so-called technocratic state based on universal standards that contrast with the personalistic and particularistic criteria that appear to govern most traditional, preindustrial societies.

Another similar way that societies may be conceptualized is by means of a perspective I label the "moral field" (Simić 1975:48–78). A moral field can be described as an interactional sphere where the actors behave toward each other with reference to a common set of ethical imperatives, that is, with respect to rules that are accepted as being typically "good," "proper," "God-given," "natural," and the like—rules that do not require instrumental or even logical validation. Moral fields most frequently encompass a population whose membership is effectively determined by rules of recruitment that exclude others. In traditional societies these criteria are most often based on ascriptive qualities such as kinship, caste, ethnicity, place of birth, etc. Moreover, in such settings there commonly exist a number of bounded moral fields exhibiting a variety of social purposes, each with its own exclusive membership. The individual might be portrayed in this context as belonging to several such fields each with its specific purposes, fields that could be rendered graphically as concentric circles or as a number of circles within larger circles. No matter at which level of magnitude these moral fields are conceptualized, they will generally stand in opposition to similarly defined entities outside their boundaries. Moreover, within such a strong, multipurposed moral field, members will tend to act toward each other with reference to common values by which behavior is structured and evaluated. While conformity need not necessarily result, deviation will be judged in terms of ideas of immorality. In contrast, the members' activities outside the field can be regarded as *amoral* in that they are unpredictable, capricious, instrumental, and not subject to the same imperatives that govern the moral field. Thus, in terms of the individual, those belonging to other moral fields can be said to be part of his or her amoral sphere.

Contrary to the preceding model of traditional society, the more universalistic a social system, the greater will be the tendency for its members to participate ideologically in the *same* moral field. In other words, there will be a commonly held belief that everyone should be judged by the same set of standards. Similarly, the more universalistic a society and the greater the division of labor, the higher will be the probability that the separate moral fields that do exist will be limited or even single-purposed, relatively open in terms of recruitment, and weak in respect to the imperativeness of their moral dictates. Thus each actor's interests will be fragmented among a number of interactional arenas, and in this way the moral and social solidarity of any given corporate group will be effectively weakened.

The idea of the moral field (which is in fact only an elaboration of the conventional in-group–out-group concept) was first suggested by the controversial study of Banfield (1958), which sought to explain the low level of political participation in an impoverished Lucanian town in terms of what he labeled "amoral familism." He described what is, in essence, a moral field consisting of only the nuclear family, a field so intense as to seriously endanger all cooperation outside its boundaries.[3]

In the case of the Balkans, the moral fields generated by Dinaric tribal society and the *zadruga* were considerably more extensive than those described by Banfield in southern Italy. Moreover, these kinship groups existed within a broader moral concept tied to ethnicity and nationalism, making possible larger-scale social organization for certain limited purposes. In this respect the South Slav corporate family provides an instance of concentric moral fields. The *zadruga* frequently consisted of a number of nuclear families that, aside from their exclusive procreative functions, comprised relatively weak moral fields. On the other hand, the *zadruga* as a whole constituted a very strong moral field owing to its ritual and economic corporacy. Its members, who consisted of a number of agnates (tracing common descent from a founding ancestor) with their wives and children, were tied together by many-stranded obligations and concerns. For the most part their dealings with the outside world were essentially competitive and even hostile in nature, and relations between *zadrugas* might be likened to diplomatic negotiations between potential enemies. In this respect, during the traditional period prior to the turn of the century, the idea of "friendship" probably did not generally exist in the modern sense but, rather, was defined, if at all, in the context of alliances of marriage and fictive kinship. This is indirectly evidenced by the fact that the contemporary Serbo-Croation word *prijatelj*, now vaguely synonymous with the English "friend," is simply derived from the word for "affine." Moreover, outside of the rather weak and precarious moral obligations created by marriage and ritual sponsorship, ethnicity circumscribed the parameters of the ultimate moral boundaries. Since many communities were ethnically homogeneous, this final moral boundary remained an ideological construct only occasionally activated in practice. Nevertheless, when evoked, ethnicity proved to be a rigid and impenetrable moral barrier. For instance, Milovan Djilas, in his work *Land without Justice* (1958), describes the dispassionate manner in which Montenegrin Christians and Moslems slaughtered each other out of a sense of moral obligation. Stated simply, the concept of humanity, and by extension morality, did not transcend ethnic boundaries.

The positive aspects of the moral fields generated by the traditional South Slav kinship system in a time of transition have already been described. It has also been pointed out that kinship has shown considerable adaptability in response to increased geographic and social mobility, principally in the form of greater selectivity and individuality in the activation and cultivation of specific links. Thus kinship relationships have become somewhat less rigid, though they retain a morally imperative character when activated. In other words, with urbanization traditional moral fields have become broader, allowing greater leeway for personal predilection. In contrast to the former preponderance of tight-knit co-resident corporate groups, there has been a shift in the direction of ego-centered networks of reciprocity. Though ascription still plays a dominant role, the element of achievement has been introduced, and in this respect the social system must be regarded as more universalistic now than previously. However, in spite of such shifts toward a more contemporary model, traditional ideas about the nature of social relationships have remained strong, significantly inhibiting the rationalization of the economy and bureaucracy. These negative aspects can be observed at every level of society ranging from personal adjustment to city life to the functioning of the national bureaucracy. This is underscored by Duško

Doder, a Yugoslav-born American journalist who was stationed for some years in Belgrade (1978:63): "For those who had expected the old ways to disappear in the advance of consumer society, progress, rapid industrial development — or whatever label one attaches to Yugoslavia's entry into the modern world — evidence to the contrary pours in daily. . . ."

The conflict between "the old ways" and the exigencies of urban-industrial life can in fact be observed at every turn in Yugoslavia. For example, in terms of the individual transplanted from a village environment characterized by intimate and highly personalized relationships, the city with its anonymous and more universalistic standards is, at the same time, both threatening and a potential avenue for unencumbered exploitation. One requirement of the urban setting is that one must by necessity transact a variety of exchanges with persons he has never seen before and with whom he may never have future dealings. The only expectation that can reasonably be held about these contacts on the basis of prior experience in a traditional village is that they are fraught with danger and the portent of deception and exploitation. These fears were clearly articulated with surprising regularity by my Belgrade informants, and the following statements are typical:

How can you depend on people you don't know?

At every turn strangers will fool you!

You never know who people in the city are, or if you can trust them. They enjoy deceiving you (vole da vas prevare)!

In the end, one can only depend on his own!

In the city people can get away with anything!

In the city one needs allies, and these are usually kin!

An area of particular apprehension was that of sex-role behavior and the choice of a marriage partner. In this regard a number of rural migrants had returned to their native villages to take brides, and others had married peasant girls from villages other than their own rather than from the city. The lack of intimate social controls in Belgrade, combined with the anonymity of urban life, created insecurities about women's reputations and their future fidelity in marriage. As one informant phrased it, "As for Belgrade girls, one never knows what he is getting — in my village, you could spend ten years, and never see a couple kiss or even hold hands in public!" Contrary to the city, in the countryside reputation is everything, and one is judged not only by his own behavior but also by that of his family and kin.

Freed from the intimate social controls characteristic of the village, one is liberated in the city to behave in any way perceived as momentarily rewarding toward those outside his moral field. Therefore, it is not surprising that Yugoslav urbanites feel a deep distrust of impersonal relationships, nor is it paradoxical that they behave in the very same manner that they most fear from others. It is in this context that the rudeness, obstinance, and indifference that characterize many instrumental, single-stranded transactions with clerks, waiters, and petty officials become understandable. The frequent difficulty of transacting even the simplest bureaucratic procedure is explicable if the purveyor is viewed as the controller of services and/or favors, and his ability to facilitate or obstruct a negotiation as a weapon for self-aggrandizement or personal gain.

It is notable that in contrast to Banfield's (1958) description of southern Italy, today's urban Yugoslavia is typified by the presence of a number of different types of voluntary associations and social service institutions. However, the attitude of Yugoslavs toward these is consistent with their world view regarding both impersonal relationships and authority. As Doder (1978:75) observes, in Yugoslavia people have traditionally believed that "public life is a fraud, regardless of who is in power, and . . . men seek power and influence to get rich, which they do through stealing and corruption." Moreover, there is an extension of this sentiment to all forms of impersonal cooperation, that is, to all exchanges except those typified by close personal ties maintained on the basis of intense moral and material reciprocity. An example of the ramifications of such attitudes can be seen in the manner in which apartment houses are managed. Each building within the socialist sector of the economy is ostensibly governed by a "house council" *(kućni savet)* chosen by the residents. However, though such councils are theoretically charged with making and implementing decisions regarding a variety of concerns including maintenance, action is more often than not paralyzed by the inability and unwillingness of members to cooperate or sacrifice personal interest in favor of group welfare or abstract principles. The following illustrations are typical of cases I personally observed in Belgrade or that were reported to me by informants:

> Although there is an acute housing shortage, an apartment had been empty for over a year. This was well known to the house council, but the members had refused to take action since each obstinately insisted that the apartment be awarded to either a relative or to fulfill some personal obligation. Clearly, the unutilized space was regarded as preferable to an impersonal compromise or a solution that favored one family over another.

> The corridor lights in a large apartment building had not functioned for some months. Prolonged discussions and heated arguments at meetings of the house council had failed to resolve the issue of repair. Convinced that no agreement would ever be reached, each family simply illuminated its own entranceway with a naked bulb at the end of a long extension cord run from the apartment interior. This was consis-

tent with attitudes regarding the filthy and ill-maintained corridors, which were viewed as communal property and thus no one's concern.

Similarly, many (perhaps most) urban informants regarded membership in the League of Communists (Savez Komunista) in instrumental terms related to political advantage or social mobility rather than as either an ideological commitment or a dedication to the general betterment of social and economic conditions. As one Belgrade construction worker phrased it, "I feel no more obligation from my party membership than I do from belonging to the Red Cross" (membership in the Red Cross consists of giving a small yearly donation at one's place of employment). In another case, when questioned as to what kind of person he most admired in his factory, a mechanical engineer replied, "He who makes the most, does the least, and takes care of his own." These and similar attitudes expressed by urban Yugoslavs tend to substantiate Banfield's (1978) hypothesis that at least one condition of successful organization is that members not only have some trust in each other but also identify with the purpose of the organization as an activity of intrinsic value.

In all fairness it should be pointed out that the Yugoslav bureaucracy functions somewhat better than the statements of informants would indicate; that is, there appears to be some discrepancy between what people believe and what actually occurs. For example, in many cases impersonal transactions can yield the desired results, and bureaucratic procedures can be negotiated according to the formal rules. However, the high level of insecurity about such relationships undoubtedly stems, at least in part, from the unpredictability of their outcome.

The statements of both urban and rural imformants overwhelmingly affirm the belief that where no moral obligation is involved, people act only out of personal interest. In other words, altruism does not form an explicit element in the folk mentality, though it very well may exist, however defined. Thus, exchanges that are not underwritten by strong reciprocal ties or evident personal interest produce both doubt as to the outcome and apprehension regarding the eventual cost. Not only is bribery regarded as a proper and efficacious manner of facilitating impersonal transactions, but it appears to be frequently proffered even when it is not solicited. In this way the petitioner feels assured that the purveyor of a service is acting out of predictable personal interest. The following examples are typical of the many case histories collected in Belgrade and other Yugoslav urban centers:

> A secondary school teacher stated that parents frequently offered bribes or favors in exchange for high grades for their children. Such bribes were proffered even when the students in question were excellent scholars.

Customs agents allowed two Montenegrin brothers to import large quantities of goods, including illegal guns and ammunition, from Italy in exchange for "favorable treatment" by the young men's uncle, who was an important official in Belgrade.

Informants stated almost universally that adequate medical and dental care under the socialist system was virtually unobtainable without bribery, the exchange of favors, or personal contacts. A middle-aged bank teller reported that when her 75-year-old mother broke her hip, an orthopedic surgeon agreed to operate only after gifts had been relayed to his two daughters through a mutual acquaintance. Later it was necessary to bribe hospital orderlies and nurses to obtain a bed for the elderly woman, who had first been placed on a thin and tattered mattress on a corridor floor.

A university professor had been on a waiting list for an apartment for almost five years. After noting that a number of individuals with less seniority had already received housing, he approached the bureaucrat in charge of allocation. For "consideration of his housing problem" the professor obtained a job in his institute for the official's daughter.

While carrying out fieldwork in Yugoslavia I regularly sent packages of books to America. This was a complicated and time-consuming process that required customs inspection and the affixing of seals. A customs agent with whom I regularly dealt invited me for drinks in a nearby café, and suggested that the payment of an additional fee that he had "forgotten" could greatly facilitate the procedure.

On another occasion I attempted to send an unusually heavy envelope containing newspaper clippings from a Zagreb post office. The clerk demanded that I open it for inspection, and when I indignantly retorted that "this was never done in Belgrade," she replied with a smile, "Ah, but they know you there!" The issue was resolved by my agreement to mail her a Playboy calendar from America for her son.

Evidence regarding the failure of the Yugoslavs to develop a universalistic ethic in the public sphere is underscored by the almost daily accounts in the press of bribery, corruption, and economic crime. For example, the October 7, 1968, issue of *Politika* reported that the directors of a school for professional drivers in the Bosnian capital of Sarajevo were earning large sums of money by selling diplomas. Similarly, on October 9 of the same year *Politika* revealed the extensive sale of trade-school diplomas in the town of Brčko, also in Bosnia. In the same issue there appeared an article disclosing the use of "state funds" by government officials to purchase private homes. Though such reports assume a reformist attitude, a highly placed informant stated that official opposition to corruption is not always out of principle but, rather, is frequently motivated by "personal political and professional ambition, the desire for revenge against adversaries, or simply envy."

While bribery is widely accepted, the creation of intimate relationships based on intense personal ties and reciprocity constitutes the preferred means of seeking advantage in Yugoslav urban society. In respect to these relationships, it is the family and kinship group that provide the principal model for structuring ties between friends, colleagues, co-workers, patrons and clients, and so forth. For example, important extrafamilial relationships exhibit almost the same intensity, the same requirement of constant revalidation through frequent contact and exchange of goods and services, and the same moral imperativeness that characterize ties between kin. Furthermore, except in the case of patron-client relationships, there is the expectation of an equilibrium or parity between partners. In other words, colleague ties tend to act as leveling mechanisms. For example, a Belgrade university student related that "best friends should be equals in all things including grades." In another case a university student related that she had severed ties with her best friend because "she had studied secretly and received a better grade" than the informant.

While all societies operate in terms of both the official institutional framework and a system of informal relationships and understandings, the gap between the two in urban Yugoslavia appears quite broad when judged by northwestern European and American standards. It is probably not an exaggeration to state that South Slav public life could not function at all without reliance on a series of informal, personalized links that are known to every Yugoslav as VIP (*veze i poznanstvo,* "connections and acquaintance," or *veze i protekcija,* "connections and favoritism"). The manner in which VIP functions is vividly summarized by Doder (1978:75):

> This is the magic *veza,* which translates literally as connection but which means much more than that. *Veza* is influence, pulling strings, an alternative bureaucratic system comprised of networks of clan and family links, old friendships, as well as of extended graft, bribery and corruption. If a man has *veza,* then everything is possible. He can get a low-cost apartment, a job for a distant cousin, he can fix and finagle things and obtain just about any service offered by society.

The widespread acceptance in Yugoslavia of the unofficial system of VIP is rationalized not only as a pragmatic expedient but as a moral imperative. Bribery and favoritism are more often than not simply interpreted as what Moore calls "the fruit of friendship" and "the price of allocation" (1973:727–28). Her analysis of the informal system governing relationships between workers and management in the New York garment industry is equally valid for the interpretation of the Yugoslav case (1973:727):

All these extra-legal givings can be called "bribery" if one chooses to emphasize their extra-legal qualities. One could instead use the classical anthropological opposition of moral to legal obligations and call these "moral" obligations, since they are obligations of relationship that are not legally enforceable, but which depend for their enforcement on the values of the relationship itself. They are all gifts or attentions calculated to induce or ease the allocation of scarce resources. The inducements and coercions involved in this system of relationships are founded on wanting to stay in the game, and on wanting to do well in it.

What is perhaps most perplexing about the VIP system is the relative importance attached to the relationships themselves in opposition to the instrumentalities that they generate. In a comparative framework it is interesting to note that middle-class Americans very often feel that material reciprocity, such as the lending of money, endangers friendship. In contrast, Yugoslavs, rural and urban alike, believe that true friendship can only exist in the framework of such exchanges. Thus, in the Yugoslav case it is all but impossible to disassociate the values of friendship from those attached to the material benefits derived from it. However, it is evident that such a system is inimical to the creation of what we have labeled a "rational economy and bureaucracy." Moreover, the situation is exacerbated by the essentially circular relationship between the folk ideology and the functioning of large-scale urban-based institutions. The greater the belief that such impersonal institutions are incapable of fulfilling their overt purposes, the greater will be the reliance on alternative social structures rooted in traditional ideas of kinship solidarity and personalism.

The Yugoslav model poses a number of questions regarding the future direction of urbanization and modernization in the world. For example, do the moral fields described here, and the kind of personalism they engender in public life, place real limits on development? Does the South Slav case, in which models appropriate to small-scale social organization are projected into the functioning of the national bureaucracy and economy, simply represent an intermediate phase in the transformation from a peasant-agrarian people to an urban-industrial state? Given the relatively pathology-free integration of millions of peasants into Yugoslav life, can we interpret many of the commonly held "rationalistic" goals of modernization as maladaptive in terms of human psychological and nonmaterial social needs?

The case of Yugoslavia is one of particular interest for the cross-cultural study of urbanization and modernization. In many ways it may prove typical of societies in which innovation and change have come about very rapidly. The precipitous rush of the South Slavs into the twentieth century has not been an isolated phenomenon, but one that has characterized the recent history of not only most of the former colonial world but also of much of the Mediterranean as well. What has occurred in the Balkans represents a major theme of our time, the metamorphosis of tribalists and peasants into an urban proleteriat. In many areas, such as northern Europe, traditional society has all but disappeared. Thus, it is in *developing nations* like Yugoslavia that the social scientist is provided with a living laboratory for the study of the dynamics of rural-urban migration, urbanization, and industrialization. Perhaps one of the most significant questions to be posed is whether the modernization process will lead inevitably to a single world culture, or whether each society will follow its own line of development.

NOTES

1. For example, the Belgrade newspaper *Ekspres Politika* of Feb. 10, 1974, reported the existence of a family *zadruga* of 105 co-resident members in the village of Nivokaz near Djakovica in Kosovo (southwestern Serbia). Similarly, Kosovofilm recently produced a documentary entitled "117" depicting the life of a household of this size. It should be noted that the majority of such large *zadrugas* now occur among the Albanian minority in Yugoslavia, and extended families among Serbo-Croatian speakers tend to be much smaller as a rule.
2. An original urban sample of 158 persons was obtained in 1961 and supplemented during subsequent visits. Random sampling in Yugoslavia is very difficult outside the context of official investigations, the more so because of a general public suspicion of such impersonal contacts and techniques. Thus I depended to a large extent on the same strategy used by anthropologists in primitive and peasant communities; I worked with those people willing to cooperate with me, depending mainly on personal relationships to establish further contacts. Nevertheless, in spite of these limitations, the original sample represented a fair spectrum of Belgrade societal types and included: 26 professions, 26 white-collar workers, 22 skilled workers, 31 unskilled workers, 18 housewives without other employment, and 40 students of various kinds (university, trade school, etc.). Of my informants, 79 were rural migrants, 47 were city-born, and 32 had moved to Belgrade from smaller towns. Those interviewed during later fieldwork in Belgrade and elsewhere in Yugoslavia represented essentially the same mix.
3. For a criticism of Banfield's concept of amoral familism, see Miller (1974).

REFERENCES

Andrić, Nada, *et al.*
    1967   *Beograd u XIX veku* (Belgrade in the nineteenth century). Belgrade: Muzej Grada Beograda.
Banfield, Edward C.
    1958   *The moral basis of a backward society.* New York: Free Press.
Barić, Lorraine
    1967a   Levels of change in Yugoslav kinship. In M. Freedman, ed., *Social organization.* London: Cass, pp. 1–24.

1967b   Traditional groups and new economic opportunities in rural Yugoslavia.
         In R. Firth, ed., *Themes in economic anthropology.* London: Association of
         Social Anthropologists of the Commonwealth, pp. 253-78.
Berger, Peter L.
1976   Ideologies, myths, moralities. In I. Kristol and P. Weaver, eds., *The
         Americans, 1976: An inquiry into fundamental concepts of man underlying various
         U.S. institutions. Critical choices for Americans,* vol. 2. Lexington, Mass.:
         Lexington Books, pp. 339-55.
Burić, Olivera
1976   The zadruga and the contemporary family in Yugoslavia. In Robert F.
         Byrnes, ed., *Communal families in the Balkans: The zadruga.* Notre Dame:
         University of Notre Dame Press, pp. 117-38.
Caro Baroja, Julio
1963   The city and the country: Reflections on some ancient commonplaces. In
         Julian A. Pitt-Rivers, ed., *Mediterranean countrymen: Essays in the social an-
         thropology of the Mediterranean.* The Hague: Mouton, pp. 27-40.
Denich, Bette S.
1969   Social mobility and industrialization in a Yugoslav town. Ph.D. disserta-
         tion, University of California at Berkeley.
Djilas, Milovan
1958   *Land without justice.* New York: Harcourt, Brace.
Doder, Duško
1978   *The Yugoslavs.* New York: Random House.
Durkheim, Emile
1933   *The division of labor in society.* New York: Macmillan.
Eisenstadt, Shmuel N., ed.
1968   *The Protestant ethic and modernization: A comparative view.* New York: Basic
         Books.
Ekspres Politika
1974   Porodica od 105 članova (A family of 105 members). Feb. 10.
Halpern, Joel M.
1963   Yugoslav peasant society in transition: Stability in change. *Anthropological
         Quarterly* 36:156-82.
1965   Peasant culture and urbanization in Yugoslavia. *Human Organization*
         24:162-74.
Halpern, Joel M., and David Anderson
1970   The zadruga: A century of change. *Anthropologica* (n.s.) 12:83-97.
Hammel, Eugene A.
1968   *Alternate social structures and ritual relations in the Balkans.* Englewood Cliffs,
         N.J.: Prentice-Hall.
1969a   Economic change, social mobility, and kinship in Serbia. *Southwestern
         Journal of Anthropology* 25:188-97.
1969b   *The pink yo-yo: Occupational mobility in Belgrade ca. 1951-1965.* Berkeley: In-
         stitute of International Studies, University of California.
Hammel, Eugene A., and Charles Yarbrough
1973   Social mobility and the durability of family ties. *Journal of Anthropological
         Research* 29:145-63.
Lewis, Oscar
1952   Urbanization without breakdown. *Scientific Monthly* 75:31-41.
Miller, Roy A.
1974   Are familists amoral? A test of Banfield's amoral familism hypothesis in a
         South Italian village. *American Ethnologist* 3:507-27.

Moore, Sally Falk
1973 Law and social change: The semi-autonomous social field as an appropriate subject of study. *Law and Society* (Summer):719–46.
Redfield, Robert
1941 *The folk culture of Yucatan.* Chicago: University of Chicago Press.
1953 *The primitive world and its transformations.* Ithaca, N.Y.: Cornell University Press.
Sapir, Edward
1964 *Culture, language and personality.* Berkeley: University of California Press.
Simić, Andrei
1967 The blood feud in Montenegro. In William G. Lockwood, ed., *Essays in Balkan ethnology.* Kroeber Anthropological Society, Special Publication no. 1. Berkeley: University of California, pp. 83–94.
1972 *The peasant urbanites: A study of rural-urban mobility in Serbia.* New York: Seminar Press.
1973a Kinship reciprocity and rural-urban integration in Serbia. *Urban Anthropology* 2:205–13.
1973b The best of two worlds: Serbian peasants in the city. In George M. Foster and Robert V. Kemper, eds., *Anthropologists in cities.* Boston: Little, Brown, pp. 179–200.
1974 Urbanization and cultural process in Yugoslavia. *Anthropological Quarterly* 47:211–27.
1975 *The ethnology of traditional and complex societies.* Washington, D.C.: American Association for the Advancement of Science.
1977 Aging in the United States and Yugoslavia: Contrasting models of intergenerational relationships. *Anthropological Quarterly* 50:53–64.

Sjoberg, Gideon
1960 *The preindustrial city.* New York: Free Press.
Socijalistička Federativna Republika Jugoslavija
1965 *Popis stanovištva* 1961. Vol. 10: *Stanovništva i domaćinštva u 1948, 1953, i 1961* (Population census 1961, Vol. 10: Populations and households in 1948, 1953, and 1961). Belgrade: Savezni Zavod za Statistiku.
Tönnies, Ferdinand
1957 *Community and society.* East Lansing: Michigan State University Press.
Weber, Max
1930 *The Protestant ethic and the spirit of capitalism.* London: George Allen and Unwin.

Chapter **8**

Rural-Urban Migration in Greece

Susan Buck Sutton

Greek villagers have moved to the capital city, Athens, and to certain provincial centers in steadily increasing numbers since the mid-nineteenth century. This rural-urban migration has profoundly changed the nature of
Greek life and is important to anyone interested in Greek cities. One could
comprehend neither the giant conglomeration of greater Athens nor the
much smaller regional towns without a knowledge of the migration that has
gone into building and shaping them. The new grey and white houses and
apartments that cover the Attic plain and spill out beyond the surrounding
mountains contrast with the older buildings clustered around only one or
two main squares in many other cities, attesting to the greater attraction of
Athens. All Greek cities stand in even starker contrast, however, to the
scores of rural villages where houses are empty and fields lie untilled,
monuments to the massive recent exodus of peasants. Predominantly rural
50 years ago, the Greek population is now over 50% urban. Athenian
growth has overshadowed all others during this period; the city has risen
from only 5,000 to almost 4,000,000 people or 40% of the current national
population (see Table 1).

This chapter examines these dramatic demographic shifts from the perspective of existing anthropologically oriented research on Greek rural-
urban migration, research that focuses on the experiences of one group of
people, considers the perceptions of actors as well as observers, and/or employs a holistic and cross-cultural perspective.[1] Such research complements
other perspectives on Greek rural-urban migration. The excellent economic, geographic, and demographic studies of the phenomenon[2] provide essential knowledge of the volume of migration as well as the larger
economic and political systems involved, whereas the anthropological
studies tend to reveal how these forces affect decision making among specific
groups of people. With the notable and valuable exceptions of Vermeulen's
work (1970) on the entire Serres region and Gutenschwager's (1971) and
Hirschon's (1970) on neighborhoods in Athens, most anthropological research on Greek rural-urban migration has concentrated on how the inhabitants of one particular rural village have undertaken migration (see especially Allen 1973, Dubisch 1977, Friedl 1976, Sutton 1978). Such research has

Table 1. Greek Urbanization, 1828–1971

Date	Greek National Population[a]	Urban Population	Urban Proportion of National Population	Athenian Population	Proportion of National Population Living in Athens
1828	753,400	- -	- -	5,000[a]	0.7%
1840	850,246	- -	- -	29,700[c]	3.5
1853	1,035,527	- -	- -	36,594[d]	3.5
1861	1,096,810	- -	- -	49,823[d]	4.5
1870	1,457,894	262,421[a]	18.0%	59,154[d]	4.1
1879	1,679,470	352,689[a]	21.0	90,295[d]	5.4
1889	2,187,208	481,186[a]	22.0	144,924[d]	6.6
1896	2,433,806	681,466[a]	28.0	179,755[d]	7.4
1907	2,631,952	710,627[a]	27.0	250,000[d]	9.5
1920	5,016,889	1,354,560[a]	27.0	453,042[d]	9.0
1928	6,204,684	1,931,937[b]	31.1	802,000[d]	12.9
1940	7,344,860	2,411,647[b]	32.8	1,124,109[d]	15.3
1951	7,632,801	2,879,994[b]	37.7	1,378,586[b]	18.1
1961	8,388,553	3,628,105[b]	43.3	1,852,709[b]	22.1
1971	8,768,641	4,667,489[b]	53.2	2,540,241[b]	29.0

[a]Great Britain (1944:2:3, 378) (urban proportion calculated on basis of population of all settlements over 5,000 people).
[b]Greece (1973a:16, 18, 21) (urban proportion calculated on basis of population of all settlements over 10,000 people).
[c]Miller (1926:24).
[d]Ward (1962:66).

contributed to our understanding of how rural-urban migrants have responded to the range of conditions in which they have found themselves and, in turn, how their actions have sometimes changed the conditions to which they were responding in the first place.

Although the anthropological work done on Greek rural-urban migration is thus of considerable value, it also has some shortcomings. There have been relatively few studies done, especially in contrast with the number focusing on rural Greece. Furthermore, the research that has been done concentrates on Athens almost to the exclusion of any other urban destination, a bias reflecting the fact that Greek rural-urban migration has increasingly become synonymous with rural-Athenian migration. Discussion here must thus be limited to what is known about migration to Athens, and the reader should bear in mind that provincial towns probably vary from the capital city. The anthropological literature on Greek rural-urban migration also suffers from very little synthesis of the different studies and from articulation of this body of information with what is known about the national and international political and economic forces that have gained influence over Greek life in the last two centuries. Just as Greek peasants have been drawn more and more into larger political and economic systems, anthropologists must similarly expand their theoretical frameworks beyond the individual village or neighborhood level.

It is the purpose of this chapter to attempt such a synthesis of existing anthropological work and to present it in a framework that will make clear its articulation with what is known about the national and international contexts of Greek rural-urban migration. This discussion will begin with a brief history of the modern Greek state that outlines the major political and economic forces that have come into play since its creation a century and a half ago. Second, the decision of some villagers to migrate will be considered in light of these forces. The next three sections of the chapter will present migrant actions after making the decision to leave the village: the first steps migrants use in establishing a place for themselves in the city, the processes of their long-term settlement there, and their continuing relationships with their rural areas of origin. Finally, the changes engendered by these migrant activities in the systems that spawned migration in the first place will be analyzed.

One theme runs throughout this presentation: Greek rural-urban migration began by connecting previously isolated settlements in a changing national system and then contributed to the growth of a few key settlements at the expense of others. In short, it contributed to what Kayser (1976) has called simultaneous processes of integration and disintegration within the Greek state. We are thus led to recognize that Greek rural-urban migration matches in many respects that of other economically underdeveloped and politically dependent nations. Migration in these countries has been spawned by national and international realignments, including governmental centralization, lack of internal economic development, growth of wage labor, and increasing dependence on foreign nations and multinational businesses. Such conditions have led to the growth of a few key cities at the expense of the rest of the nation and to the particular patterns of urban migrant behavior found in many of these nations. At the same time, rural-urban migration feeds back into the changing system, adding to regional disparities, linking less developed areas with more developed ones, and changing the nature of urban life. In sum, while the migration here described has a particular Greek character, it is also an odyssey that others will recognize because the larger-level forces operating on Greece affect many nations in the contemporary world system.

THE CHANGING GREEK STATE

Creation of the modern Greek state in 1827 both changed the nature of Greek political systems and ushered in the era of direct northern European and American economic penetration of the area. Such changes form the matrix in which Greek rural-urban migration has occurred and thus constitute the logical starting point for an analysis of such migration.[3]

Prior to the Greek War of Independence, there was no nation corresponding to modern Greece. People who were ethnically Greek lived in several provinces of the Ottoman empire spread throughout the Greek peninsula, the Balkans, and Anatolia. Although these provinces were ultimately under the control of the sultan in Constantinople, there was considerable local autonomy in most areas. The sultan extracted taxes and miltary labor but otherwise often left Greek regions alone. Greek topography and prior political organization had resulted in a large number of small, distinctive regions where local Greek landowners, religious and military leaders, merchants, or civic councils directed the affairs of the population. Most Greeks worked on agricultural estates belonging either to private individuals or to the Orthodox church. Except in parts of northern Greece, these estates were not oriented toward the production of large-scale surplus or toward cash cropping. Peasant families subsisted largely on what they produced themselves with the remainder going to the landowner or the Ottoman administration.

This political and economic system was reflected in the Greek settlement pattern of the early nineteenth century. Most Greeks lived in small, rural villages surrounded by the fields they worked. The urban population was slight in comparison and distributed fairly evenly among the many provincial towns, each about 50 kilometers from the next. These small cities served as market and manufacturing centers for the agricultural regions around them and as homes for Turkish officials. Each bore the architectural stamp of its region; the compact island towns were perched in high locations safe from piracy, while the broader streets of the inland cities surrounded a larger central square. Only a few cities, most notably Salonika and Constantinople, were major trading centers characterized by a large, cosmopolitan population.

Certain patterns of Greek social organization had developed by the end of Ottoman domination that insulated individuals against such a large, predatory, imperial system.[4] Most Greeks sought ultimate refuge in the family unit, whose interests were held to be paramount and whose members worked jointly for those interests.[5] Families tried to establish their children well; the inheritance that passed to daughters at marriage through dowry and to sons later in the life cycle through patrimony was a major focus of these efforts. Kin were generally considered more trustworthy than other people. Although different families interacted with some antagonism within the village, they generally presented a united front to outsiders and identified strongly with their local areas. Finally, political and economic relationships generally followed a patronage model by which less powerful people tried to temper the actions of those above them by offering loyalty and support.

Following the Greek War of Independence (1821–27) new national and international systems began to take shape. Independence had been won with the assistance of England, France, and Russia, who then sought roles in shaping the new Greek nation. They insisted upon creation of a nation-state along northern European lines and established an absolute monarchy to be initially occupied by the second son of the Bavarian king. In this new state the longstanding regional differences and semiautonomy of local areas were to be subordinated to a strong central government with authority to control and administer all settlements within national borders. The powers of most communities were to decrease while those of administrative centers were to increase. The newly named national capital of Athens was to house a government with more direct control over local areas than the sultan had previously had.

This centralization soon became as much fact as bureaucratic plan. The 150 years since the founding of the Greek state have seen increasing strength for the central government accompanied by decreasing power for local communities. Rural-urban migration was one factor contributing to this process. Also involved were support of the central government by foreign nations and the Greek elite, who wrested a place in it from the first king; increasing expansion of this government into education, medical care, social services, communications, and public works; and reduction of the responsibilities vested in local governments. Government-sponsored land reforms not only provided land for every peasant but further reduced the power of the traditional local leadership.

The new Greek nation was subject to considerable economic reorientation as well. The break-up of most large farming estates led to the proliferation of small, unmechanized, freeholding operations by the early twentieth century. At the same time, improved communications and increased penetration of Greece by foreign markets led to different expectations on the part of villagers (Aschenbrenner 1972, Baxevanis 1972:56–61, Friedl 1962, Sanders 1962:296). Greece became a nation of consumers before it had become a nation of producers (Meynaud 1965:456). Freeholding peasants were soon caught in annual cycles of debt to urbanites, as they attempted to acquire more manufactured goods and to convert their operations to cash production. Certain areas of Greece were able to mechanize their farming operations (i.e., the plains areas of Thessaly, Boetia, Macedonia, Thrace, Peloponnesus, and Crete); however, other areas remained unable to achieve the transition on a large scale.

At the same time that Greeks became increasingly oriented toward using manufactured goods, Greek industry remained in a subordinate position to that of northern Europe and the United States. For example, between 1938 and 1959 industrial output grew from 20.7% to only 26.5% of the gross domestic product, and 84.9% of Greek manufacturing establishments at the end of that period employed five persons or less (Coutsoumaris 1963:36–37, 55). The last two decades have seen greater growth in Greek industry, but such industry as does exist is heavily concentrated in a few cities (especially Athens and Salonika) and produces largely for consumption in the immediate area. These patterns have resulted in an unfavorable balance of trade for Greece, only somewhat mitigated by tourism, shipping, and remittances from those migrants who have gone abroad.

In the midst of such economic and political changes, certain settlements have become more important as nodes in the new networks than others. Those cities with administrative functions in the new governmental system and those that were centers for the importation and distribution of foreign manufactured goods increased in importance. Athens, the apex of both these systems, became a primate city, followed at some distance by the other large cities of Salonika, Patras, Iraklion, Volos, Larissa, and Kavalla. In 1971 the greater Athenian population was five times that of Salonika, and all but a few other cities had fewer than 100,000 people (Greece 1973a:21). Most provincial towns and villages have decreased in importance, no longer providing the political or economic leadership they once did and now serving largely as points of communication with Athens (Kolodny 1974: 1:401–21).

THE DECISION TO MIGRATE

It was to such changes that those who have migrated from village to city have been responding. The reorientation of national political and economic systems has gradually refocused people outside their villages. At first, migration served to spread networks of familism, localism, and patronage over wider geographical distances, thus connecting villages to centers of power and wealth. As the gap in development between city and countryside has progressively widened, however, these networks served as much to draw people out of villages as to filter goods and services back to them. These processes will now be elaborated, especially as they pertain to the decision to migrate.

The first four decades of the new Greek state constituted a period of small-scale, exploratory mobility involving relatively few people. The events of this period, however, reinforced certain conditions that later led to increased migration. There were a variety of migration streams during this period, not all rural-urban (Kolodny 1974:1:108–9, 186–92; Sutton (1978:68). For example, some uninhabited islands were colonized by peasants, and many Greeks left lands still under Ottoman control to settle in the

Greek countryside.[6] Until 1870 rural-urban migration attracted mainly the local leaders, large landowners, and merchants interested in attaching themselves to new political and economic structures (see especially Petropoulos 1968). Provincial capitals, Athens, and the boom-town port of Ermoupolis (Siros) were the major urban migrant recipients (Kolodny 1974:1:107–9). These latter two cities grew to populations of approximately 60,000 and 20,000 respectively during this early period. Greek political leaders soon established a place for themselves in the new governmental structures by gaining control of the bureaucracy as well as demanding that the Bavarian king establish a national legislature and then running for office in it. The Greek economic elite simultaneously found places in shipping and international commerce.

Because they legitimated new political and economic structures, these actions set the stage for large-scale migration by less influential rural dwellers, only a few of whom had already come to cities to service the elite, construct new governmental buildings, and seek an education. The spread of rural-urban migration to a larger segment of the Greek population is reflected in Table 1. Despite a positive rate of natural increase (Valaoras 1960), rural areas have steadily lost population since 1870. Rural-rural migration has been outstripped by rural-urban, with 60% of the internal migration between 1956 and 1961 and 63% between 1965 and 1971 being of the latter sort (Greece 1973b:123, Kayser 1963:198).[7] The only rural areas to maintain population have been those where large-scale mechanization and cash cropping have been established (Campbell and Sherrard 1968:323, Kayser and Thompson 1964:213–16). Other rural areas, especially the mountains, Epirus, the Peloponnesus, and the islands, have experienced severe and increasing population decline.[8] For example, since World War II the Peloponnesian population has declined by 22% (Baxevanis 1972:15). Over time this rural-urban migration has focused almost exclusively on Athens and a few other cities. The provincial towns have ceased expanding and have even lost population; of 53 provincial cities, only 13 had a positive migration balance between 1956 and 1961 (Kayser 1963:198). The major provincial urban recipients of migration have been coastal and crossroads towns that provide access to larger centers (Kolodny 1974:1:265–74, 2:473–86). All internal migration streams pale when contrasted with the volume directed toward Athens, a city that now contains 40% of the national population.

Such migration figures reflect the response of Greek villagers to the changing conditions of the Greek state after 1870. Land reform, compulsory schooling run by the national government, improved communications, a military draft, taxation, and increased central governmental activities all contributed to the steady breakdown of local power structures and decreased isolation of rural areas. The products and lifestyles of northern Europe, the

United States, and Athens became better known to villagers, who incorporated them as part of their personal and familial goals. Small-scale farming operations and the inability to expand or mechanize these led peasants in many areas to devalue rural life and to look outside the village for attainment of their goals (Allen 1973, Dubisch 1977:70, DuBoulay 1974:233–36, Friedl 1976:276, Kasperson 1966:99–100, Sutton 1978, Vermeulen 1970). Interviews with recent rural-urban migrants add weight to this analysis; most left their villages to find work that paid cash, to seek an education, to marry an urban spouse, and/or to find a more exciting lifestyle (Baxevanis 1972:60, DuBoulay 1974:233–36, Friedl 1976:369, Moustaka 1964:60, Sandis 1973:91, Sutton 1978:157–72).

This large-scale rural-urban migration began with an entrepreneurial or pioneering stage (Friedl 1976, Sutton 1978:59–78). The first waves of migrants were generally among the wealthier villagers, people whose families could spare their labor and afford to risk the trip to the city. The move often stemmed from the family's plan to advance their children; sons were sent to obtain an education or earn cash for the family (see also Kasperson 1966:38), and daughters were sent to marry an urban husband or to enhance their dowries by working before marriage (see also Miller 1905:195). These early migrants acted in an entrepreneurial fashion to connect the declining village to new sources of power and wealth. A few of these early migrants also came from among those peasants most marginally established in a village, those who had only recently come to the village and had few roots in it.

Such entrepreneurial migrants opened the way for subsequent migrants who used the connections thus established. Many villagers wished to migrate; however, those with relatives already in a city felt more secure in doing so than those with none (Allen 1973, Dubisch 1977:73, Friedl 1976:372, Mendras 1962:20, Moustaka 1964:50, Sutton 1978:164–67). Siblings followed siblings, nephews and nieces followed aunts and uncles, and spouses followed spouses. Early migrants gave later ones detailed knowledge of what to expect and eased their entrance into the city. As migration has continued, such links have increased in number, thus creating more opportunities for migration among village populations. For example, the proportion of island villagers Sutton studied, with at least one sibling in Athens, rose from under 10% in 1900 to almost 50% in 1975. These ties have allowed a greater number and variety of villagers to migrate than before (see also Dubisch 1977:71).

In the last two decades another factor impelling migration has joined those already mentioned. With severe rural depopulation and collapse of local political and economic structures, some villagers who might otherwise not have migrated are now doing so. Allen (1973:75) points out that some villagers now go to cities not because they wish to but simply to be near their relatives who are overwhelmingly concentrated outside the village. For example, elderly villagers move to be cared for by their children, none of whom remain in the village (see also Kolodny 1974:2:604, Sutton 1978:162). Kinship networks that at first connected the village to urban resources have now come to drain the countryside and support further urban growth.

Athens has come to occupy a dominant position in this migration. Although provincial towns at first drew migrants, no city can now match the attraction of the capital. Almost half the internal migration between 1956–61 and 1965–71 was directed toward Athens (Andreadis 1963:319, Greece 1973b:123). Most recent internal migrants in both Sandis's study (1973:80) and mine have gone directly to Athens with no temporary, intermediate destinations. As Greece has remained largely nonindustrialized, only Athens could provide any semblance of what migrants sought. Rapidly ramifying kinship networks connecting the capital to many rural areas have only added to Athenian importance.

Throughout this history migrants have been concentrated in the young adult ages (15-35 years of age), although this has been tempered recently as more elderly and more children have been drawn into cities. The elderly migrate, as already mentioned, to be with their migrant children, while the children are sent to attend postprimary schools, most of which are only found in cities. Higher education is seen as a means to social mobility, and many village families attempt to give at least one of their children such an opportunity (Allen 1973:32; Baxevanis 1972:68–69, 71–73; Friedl 1976). Marriage to an urban spouse similarly provides mobility, and indeed many village families attain mobility for their daughters by providing an urban dwelling as dowry in order that they marry an urban spouse (Allen 1973:87; Friedl 1963a, b, 1976).

War refugees constituted another major source of urban migrants in Greece, although they moved for reasons obviously different from those just described. There were two major streams of refugees. The first and larger followed the Balkan wars and World War I, stemming from a series of voluntary and forced population exchanges among Greece, the newly formed Balkan nations, and Turkey. Between 1920 and 1928 approximately 1.2 million Greek refugees entered Greece (Kayser and Thompson 1964:204, Pentzopoulos 1962). Of these, 60% were settled in Athens and Salonika, with the capital city receiving the majority. Most of the remainder were settled in the countryside, largely in Macedonia and Thrace; many had been urban dwellers in Turkey, however, and soon left their new villages for the cities (Ladas 1932:645–46). A second wave of internal, rural-urban refugees was engendered, especially in northern Greece, by the events of World War II and the Greek Civil War (see Common 1958:262, Kayser 1963:194, Kayser and Thompson 1964:204, Vermeulen 1970, Wagstaff 1968:179).

SETTLING IN THE CITY: FIRST STEPS

Most Greek rural-urban migrants thus move in the hopes of bettering the position of themselves and their families in a shifting national system that gradually eroded village vitality in favor of a few key cities. Their success in achieving these goals and their continued maintenance or rejection of them rest on what occurs as the migrants establish themselves in the city. This settlement process can usefully be divided into two phases. The first phase covers the initial steps a newly arrived migrant takes in gaining a toehold in the city and is considered in this section. The second phase covers a migrant's subsequent attempts to branch out from this position and is examined in the next section. Unfortunately, once again the data that inform these two sections are heavily biased toward settlement in Athens, and these discussions must be taken as referring to the capital alone. Salonika, Patras, and a few other cities may share Athenian patterns of migrant settlement. Settlement in other cities, however, has most likely differed from that in Athens owing to their more limited resources, smaller population sizes, different economic bases, different positions in national systems, and the fact that migrants in these cities have often subsequently moved to Athens and Salonika.

Newly arrived rural Athenian migrants use egocentric social networks to ease the problems of initial settlement. Such networks allow even the poorest villagers some success and security in moving to and living in Athens. Three major networks are used in this manner: those based on kinship, those based on local or regional ties, and those based on economic position. All three types involve both relationships strictly among migrants and relationships between migrants and native-born urbanites. Each of these three types will now be discussed; then the operation of the networks in finding housing and jobs will be examined.

The patterns of familism that influenced villagers to migrate are also a means by which many effect their early adaptation to Athens. This is true for people of all economic classes and regional origins. As mentioned above, the presence of kin in a city is important in deciding to migrate. These kin help newly arrived migrants (Allen 1973:65, 111; Dubisch 1977; Friedl 1976; Sutton 1978:104, 130–34). As migration has increased, the pool of such kin available to help any newly arrived migrants has also grown larger.

Migrants to Athens also use networks based on area of origin to settle in the city. People from the same rural area often seek each other out for information and aid. These regional and local networks have changed over time, if one judges by the case of the Cycladic villagers Sutton studied. In the early stages of migration, the regional networks of these villagers represented large geographical areas (i.e., all of the island, and sometimes the Cyclades in general). There were then few migrants in Athens, and they were thus compelled to look beyond their own village to find people with whom they felt some mutual regional obligations. Later, as more and more migrants entered the city, such wide-flung regional networks have been supplemented by smaller, closer-knit networks based just on the small section of the island where the village is located.

Four institutions have frequently arisen from these regional and local networks in Athens, institutions that both stem from the networks and keep them operative. First, there are usually one or two coffee houses *(kapheneia)* in Athens, owned and frequented primarily by migrants from a particular area of origin (Andrews 1967:28; Kenna 1978; Sutton 1978:104, 133). These coffee houses generally bear a name identifying the region they represent. They serve as places to relax, as arenas for social interaction, and as communication centers for news of the home area, other migrants, job opportunities, and politics. They are patronized almost exclusively by men, who then convey the information to their wives, who further convey it to other women through home visits and, more recently, telephone calls.

Second, Athenian neighborhoods often develop in which migrants from a particular area are concentrated (Allen 1973:66; Andrews 1967:28; Andromedas 1963; Kenna 1976; Kolodny 1974:2:604; Miller 1905:187; Moustaka 1964:35, Sutton 1978:101, 131). Several neighborhoods have sometimes successively represented one area of origin, each having been formed at different periods in Athenian expansion. Such neighborhoods are neither geographically distinct nor composed exclusively of migrants from one area. Nor do all migrants from an area live in them. In addition, some migrant groups have not even had such neighborhoods (Dubisch 1977, Friedl 1976). Those that do exist, however, are symbolic centers for these migrants in Athens and generally contain the coffee house. Newly arrived migrants tend to be more heavily concentrated in them than those who have been in the city longer.

Third, regional networks in Athens have also spawned and been maintained by regional voluntary associations, which have done only a little to help newly arrived migrants and are discussed more appropriately and in more detail later. Fourth, in recent years regional newspapers have appeared in Athens (Kolodny 1974:1:122, Sutton 1978:177). These papers convey news of the home area and migrant activities as well as carry advertisements for businesses run by migrants from the area. They generally represent fairly large geographical areas.

The final type of network used by newly arrived migrants has been based on economic position. Migrants soon meet people outside familial and regional networks at work, in school, or in their neighborhood, contexts which generally segregate people according to economic position. Migrants from different areas of origin show little prejudice toward each other and form some bonds with new people in these contexts, thus laying the groundwork for new social networks and class formation. From the start, the group forming the strongest bonds and holding themselves most apart from others has been the elite (Campbell and Sherrard 1968:92, Legg 1969:110–14, Miller 1905:191–203). The leading politicians, merchants, shippers, and bankers together with the religious hierarchy have come to form a closely knit network, mixing as much with foreigners as with other Greeks.

All three types of networks have aided newly arrived migrants in finding both housing and work in Athens. Adequate housing for new migrants has rarely been a problem in smaller cities that received few migrants. The great influx to Athens, however, has caused shortages from time to time, resulting in some squatter settlements since the mid-nineteenth century as well as escalating and inflationary housing prices (Andrews 1967:13, Papageorgiou 1967:88, Wagstaff 1968:177–78). Thus the information and assistance provided to newly arrived migrants through their social networks are of considerable value. Adult migrants frequently stay with relatives or friends until they find housing of their own, while migrant school children often live with relatives throughout the duration of their education. When migrants move out on their own, they are influenced by the information conveyed by these networks as well as by what is available for rent or sale by people they know.

Such networks are similarly used by migrants seeking work. The early, entrepreneurial migrants found work without extensive use of pre-existing networks, developing whatever they could (Campbell and Sherrard 1968:92). Later migrants, however, often have a job prearranged by relatives or fellow villagers in Athens before they arrive (Moustaka 1964:51) or make use of their networks once in the city. Certain occupations in Athens have sometimes been known for high concentrations of people from the same region working in them (About 1857:38, 501; Allen 1973:112; Andrews 1967:54; Andromedas 1963:277; Miller 1905:184–89; Sutton 1978:104). The realtively low level of manufacturing in Greece has meant that relatively few people were employed in this sector. Even in Athens only one-quarter to one-third of the labor force has worked in manufacturing since 1961 (Greece 1973a:74, Papageorgiou 1967:91–95). Construction and services have consistently provided the largest sources of urban employment, while, over time, shipping and tourism have also grown in importance (Kolodny 1974:1:325–74, 423–41).

The Anatolian refugees who streamed into Athens, Salonika, and some other cities after World War I had to establish themselves without the aid of relatives or friends already there and without many financial resources of their own. In lieu of pre-existing social networks in Athens such as those just described for other migrants, they formed cohesive mutual-aid networks among themselves to aid in their initial settlement (Gutenschwager 1971:46, Legg 1969:86, Pentzopoulos 1962). Many had left all their belongings behind as they fled in fear of their lives before the Turkish army. They arrived in a state of anger and shock with little except the clothing on their backs. Their large numbers overtaxed the immediate abilities of Greek cities to house them. Government assistance programs were slow and inadequate to serve everyone involved. The refugees turned to each other for assistance. Squatter settlements arose where public housing did not, and mutual resources were shared among relatives and friends.

SETTLING IN THE CITY: THE LONG RUN

Having established a toehold in Athens, migrants are then faced with the decision of whether to stay in the city or not and, if the former, how to effect their long-term settlement there. As will be seen in this section, these involve somewhat different patterns of behavior from the steps toward initial settlement.

In the early years of rural-urban migration villagers often moved back and forth between the village and Athens before deciding where to settle on a long-term basis. Most villages were still viable, and the migrants had more kin there than in the city. A brief stint in Athens was often seen simply as a means for earning cash to improve a migrant's position upon return to the village. The women who worked as seamstresses and servants to improve their dowries and the men who migrated only for seasonal construction work attest to this (Dubisch 1977:70, Kenna 1976:347, Sutton 1978:105). Friedl has noted other sorts of early migrants who spent periods of time back in the village (1976:372–74). During the nineteenth century over half the migrants from the Cycladic village Sutton studied eventually resettled in the village.

As the balance between the village and city has become more heavily weighted toward the latter, decisions not to return to the village have been made more quickly, with less ambivalence, and by more migrants. The back-and-forth patterns just mentioned have decreased in frequency, and there are now very low rates of return migration (e.g. Allen 1973:79, Kenna 1978). Although migrants have increasingly decided not to return to the village, not all stay in the city to which they first move. Those in provincial towns frequently move to larger cities or abroad. Even many of those in Athens and Salonika hold open the possibility of emigration. The ability of even those cities to provide jobs has been limited, especially in light of low industrial development. Since the late nineteenth century, unemployment has been relieved primarily through the safety valve of large-scale emigration to more developed nations (Kasperson 1966:94, Kayser and Thompson 1964: 217, Kolodny 1974:2:569–92, Valaoras 1960, Vermuelen 1970).

Those migrants who remain in Athens have generally achieved some upward mobility according to their familial and personal goals (Friedl 1976, Sandis 1973:60). They have succeeded in entering the market economy, establishing residence in the nerve center of the nation, and acquiring a higher standard of living than they had in the countryside. As Friedl and Sandis point out, however, few achieve great mobility, and the relative economic standings the migrants held in the village with respect to each other are often repeated in Athens. Their mobility and the belief that urban life offers greater opportunities to their children have convinced these migrants that the decision to move was correct and have committed them to long-term residence in Athens (Moustaka 1964:71, 75; Sandis 1973:94). Although they recognize that the village was more peaceful and a few wish to retire there, the odds are increasingly in favor of continued urban residence.

The same social networks facilitating initial migrant adaptation to Athens also facilitate long-term settlement. These networks provide personal assistance to long-term settlers and are also the means by which they learn new information, judge their own behavior, and conduct a satisfactory social life. Family ties remain important to migrants even after decades of urban residence (Campbell and Sherrard 1968:366, Friedl 1976, Moustaka 1964:41, Safilios-Rothschild 1976, Sandis 1973:103). Closely related kin often live nearby, make daily house visits or telephone calls, and take periodic group excursions to tavernas and the beach. In the case of migrant-owned stores and workshops, small kin groups often work together as well. Regional networks and institutions have also been maintained by long-term migrants (Sutton 1978:177–80). The regional voluntary associations seem to be run by migrants who have been in Athens a decade or more. Many migrants also continue to live in regional neighborhoods. Even when migrants move to another part of the city, the men return to the regional coffee houses from time to time to keep in touch.

While maintaining such networks, most migrants also attempt to expand their ties to other people in Athens, generally to people of the same or higher economic position (Friedl 1976:372). Such relations are extended through work, school, neighborhood, and church connections or through friends or relatives. An important mechanism of network extension is, frequently, marriage.

The decision to stay in Athens is often signaled and solidified by a migrant marrying and beginning to raise children there. This step expands a migrant's networks of mutual obligation in the city. This is especially important for the two-thirds of the migrants who marry a spouse from outside their own village (Allen 1973:104; Friedl 1976:373, 375; Sandis 1973:50; Sutton 1978:107, 135, 130). Marriage also provides migrants with additional economic resources, in the form of the spouse's income, dowry, or patrimony. Finally, marriage makes return to the village more difficult for those migrants whose spouses are not from their region and do not wish to move to a village in which they know few people. Marriage is generally soon followed by having children, a step further extending migrant networks and committing them to urban life. Most migrants feel their children will have a better future in Athens than the village because they can receive better education and medical care there and more job opportunities are open to them (Moustaka 1964, Sutton 1978:183). In addition, their children generally oppose return to the village and have formed friendships with schoolmates, further integrating them into the urban setting.

Few migrants remain exactly as they were when they first moved to Athens; most use the social networks just mentioned to effect job and residence changes. The working male migrants generally seek a higher paying, more skilled job, or decide to open their own store or workshop (Campbell and Sherrard 1968:374, Moustaka 1964:55, Sutton 1978:182–83). Over half the migrants Sutton studied and 30% of those questioned by Moustaka made such shifts, generally after a decade or more of urban residence. The migrants entering Athens as school children generally found a place for themselves in the growing ranks of professionals and office workers (Campbell and Sherrard 1968:370). At the first pregnancy, if not before, migrant women almost always become full-time housewives and cease working for wages outside the home (Moustaka 1964:46, Sandis 1973:56, Sutton 1978:183).[9] This pattern may stem from the scarcity both of people (especially grandparents) who can tend children during the day and of adequate job opportunities.

Most migrants in Athens change residence at least once (Friedl 1976, Sandis 1973:93, Sutton 1978:175). The ownership of urban property is seen as a safe investment in an otherwise tenuous economic situation, and Greek cities have a high degree of home ownership (Sandis 1973:145, Kenna 1978, Ward 1962:28). Migrants make every attempt to own their housing, and marriage to a spouse with a dwelling is highly valued in this regard. The institution of dowry remains strong in the city as a means by which a young couple can get a good start (Allen 1973, Gutenschwager 1971:84–89, Hirschon and Thakurdesai 1970, Lambiri 1965:265, Friedl 1976, Safilios-Rothschild 1976, Sutton 1978:175). Since migrant women rarely work after marriage and thus do not contribute cash to the household (although they do, of course, contribute unpaid labor), they are expected to contribute to the family at marriage through dowry. The most preferred form of dowry is an urban dwelling, and wealthy village families provide their daughters with land or housing in Athens to ensure their marrying an urban husband. Although such dowries are the ideal, they are probably achieved less than half the time. A less common pattern is for the husband to purchase or inherit a house or apartment before marriage and for his wife to move there. When neither pattern occurs, the migrant couple attempts to save enough money after marriage to acquire their own residence.

However they obtained it, migrants generally prefer to choose housing near their relatives in Athens (Friedl 1976:23; Sutton 1978:133, 175–76).

This involves either building new single-family houses on open land, subdividing existing houses, or replacing houses with apartment buildings in which several apartments are owned by close relatives (Hirschon and Thakurdesai 1970, Sutton 1978:175–76). When land and housing are still available in the regional neighborhood, this often leads to a continued concentration of migrants from that region there. As Athens has become more densely populated and land values have risen, many migrants turn from the regional neighborhoods to build in the newest ring of housing surrounding the city; land values generally decline as one moves outward from the center of Athens. The city has gradually expanded across the Attic plain surrounding the old Turkish city, a plain that less than a century ago was given over to olive groves and wheat fields.

Most migrants remain official citizens of their village for several years after settling in Athens, a pattern signifying they have not yet decided to settle permanently in the city and, during the 1950s, also reflecting official government policy (Meynaud 1965:52–59, Sutton 1978:135). They thus continued to vote for candidates in the village for several years after they left. Eventually, however, most change their official registration to Athens and vote there because they have committed themselves to the city, and they dislike the long trips back to vote.

It is unclear if migrants have changed their political views as a result of Athenian residence. Certainly they removed themselves from political patronage networks operating in the countryside (Meynaud 1965:168). Most migrants with whom I spoke, however, did not feel they had changed their political ideology. They have not reorganized themselves politically in the city, a point given support by only minimal development of a labor movement among migrants (Campbell and Sherrard 1968:377, Legg 1969:116). Most ideological changes seem to have occurred among those migrating to the city as school children; students have been a major left-wing force in Greek politics (Legg 1969:211–13). The Anatolian refugees were one major migrant group also making a leftward political swing; this was a response to the helplessness and abandonment they felt (Legg 1969:115, Pentzopoulos 1962:171–95).

Settlement patterns among Anatolian refugees generally exhibited some distinctiveness stemming from the peculiar nature of the refugee situation. The refugees maintained themselves as a somewhat separate group long after their arrival (Pentzopoulos 1962:204, Gutenschwager 1971:57). They recognized common cultural and historical experiences with each other. They sometimes regarded marriage into other groups with suspicion, and many continued to live in the refugee areas where they originally settled (Andrews 1967:26, Hirschon and Thakurdesai 1970:187, Sandis 1973: 37–40, Gutenschwager 1971). The regional ties that had helped them weather their traumatic initial settlement proved durable. Most refugees did not remain impoverished but gradually improved their economic condition. Using skills brought from Turkey, many established small carpet, textile, and pottery workshops (Coutsoumaris 1963:22, Great Britain 1944:2:104, Gutenschwager 1971:73–83). Such small-scale manufacturing not only helped the refugees but also gave Greek industrialization a major boost.

CONTINUING TIES WITH THE HOME AREA

Greek rural-urban migration has seen a gradual spreading of social networks between countryside and city; migrants rarely sever their connections to their home areas. These ties and obligations continue to influence their behavior and constitute an informal but important connection between city and countryside.

Among the earliest ties between migrants and their home areas were those maintained by the leaders who migrated to provincial capitals and Athens soon after Greek independence. These migrants moved to gain a place in the new political and economic structures and soon succeeded in their goals. By maintaining patronage ties with villagers in their home areas, these men became intermediaries between the new centers and their home areas. The Greek elite thus expanded the old political patronage hierarchy from its rural locus to one spanning countryside and city and fitting with the new centralized system (Campbell and Sherrard 1968, Legg 1969, Petropoulos 1968). Such patronage links between rural areas and cities have been maintained (see also Meynaud 1965).

As less elite migrants moved to cities, however, these patronage networks were supplemented and undermined by others giving most villagers more direct, more trustworthy links to urban resources. Most migrants have maintained contact with their close kin in the village, especially parents and siblings (Allen 1973; Dubisch 1977; Friedl 1959, 1962, 1963a, b, 1976; Sutton 1978). Allen (1973:117–35) notes a tendency to overlay actual migrant-villager kinship relationships with fictive ones to strengthen them (see also Kenna 1976:347).

Migrant-villager kinship links are maintained in two ways. First, migrant and village relatives maintain communication by personal visits, letters, or, where possible, telephone. Most migrants with close relatives in the village return at least once a year to visit them. Such visits generally occur in spring, summer, and early fall when travel to and life in the village is easier; they also coincide with important village festivals. On these occasions the villages are swelled by the influx of visiting migrants and exhibit a demographic vitality they do not truly have. Through these channels migrants and villagers maintain bonds among themselves and convey information. Villagers keep migrants up to date on events in the village; migrants inform villagers about the success or failure of other migrants and about new ideas and goods they have encountered (see also Evelpidis 1963:203). Until the advent of radio around World War II, such networks were the major source for villagers to learn about the outside world.

A second contact between migrant and village kin is the exchange of gifts and favors. Villagers send urban relatives food staples; migrants send village relatives manufactured goods and money (see Kayser 1963:194). Although rarely on a large scale, this exchange enables villagers to translate subsistence produce into items for which they would otherwise need cash and also enables migrants to obtain staples they would otherwise have to buy. In some regions people earn a living as private couriers transporting these gifts (Andrews 1967:29, Dubisch 1977:70, Kolodny 1974:1:100-101, Sutton 1978:107). Migrants and village relatives also do favors for each other: both offer the hospitality of their homes for visits; migrants attend to governmental or medical business for village relatives (see also Campbell 1963:143); villagers care for migrant relatives' land and houses. In such ways some resources of both city and village are open to both, and personal links are substituted for more distant, patronage ties (Campbell 1963:145, Dubisch 1977, Friedl 1962:74).

Migrants tend to keep land and houses they have inherited in the countryside (Allen 1973:173-75), Dubisch 1977:76-77, Kenna 1976:347, Sutton 1978:136, Vermeulen 1970, Wagstaff 1968:179). In regions with declining population and poor terrain, migrants have little opportunity to sell either houses or land. Furthermore, such property provides a measure of insurance for migrants in case of failure in the city. The land is sometimes worked by relatives or other villagers who keep a portion of the produce and give the rest to the migrant; at other times it is left uncultivated. The produce rarely provides more than olive oil and other food staples for the migrants; only in exceptional cases is it a major source of income. Migrants generally leave their village houses empty to be used for their periodic trips to the village or to be rented to occasional tourists.

A final way migrants maintain ties with their rural homeland is by establishing regional associations to work for the improvement of the home area (Allen 1973:166, Dubisch 1977:77, Kenna 1978, Sutton 1978). Such associations are found only in major cities and primarily in Athens. Their activities on behalf of newly arrived migrants are less than those on behalf of the village. Instead, they lobby with the national government to gain more public works and social services for the villages, and they collect and relay money from migrants to the villages. They also sponsor social gatherings, which reinforce regional networks in the city and remind migrants of obligations to the home area. These associations began appearing in the late nineteenth century and have steadily proliferated. They attempt to counteract the political and economic imbalance that characterizes the relationship between city and countryside in Greece.

CONSEQUENCES OF GREEK RURAL-URBAN MIGRATION

Thus have migrants responded to the changing structure of the modern Greek state. As already stated, rural-urban migration such as occurs in Greece does not simply conform to a static status quo but instead feeds into the complex dynamics of national changes. Greek migration began by connecting villages to new sources of power and wealth but has over time contributed to the devolution of these same villages in favor of fewer and fewer key cities. This process will now be considered in terms of four systems: individual, urban, village, and national.

The move from village to city enables individual migrants to leave low-cash-producing, low-power situations and enter ones with more possibilities for earning money and being close to the decision makers in Greek society. The move entails much personal cost to the migrants: they have left the close relatives, friends, and familiar situations that afforded them a measure of peace and security. Despite such losses, however, most migrants have committed themselves to their new life. They do so to achieve some of the personal goals they have set for themselves. Their success stems from supportive, egocentric social networks facilitating their settlement in the city and the balance that has thus far existed between employment opportunities and emigration. The continued well-being of these migrants is more in doubt, however, as more and more migrants enter Athens and as the structural weaknesses inherent in Greece's underdevelopment and dependence make themselves felt more strongly.

Rural-urban migration has affected those cities receiving migrants differently from those that did not. This differential effect has increased over time as a few cities became centers and received the bulk of the migration. Those cities receiving few migrants have dwindled in size and importance; those receiving many have developed in the opposite direction. In most such recipient cities at least 50% of the population since the mid-nineteenth century have been migrants (Kayser and Thompson 1964:219, Sandis 1973:15, Sutton 1978). The influx has changed the nature of these cities. Their populations are now larger and contain relatively fewer elite. The migration has reinforced Greek political centralization in these cities. Finally, their economic systems have become oriented in two directions: toward providing buildings and services for newcomers, and toward participating in international trade networks from a disadvantaged position.

Migration has similarly affected those villages losing much population differently from those that have not. The late nineteenth and twentieth centuries have witnessed migration's increasing impact on areas not converting to cash production. All villages have lost population to cities, but these have lost considerably more than the rest. These villages have experienced mixed effects from the out-migration. On the one hand, it has connected them to sources of wealth, power, and information to which they otherwise had access only through unsympathetic and remote political patronage networks. On the other hand, it has also weakened them demographically, politically, and economically (see Allen 1973 for a comprehensive account). Many have been abandoned, and others have experienced severe decline and aging of their population (Baxevanis 1972:39, Evelpidis 1963:204, Kolodny 1974:2:611–54, Sutton 1978:158, Wagstaff 1968). Traditional local economic and political structures have disintegrated, labor shortages have arisen, and the villages have focused in a dependent manner on major cities and abroad (DuBoulay 1974:427–29, Kasperson 1966:32, Vermeulen 1970).

Rural-urban migration has played a key role in reinforcing the national processes set in motion by the creation of modern Greece. First, it has contributed to the formation of a tightly knit, highly centralized state. The migration has supported the decrease in power of local areas and increase in power of the central government. Second, the migration has increased demand for foreign manufactured goods in an underdeveloped economy subject to outside pressure. Migrants have committed themselves to the new economic system and transmitted their goals to their rural relatives. Finally, by concentrating population and resources in them, the migration has reinforced the pre-eminence of some settlements, such as Athens, as key centers in the new systems.

In sum, Greek rural-urban migration represents the attempt of peasants to participate more fully in the new systems set in motion as Greece changed from an imperial, feudal system to a capitalistic, national one. Although achieving some mobility for themselves and channeling some resources back to the countryside, migrant actions have largely reinforced the inequities of the new system thus far. Migrants have taken such actions as they could to improve their position within this system but have generally done little to structurally alter it despite the problems it poses for them.

At the same time rural-urban migration has reinforced the new system, it may also have laid the groundwork for other changes, some of which may eventually lead Greece in other directions. There has been some democratization of the political system and the development of a labor force ready to participate in indigenous industrialization. From the start, migrants were concerned with increasing their ability to participate in the political system: creation of a parliament, entry of the middle class into electoral politics, ousting of the king, and by-passing of patronage networks have all been testaments to this. At the same time, migrants were concerned with developing occupations providing them access to goods they wanted. Such tendencies continue to grow and are progressively being channeled in new directions as new ways of viewing national development are examined by the growing student and second-generation migrant populations. This latter group may decide that what satisfied their parents will not satisy them, and recognize the limits of the underdeveloped, overcentralized national system in which they live. Migration provided their parents with some semblance of mobility; growing up in the city has not necessarily done the same for the second generation, who often have greater feelings of both frustration and class consciousness than their parents. As second-generation migrants may soon for the first time constitute a larger population in the major Greek cities than first-generation migrants, the ways in which they decide to act upon these perceptions may well be a major source of change in Greek life.

NOTES

1. See Gulick (1974) for a good discussion of the range of urban anthropological research.
2. See especially Baxevanis (1972), Kayser and Thompson (1964), Kolodny (1974), and numerous publications by the Greek National Statistics Service. Work in progress and raw data may be found at most Greek social science organizations, especially the National Center of Social Research, the National Center for Economic Planning, the National Statistics Service, and the Athens Center of Ekistics.
3. My account of the changing nature of the Greek state is compiled from several excellent political and historical works on the topic, especially Campbell and Sherrard (1968), Legg (1969), Petropoulos (1968), Mouzelis (1978), Kayser and Thompson (1964), Kolodny (1974), Meynaud (1965), Vacalopoulos (1976), and Sanders (1962).
4. For more extensive discussions of kinship, localism, and patronage, especially in contemporary times, see Campbell (1964), DuBoulay (1974), Friedl (1962), and Loizos (1975).
5. Different types of family structures and kinship systems characterize different regions of Greece. When I use the term "family" in this chapter, I am referring to the smallest, core family unit in an area, generally either an extended or a nuclear family.
6. The original modern Greek state covered only a small portion of its present territory, the southern part of the Greek peninsula. As the Ottoman empire was gradually dismantled during the nineteenth and twentieth centuries, Greece grew to its present geographical dimensions and received the in-migration of many Greek ethnics who remained outside its borders but within the eastern Mediterranean area. See Crawley (1967:98) for a brief overview of this process.
7. Much rural-rural migration occurs over short distances when people from two nearby villages marry.
8. For detailed discussions of depopulation and the concentration of migration streams on Athens as a destination, see Allen (1973), Andromedas (1963), Baxevanis (1972), Common (1958), Dubisch (1977), Evelpidis (1963), Friedl (1976), Kayser (1963), Kayser and Thompson (1964), Kolodny (1974), Sutton (1978), Vermeulen (1970), and Wagstaff (1968).
9. This pattern contrasts with most village patterns whereby women work outside the home in the fields on a daily basis.

REFERENCES

About, Edmond F. V.
   1857   *Greece and Greeks of the present day.* New York: Dix, Edward and Co.
Allen, Peter Sutton
   1973   Social and economic change in a depopulated community in southern
           Greece. Ph.D. dissertation, Brown University.
Andreadis, Stratis G.
   1963   Discontinuités sociales et problèmes de developpement économique en
           Grèce. In John G. Peristiany, ed., *Contributions to Mediterranean sociology.*
           Paris: Mouton, pp. 315–24.
Andrews, Kevin
   1967   *Athens.* London: Phoenix House.
Andromedas, John
   1963   The enduring urban ties of a modern Greek folk subculture. In John G.
           Peristiany, ed., *Contributions to Mediterranean sociology.* Paris: Mouton, pp.
           269–73.
Aschenbrenner, Stanley
   1972   A contemporary community. In William A. McDonald and George R.
           Rapp, Jr., eds., *The Minnesota Messenia expedition.* Minneapolis: Univer-
           sity of Minnesota Press, pp. 47–63.
Baxevanis, John
   1972   *Economy and population movements in the Peloponnesus of Greece.* Athens: Na-
           tional Center of Social Research.
Campbell, John
   1963   Two case studies of marketing and patronage in Greece. In John G. Per-
           istiany, ed., *Contributions to Mediterranean sociology.* Paris: Mouton, pp.
           143–54.
   1964   *Honour, family and patronage.* Oxford: Oxford University Press.
Campbell, John, and Philip Sherrard
   1968   *Modern Greece.* New York: Praeger.
Common, R.
   1958   Some recent developments in Greece. *Tijdschrift voor Economische en sociale
           Geografie* 49:253–66.
Coutsoumaris, George
   1963   *The morphology of Greek industry.* Athens: Center of Planning and Economic
           Research.
Crawley, C. W.
   1967   Modern Greece, 1821–1939. In W. E. Heurtley, H. C. Darky, C. W.
           Crawley, and C. M. Woodhouse, eds., *A Short History of Greece.* Cam-
           bridge: Cambridge University Press, pp. 91–134.
Dimen, Muriel, and Ernestine Friedl, eds.
   1976   *Regional variation in modern Greece and Cyprus.* New York, New York
           Academy of Sciences.
Dubisch, Jill
   1977   The city as resource: Migration from a Greek island village. *Urban Anthro-
           pology* 6, no. 1:65–82.
DuBoulay, Juliet
   1974   *Portrait of a Greek mountain village.* Oxford: Clarendon Press.
Evelpidis, Chryssa
   1963   L'exode rural en Grèce. In John G. Peristiany, ed., *Contributions to Medi-
           terranean sociology.* Paris: Mouton, pp. 201–5.

Friedl, Ernestine
    1959   The role of kinship in the transmission of national culture to rural villages
            in mainland Greece. *American Anthropologist* 61:30–38.
    1962   *Vasilika.* New York: Holt, Rinehart and Winston.
    1963a   Lagging emulation in post-peasant society: A Greek case. In John G.
            Peristiany, ed., *Contributions to Mediterranean sociology.* Paris: Mouton, pp.
            93–106.
    1963b   Some aspects of dowry and inheritance in Boetia. In Julian A. Pitt-
            Rivers, ed., *Mediterranean countrymen.* Paris: Mouton, pp. 113–35.
    1976   Kinship, class and selective migration. In John G. Peristiany, ed.,
            Mediterranean family structure. Cambridge: Cambridge University Press,
            pp. 363–88.
Great Britain, Naval Intelligence Division.
    1944-45 *Greece.* Geographical Handbook Series B.R. 516. London.
Greece, National Statistics Service
    1973a   *Statistical yearbook of Greece.* Athens.
    1973b   *Results of the population and housing census of 14 March 1971: Sample elaboration.*
            Athens.
Gulick, John
    1974   Urban anthropology. In John J. Honigmann, ed., *Handbook of social and
            cultural anthropology.* Chicago: Rand McNally, pp. 979–1029.
Gutenschwager, Mary C.
    1971   Nea Aeolia: Persistence of tradition in an urban Greek community.
            Ph.D. dissertation, University of North Carolina at Chapel Hill.
Hirschon, Renée B. and Thakurdesai
    1970   Society, culture and spatial organization: An Athens community. *Ekistics*
            30:187–96.
Kasperson, Roger
    1966   *The Dodecanese: Diversity and unity in island politics.* Chicago: University of
            Chicago Press.
Kayser, Bernard
    1963   Les migrations interieures en Grèce. In John G. Peristiany, ed., *Contribu-
            tions to Mediterranean sociology.* Paris: Mouton, pp. 191–200.
    1976   Dynamics of regional integration in modern Greece. In Muriel Dimen
            and Ernestine Friedl, eds., *Regional variation in modern Greece and Cyprus.*
            New York: New York Academy of Sciences, pp. 10–15.
Kayser, Bernard, Pierre-Yves Pechoux, and Michel Sivignon
    1971   *Exode rural et attraction urbaine en Grèce.* Athens: National Center of Social
            Research.
Kayser, Bernard, and Kenneth Thompson
    1964   *Economic and social atlas of Greece.* Athens: National Statistics Service.
Kenna, Margaret
    1976   The idiom of the family. In John G. Peristiany, ed., *Mediterranean family
            structure.* Cambridge: Cambridge University Press, pp. 347–62.
    1978   The occupational culture of building workers in Athens. Paper delivered
            at Social Science Research Council Seminar on Anthropological Re-
            search in Europe.
Kolodny, Emile Y.
    1974   *La population des iles de la Grèce: Essay de géographie insulaire en Mediterranée
            orientale,* vols. 1–2. Aix-en-Provence: Edisud.

Ladas, Stephen P.
  1932   *The exchange of minorities in Bulgaria, Greece and Turkey.* New York: Mac-
            Millan.
Lambiri, Ioanna
  1965   *Social change in a Greek country town: The impact of factory work on the position of
            women.* Athens: Center of Planning and Economic Research.
Legg, Keith R.
  1969   *Politics in modern Greece.* Palo Alto, Calif.: Stanford University Press.
Loizos, Peter
  1975   *The Greek gift.* Oxford: Basil Blackwell.
Mendras, Henri
  1962   *Six villages d'Épire.* Paris: UNESCO.
Meynaud, Jean
  1965   *Les forces politiques en Grèce.* Etudes de politique no. 10. Lausanne.
Miller, William
  1905   *Greek life in town and country.* London: George Neunes.
  1926   *The early years of modern Athens.* London: Anglo-Hellenic League.
Moustaka, Calliope
  1964   *The internal migrant.* Athens: National Center of Social Research.
Mouzelis, Nicos P.
  1978   *Modern Greece: Facets of underdevelopment.* New York: Holmes and Meier.
Papageorgiou, G.
  1967   Changes in the capital of Greece. *Ekistics* 24:81–95.
Pentzopoulos, Dimitri
  1962   *The Balkan exchange of minorities and its impact upon Greece.* Paris: Mouton.
Peristiany, John G., ed.
  1963   *Contributions to Mediterranean sociology.* Paris: Mouton.
  1976   *Mediterranean family structure.* Cambridge: Cambridge University Press.
Petropoulos, John Anthony
  1968   *Politics and statecraft in the kingdom of Greece.* Princeton, N.J.: Princeton Uni-
            versity Press.
Safilios-Rothschild, Constantina
  1976   The family in Athens: Regional variations. In Muriel Dimen and Ernes-
            tine Friedl, eds., *Regional variation in modern Greece and Cyprus.* New York:
            New York Academy of Sciences, pp. 410–18.
Sanders, Irwin T.
  1962   *Rainbow in the rock.* Cambridge, Mass.: Harvard University Press.
Sandis, Eva E.
  1973   *Refugees and economic migrants in greater Athens.* Athens: National Center of
            Social Research.
Sutton, Susan Buck
  1978   Migrant regional associations: An Athenian example and its implica-
            tions. Ph.D. dissertation, University of North Carolina at Chapel Hill.
Thompson, Kenneth
  1963   *Farm fragmentation in Greece.* Athens: Center of Planning and Economic
            Research.
Vacalopoulos, Aspostolos E.
  1976   *The Greek nation, 1453–1669.* New Brunswick, N.J.: Rutgers University
            Press.

Valaoras, Vasilios G.
  1960   A reconstruction of the demographic history of modern Greece. *Milbank Memorial Fund Quarterly* 38:115–39.
Vermeulen, Cornelis J. J.
  1970   *Families in urban Greece.* Ph.D. dissertation, Cornell University.
Wagstaff, J. M.
  1968   Rural migration in Greece. *Geography* 5:175–79.
Ward, Benjamin
  1962   *Problems of Greek regional development.* Athens: Center of Planning and Economic Research.

PART THREE: CASE STUDIES

Chapter **9**

The Meaning of Urban Life: Pluralization of Life Worlds in Seville

David D. Gregory

INTRODUCTION

In barely a decade the inexorable demographic and economic trends of the 1960s propelled Spain from a nation of rural countrymen to urban dwellers caught up in the anxieties of an impressive if unstable industrial development. By 1970 Spain had become the tenth industrial power of the world. In particular, the massive exodus from the countryside to the cities radically changed both the distribution and the composition of the population.[1] By July, 1971, the Comisión de Estructuras y Servicios Urbanos del Plan de Desarrollo predicted that in 1980 half of Spain's population would live in metropolitan areas and that one out of every three Spaniards would live in Madrid, Barcelona, Valencia, Seville, or Bilbao. In the southern region of Andalusia the capital cities of its eight provinces drained the population from their surrounding hinterlands. This urbanization process was particularly intense in the provincial capital of Seville. Since 1900 this city's population has grown by nearly 400%.

This vast number of immigrants cannot be considered as a separate population — people who are somewhat less than full members of Seville's traditional existence. Nor should they be viewed as passive figures caught up in a cityscape that forces them to transform every aspect of their lives. In an excellent book on Seville, oriented more toward the general study of urban anthropology than Hispanic studies *per se,* Irwin Press concentrates upon the effect the city has upon those who are its inhabitants. It is portrayed as a classic orthogenetic city functioning like a well-oiled, self-moving machine with its own generator.

> . . . in Seville ideological factors exert powerful influences upon behavior. They promote provincialism, chauvinism, complacency, and conservatism in all sectors of Sevillano society. In turn, these factors have discouraged industrial development and encouraged patronism and a particularistic orientation to economic recruitment. This lack of new economic opportunity has minimized significant migration from other areas of Spain. Consequently Seville has developed as a culturally ho-

mogeneous and self-consciously official repository of custom. (1979: 282)

Seville's migrants, however, have not merely fallen into a new urban environment that compels their adaptation. To the contrary, during the past 30 years Seville's immigrants have been a steady tide eroding the city's basic ecology and organization. This influx has led to the breakdown of the inner city's barrios — which gave Seville its traditional cultural identity — and the growth of sprawling precincts or *barriadas* outside the city's ancient walls. Therefore, in studying the urbanization process of a city like Seville, the anthropologist should be cautious that the professional search for "cultural areas" and "superorganic" explanations does not totally overshadow the migrant's effect upon the city. In an introduction to a series of studies on the behavior of migrant populations in new environments, Eugene Brody emphasizes how difficult but necessary it is to

> . . . separate the impact of a host environment from the nature of the experience, talent and equipment the migrant brings to it. His initial attributes include those which may be subsumed under personality and health, socioeconomic status, demographic features, and such items as the length of time since his last move. He has certain goals and he searches the opportunity structure of the new environment in order to attain them. He encounters a proximity structure, an institutional structure and a personal network structure. This last may include relatives or friends who have gone before. The range of alternatives open to him depends in part on the perceived support or cohesiveness of others like him. (1970:18)

The following is not a total explanation of Seville as the archetypal urban center of southern Spain.[2] Rather, it is a brief attempt to portray the urbanization process of a city that has once again entered another major transition period in its long history. This process is portrayed by focusing upon the lives of four families who have at one time or another in the past all lived in the same rural agro-town but now find themselves residing in the provincial capital. The interactive role played by these families is seen from the perspective of four different social groups: the gentry in transition, the pressured upper middle class, the traditionally insecure and dependent worker always on the verge of impoverishment, and a new urban proletariat. These families, and thousands like them, are not merely passive actors playing fixed roles in an eternal city. They are the forces of change greater than the seeming fixity of the city. In concentrating upon these four families, we can see the urbanization process as once again emphasizing Seville's growing heterogeneity. These cases demonstrate that there are not only many concepts of the city for different classes of people, but that there are different concepts of the city for the same individual, depending where he is situated in his "life plan."[3]

While much of the traditional structure and ideological order that once provided the city with a number of centralizing and homogenizing value patterns is breaking down, the mythic image of what Seville represented has remained strong in the consciousness of the people in the countryside. Attracted by the city, they have come with the expectation of better employment. For the most part their expectations have ended in substandard housing, unstable employment, and a lack of schooling for their children. Regardless of the cultural lag between image and reality, and the repeated disappointment it engenders, the city continues to open up new horizons. City living, as Peter Berger has repeatedly emphasized, challenges the new urban dweller's most fundamental sense of his own identity and consciousness of daily living. This challenge of city life, which forces people to make new efforts to successfully overcome restrictions and rejections, can also increase their sense of the value of self-effort and personal freedom.[4]

CITY TYPE

To understand the synergistic effects of the urbanization process upon the lives of the people and the structure of the city, one must take into account, first, the uniqueness of the city type and, second, its process of growth. As Fox (1977) has clearly shown, the city cannot be treated as an external backdrop needing no analysis by anthropology. Nor is it sufficient to merely consider the size of the population, which only indicates the degree of urbanization. Rather, it is necessary to understand the city according to the dominant economic activities of its people and its position in the nation's urban hierarchy.[5]

Seville, the symbolic capital of the eight Andalusian provinces, is the fifth-largest urban area in Spain after Madrid, Barcelona, Valencia, and Bilbao. Since the "siglo de oro" it has received the international attention of more painters, dramatists, writers, musicians, and poets than any other city in Spain. Their encounters with Seville have left us with the romantic images of "'la ciudad de la manzanilla' (alegria), 'la amorosa ciudad' (acogedora), 'la ciudad de cristal' (fragil), 'la ciudad cristalina' (transparente), 'la airose maravilla' (elegante y fina), 'la ciudad del toro' (viril), 'la ciudad de Mayo' (luminosa y de las flores), 'la ciudad del ala' (ligera), and 'la ciudad de las muchachas' (juvenil) . . ." (Morales 1975:13).

These romantic qualities of the old inner city clearly derive from the juxtaposition of urban styles (Moslem/Christian, tower/turret, garden/fountain) referred to by Michael Kenny and Mary Knipmeyer in Chapter 1.

Still concentrating on the inner city, Irwin Press believes that "Seville appears to be almost archetypically urban . . . this urbanity coexists with Seville's ethnic homogeneity and provincialism, its relative lack of capital flow and industry, and the various particularistic mechanisms which soften impersonality" (1979:285).

Seville is a city originally created by its historic river, the Guadalquivir. A view of the city's 141 square kilometers from the air gives the impression of a labyrinthian, chaotic, cellular growth. In the past it was a world-famous port in the center of one of the wealthiest agricultural areas in Spain. Because of Seville's monopoly on trade with the Americas in the sixteenth century, it became the most important city in the country. Ruth Pike, in the words of a native son of the period, says that it was "not a city but a world. . . . " Between 1534 and 1588 she shows that Seville's population grew from 9,040 to 25,986 *vecinos*. It became the largest city in Spain. If the undocumented floating population were included, the city's total population was probably over 100,000. Her work strongly documents the early heterogeneity of a boom town like Seville during its first period of rapid urbanization in the 1500s. "Seville, because of its size, cosmopolitanism, and economic-boom atmosphere naturally attracted all kinds of diverse elements. It provided a haven for the unassimilated and the social outcasts and a favorable environment for the enrichment and rise of *conversos* (Jewish converts and their descendants) and commoners" (1972:vii). She documents the in-movement of Spaniards from the north and center along with foreigners: Genoese, Germans, Flemings, and Portuguese. Along with these groups were the hordes of landless peasants from the hinterlands and the Moriscos from Granada. In sum, Pike's work demonstrates that during Seville's first great urbanization heterogeneity characterized all levels of its society.

After the stagnation and disastrous plagues of the seventeenth and eighteenth centuries Seville entered another phenomenal growth period between 1797 and 1857. Carlos Alvarez Santalo (1974) has made a detailed demographic study of the growth of Seville's parishes between 1800 and 1833 and attributes Seville's astounding demographic recovery to immigration. His analysis of the marriage records shows that 46.3% of the male immigrants and 62.8% of the female immigrants came from the province of Seville, the adjoining provinces of Huelva and Cadiz, and Extremadura and the other five Andalusian provinces. The remaining 53.7% of the men and 37.3% of the women came from all other areas of Spain. He also shows a direct relation between immigration and those parishes of Seville with significant industry. On the other hand, there appears to be an inverse relation between those parishes dedicated to agricultural activities and in-migration.

Today Seville is no longer an important port or a city dedicated principally to agriculture. Nor can it be characterized as a spiritual site, military base, university center, or financial and industrial capital. Rather, it is an urban center of multiple functions in which the service component and administration predominate. In 1970, out of an officially registered active population of 191,152, 1.8% were employed in the agricultural sector, 37.8% in industry, and 60.4% percent in services. In terms of finer occupational distinctions, 39% of the work force was considered as members of an urban middle class. The majority of Seville lives from the salaries the functionaries send from Madrid, industrial delegations from Catalonia or the Basque provinces, the large warehouses that forward agricultural products to be processed outside the region, small commercial establishments, and some industry.

The fallacy of thinking that urbanization represents a national unifying tendency or homogenization process with respect to life and work is dramatically portrayed by two figures. The first indicates that in 1930 Seville's industrial sector was nearly double that of today (61.9%). The second figure focuses on average annual income and demonstrates that while there was an average difference of 12,157 pesetas between a city like Bilbao and Seville in 1955, by 1970 the gap had widened to 39,521 pesetas in Bilbao's favor. All figures indicate that while the Sevillanos have a higher income than in the past, they are not keeping up with the national average, and the industrial cities to the north are rapidly leaving Seville behind (FOESSA 1970:1238–59).

Most of the industries in Seville owe their existence to government decisions and continuing state aid. In 1964 Seville was established as an industrial development pole. The objective was to stimulate the local economy, create employment, and spread industrialization to the hinterlands. The plan offered firms tax relief and low-interest loans if they conformed to certain predetermined limits and standards. The results have been disappointing. The businesses securing the largest loans were prestigious local enterprises in financial difficulties. After four years the number of jobs created amounted to 4,750, the number of posts eliminated 2,602. By 1974 less than 37% of its stated objectives had been realized, more than 25,000 people left Seville for other areas of Spain, and another 17,000 temporarily migrated to Germany and Switzerland. In sum, the industrial development pole was a convenient way for certain undertakings to qualify for state aid rather than a means of creating a powerful industrial focus.

URBANIZATION PROCESS

It has often been maintained that "urbanization is an ecological aspect of industrialization and professionalization." Hans Buechler in Chapter 5 states that urbanization in Spain " . . . is largely the product of the development of areas characterized both by a long history of industrial and mercantile development and by close proximity to markets elsewhere in Europe." While Seville is quite distant from European markets, its growth process in the twentieth century is certainly the result of a series of historic illusions founded on the mirage of contemporary development. Antonio Burgos (1974:27) compares the city to the old "picaro" who, though always hungry, covered his beard with bread crumbs to create the impression that he had just eaten well. While the growth of cities like Barcelona and Bilbao had a basis of wealth that offered jobs, the growth of Seville was based upon the existence of its historical image and false information. Throughout the 1960s Seville lived and speculated upon illusions and promises that never materialized: the construction of the Seville-Bonanza canal, which was to revitalize the port (never built); the plans to locate a major foundry and steel-working complex (built in Valencia); the all but assured construction of the new Ford automobile factory (finally built in Valencia); the development of the industrial pole that never really developed anything. Of course, not all were taken in by this false image. Paradoxically, during this century of Seville's explosive growth Andalusia as a whole was being depopulated. From 1900 to 1940 Andalusia lost 360,671 of its inhabitants. During the following 20 years the rural exodus from the region was nearly 800,000. In the ten years spanning 1960 and 1970, 850,000 more people entered this migratory flow. Between 1971 and 1972 over 100,000 emigrants abandoned the south.

The urbanization process in Seville can be divided into three phases: 1900–1939, 1940–59, and 1960–75. At the beginning of the century Seville registered a population of 148,315 residents living mostly between the river and the old walls (Figure 1). The construction of the world-famous 1929 Exposición Iberoamericana attracted the first heavy wave of migrants, and the city grew to 228,729 inhabitants by 1930. After the exhibition Seville's economy collapsed, leaving the people without jobs or housing, and the social unrest of the pre–Civil War period began.

Until 1939 the 11 barrios, known by the names of the saints of their respective parishes, formed the city. They were the units people used for self-identification through membership in the local religious brotherhoods, bull-fighting clubs, or football casinos. The 21 barriadas, or precincts outside the city walls, harbored few inhabitants, and Seville was surrounded by ample rural areas.

It was working in one of the inner barrios during the transition period between the late 1960s and early 1970s that led Irwin Press to highlight the shared values that gave the inner city of Seville its seemingly "great cultural homogeneity." This homogeneity is dramatically displayed in the relationship between the barrios and their religious fraternities (hermandades) and brotherhoods (cofradías), both of which date from the Middle Ages. These fraternities and brotherhoods also partially define the city's structure. Until the 1700s Seville was divided into guilds, groups of artisans who lived and worked in specific city streets, and the fraternities were composed of men who shared similar class backgrounds and professions. Today the guild sys-

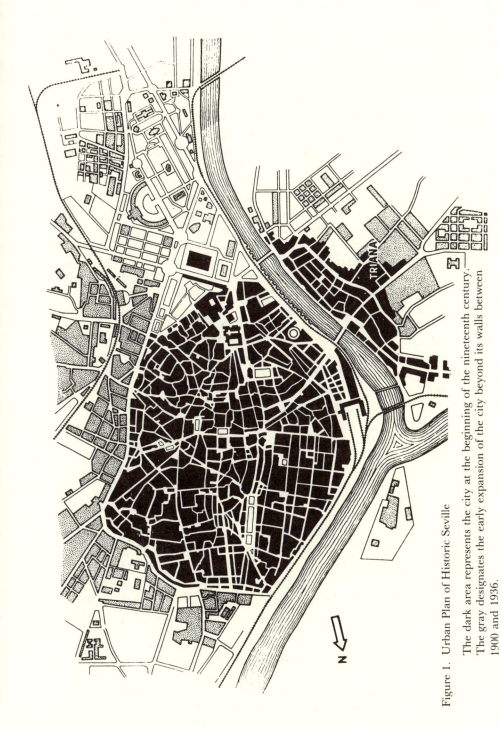

Figure 1. Urban Plan of Historic Seville

The dark area represents the city at the beginning of the nineteenth century. The gray designates the early expansion of the city beyond its walls between 1900 and 1936.

From Vicens Vives 1961.

tem has become a network of barrios. Within the barrios each religious fraternity is a group of men associated with a parish church and its images. The group functions as a sort of lay order, encouraging its members' spiritual growth, promoting the worship and celebration of its cult images, and performing charitable works. In 1977, 70,000 of the 281,000 men in Seville belonged to religious fraternities. *Cofradías* are made up of those members of the fraternities who parade with the fraternities' images during Holy Week. One Sevillano in six belongs to a *cofradía* (Gregory 1978:52).

The great transformation of Seville and the area outside the inner barrio structure began in 1940 and paralleled the mechanization of agriculture. Between 1940 and 1958 the city grew by 170,000 people. The poor, rural proletariat who were forced to abandon the countryside were attracted by the myth of Seville's past prosperity as the port of the Indes, the capital of Andalusia, and the emporium of the Guadalquivir. One hundred thousand of these arrivals packed themselves into the old city, sharing or renting space from friends or relatives. The other 70,000 illegally occupied land in the surrounding rural precincts and began to construct *barracas* or *chozas* in areas completely devoid of public services. The majority never found anything but temporary employment and subsisted off charitable agencies that distributed powdered milk and "synthetic" cheese from America.

In 1948 people also began to abandon the old city as thousands of its houses were declared in ruins. Local officials finally recognized the exterior population areas and began constructing blocks of relatively low-cost housing outside the city. The location of new *barriadas* was not determined by any urban planning other than the cheap availability of land and the profits to be made from speculation. The first constructions were carried out under the orders of General Queipo de Llano to provide work for the army of unemployed. In the 1940s building was supported by the National Institute of Housing and other municipal, governmental agencies. From 1960 onward official support declined and construction was taken over by private enterprises.

The third period between 1960 and 1975 was the result of Seville's designation as a pole of industrial development. People were attracted by the outrageous propaganda, which created the illusion that there would soon be work for everyone — especially if they got to Seville first. The city grew by 147,421 more inhabitants. By 1975, 43% of the entire population of the province (589,721 out of 1,378,543) lived in the metropolitan area. Seville now truly passed from being a city of barrios to one of *barriadas,* and the break with its past was almost complete. Its two worlds of gentry and workers were now transformed into the world of the decaying, official city for tourism within the walls, and the world of the 60 *barriadas* outside, in which 84% of the population now resided (Figure 2). In the 1963 Plan General de Ordenacion Urbana de Sevilla, 69% of the city's buildings were two or less sto-

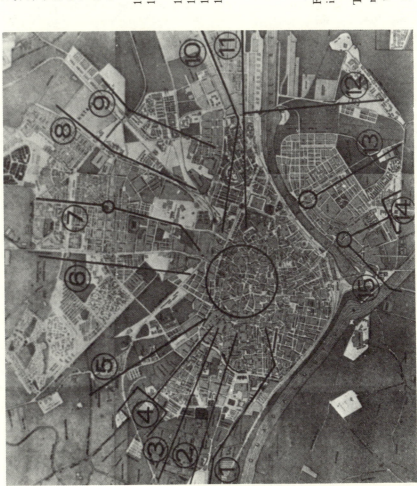

1. Sánchez Pizjuán
2. Doctor Fedriani
3. Cruz Roja
4. Miraflores
5. Carmona
6. Luis Montoto
7. Eduardo Dato
8. Ramón y Cajal
9. Felipe II – Autopista Universidad Laboral
10. Borbolla – Manuel Siurot
11. Delicias – Victoria – Carretera
    a Cádiz
12. García Morato
13. República Argentina
14. San Jacinto
15. Castilla (c. a Huelva)

Figure 2. Urban Plan of Seville
in the Twentieth Century

The numbers 1 through 15 indicate the
main thoroughfares of expansion beyond
the inner city from 1900 to the present.

From Banco Urquijo 1973.

ries in height while only around 5% reached higher than four stories (1:143). By 1970 the old city was almost totally surrounded by towering, cement blocks of condominiums.

Irwin Press, who studied the *corrales de vecinos* (tenements in which numerous one- and two-room apartments front upon a common courtyard with but one street entrance, where the majority of Sevillanos lived 30 years ago), did so with the intention of laying bare the foundations of modern Seville life (1979:xii). On a return visit in June, 1980, he discovered that most of the *corrales* were gone. "When I went back in June there was nobody left there that I knew. . . . now there were two hippies with beards and earrings — living with an American girl." Beyond the tenant-owned condominiums into which the majority have packed themselves, there have formed two belts of "dormitory" cities. In 1970 the first and second belts totaled another 193,312 and 134,697 persons.

The majority of migrants who have entered Seville during the 1960s were quite young.[6] They in turn have had a direct effect upon the age structure of the city. By 1971, 43% of the population was less than 20 years of age, a figure higher than that for both the region (40.5%) and the nation (35.8%) at the time. The older generations who have stayed behind in the countryside seem to represent a disappearing culture. Each year they have less effect upon the socialization process of the young, who seek to reject the ethnic stereotypes of the south.[7]

At the end of the 1960s Seville still seemed to be able to function as a city. Press found that "services and bureaucracies were well organized, predictable, dependable, familiar to all, and heavily utilized in the survival strategies of all classes" (1979:284). Since that important transition period, however, there appears to have been a steady deterioration. In that less than 42% of Seville's inhabitants pay municipal taxes, the attempts by local government to marginally maintain the exterior *barriadas* have been ineffectual and have had direct repercussions on its ability to care for the central city itself. Furthermore, the newly elected municipal officers inherited a virtually bankrupt city government from the outgoing Franco appointees in a period of economic decline. Therefore, the problems of meaningful employment, congestion, contamination, public transportation, and other services have all come to a head. The lack of sufficient schools in a city with one of the highest illiteracy rates in Spain has been particularly detrimental. Hospital facilities are overburdened. Alcoholism (with the major shift from wine and beer to scotch and rum) has become a growing social problem. Crime among the younger age groups has upset the city's traditional feeling of security. While I lack the numerical breakdown for the city, the relative suicide rate in the province has become the highest in the nation.

LIFE WORLDS

Cities exist as a cultural type only in a historical domain. What of the individual lives that collectively define the type of city and contemporary process of transformation that is Seville?[8] Recent studies of the life of individuals in cities are once again employing a modified phenomenological approach that views society as a dialectic between objective givens and subjective meanings. The life histories of the individuals composing the various social groupings of a city are being compiled in terms of the reciprocal interaction of what is experienced as outside reality (the world of institutions, demographic processes, etc.) and what is experienced within the consciousness of the individual actors. This approach leads to a renewed emphasis upon the plurality of "life worlds" for the individual inhabitants of many twentieth-century cities.[9]

The following telescoped life histories demonstrate that the experience of living in Seville is quite variable for its inhabitants. The city means different things to different individuals, depending not only upon their social grouping but also upon where they perceive themselves to be in their life plan. In other words, what meaning is actually invested in the city depends considerably upon how an individual's experience of living in Seville articulates with his life plans. In considering the following four families, we can see that "where you are going" is equally as important as "where you are coming from" in creating the intrasubjective maps of the city (Alverson 1978:215).

Gentry in Transition: Don Manuel

The family of Don Manuel is archetypal of Seville's titled gentry. While not migrants, they certainly are commuters among their agro-town, Seville, and the Costa del Sol, where they maintain homes. In the town Don Manuel and his brothers work a 600-hectare estate. One of the main streets is named after their father, who in 1936 flew a one-engine plane from Seville and dropped three bombs out of the cockpit upon the communist barrio of agricultural workers. Like his father, Manuel is a member of Seville's most exclusive casino, the Royal Club of Andalusia, which was founded during the first part of the century by civilian and military pilots who practiced flying as a sport. Within Seville the club's members are considered those "who have and who command" in the city. Don Manuel, however, informed me that it is just another of the public's crude myths. "It is a place to read the paper, play cards, drink and meet a friend. It is one of the few places that one can escape the streets and prying habits of the public." Don Manuel lives in an invisible world of home, chauffeured cars, casino, bank, and business.

In 1968 he moved his family out of Seville to Marbella. "You can only lead the old traditional life in the tourist areas these days," he said. Manuel tore down the palace built by his great-great-grandfather in the middle of the city and left the lot vacant to take advantage of spiraling land prices. He sold the beams, doors, windows, etc., to local antiquarians. The proliferation of this activity among other members of his class has left wide clearings in the center of the city that become focal points for neighbors' garbage and armies of rats. By 1973 the old artistic palaces and homes of Seville were disappearing so rapidly that the Instituto de Bellas Artes, with the support of the Ministry of Tourism in Madrid, declared many of the abandoned structures artistic monuments and part of the national patrimony in order to save them from real estate speculations.

In 1974 he moved back to Seville and rented a restored palace. "No, we are not coming back," his wife said. "In fact, Manuel has just sold the business to some Americans. We are only here for four more years so that our daughters can move in a proper social circle and make good marriages. We prefer living on the coast, but there you can never really be sure of a person's fortune or family background."

For Don Manuel there is no longer a Seville of business or speculation, only of exclusiveness and match-making. The *señorial* city of which he is supposed to be a symbol is dead in his mind and has no place in his future. Not since the Civil War has Seville's gentry dominated the city. They augmented their fortunes during the Franco years but lost their power to men from Madrid. Now the socialist upsurge in the *barriadas* indicates to them that their fortunes in this city might also be in jeopardy. "It is time to leave the city to the Spanish socialists and the American businessmen," he concluded.

Working Class: Antonio

Until 1958 Antonio worked on Don Manuel's estate in the agro-town, at which time he and his mule were replaced by a tractor. Antonio and his family of three had been living in the house of his mother-in-law. After nine months without work he migrated to Seville, where he took residence in an inner barrio with his uncle's family of four. Antonio's life plan was to make enough money to return and build a house in his native town. He was extremely devout and hoped to take over his father-in-law's job as *sacristán* when the old man retired.

While he found work, he soon discovered that it was little different from that of a fieldhand. The building sector — which played a traditional role in Seville as a transition between agriculture and industry — was also subject to a hazardous market and seasonal variations. Workers were taken for specific jobs and then laid off. Antonio became a temporary worker on a team contracted by a foreman from a large construction company. By only maintaining the foreman as an employee, and not the team members, who were the foreman's responsibility, the firm evaded the payment of social security charges, which now amount to 60% of the gross wage. This system allowed the firms to dismiss workers at will. Though Antonio had no protection against unemployment, accident, or illness, he approved of the covert system because there were no deductions from his salary.

On November 25, 1961, the river El Tamarquillo overflowed its banks and backed up into Seville's sewer system. By December 12 Antonio and his uncle, along with 30,000 other Sevillanos, were forced to abandon their houses. Antonio, whose major goal was a search for decent housing, entered the Seville of *los refugios:* 26 temporary shelters set up around the city in warehouses, abandoned buildings, and factories. Antonio spent the next two years living in the Brazilian Pavilion, which had been built for the great fair of 1929. "There were twenty-six of us sharing one area," he complained. "I divided my family from the others with paper cartons and blankets. The barrio with my uncle had been wonderful, and I began to forget about life in the country. But the *refugio* was like living out on the farms during the olive harvests. I had lost everything, but the brothers of the *cofradía* in the old barrio gave me clothes and money."

The Sevillanos jokingly referred to the shelters as "purgatory" because they were places where men waited patiently and in suffering before passing to the glory of a meritorious apartment. But it was no joke; over 100,000 inhabitants passed through "purgatory" between 1961 and 1971—not only flood victims but people from housing that continued to collapse or was declared unsafe in the central city.

In 1963 Antonio went to Don Manuel and obtained permanent work as a sweeper in his factory. He lived in a small apartment provided by the state outside the city center and lost contact with the *cofradía* in his uncle's barrio. In 1968 Antonio lost his hand in an accident. He discovered that the factory had not insured him properly. In order to avoid a lawsuit, Don Manuel, with the help of his friend Don Carlos, found a position for him as a doorman in a luxury apartment complex in the elite, middle-class *barriada* of Los Remedios on the other side of the river.

Upper Middle Class: Don Carlos

Don Carlos is a member of the province's rural, untitled, but long-term residential gentry. He went to the University of Seville in 1959 and in 1964 moved his widowed mother, sister, wife, and first of six children to the wealthy *barriada* of Los Remedios. Unlike his friend Don Manuel, who commands greater wealth and a title, Don Carlos sees his future in the city. People like him make every attempt to remain gentry in the city by maintaining all their traditional roles and seeking every available means to add to their prestige. He is against the Church hierarchy but a supporter of his local *cofradía*; he has held numerous government posts in the city but supports the far right Andalusian movement, Alianza Nacional 18 de Julio.

His first cousins have followed him to Seville, and 19 relatives are divided among four floors of his apartment complex; they live like one large extended family. The women's roles remain much the same as in the countryside. All the younger children attend the same private school, where they meet more distant cousins who are always potential marriage partners, no matter what the age. While the poorer migrants expect and are ready for change in the city, gentry like Don Carlos think that change can be resisted and the status quo of the Franco years maintained. For Don Carlos, Seville means the inner city (where he does not live) — tradition, stability, and privilege: "Seville can and should be the cultural capital of Andalusia . . . but it must support a stronger central government than we now have. Otherwise regionalism will destroy the city by allowing it to fall into the hands of the capitalists or be ripped apart by the hate and abuse of the marxists. The growth and future of Seville must be based upon the traditional doctrines of José Antonio. Only in this way can order be maintained and the right for everyone to work be defended against the communists."

Working Class: Juan

Juan, at the age of 34, was forced out of the agro-town and attracted to Seville in 1964. Being less traditional and more aggressive than the type of worker represented by Antonio, he had lodged a formal salary complaint with the government syndicate against a local landowner. He collected his salary but was frozen out of the labor pool. The industrial pole was beginning in Seville, so he sold his wife's share of her house to his brother-in-law and moved to the city with his wife and two children. They settled in the impoverished *barriada* Torreblanca la Nueva, where 40% of the families had four or more children and monthly incomes of less than 6,000 pesetas.

After facing his disappointment in not being able to find work, and realizing the industrial pole was a myth, he and thousands like him migrated to Germany. Thanks to work in Western Europe, the old ills of the *barriadas* began to disappear. After nine months Juan sent his wife enough money to pay her way into a private apartment complex closer to the city. He continued working in Germany until 1972, making monthly payments on his apartment in Seville. When he returned, he purchased a taxi and another apartment in the *barriada* of Los Remedios, which he rented only to wealthy foreigners. He had acquired this idea from the way the gentry had often worked their land back in his home community. His older son found a job in the metal-working industry and the younger boy was studying at the University of Seville with a scholarship from the Institute of Migration. While one might doubt that Juan actually lived in Seville, until 1972 it was the central focus of his life plan for himself and his family — a life plan that became the source of his identity even in Germany.

In 1976 all three men became involved in a series of labor conflicts. Juan and other independent drivers began fighting for their own free union.

His son in the metal-working firm became a member of the communist syndicate and lost his job when he led his fellow workers out on a sympathy strike with men from the Recalux plant. The younger brother, along with 500 university students and 300 teachers, provided the Recalux workers with further support and demonstrations.

While Seville might be the city least interested in politics according to a national survey in the 1970s, it is the city with the most labor conflicts in southern Spain. Merely during the month of December, 1976, over 12,000 Sevillanos participated in strikes or work slowdowns: railroad workers, bank clerks, electrical workers, and employees of the municipal government.

Juan and his sons display an intensity and drive that lead them into conflict not only with traditional authorities but also with their fellow workers like Antonio, who timidly seeks to modify his life through traditional channels of patronage. These younger men refuse to accept the disassociation between official rhetoric and the social realities of city life. Their new hunger is not for the possession of land but for services that make a city livable.

CONCLUSION

The four case studies highlight the changing role of the city of Seville as a cultural type and its process of urbanization. They emphasize the fact that the problem is not merely how people operate in a city but how they must contend with each other during a period of transition in which the traditional basis for social life is changing. Even before Franco's death on November 22, 1975, the Spanish people sensed the beginning of even more dramatic changes. Over the past 30 years they had shifted from a nation of rural to urban dwellers, which has changed the social conditions for the majority of the population. In these new urban environments they have had to live with six new realities: "an economy that was in decline after years of growth; a rapid increase in strikes for higher wages; the constant threat of violent action by the extreme right; the subtle, but steady withering away of the corporate institutions of Franco, especially in economic life, before new forms had been legalized or established; the pressure of constant demands for regional self-government; and terrorism by separatists and extremists of the left" (Menges 1980:3). Periods such as these make it extremely difficult to treat a city holistically. In particular, the problem of homogeneity versus heterogeneity in an analysis of city living becomes a very delicate issue.

Irwin Press, who has written one of the most interesting and serious books on urban anthropology in Spain, has stressed the cultural homogeneity of Seville (1979). His holistic view of Seville as an urban community sensitively emphasizes the linkage between the homogeneity of values (the city's dominant ideology) and behavior. By focusing upon the context of the city and its more stable inhabitants in the inner barrios, his work is anchored more firmly in the study of urban anthropology than my own, which emphasizes the process of urbanization and the role of the first generation of migrants. Kenny and Knipmeyer wonder about the representativeness of his sample: " . . . even Press dwells longer and more comfortably on a specific part of the city—a tenement housing complex *(corral)*." Nevertheless, many of the experiences and ideological factors he describes correspond to my own impression of Seville in the 1960s. If there are major contradictions between our points of view, they might grow out of working in a period of transition—a problem that plagues most contemporary monographs and generalizations about Spain.

It is my contention that Seville is once again emphasizing its heterogeneity. There has always been a more inherent degree of social differentiation in Seville than stressed by Press.[10] Antonio Burgos, a resident of and astute social commentator on Seville, believes that there have always been two Sevilles: that of the gentry and that of the workers. During most of its history there was very little real social mobility between these two classes. The aristocrats, like Don Manuel, and the nontitled gentry, like Don Carlos, owned the land and lived off their agricultural rents. The rest of the society—virtually ignored by the elites—lived off their labor (1974:22). The bloody class struggle during the Civil War accented the division between these two worlds. It is probable that the seeming homogeneity that occurred between the end of the Civil War and 1973 was the result of the structure of corporate institutions of the Franco years. *The dominant expression originating from the top of the society was based upon the lack of power at the bottom.* The labor unrest, strikes, and political shift to the left in Seville would make me more cautious in asserting that in the 1980s "the lower [class] link themselves with the upper levels as sharing membership in a single socio-moral system . . ." (Press 1979:176).

Everywhere in the city it seems that the real and symbolic reference points of old Seville are vanishing. The lives of Antonio and Juan demonstrate how the influx from the countryside has lead to the deterioration of the old city and the mushrooming of the precincts beyond the walls. Nicolas Salas, chief editor for the newspaper *ABC* of Seville, commented on this growth: "Today, it is sad to realize that the fundamental values that made Seville one of the most celebrated, universal cities, are in danger" (1974:41). He sees the new barrio of Los Remedios, the residence of Don Carlos, as the worst urban calamity in Seville's history. It signifies a basic change in values from a house with a patio, marble sculpture, flowers, fountains, and separate entrances to an apartment complex with only pretentious distinctions, in an area where the sun barely shines into many of the streets, the repugnant odors from the river and industrial zones fill the air, and there are few green zones and parks for the children (1974:40).

In the lives of all the men, except Don Carlos, we can also witness a weakening of the city's overarching canopy of religious symbols associated with its brotherhoods *(cofradías)* and ritual participation in Holy Week, which in the past attempted to integrate the lives of all Sevillanos by presenting the institutional order as a symbolic totality. In October, 1973, Bishop Montero said: " . . . now only 30% of the diocese maintains habitual contact with the church, and the rest are not Christian actors but spectators; likewise, one can say that anticlericalism is being surrendered to in Seville as equally among the most wealthy as among the working class" (Salas 1976:433). Increasingly the new overarching activity is politics, even though a national survey in 1975 by "Metra Seis" for "La Vanguardia" ranked Seville as the city least knowledgeable and interested in politics in all of Spain.

Until the death of Franco in 1975, the Anadaluz had been notoriously reluctant to publicly express his political views like the Basque or Catalan. Many seemed to share Antonio's view: "My father taught me that if I were to survive in Spain, I had to learn how to walk quietly between two giants . . . never disturbing either one. The church and the state!" While walking softly, the older Sevillanos like Antonio knew how to use their friends and contacts with the other classes (like Don Manuel) to get by within the system. The younger and more aggressive migrants like Juan and his sons, however, participated in "group actions" for better wages and basic necessities of urban life such as stoplights, sanitation, schools, etc.[11] The new associational activity discussed by Kenny and Knipmeyer (pp. 44–45) and Hans Buechler (pp. 150–54) have taken shape not only in the *barriadas* but equally in the barrios of the inner city.

With the elections of 1977 and 1979 many of these actions took on a larger political significance. In the local elections of 1979 all eight provincial capitals of Andalusia were won by the left: the Spanish Workers Socialist party (PSOE) took six, the Communist party (PCE) took Cordoba, and the Andalusian Socialist party (PSA) took Seville. One of the first acts of the new city government was to reduce the number of slots for reserved official parking at the famous senorial April *feria* from 300 to 70. The second was to open the Municipal Pavilion to the entire public, "without any class distinctions." During the Franco years the pavilion was strictly reserved for those with high political offices, the gentry, and outlying political bosses (*Cambio 16* 1979:16).

It is difficult to say how the urbanization process and political events occuring in Seville will eventually blend and "unite" Seville with the rest of Spain. The FOESSA studies (1970–75) and the detailed investigation of the social structure in Spanish cities by Martin Moreno (1977) both imply that the urbanization process throughout Spain is not homogeneous with respect to work and lifestyle. Amando de Miguel has shown that the rural exodus differentially determines both the rhythm and the level of urbanization, as well as the type of economic development, for each region of Spain (1976). After four decades of political dependence upon Madrid, Seville is spearheading the new regional Andalusian movement for greater autonomy.

In sum, until the late sixties and early seventies, Seville's governing elite was able to maintain the more traditional aspects of the city. Therefore, it is somewhat difficult to talk about the attraction of the rural population into the city in terms of the "lure of modernity." Rather, it has actually been the influx of migrants into the city that has gradually forced the city to change — "modernize" does not seem to be the correct word in this case. What we will continue to witness throughout the next decade is the clash between the migrants' growing aspirations toward a better life and the traditionalism of Seville's commercial elite and newly elected officials who cannot change the economy.

NOTES

1. For a comprehensive description of these changes in all of Spanish society, see the studies by FOESSA (1970, 1975) and Amando de Miguel (1976).
2. For a full description of Seville as an orthogenetic city, see Irwin Press (1979).
3. Human behavior expresses a great deal more "intentionality" than is fashionably accepted in much of the social sciences. Berger's use of the concept "life plan" implies that every individual has a realistic understanding of the life career provided by his society. He has a " . . . map of society within which he can locate and project himself in terms of both past biographical recollection and future projects. The individual's life is perceived as a trajectory across this 'map.'" The "life plan" becomes the totality of all the "relevant timetables" associated with this trajectory and gradually becomes the primary source of an individual's identity (1974:71–73).
4. I am indebted to the theoretical insights and writings of Alfred Schutz (1962–66) and Peter Berger (1974) in this attempt to understand the different levels of urban life in the city of Seville. Hoyt Alverson has carried this approach further in anthropology than any other scholar I am familiar with. He has provided me with a great deal of collegial stimulation both in conversation and in his most recent book (1978).
5. As will be apparent from the text that follows, I have relied heavily upon the research reports of the Banco Urquijo (1973) and the writings of Nicolas Salas (1972, 1974, 1976).
6. In an earlier study I showed that internal migrants are younger, greater risk takers, and more alienated from the traditional social structure of their communities than are the first-term external migrants to Western Europe (Gregory 1978b).
7. In a personal communication Press stated that he does not really believe that the movement from the countryside bodes ill for the homogeneity of Seville, since the majority of the migrants come from Andalusia. It is difficult, however, to speak of Andalusia as a natural region in the sense of Galicia, a cultural region like the Basque area, or an area in which the people are aware of their ethnic identity and self-interest like Catalonia. The elections of both 1977 and 1979

seem to emphasize the variety rather than the singularity of Andalusia (Gregory 1976).

8. The term "life world" implies that all men must live in " . . . a reality that is ordered and that gives sense to the business of living." Its origin is socially determined in that the order it provides is established and maintained through collective consent (Berger 1974:63).

9. Alfred Schutz believed that multiple realities were a constant and probably necessary feature of human consciousness at all times. Peter Berger, however, indicates that the sharing of multiple realities is increasingly a contemporary phenomenon associated with the explosive urbanization of the world population. The life world of the average person in the city is quite different from that of the rural villages and towns from which they or their parents migrated. Different sectors of their everyday life bring them repeatedly into vastly different and discrepant worlds of experience and meaning. Modern life in the city is, therefore, typically more segmented than in the countryside. This segmentation, which is clearly observable in the interaction between the various social classes, is also manifest in the levels of the individual's consciousness. Therefore, Berger believes that in modern cities the creation of a shared symbolic universe becomes much more difficult in that different realities are defined and legitimated in many different ways.

10. It is not my intention to go into a detailed discussion of class relations in Andalusia. For a general description, see the works of Cazorla (1973), Gilmore (1976), and Corbin (1979).

11. It is difficult to ascertain to what degree the lives of men like Juan are examples of significant upward social mobility in Andalusian society. In the south of Spain there is a growing disparity among class, status, and power in the Weberian sense. Higher wages, a modest apartment, a television set do not markedly change a man's status. Only through marriage can one break through the protective walls of title, family name, land, etc. Those men with both class and status, like Don Manuel, have witnessed the steady erosion of their power, first to the Franco political appointees from Madrid, and currently to the socialist and communist parties.

REFERENCES

Alvarez Santalo, Carlos
    1974   *La población de Sevilla en el primer tercio del siglo XIX.* Seville: Diputación Provincial de Sevilla.
Alverson, Hoyt
    1978   *Mind in the heart of darkness.* New Haven, Conn.: Yale University Press.
Banco Urquijo
    1973   *Estudio general sobre la economía de la provincia de Sevilla.* Madrid: Editorial Moneda & Credito.
Berger, Peter L.
    1974   *The homeless mind: Modernization and consciousness.* New York: Random House.
Brody, Eugene B.
    1970   *Behavior in new environments: Adaptation of migrant populations.* Beverly Hills, Calif.: Sage Publications.

Burgos, Antonio
   1974   *Guía secreta de Sevilla.* Madrid: Editorial Al Borak.
Cambio 16
   1979   Los rojos están de feria. No. 387 (May).
Cazorla, Jose
   1973   *Problemas de estratificación social en España.* Madrid: Cuadernos para el Diá-
            logo.
Checa Godoy, Antonio
   1978   *Las elecciones de 1977 en Andalucia.* Granada: Aljibe.
Corbin, J. R.
   1979   Social inequality in an Andalusian city. Unpublished ms.
FOESSA
   1970-75 *Informe sociológico sobre la situación social de España.* Madrid: Editorial
            Euroamerica.
Fox, Richard
   1977   *Urban anthropology: Cities in their cultural settings.* Englewood Cliffs, N.J.:
            Prentice-Hall.
Garcia Barbancho, Alfonso
   1975   *Las migraciones interiores españolas en 1961-1970.* Madrid: Instituto de
            Estudios Economicos.
Gilmore, David
   1976   Class, culture, and community size in Spain: Relevance of models.
            Anthropological Quarterly 49, no. 2:89-106.
Gregory, David D.
   1976   A house divided: Ethnicity and class in southern Spain. *Iberian Studies*
            5:56-62.
   1978a   Semana Santa in Seville. *Natural History* 87, no. 4:44-56.
   1978b   *La odisea Andaluza: Una emigración hacía Europa.* Madrid: Editorial Tecnos.
Martin Moreno, Jaime
   1977   Algunos aspectos de la estructura social de las ciudades españolas. Xe-
            roxed monograph. Granada.
Menges, Constantine
   1980   Spain—A hopeful 'alternative emphasis' forecast:1980-83. *International
            Strategic Issues* 1, no. 6:1-4.
Miguel, Amando de
   1976   *40 millónes de Españoles 40 años después.* Barcelona: Ediciones Grijalbo.
Morales, Francisco
   1975   *Visión de Sevilla.* Seville: Real Academia Sevillana de Buenas Letras.
Pike, Ruth
   1972   *Aristocrats and traders: Sevillan society in the 16th century.* Ithaca, N.Y.: Cor-
            nell University Press.
Press, Irwin
   1979   *The city as context: Urbanism and behavioral constraints in Seville.* Urbana:
            University of Illinois Press.
Salas, Nicolas
   1972   *Andalucia: Los 7 círculos viciosos del subdesarrollo.* Barcelona: Editorial Pla-
            neta.
   1974   *Sevilla: Complot de silencio.* Seville: Universidad de Sevilla.
   1976   *Sevilla: Crónicas del siglo XX.* Seville: Universidad de Sevilla.
Vicens Vives, Jaime
   1961   *Historia de España y América,* vol. 5. Barcelona: Editorial Vicens-Vives.

Chapter **10**

The Contradictions of Social Life
in Subproletarian Naples

Thomas Belmonte

HISTORICAL BACKGROUND

Although the city did not originate in the Mediterranean as a pristine development, it achieved a cultural hegemony there never attained by its northern European counterparts. The city is no intrusive afterthought on the Mediterranean scene. It is, rather, the template of all other major communal forms. In the Mediterranean, urbanization and humanization mean the same thing. *Zoon politikon* finds his proper niche — makes his living and puts forth his views — in the city.

Along the shores of the Mediterranean, neotechnic man developed an ecotype based upon barley, wheat, olives, and wine. Trade and the subsequent monetization of local economies, peasant and pastoral, brought the world's first true business civilization into being. The production of commodities for exchange, the transformation of money-making into an art (Aristotle's chrematistics), the destruction of the ancient *oikos,* and the rise of the preindustrial city as headquarters of a mercantile and absentee landlord elite were the interlocking features of a long-enduring institutional gestalt. Exit Homer and his *aristoi.* We are in the world of merchant capital and rent capital, where even the house of God is a sacred bank (Houston 1967:117–25; Marx 1977:253n; Else 1965:67; Finley 1954, 1973).

Although far more stationary and resistant to change than industrial capitalism, the world of merchant capital was capable of generating contradictions no less striking. Democracy could thrive among slaveholders. Universalistic religions of brotherhood and mercy might arise in the midst of moneychangers and thieves. Exuberant sociality and venal trickery became ubiquitous and ever-present habits of being. Perhaps nowhere else on earth have the imperatives of social life spawned so much tension between neighbors. Moreover, although the relationship between the various classes of Mediterranean society was ruthlessly antagonistic, amounting to a kind of chronic guerrilla warfare lasting for centuries, there was never, as Fernand Braudel has observed, any decisive confrontation between them, no "final cataclysm" (1973:735).

In the countryside, rent capitalism sapped the peasant of his strength, the soil of its fertility, and the village community of its cohesion (see Bobek 1962). In former breadbasket regions like western Sicily, the depredations visited upon land and peasants alike by a leisured absentee elite left a vacuum of commerce and security that was gradually to be filled by a "new class" of gun-toting estate managers and broker capitalists. The cultural and symbolic associations of rural life were transformed as this new class re-adapted earlier codes of honor, roguery, and friendship to their emergent purposes as *mafiosi* and bourgeois strongmen (Schneider and Schneider 1976).

In the preindustrial city a restless and precariously surviving mass of artisans, laborers, street hawkers, and jobless took what they could from the luxury-based service economy of the elite, exercising their one right to riot only when there was nothing left for them to trade and very little left to lose. The city poor felt little empathy for their impoverished rural brethren. Indeed, the subproletariat resembled not the peasantry so much as those other "displaced persons" of Mediterranean society, the bandits and brigands of the hills. Like the elite, and like the brigands also, they too were reliant on the parasitic exploitation of the countryside, eager in their misery for some miniscule fraction of whatever surplus their masters could skim from peasant toil (Hobsbawm 1959:115). Taken together, these various trends make up the eroded palimpsest upon which life in contemporary Mediterranean cities must be understood.

In modern Naples the legacy of this past is discernible at every turn — in the serene grandeur of the monuments and in the squalor over which they continue to preside, in the profusion of small vendors monopolizing the sidewalks, and in the din of chatter, argument, and song that reverberates from every courtyard. It is apparent also in the statistics of unemployment and infant mortality, among the highest in Europe, and in the thriving black market, so integral to the local economy that the contrabanders have had the temerity to form a union (Manning 1978:21). But most of all it is apparent in the lifeways of the people, as they struggle still, against the whole oppressive current of their history, to live active, decent lives, redeemed by some small measure of comfort and conviviality.

FIELDWORK IN NAPLES: RESEARCH GOALS, METHODOLOGY, AND THE SITE

The goals of my fieldwork in Naples were twofold. I wanted to gather standard ethnographic data on the details of economic and social organization in the lower-class districts. But I also wanted to discover something of the relationships between mind and society in a setting that had been urban and poor for two millennia. How had the historical experience of poverty in the city affected personality, styles of interaction, and the world view of the people?

After encountering various obstacles to entry, centering around suspicions that I might be a police agent of some sort, I managed to settle in a small, grotto-like apartment in a district that I refer to as Fontana del Re. I resided there for one year, from May, 1974, until May, 1975. The district was notorious in Naples as a dangerous zone, a den of thieves, roughnecks, and prostitutes. I cannot vouch for the uniqueness of the neighborhood as a high-crime area, since prostitution and thievery were common elsewhere. There were, however, fewer self-employed artisans in Fontana del Re than in other lower-class districts. Perhaps because of the proximity of a small cardboard-recycling plant, a disproportionate number of the inhabitants earned their living collecting cardboard and junk.

I realized at the outset of my fieldwork that I could not expect to get very far with a notebook-in-hand approach. My Neapolitan informants were resistant and hostile to my early attempts to elicit genealogical and census data from them, viewing these as direct invasions of their privacy. I decided, therefore, to learn what I could by listening, participating, and observing, and finally by involving myself in the quasi-autonomous world of my informants' inner lives.

Despite its empirical limitations, however, I would still defend "pure" participant observation as the most effective and honest means available for learning about the lives of oppressed people anywhere, but especially in cities. First, urban poor people correctly associate more structured and arbitrary modes of inquiry with the overarching power structure and the implacable will to knowledge of that power structure. Second, if it does not cause his ejection from the field site, the imposition of a strange and alien research program on the people often serves to mystify the humanity of the anthropologist and thus cuts him off from the spontaneous flow of messages about ordinary events and feelings that informants casually "send in" when they are relaxed and comfortable. Third, in an urban environment one has the choice of knowing a few people well or a great many people hardly at all. The anthropologist's situation is very far removed from that prevailing in a tribal or peasant village, where statistical frequencies can be established and checked. Generalizations, therefore, will tend to be cautious and useless or fearless and falsifiable.

Finally, although etic operations are necessary and certainly more productive and predictive for certain classes of data (demography, nutrition, housing), they do not always enable and may block access to the meaning of lived experience for those we study. No doubt, what we know depends on how we know, and the fieldworker makes his choices. In Naples I chose to study, or rather grapple with, the problem of social character. Anthropology, for me, became an art form. If our objectives are formulated in technical terms, as problems of social engineering, I don't think that art or love can have much of a place in our handbooks. But if, following in the footsteps of Benedict and Radin, we envision our task as one of interpreting the cultural movement of lifetimes, then the intimacies and reserves of anthropological friendship must take precedence over a more etic methodology.

ECONOMIC STRATEGIES

The people of Fontana del Re were "urban foragers" who continually recombined a variety of legal and illegal activities in order to fund their daily lives. For example, it was not uncommon for a young man to be a mechanic or repairman during the day and a sailor's guide at night. A part-time waiter or bartender might hawk stolen clothes in his spare time. The owner of a small sundries store broke up junk with the help of his children, provided a chauffeur service to local prostitutes, and then sold them cosmetics along the way. A parking lot attendant doubled as a skilled and daring cat burglar. An old widow received a small pension, took in laundry, sold sandwiches, beer, and condoms, and still found time to play (and win) at the numbers game. At Fontana del Re, if there was something to sell it was sold, and so it went, until every available niche in the local economy was filled. The concept of a single job had little practical meaning, and the working day itself (the measure of all life time in industrial capitalist society) was differently conceived in Naples as a more varied and self-determined, if sometimes futile, expenditure of labor power.

Many of the characteristic behaviors and attitudes of the people at Fontana del Re seemed to obey Leibig's ecological principle of the minimum; i.e., they were adjusted to minimal and not optimal conditions. For example, many of my friends often spent surplus funds as if they would never have the opportunity to do so again. They often feasted and ate to excess as though they were about to starve. They often spoke in loud tones as if they would not otherwise be heard. They indicated states of emotional distress with volatile or tantrum-like reactions as if no one would pay attention to anything less dramatic. They managed friendships with the understanding that eventual betrayal and not greater trust would be the inevitable outcome and even regarded kin relations as something less than eternal. Their morality was pragmatic, flexible, and ultimately self-referential in Godel's sense. An ethnosemantic analysis of their ethical system would probably disclose a tenth commandment casting the other nine into doubt.

In sum, then, the people of Fontana del Re were fiercely opportunistic in a setting offering few opportunities. They were determined to survive in a city where to assume survival was to significantly lower one's chances. The people were bound to one another like players around a gambling table — as bidders and competitors, creditors and debtors, cheaters and cheated. The relations of production in Naples provided little in the way of mechanical solidarity. Participation, however, in a common urban cultural and linguistic tradition and long-term co-residence as neighbors in an "open-air" city lent a small-town quality to subproletarian quarters and neighborhoods.

THE NEIGHBORHOOD

Fontana del Re could easily be described as an urban village, a small, insular compound where approximately 200 people interacted with one another daily, year in and year out, greeting one another across clotheslines, chatting, visiting, marketing and sharing food, feasting together, and presenting a united and silent front against tax collectors and the police. Within the familiar precincts of the local neighborhood, children played and squabbled and learned how to be street-wise, while older youths formed themselves into amorphous peer groups, more solidary than a network but less corporate than a gang. These young male adolescents cooperated with one another in various delinquent expeditions and escapades. It was they who actually "defended" the neighborhood against intruders and outside aggressors from other zones (on defended neighborhoods, see Suttles 1972). More than any other category of the population, they expressed sentiments of allegiance and loyalty to Fontana del Re, viewing it as a place of refuge where they could rely on the protection and support of their friends.

Warm and convivial interaction was commonplace at Fontana del Re. With the arrival of the street vendors every morning, the local women had occasion to greet each other and exchange news. On hot summer afternoons the elderly women of the district converged to set up their chairs and take the sun, as they reviewed and collocated all new items of gossip that had surfaced in the preceding 24 hours. The older men gathered nightly, weather permitting, to drink and play cards. In the summer, people joined up for picnics on the beach, and in winter they huddled around makeshift fires to warm themselves and perhaps exchange a cigarette and a joke. Humor lightened the pace of most interactions. Everyone knew everyone else and most people had a nickname. The right to privacy was proclaimed loudly and repeatedly. "Mind your own business!" was a frequent refrain only because it was taken for granted that no one would.

But as often as they engaged in positive interactions, the people of Fontana del Re were suspicious and predatory with one another. Not the neighborhood and not the family but the individual was the absolute and fundamental unit of social life, and his petty, short-term advantage the first premise of the social philosophy. The ideal individual was supposed to be tough, wise, and false, capable of monopolizing and ready to wield physical force. (Cunning and aggression were traits admired in mature women and males of all ages.) In other words, it was a world where the bully was hero and the swindler was assumed. Here was a personal community, in many ways a moral community, but one long familiar with privation and the morally transfigurative power of money (see Marx 1964). It was an intensely social world — never indifferent — where people mattered enough to one another to argue and feud and seek out revenge. In these respects community in the back streets of Naples was not unique. Community in the Mediterranean is usually a strikingly dialectical proposition, involving a clash of opposing social tendencies, constituting a sociological paradox, a kind of "Hobbesian gemeinschaft."

According to Clyde Kluckhohn, all cultures condemn stealing within the in-group (1962:294). But at Fontana del Re stealing was a social habit. Not everyone was a thief, but there was no one who was not a suspect. Almost everyone had been robbed at some point and all harbored suspicions about the potential culprits. The motivations for robbery varied from sheer economic desperation to punishment, repudiation, or revenge. The less capable one was of retaliating, the greater were the chances of frequent victimization. Because the individual might at any point redefine the surrounding in-group as an out-group, all social intercourse was laced with the expectation of thievery, trickery, and deception.

I was subject to robbery at Fontana del Re only after I had achieved near-complete integration into the flow of ordinary social life (after about eight months of continuous residence). Before that I had enjoyed a sort of diplomatic immunity as an exotic guest. The burglarization of my apartment by a close friend signified not rejection but, rather, my incorporation into the realm of the profane and the commonplace. Indeed, I never felt so much a part of the local scene as when I had been robbed! The resultant outpouring of commiseration and the crazy-quilt pattern of pointing fingers and whispered accusations effectively naturalized me as a "citizen" of the neighborhood, who could now partake of the privileges and perils attending that status.

Kluckhohn's generalization might well hold for the Neapolitan poor if we were to consider only the most superficial and obvious level of their morality. Everyone at Fontana del Re was certainly unanimous in condemning the stealing that they said was taking place with increasing frequency inside the quarter. Nevertheless, the violent realities of street life and the futility of cooperation in what was, in essence, a wasteland of the European world system generated a greater than random frequency of predatory and otherwise agonistic interactions. In other parts of the Italian south the code of cunning (*furberia*) exists as one term of a cognitive trinity that also includes friendship and family honor (see Schneider and Schneider 1976). But in subproletarian Naples the codes of friendship and family honor have been allowed to wither on the bud while that of cunning has flourished like an exotic *fleur du mal*. More than a survival strategy, *furberia* (like the *picardía* described by Braudel 1973 and Miller 1967) is an existential game of chance. To play it well you need a keen eye for human vulnerability, a good sense of humor, and a grim temper to deal with defeat. The instrumental use of cunning is not seen by the poor Neapolitan as a mark of ethical failure. Its every manifestation among children is applauded by adults. For them it forms part of a harsh but indestructible humanism that is, in turn, based upon a depth psychology of desire, weakness, and vice. Lifelong training in cunning served my informants well whenever they had to be predatory or aggressive, but it also resulted in people who were tolerant of human failings and knowledgeable about human nature. Theirs was a philosophy of life and motivation based on a dialogue between a murderer and a clown. It follows that both innocence and moral naiveté would be shortlived in such a world and that enduring relationships would be compromised by the need to constantly renegotiate a position of strength. Unni Wikan's characterization of social life in the back streets of Cairo works well as a description of Fontana del Re:

> The back streets become a *hostile* environment to the individual. Because everybody is *always* actively undermining *somebody* else, people's talk flourishes, all social relations are threatening and precarious, and the folk generalizations that people are false and deceitful, and never want anything good for each other, are created and confirmed. Thus the neighborhood reproduces its characteristic social organization: small, divisive coalitions and enmities in a sea of strangers; unstable, scattered circles of acquaintances in spite of limited geographical mobility; a low level of integration and adherence to positive norms in spite of intense gossiping. (1980:147)

What can the word "friend" mean in such a setting? My major informant, Stefano, a local junkman, once described for my benefit that facet of his world view pertaining to friendship. Because his views on this matter were not idosyncratic but were echoed in so many conversations at Fontana del Re, I think it fitting to quote him at length here:

> The *popolino*, Tom, not *i grandi signori*—they have their honor—but the *popolino* of here, and of places like Forcella; you know how we are made? Tonight, today, I have some money, so I offer you to eat. But tomorrow if I'm broke, and I and my family have to eat, I'll try to rob you and trick you. I'll send you a letter in America and tell you my son is dying, and I need money terribly, and of course, as a *grande signore,* you'll respond. I would try to rob and trick my own brother. But it's easier with friends. Family doesn't help you out anyway, and then, between brothers, if you lend him a hundred thousand lire and he can't pay you back, what can you do? A friend, you can beat his head in. A brother, no. A friend, you can revenge yourself against. Don't ever trust anyone Tom, not even me! (Belmonte 1979:48)

Stefano's words lament the failure of trust in a world where class, money, and the rules of the market game have had ample time to invade all the inner sanctums of social life. For the subproletarian urban poor, the facts of scarcity and chronic economic insecurity impose an especially brutal and reductive logic on all social interactions. Although more difficult to measure than more obviously "etic" indicators of hardship, the erosion of dyadic and communal bonds was a major cause of anguish and suffering among the people of Fontana del Re. Stefano, for one, does not shrink from the implications. Such are the bitter residues that lie encrusted at the bottom of all societies founded on antisocial modes of production.

REFERENCES

Belmonte, Thomas
    1979   *The broken fountain.* New York: Columbia University Press.
Bobek, Hans
    1962   The main stages of sociocultural evolution from a geographical point of view. In Philip Wagner and Marvin W. Mikesell, eds., *Readings in cultural geography.* Chicago: University of Chicago Press, pp. 218–47.
Braudel, Fernand
    1973   *The Mediterranean and the Mediterranean world in the age of Philip II,* vol. 2. New York: Harper and Row.
Else, Gerald
    1965   *The origin and early form of Greek tragedy.* Cambridge: Harvard University Press.
Finley, M. I.
    1954   *The world of Odysseus.* New York: Viking.
    1973   *The ancient economy.* Berkeley and Los Angeles: University of California Press.
Hobsbawm, Eric J.
    1959   *Primitive rebels.* New York: Norton.
Houston, J. M.
    1967   *The western Mediterranean world.* New York: Praeger.
Kluckhohn, Clyde
    1962   Education, values, and anthropological relativity. In Richard Kluckhohn, ed., *Culture and behavior.* New York: Free Press, pp. 286–300.
Manning, Robert
    1978   Italy, politics fester, the economy founders. In *Working Papers for a New Society* (May–June).
Marx, Karl
    1964   The power of money in bourgeois society. In *The economic and philosophical manuscripts of 1844.* New York: International Publishers.
    1977   *Capital,* vol. 1. New York: Vintage Books.
Miller, Stuart
    1967   *The picaresque novel.* Cleveland: Press of Case Western Reserve University.

Schneider, Jane, and Peter Schneider
    1976   *Culture and political economy in western Sicily.* New York: Academic Press.
Suttles, Gerald
    1972   *The social construction of communities.* Chicago: University of Chicago Press.
Wikan, Unni
    1980   *Life among the poor in Cairo.* Trans. Ann Henning. London: Tavistock
             Publications.

Chapter **11**

On the Fringe of the Town

Slavko Kremenšek

The settlement of Zelena jama, treated in this chapter, is a part of Ljubljana, the capital of the Socialist Republic of Slovenia, lying in the northwest of Yugoslavia. Nowadays this settlement of about 2,900 inhabitants is a part of the densely built urban agglomeration. At its beginnings, at the turn of the twentieth century, it was considered to be outside the town, yet not far away, about half a mile from the Ljubljana railway station and about one mile from the center of the town. Even from the point of view of administration Zelena jama first belonged to one of the Ljubljana suburban communities. In 1935 it was, however, officially incorporated into greater Ljubljana, which then had about 80,000 inhabitants.

In the second half of the nineteenth century Ljubljana started to grow beyond its former urban and suburban boundaries set long ago in the feudal system. At first, population growth and the expansion of the town were rather slow. Then, in the wake of a major earthquake in 1895, the pace of growth quickened and new settlements arose. Postearthquake construction was facilitated in numerous ways, including favorable loans and tax abatements. In addition, Ljubljana experienced an influx of immigration from the rural hinterland.

World War I slowed down the growth of the Ljubljana population. Yet this stagnation was mainly confined to the town center. The suburbs continued to grow, with the pace of growth quickening since the beginning of the thirties. Meanwhile, the residents of the old town center increasingly moved to other parts of the town. Indeed, even in 1910 the old part of town encompassed only 16% of the whole Ljubljana population.

With the decay of the Austrian empire and the creation of the state of Yugoslavia, Ljubljana as the Slovene capital became an important administrative and especially cultural center. This position is reflected in the city's occupational and social characteristics. Officials, minor merchants, and tradesmen comprised an important part of the Ljubljana population. It was not until after World War II that Ljubljana assumed a more industrial character.

Since the end of the nineteenth century both the increase in population and the growth in construction of Ljubljana were particularly evident in the

emergence of new suburban settlements. Many of these new urban and suburban quarters were differentiated, marked by the social status of their inhabitants. In addition, there were various transitory areas with a less specific
social profile. It was at this time that Ljubljana underwent the process of full
urbanization. An important factor in the construction of this period were
town villas. These were residential houses, mainly owned by petty bourgeoisie, that with their accompanying gardens covered a large area. They were
scattered all over town. The fringe of these areas often bordered on areas of
smaller, mainly workers' houses. These two types of residences were often
intermingled. This coexistence of villas and more modest residential houses
could be compared to the suburban mixture of old farmers' houses, villas,
small residential houses, and industrial buildings. Owing to this interweaving and for some other reasons, the external aspect of individual quarters as
well as the structure of their population used to differ very much. Among the
most poor were improvised groups of shacks that emerged in several parts of
Ljubljana and its suburbs. Zelena jama, the focus of this chapter, used to be
a typical workers' settlement, yet it never showed any slum characteristics.

Some years ago an ethnographic study was made of Zelena jama to determine the ethnologically interesting features of this type of settlement. Until then Yugoslav ethnologists had studied the cultural patterns of chiefly
rural localities. The main focus of such studies was on traditional cultural
features. Zelena jama, on the contrary, represents a settlement that has developed anew, without any historical rural roots. And, what is most important, it has an urban character. Until recently no Yugoslav ethnologist has
taken an interest in newly developed urban settlements. At present the situation is quite different, for there are several such investigations in course,
some of them even in Ljubljana.

The results of this investigation were published in the book *The Ljubljana
Settlement of Zelena jama as an Ethnologic Problem* (1970). I shall try to cull from
this work all those findings related to the problem of a suburban settlement,
to the conditions of its origin, and to the reasons for its gradual decay. Accordingly, my attention will be focused on the cultural identity of the settlement,
which has been shaped under special suburban circumstances. I inquire into
the forces that have conditioned the formation of the community and I discuss those cultural events that have kept it alive. Moreover, I recount the
process whereby the communal ties that had once united the inhabitants of
this settlement began to weaken.

In reviewing the origin and the growth of the settlement, three periods
can be distinguished: before World War I, between the two wars, and after
World War II. At the turn of this century, on a field near both the railway
and a glue factory, the settlement of Zelena jama sprouted, growing to include over 70 houses. It was named after a long-abandoned nearby quarry.

During the war and even some years after it the settlement saw no expansion; in subsequent years, by the period of the national liberation struggle, however, its population had increased considerably to nearly 3,000 inhabitants and more than 700 families, including about 200 house owners and about 500 tenants. After World War II Zelena jama continued to grow, yet at a reduced rate owing to lack of space, resulting from the fact that the settlement was caught between communication lines and industrial buildings constructed before World War II. After the war the remaining land was built up, mainly with blocks of flats. In spite of these new flats and some smaller buildings, the number of inhabitants after the war did not surpass the prewar population size. In recent years the external appearance of Zelena jama has undergone no significant change, which is partly due to the fact that this area has been reserved for industrial buildings and partly due to the national protection of monuments.

At its origin Zelena jama was located on the fringe of Ljubljana. In those years even the inhabitants of Zelena jama and similar settlements imagined that Zelena jama represented the end of the town where a different world was supposed to begin. Zelena jama was a suburban settlement of workers, especially railwaymen and their families. It passed for a railwaymen's colony. For this reason it differed from some other, even neighboring workers' settlements. In the mind of the Ljubljana townsfolk Zelena jama was regarded as the residence of the lowest classes of society, distinct from other suburban settlements. It was characterized by its own cultural features. What were they and what accounted for them?

As already mentioned, in the initial period the houses in Zelena jama were mostly built or owned by railwaymen. About three-quarters of the house owners were employed in various railway occupations. Foremost were railway guards and stokers, who encouraged each other to build their houses in Zelena jama. People of these occupations constituted the majority in Zelena jama. It was only in individual exceptional cases that people of a social status higher than that of the railwaymen were found. The families of engine drivers, chief guards, and the rest of the better paid railwaymen were rather rare during this first period of Zelena jama's development.

Another question relevant in this context concerns the origin of the inhabitants of Zelena jama. The first generation came almost entirely from the Slovene countryside, hence from village environments. The majority of them belonged to a wider Ljubljana rural backcountry. These were originally peasants. A great many of the newcomers came from small or medium-size farms with numerous children. In addition, many were children who came from decaying or degenerated farms, in several cases sons and daughters or parents who had had only a small holding of land or none at all.

In general, the newcomers did not come to Zelena jama directly from the countryside and from peasant work. At the time of their settlement the first generation already had some practice in other, rather different occupations. Thus some of them turned from herdsmen and farm laborers to factory workers or railway storage workers or even to stokers, switching yard workers, or railway guards. Before World War I they had, at most, a primary school education. Educated people, originally from the countryside, did not choose to live in Zelena jama. Likewise, few people there were trained in a particular craft. In general, this generation had left home rather young, without taking up any professional training in their native village. However, the lives of boys coming from the country were greatly influenced by their military service.

Accordingly, for the great majority the process of cultural accommodation at the transition from village to town was already completed prior to their settlement in Zelena jama. Most of them had been separated from their rural homes and the village atmosphere long before. To a large extent they had already tried to adjust themselves to the new, sometimes seemingly strange or at least unintelligible environment prior to settlement. Owing to their shortage of money as well as their different customs, they did not take advantage of the possibilities of a more extensive life offered by the town. Thus the endeavors of these rural people of peasant origin, mainly railwaymen, people without special or higher education, were at first characterized by the struggle for the solution of their fundamental existential problems. Chief among these was housing, a problem that provided the main impetus for their settlement in Zelena jama.

The people building their houses in Zelena jama were primarily driven by their strong wish to live under a roof of their own. Accordingly, with very little means at their disposal and following their unpretentious requirements, they built houses strongly resembling each other. This was the product of the skill and the common building techniques employed by trained bricklayers from the neighborhood, following the traditional style of suburban houses. There were mostly single-story homes of simple external appearance. The interior arrangement of rooms changed continually. In many cases they first built only a flat for themselves, later extending it by built-on garret lodgings for tenants. Not being too demanding, and fleeing from rented flats to be under a roof of their own, many families were satisfied to have a kitchen and a bedroom. These one-room flats, often without a larder, always without a bathroom, and commonly also without any entrance corridor, were for many a noncodified housing standard. Although many house owners possessed two rooms and a kitchen, the flats to let were mainly one-room. Yet because the owners of two-room flats used to let one room to tenants, the families of Zelena jama actually lived exclusively in one-room flats.

Like the home owners, the tenants of flats or rooms were also chiefly railwaymen, often known to the house owners through their jobs. For them, too, Zelena jama was attractive, especially because of its proximity to their workplaces. Families belonging to other occupations were much less frequently represented among the tenants. These were mainly families of factory workers, of whom only a few owned a house in Zelena jama.

Nearly all inhabitants of Zelena jama depended on their own wages or, rather, on the wages of their breadwinners to pay off the loans invested in the building of their houses or to pay the rent and other costs of living. Few of them earned their living through a trade or self-employment. The wages the railwaymen, for example, received for their work depended on their work position, and in certain cases also on their personal performance. In fact, in railway jobs personal efforts for promotion were highly encouraged. Accordingly, thanks to promotion, the railwaymen could get access to new, quite diversified work posts. The inhabitants of Zelena jama worked mainly as brakemen, stokers, switching yard workers, freight car recorders, luggage room attendants, and railway guards of different grades.

In principle, women were not employed. After marriage and the birth of their first child they stayed at home, devoting themselves to housekeeping and child care. Yet in most cases they found additional work. The most typical ways of earning extra money were gardening, tilling rented fields, and breeding domestic animals. Houses were almost necessarily accompanied by gardens. Everybody looking for a building location sought to have his house surrounded by a yard and a garden. As a rule, the garden was mainly tilled by the owner's family. On the other hand, almost everywhere a part of the garden was reserved for tenants, who used it to grow some vegetables. Where the gardens were larger, families were able to provide most of their food during the summer from them. Potatoes, cabbages, and beans were grown in fields rented in the surrounding area. The produce was also used as food for pigs, bred by most house owners and even some tenants. In addition, breeding of poultry, rabbits, and, to a certain extent, goats was quite widespread.

Beside tilling gardens and breeding domestic animals, women used to find other employment. Some of them did laundry, for example, for soldiers, or some sewing both for merchants and for the factory. Others took up petty trade, many selling vegetables and flowers in the town market. More rarely they went to town as charwomen.

Initially the foodstuffs and other necessities people could not produce themselves were provided in nearby shops or in the town. It did not take long, though, before Zelena jama got its first public taverns, owned by the railway people. The first were a pub and some brandy- and wine-houses.

It was in this context that the social relationships of the inhabitants of Zelena jama at the first stage of its development were based. Owing to the considerable social and professional uniformity of this rather small settlement, the social relations there were considered by the inhabitants to be good. As a matter of fact, some social differentiation, based on the individual's professional position and personal income, already existed, although in that period it was not really evident. A certain resistance was felt toward newcomers who, because of their better knowledge of the German language, made career advances more easily and quickly. Differences in the degree of religious devotion did not affect social relations.

When a house was being built and on many other occasions, people regularly used to help each other. Especially in construction work, the railwaymen could count on the assistance of their workmates. Likewise, their neighbors took part in the preparatory work. Inhabitants of the settlement used to visit each other without any formality. There was no seclusion into one's own family circle or one's own yard. The relations between individual families were based on friendship, in certain cases resembling family relations. This emotional closeness was partly due to the proximity of houses, yards, and gardens. Families lived without any special attempts at privacy. Some of the houses even began to receive certain forms of given names. Whenever a member of the settlement died, a representative of each house necessarily took part in his funeral. To a certain extent even general customs reflected the life of the whole settlement. Among the customs of the year there were some that brought together most of the settlement or at least the children. Such was the case of the festivities of Shrove Tuesday or New Year's Eve, when numerous inhabitants of Zelena jama gathered in the pub to celebrate the coming of the new year.

In spite of the domestic atmosphere, some inhabitants of Zelena jama nevertheless felt that life in the settlement was more "secluded" than that in their native village. On the other hand, there were some who, owing either to their social origin or to their slightly higher social position or for other reasons, sought seclusion from the community. Yet in the initial period such cases were still rare.

In their social relations, expressed in the extent of mutual familiarity and reciprocal help, many felt life in the settlement of Zelena jama was "as in the country." The inhabitants knew each other, helped each other at work, and borrowed from each other whatever they needed. Those who did not have a well at home went to fetch water from their neighbors. Some of them saw this as a form of village life. Yet the question arises whether these relations and this feeling resulted from people's rural background and education or, on the contrary, were as much conditioned by the way of life found on the fringe of the town itself. Both possibilities should be admitted, although many features indicate that the local conditions were of primary importance. The inhabitants were rather homogeneous in their social and occupational character and mainly alike in their origin. Their general cultural level was more or less the same and so were their cultural needs. Because the settlement was small, people could know each other better. All this contributed to the uniformity of the settlement and, moreover, created the consciousness of a definite community that was, half seriously and half not, referred to as the special Zelena jama "republic."

But to what extent did this sense of the particularity or integrity of the settlement manifest itself externally? In its territorial aspect and according to its external architectural style, Zelena jama belonged to the fringe of the town, as has already been mentioned. As regards food, the first generation of Zelena jama still retained numerous components from the diet of their original home, but they came much closer to the town in their clothing. The reasons for this difference lie in the fact that while the daily food was largely determined by the domestic economy, clothing was affected by the proximity of the town. Upon settlement in town the originally peasant newcomers to Zelena jama were trying to shake off their peasant features. They did not feel any need to publicly display their origin. Accordingly, they wanted to adapt themselves as soon as possible to the manner of clothing that prevailed in the town. Hence, in this respect Zelena jama belonged to the urban agglomeration. Yet, although the inhabitants never tried to emphasize its particular physiognomy, this was nevertheless present in the consciousness of Ljubljana townsfolk.

The relatively homogeneous status of the inhabitants of Zelena jama gave rise to similar illusions, needs, and wishes. Moral attitudes arose that had a specific tinge of locality. The actions of individuals were always subject to an autochthonous view of the society, with its evaluations and condemnations. In the settlement as a whole everything was known about the life of each family. The unofficially constituted community of Zelena jama determined the life of its members in such respects as clothing, consumption of goods, work, and general behavior. Individual gestures out of tune with the norms met disapproving responses on the part of the settlement as a whole. Conversely, solidarity with other residents meant help in case of need and hardship. This was the environment in which the inhabitants of Zelena jama felt at home. Zelena jama was a world of people similar in status and thinking. In the settlement they felt relaxed; they did nothing to conceal their way of life and their culture, for as a rule their neighbors were in no respect better off. However, it should be stressed that all this relative peculiarity, even seclusion, of the settlement of Zelena jama did not result from any weaker ties with the existing socioeconomic and cultural development process as a whole. On the contrary, it was the result of this very process. On the basis of their social status, the inhabitants of Zelena jama were pushed to the fringe of the town in the widest sense of the word. Their material status as well as their material and spiritual culture were a direct expression of definite social relations. This should be constantly taken into account when discussing Zelena jama and similar settlements in terms of more or less secluded communities.

During World War I and for four or five years thereafter, Zelena jama did not exceed its prewar boundaries. This was one of the reasons why the life of the settlement remained more or less the same for a few years after the war. But with intensive building in the following years the settlement gradually increased in size and in number of inhabitants. Thus by 1940 the number of houses (just 72 before World War I) had increased to 253. At that time the settlement had nearly 3,000 people. Even in the new parts of the settlement railwaymen were still predominant in comparison to any other occupational group. According to the 1935 census, 44% of the owners of houses built between the two wars were railwaymen. Zelena jama continued to be described as a railwaymen's settlement different from the neighboring suburban areas of "workers" and "farmer-workers." Between the two wars, however, Zelena jama started to turn from a settlement with an absolute majority of railwaymen into one in which the railwaymen had only a relative majority. This was due to the fact that many newcomers were mainly artisans of various kinds as well as unskilled workers.

In 1935 the occupational structure of the heads of Zelena jama families was as follows: 25% were employed with the railways, 22% were journeymen and skilled factory workers, 18% were unskilled workers. There were also property owners and proprietresses (11%), the latter being to a large extent railwaymen's widows; 6% were clerks and various employees, followed by registered masters (4%), auxiliary staff—assistants, servants, guardians (3.5%), attendants and maid-servants (3%), police and military officers (2.5%), apprentices (2%), secondary school students (1.5%), technicians and teachers (0.8%), university graduates (0.7%), and university students (0.3%). Single girls living in their parents' families were mainly skilled workers (26%), clerks and officials (22%), workers (16%), secondary school students (15%), and apprentices (10%). Among unmarried sons living in their parents' families there were about 39% skilled workers, 22% students, and 17% apprentices. Yet, in spite of a more heterogeneous occupational pattern, Zelena jama—the settlement of railwaymen, artisans, apprentices, and workers—to a certain extent preserved its uniform social structure.

A particularly interesting problem in the change of the occupational and social structure of Zelena jama between the two wars involves the generation that had either been born or had at least grown up there. These were young people who were formed by the life on the fringe of the town, who were already in their childhood in more or less close contact with the town, even with town children, but who nevertheless led their own life. They spent their time among their equals, with children from identical or similar families. They did not lack time for playing. While these youngsters enjoyed considerable freedom, the concern of their parents for their children's future was of great importance. In their preparation for independent life most of the young generation of Zelena jama received considerable moral support from

home. The material possibilities, however, were less favorable, particularly
because of the large number of children. Yet the parents used to make great
efforts to enable their children to surpass them on the social ladder. Accordingly, only a very small percentage of sons or even daughters remained without any training. For this reason, after finishing primary school, most of the
children became apprenticed. A minority of them tried to continue their
schooling, yet many gave it up before long and entered a trade instead.
Some finished secondary school but only a few managed to get a university
education. In schools girls proved to be more assiduous than boys, yet their
parents seemed to be less inclined to continue their education. The high percentage of men as well as women trained in one of the trades reflects the predominant orientation of the generation descended from the railwaymen's
and workers' families of Zelena jama. Thus, in comparison with their
parents, the children advanced a step up the social ladder. Here the proximity of the town, providing a different environment with different standards,
gave numerous opportunities for advancement. These occupational and
social changes, however, did not have the significance they might have had
in the previous period of the settlement, for the process of proletarianization
had in this period encompassed much wider strata.

    The youths of Zelena jama in the years following World War I consti-
tuted a well-defined community. The few examples of slight isolation experienced by grammar school students who came from certain well-off families did not significantly affect this uniformity. The majority were apprenticed in different trades, especially locksmithing, with most of them looking
for jobs with the railway as well as in factories and elsewhere. Many finished
elementary school, most frequently located in the town. Thus in both their
education and their occupational goals they were very much alike. The main
aspects of their domestic education did not differ either. This generation
grew up together, played together, and remained more or less together even
in their adolescence. Their territorial limitation, common origin, and similar way of life led to intimate relationships, manifested for a time in certain
sports and cultural associations that sprang up in the settlement.

    After playing at war, inspired by World War I, with the boys from
Zelena jama constantly attacking their playmates from beyond the railroad,
the youths became very keen on sports. This interest in sports, particularly
soccer in the case of boys and a kind of handball for the girls, was not limited
to the youths of Zelena jama. It had a strong integrative effect in the settlement. In addition, people came together in mandolin groups, choirs, theater
groups, and brass bands. The common participation of the youth in sports
and various cultural activities was accompanied by other forms of intercon-
nection, imparting to the youth of these postwar years a still more uniform
character. An informal community of Zelena jama boys, which had origi-

nated in the prewar period, was strengthened during the war and came to its full expression in the postwar period. Consequently, the boys quite often chose their girlfriends from their own environment. The number of marriages between boys and girls from Zelena jama used to be rather high, reflecting and perpetuating the uniformity and common life of the youth of the settlement.

Accordingly, in the years after World War I the main bearers of the external expression of the Zelena jama community — the so-called Zelena jama "republic" — were the young people who had spent their childhood and adolescence there. Considering the fact that after marriage these native suburban youth mostly settled down in vacant flats in their parents' houses or rented other flats in the neighborhood, they represented a continuity in the settlement of Zelena jama. Yet, with intensive growth of the settlement and the numerous newcomers originating from the countryside, this stable population gradually became a minority.

A comparatively high rate of population growth, changes in the occupational structure, proletarianization and related uncertainty, as well as a fiercer struggle for existence characterized the Zelena jama community and its cultural pattern between the two wars. In addition, political-ideological forces began to impinge on the settlement. While in the first period neither the police nor the church made any particular efforts to exert their control, between the two wars both governing social forces were deeply concerned with the suburbs, hence with Zelena jama as well. They approached the community through direct measures as well as through acts of charity.

In this second period the inhabitants of Zelena jama were preoccupied with their efforts for material existence, for unemployment was present throughout the period between the two wars. In certain big families with low wages or suffering unemployment the problems of existence were often unbearable. The lack of basic means of existence led many individuals to seek work outside their occupational sphere. Thus for economic reasons tilling gardens continued to be very popular and typical for the settlement. In general, compared to the prewar situation, changes in several aspects of the way of life and of the cultural pattern of Zelena jama remained minor. They were mainly a reflection of general changes in the shaping of the community and the contents of the cultural pattern. Regarding dress, for example, residents observed the current fashion, and the slight peculiarities retained by the Zelena jama social group of the first period were now abandoned. The formerly small sartorial differences from the town now became even smaller, although the difference in quality of the material worn by local inhabitants and townspeople, of course, persisted. The particular regional features concerning everyday food, stemming from the original homes of the individuals or their families, were still alive, although the exchange of ways of preparing food added variety in the daily food in Zelena jama. Furthermore, in the sphere of furniture new elements sprang up, yet because of unimproved housing conditions they did not have any particular significance.

Housing problems in this period, including evictions, frequent moving to other flats, and renting a shared bed, were among the most significant aspects of the material features of the inhabitants of Zelena jama. Their housing conditions reflected the material capacities and to a certain extent the needs of both tenants and house and flat owners. An interesting illustration of this was the fact that many an owner's family used to dwell in the cellar or attic of their own house in order to be able to rent out the more expensive flats.

Life in Zelena jama was chiefly motivated by the concern to provide daily bread, to pay the rent, and to pay off any debts. Families were constantly haunted by the fear of losing their jobs; besides, those who had no old-age insurance suffered from the apprehension of what would happen to them when they were no longer able to work. Various cultural features of the urban center did not reach the inhabitants of Zelena jama at all, or they did so only to a degree because they could not "get used to them." This fact is of primary significance because Zelena jama was in both geographical and administrative respects a component of the Slovene national center, Ljubljana. Attending the performances of plays and operas, going to concerts, visiting art exhibitions, taking in reviews, and reading books were not among the things that attracted the inhabitants of Zelena jama, except for some exceptional cases. Consequently, the settlement was mostly deprived of artistic and other cultural enjoyments offered by the town. In this respect it still remained on the fringe of the town.

Yet the specific suburban characteristics of Zelena jama were not on the increase; they were slowly, but quite evidently, giving way to a more urban way of life. The specific suburban trades of Zelena jama, such as in its original rather homogeneous pattern, were slowly disappearing. The increasing occupational heterogeneity, the slight internal stratification, the expansion of the settlement, the process of urban incorporation, and other actions inevitably resulted in changes in the existing cultural pattern of Zelena jama. The inhabitants, belonging to the suburbs, had open access to the town, to which they would adapt themselves more and more. Consequently, a constant process inhibited any greater rooting of independent cultural features. The people were aware of changes taking place in the urban way of life and tried, according to their possibilities, to alter their own life in response. Where these changes occurred quickly, the traditions handed down from generation to generation were eroded. The people refused to be left behind by these developments; they looked not backward but ahead. They had no reason for grieving about their past. As a rule, they felt no need to refer to either their former social status or their origin. Hence there was nothing special to preserve. Their aspiration for change, for improvement of the existing cultural pattern and way of life, far exceeded any wish for conservation. Their nostalgia for the lost village way of life was in any case only a verbal expression that implied no tendencies for restitution. The inhabitants of Zelena jama did not belong to any class or social stratum that would have defended its former social position.

In spite of all the above facts, throughout the period between the two wars Zelena jama retained among other suburbs a well-defined place on the social ladder. In the opinion of the inhabitants of the city of Ljubljana proper, Zelena jama was a proletarian settlement, from the social point of view obviously lagging behind the urban areas. This was something the people of Zelena jama were well aware of. Yet, on the other hand, the Zelena jama population looked down upon the area that bordered them, which was occupationally even more heavily proletarian. Hence, in spite of the proletarian character of the settlement, the people of Zelena jama could not conceal their typical smallholding mentality.

This mentality concerning property was, of course, most directly related to house ownership. As we already know, in the second period of development of this settlement, house owners' families were in the minority. Nevertheless, apart from some more permanent and socially active tenants, it was only the house owners and their families who in the expanded settlement managed to preserve some forms of the Zelena jama community. As a matter of fact, tenants were, as a result of their frequent moves from one flat to another, a highly unstable element in the population structure. This inevitably resulted in a more complex cultural pattern of the settlement as well as in a more complex pattern of social relations. With the expansion of the settlement and the frequent changing of flats, the possibility of everybody knowing everybody else had weakened. Now the circle of those known to an individual no longer encompassed the whole settlement. Good acquaintances were possible only within the frame of a narrower neighborhood. The former openness of private life became restricted to the individual's house or flat and garden.

As a rule, the newcomers from the countryside found the life of inhabitants of Zelena jama much more secluded; they missed the familiarity found in their native village, and upon settlement they often suffered from isolation. This was especially true for housewives, who were mainly confined to home and family. Actually torn away from their former way of life, in which they took part in millet grinding, corn peeling, and going to parish fairs, public festivals, and name-day celebrations, they must have felt a great change. Men, who were very busy, expected from the settlement only a simple home, a place to rest. The youths increasingly made friends outside the narrow circle of their residence. Thus, with the expansion of the settlement the formerly more or less homogeneous community of youth became divided into smaller groups, the so-called gangs. More and more frequently, upon leaving elementary school the closer mutual contacts among children or youth weakened or completely disappeared. Likewise, courtships and subsequent marriages between Zelena jama boys and girls became more and more rare.

Gradually, the life of Zelena jama youth in particular and of the settlement in general was affected by outside forces. The settlement was influenced by the Salesian friars, who were known for their understanding of the environment and of the aspirations and needs of youth. They established a youth center in the vicinity of the settlement. They were followed by the missionary society of St. Vincent, which had organized a youth asylum in the settlement. Whenever the clergy failed through propaganda and through moral and material pressure, they extended their influence through acts of charity. These organized, politically tinged encroachments on the Zelena jama settlement resulted in certain political consequences. Among the population there were a few outstanding clerics and a few varieties of nationalists. Likewise, there were some loyal socialist and communist families. Nevertheless, the Zelena jama settlement in principle preserved its neutral, uncommitted character. It was not seen as appropriate for spreading partisan ideas. Among neighbors and inhabitants of the settlement there was practically no dispute arising from different political convictions and world outlooks. The clerical activity, however, quite strongly affected the political structure of the settlement, yet with only superficial impact on the population. People were mainly attracted only by the prospect of material advantages.

In spite of the variety of these ideological influences, many inhabitants dealt with their daily problems and those of their families by relying primarily on their own resources. Many confined themselves to their own family circle; they used to save a part of their earnings, even though these were very modest, for still more critical times to come. Saving some money was a regular habit of a number of families. Their desire to build a house of their own with a garden around it reflected their mentality as well. Wasting money, even if only on a modest scale, was not proper to them. Neither did they show off in their clothing. In their opinion, more important than showing off were their savings. Living from hand to mouth was something these families did not find to their liking. Peasant girls, who married railwaymen on account of their comparatively stable jobs, brought from the countryside the need for security, based on certain forms of property. Since their property now depended on their incessant work, they spent all their energy in this direction. Their property, consisting mostly of a house and a garden, provided them with the basis of their self-confidence. They were proud of their property, especially if their houses and gardens were big.

Differences in political views, the aspiration for gaining even some modest property and the envy arising both from the property and from the hierarchy of work positions must have affected social relations in the settlement. Besides the expansion of the settlement these elements and others, too, influenced the increasing movement toward "living apart." Nevertheless, throughout the period between the two wars the settlement of Zelena jama still preserved a few traits demonstrating the close mutual relations of the inhabitants. Thus the women, especially the older ones, used to meet and chat in front of their houses. In the evenings a smaller or bigger group often met for choral singing. Whenever an inhabitant died, a representative of almost every house took part in the funeral. Reciprocal help either with work or money was not rare. People helped each other at work to enable their neighbor "to make it cheaper." Further, they added: "In case of need, you'll help too!"

At this stage of suburban cultural development, Zelena jama became engulfed in World War II, marked by the invasion of Yugoslavia, the dismembering of Slovenia, and the occupation by Italian fascists. In Zelena jama some forms of the resistance movement against the forces of occupation were felt surprisingly soon. During the first years of expansion of the liberation front, about two-thirds of the Zelena jama families in some way or other took part in the resistance movement. The remaining third was neutral, though there were a few examples of traitors and opponents to the resistance movement.

Owing to the national and class consciousness of most of the inhabitants and as a product of joint action, similar behavior, and common fate, the Zelena jama of the liberation front developed into a close community that had no longer existed before the war. Those who as a result of their neutral position remained outside this community, or those who decided against the majority, did not pass for "ours" in this community. In those days the distinction between "ours" and those considered outsiders was of vital importance. People were becoming increasingly distrustful of the undecided and the minority of the population who opposed the liberation front. The increasing intensity of the feeling of community was accompanied by this growing distrust as well as by political and ideological differentiation within the settlement.

The local community of Zelena jama, shaped during the war, became upon the successful end of the national liberation war the force behind the whole restitution and socialist reconstruction of the settlement. The carrying out of new social tasks was related to many forms of social life that during the period of so-called administrative socialism exhibited no evident particularities of the Zelena jama settlement. The time of public gatherings, voluntary work and meetings, with its stress upon public, joint activities within the scope of commonly developed and generally accepted forms, necessarily led to a uniform way of life and cultural pattern. It was only a later phase in the development of the socialist construction — the introduction of workers' and social self-management — that again brought to the life and culture of the settlement some new elements, often eliminating certain preceding features.

This introduction of new elements was constrained by the nature of existing conditions in the community. Thus, the social structure of the postwar population was determined by the pattern of house ownership and of prewar settlement, and by the later constant shortage of flats, the postwar official assignment of vacant, often very small flats, the settlement of owners' grown-up children into formerly rented flats, as well as by other reasons. These factors, however, resulted in a very heterogeneous occupational and educational structure of the settlement. The different levels of education and the great variety of occupations make it impossible to define the occupational or the social pattern of the settlement as a whole. Accordingly, the characterization of postwar Zelena jama as a railwaymen's settlement is not justified. Even the material situation of the inhabitants became much more diversified. Consequently, after the war the suburban cultural uniformity progressively disintegrated.

Because the smallness and unsuitability of the flats in the prewar part of Zelena jama drove younger families to move out of these flats, older residents predominated in the settlement. Thus in the more recent part of the settlement the average age was 37, and in one of the oldest streets it was 49. Older residents in many respects preserved the existing way of life. Although in the wake of the social revolution the holding mentality was, at least externally, considerably weakened, people nevertheless remained strongly attached to their little houses and gardens, which they had often earned through great efforts. The changed relationships between tenants and house owners gave rise to conflicts, proving the persistence of the old suburban cultural pattern with smallholding or quasi-proletarian elements.

In their social relations people in postwar Zelena jama are probably more than ever closed behind their doors and live secluded in their family circle. This is particularly true of the people living in new blocks; in spite of their several years' residence, the majority of new residents have not become integrated into the social life of the settlement. In fact, it is only those who have moved into the new blocks from the older part who have any acquaintances among the older inhabitants of the settlement. The rest of the inhabitants know and visit each other mostly on the basis of their common jobs. Accordingly, individual flats, even if under the same roof, often represent separate units socially secluded from one another. For many people social life in the settlement ends with the family.

Compared to the years preceding World War I and to the decade after it, the common way of life — including the gangs of boys, social gathering in streets, and the negative attitudes expressed toward neighboring areas — has practically disappeared. Even in the world of children Zelena jama has lost its specific nature.

The remains of the typical features of Zelena jama are to be found only among the older generation of the population. The way of life of the younger generation, living either in the new blocks or in the older part of the settlement, is in principle more or less the same. The people in the prewar part of the settlement in one way or another refuse to accept the legacy handed down as a cultural concept. This legacy, however, also contains elements that at least for the moment have no substitute. Hence it can be concluded that Zelena jama, with its cultural pattern shaped within definite social conditions exists no more. Even the former settlement community based on these cultural features has disintegrated. The only comparatively strong cultural remains are those determined by the shortage of flats and the rather weak material position of many retired people and their families.

After examining the development of Zelena jama in terms of its identity and the social relationships of its residents, the question arises as to how typical this pattern is for other Slovene and Yugoslav urban agglomerations. The answer to this question is not simple; indeed, for the moment it is impossible, because no completed study of the same type of settlement is available in Slovenia. Furthermore, it should be stressed that for better understanding of suburban settlements one should be familiar with the contemporary cultural pattern of settlements belonging to different types, especially of typical middle-class quarters. From the point of view of class evaluation, a comparison with contemporary middle-class cultural patterns is absolutely necessary. Besides we lack analogous studies of rural regions, for those we have concentrate on traditional cultural features. Only the comparison between individual regions with special emphasis on their development could introduce us to the actual process of differentiation in way of life and culture. Accordingly, a comparison between the prewar Zelena jama and a prominent Ljubljana residential district, regarding the material situation, housing pattern, food, clothing, social relations, and cultural life in the narrow sense of the word would provide a clear picture of social differences in the former social system. A similar comparison referring to the present situation would be useful, too. A comparison of the way of life and the cultural patterns of individual regions would enable us to assess the social and especially cultural progress in its wider sense. Such investigations, however, based on historical comparison, offer a very useful insight into social relations.

No less interesting, of course, are international comparisons of the way of life and cultural development typical for approximately the same type of settlements. For this reason Yugoslav ethnologists increasingly stress the importance of ethnological investigations concerning microterritories, including those of a fully urban nature. Thus the Slovene ethnologists have already started working on a vast project, "The Way of Life of the 20th Century Slovene Population." This work will be essentially based on a monographic investigation of about 60 carefully chosen settlements of different types, including urban boroughs, industrial centers, and individual town quarters. One of the catalysts for this demanding task could certainly be attributed to the study of Zelena jama.

Chapter **12**

Under One Roof: Marriage, Dowry, and Family Relations in Piraeus

Renée B. Hirschon

INTRODUCTION

The influx into Greece in 1922 of 1.5 million displaced people from Asia Minor and Thrace had long-term consequences in economic, social, and political spheres of life. The massive increase in population (by about 20%) within a few years drastically altered the country's demography and population distribution, and the small, predominantly agricultural country became enriched and diversified with the expertise and skills of the newcomers (Pentzopoulos 1962). Through an emergency housing program numerous large settlements were established in Athens, Piraeus, and Thessalonika and in smaller provincial towns, where hundreds of thousands of families began a new life. A large proportion were themselves urban dwellers from seaports and cosmopolitan centers of the Ottoman empire (League of Nations 1926:16). The study of contemporary urban life in Greece must, therefore, take account of the specific responses and experience of the Asia Minor population, whose presence was formative and significant, though it is often neglected.

The present analysis outlines some patterns of family life that have developed in one locality of refugee origin in Piraeus. It is well to note that cultural and social patterns in these localities must be considered essentially "urban" phenomena, since the population has been established here through some four generations and over 50 years, while many were originally from urban centers; the process of "urbanization," of adjustment to the city by countryfolk, is not part of this study.

Nea Ephesus, of which Yerania, the area of detailed study, is a part, was established in 1922 on open land northeast of Piraeus harbor to shelter refugees, and by 1934, when it was incorporated as a *demos* (municipality), it accommodated about 40,000 inhabitants. Today the extended municipal boundaries include over 86,000 people (1971 national census) and four square kilometers, and it merges imperceptibly into newer residential localities where rural migrants have settled since World War II.

Despite an auspicious start (League of Nations 1926:167–71), Nea

Ephesus suffered for many years from governmental neglect; in the late 1960s public services were minimal, streets were unpaved and lighting was inadequate, no central sewage system existed, and road drainage was ineffective. Population density was high and buildings were, in the main, overcrowded. Interestingly though, social life in the area was highly integrated, and the social and personal disorganization often associated with poverty-stricken areas was largely absent (contrast Belmonte 1979). Although extensive modifications and some rebuilding have taken place, chiefly along the main roads, the distinctive housing of the original settlement is still distinguishable, and until very recently the population was predominantly of refugee origin.

Yerania is a district within Nea Ephesus, an area of 32 blocks (covering 80,000 square meters) with a population of over 3,000 people in 1971, which provided a useful starting point for an urban anthropological study based primarily on participant observation.[1] Here, unlike other parts of the settlement, standardized panel-and-frame structures were erected, intended for temporary use, but they remained for over 50 years and were subjected to various alterations, responses to culturally perceived priorities in the allocation and use of space (Hirschon and Thakurdesai 1970, Hirschon 1981).

In its original form each structure in Yerania consisted of two identical (semidetached) houses of panel-board, mirror images of each other, under a sloping tiled roof. Each block was divided into 20 plots and had 10 structures, while the amount of courtyard space allocated to each house (half-structure) depended on position in the block (i.e., corner houses had little open space but central plots were larger—see Figure 1). Each house, planned for one family, contained two main rooms (3.25 by 4 meters), a third "kitchen" room (2 by 3 meters), and outside toilet, but no bathroom. A most significant feature of the prefabricated house was the possibility of creating additional living space on the plot. The structures were set slightly above ground on plinths so that the first, easiest, and cheapest solution was to excavate rooms under the building, while additional rooms could be built in the open courtyards. Thus several families could be accommodated fairly easily on the same plot, a feature that bears directly on the provision of dowry for daughters, on kinship relationships, and on the composition of local groups.

Poverty has been endemic in Yerania. An early household survey (1930, unpublished) indicates the tenuous economic position of the majority of families: at that time only two-thirds of the family heads were recorded as being gainfully employed, the majority (40%) in unskilled jobs as "laborers," 12% as artisans, while about 30% of all family heads were recorded as having no occupation (including 12% disabled and unemployed men) and 18% of households with women heads.[2] There has obviously been a considerable improvement in income levels with the overall increasing affluence of the coun-

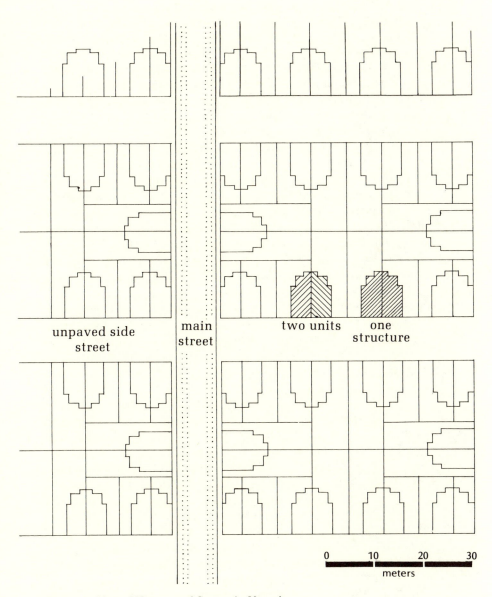

unpaved side
street

main
street

two units   one
structure

0   10   20   30

meters

Figure 1. Plan of Houses and Streets in Yerania

try, but the distribution of occupations is much as it was: manual laborers
(*ergates*) together with those involved in the construction industry comprise
42% of the working population, but more are now in skilled occupations,
20% as artisans (*technites*) and 13% in transport services (both public and private). At a time when the average monthly income per head for all Greece
was recorded as 2,720 drachmas (OCED 1972), the equivalent figure for
Yerania was estimated as 1,800 drachmas.[3] Against this background of constant economic hardship, the development of institutions in Yerania may be
viewed as reflecting culturally specified preferences expressed in and adapted
to particular material and historical conditions.

The Asia Minor refugees, it should be noted, were in all important respects, such as language, religion, and culture, essentially similar to the
Greeks of the metropolitan country. They were mainly Greek-speaking
Christians who had been long settled in Anatolia, administered under Ottoman rule as a *millet* (religious community). In this analysis of marriage institutions and family relations, the familiarity of several features usually
associated with rural Greek communities may seem surprising, but this very
fact would indicate their central cultural significance, for here we can see
how conventional forms become adapted to the urban context. The main
features of this process may be summarized as follows:

(1) Marriage is most acceptably contracted through a third party in a
formalized procedure called the *proxenio* ("marriage by arrangement"),
where an initial introduction is followed by discussion between the parents
of prospective spouses regarding material transactions associated with the
match. This procedure is flexible, however, allowing for a variety of approaches and permitting, as the final determinant of the match, the personal
attraction of the couple.

(2) The provision of dowry for a daughter is a major concern; its particular form, a separate dwelling place or "house" (*spiti*), directly affects the
composition of local groups here, as in all parts of the city. In Yerania subdivision of houses to provide living quarters for daughters' dowries results in
a number of co-resident families with links through female kin (mothers,
daughters, sisters, aunts, granddaughters), while men marry in as "strangers."

(3) This pattern of postmarital residence, under the roof of the bride's
kin, does not result in an extended family household. The term "uxorilocal,"
if applied here, should not imply any loss of authority on the part of the men.
Marriage creates a separate and autonomous conjugal unit under the
authority of its sole male head.

(4) The principle of male superiority is unaffected by the close residential proximity of the wife's kin; despite an apparent similarity, there is no
parallel with the *soghambros* in rural areas (see p. 315). Here the auton-

omy of each household is based on the premise of male authority, which remains central to kinship and domestic organization.

(5) It is commonly presumed that "traditional" practices and values, familiar in the context of rural communities, are eroded and inevitably disappear in the city, being replaced by "modern" ways that accord more closely with those of Western urban experience. Marriage and family life in Yerania, however, provide another case in which the polarity of "traditional-modern" and the corresponding set, "rural-urban," cannot be applied.

ARRANGED MARRIAGE: THE *PROXENIO*

Among three to four generations of urban dwellers the approval of, and indeed preference for, marriage conducted by the *proxenio,* usually glossed as "marriage by arrangement," may be unexpected. In essence, the *proxenio* involves a third person, a formalized introduction, the involvement of the prospective spouses' parents, and discussion of material assets, both dowry and income, that would accompany the proposed match. In the context of urban conditions all these elements can be seen to serve an important purpose: in the city reliable information about unknown families is arguably even more important than it might be in smaller rural settlements. By entering the social networks of third parties, the pool of advantageous matches is enlarged; thus it can be argued that in a locality of limited opportunity the social resources of the city are more efficiently tapped through the *proxenio* than if marriages were left to the chance meetings of young people.

Second, the procedure includes explicit investigation into the material contributions of the spouses to the new household. This interest in the economic resources of the conjugal unit reflects an enduring emphasis on family stability. The permanence of the marriage bond is of great concern in this poorer section of the urban population, so that the *proxenio* can be seen to deal with matters of economic viability in a culturally acceptable way. The prevalence of "marriage by arrangement" should not be considered an anomalous "survival" but may be seen as an effective response to conditions of large-scale urban existence in a particular cultural milieu.

The *proxenio* highlights, too, the importance of the family as the central unit of daily existence. The finality of marriage is emphasized, and, as in other parts of Greece, it is not simply the union of two independent individuals; marriage is a formal and sacramental tie, an immutable bond, ideally indissoluble (although divorce is permitted), which restructures the relationships between two sets of previously unrelated kinsmen. The emphatic expression of ideal values in advice offered to young people possibly reveals some of the stresses of contemporary life, in particular the effects of television (only recently available—in 1972 about one-third of the houses had a set). But threats to family stability are certainly not new in Yerania: excessively crowded conditions over the years have clearly contributed to conflicts, some extremely bitter, within the local group. Marriages are not always harmonious and divorce is not unknown, but there is no sign that marital breakdown is becoming accepted: the cases that have occurred are deplored and quoted as negative examples.

A principal element in family life is dedication to children's welfare, and parental devotion and obligation cease only on their successful marriages. In both moral and practical respects, parents are considered responsible for securing a proper match for a child, and it is expected that they will initiate the *proxenio* at a suitable time; until their marriages, children of both sexes remain in the parental home, not fully adult regardless of age (cf. Hirschon 1978:70–76).

A parent's active interest and guidance are considered essential because, it is believed, without it the son or daughter would fall victim to unscrupulous persons. Parents who do not initiate this process at the right time or who only half-heartedly attempt to conduct the necessary introductions are subject to criticism. Their involvement ensures the proper attention to social, economic, and practical factors without which marriage would be set upon shaky foundations.

In the context of these notions, romantic love is seen as a dangerous force because emotional factors based on individual perceptions tend to override practical issues. Love upsets the correct order of priorities for marriage; it disregards essential criteria of suitable age and background, health, and economic viability, and, for this reason, love is said to be "a catastrophe" (*i agapi einai katastrophe*). An open declaration of sentiment will prevent the parents from protecting the interests of their child, and from establishing their demands in the crucial negotiation stage of the *proxenio*.

The *proxenio* can therefore be seen as a process in which particular attributes of individuals and their families are matched, and the suitability of the prospective spouses is a central issue. Various criteria are brought to bear on the match, expressed in the imprecisely defined notion of *seira* (literally series, row) or rank. A common expression is "You will marry someone of your own *seira*" (*Tha paris kapoion tis seiras sou*). However vague, the idea of *seira* lies behind the choice of suitable partners, so that marriage in this locality is not, normatively, a means to social mobility.[4] Indeed, one of the deplored consequences of romantic love is that it may be manipulated by the unscrupulous for this very end.

Among the criteria of suitability, the economic and educational levels of the two families are very important, and an additional consideration is same place of origin (common all over the Greek world, expressed in the proverb "Shoes from your homeland, even if they are mended" — *Papoutsi ap'ton topo sou k'as einai ballomeno*). Other important considerations are per-

sonal qualities such as health, diligence, and virtue (or, rather, the reputation for it). The responsibility that the introduction of the young people is warranted in all these respects rests with a key figure, the *proxenitis* or "go-between." This is an unpaid, nonspecialist role, often undertaken by relatives, close kin, friends, or workmates, who, in any case, usually play a part in suggesting suitable partners or in discreetly verifying claims on behalf of the unmarried.

The *proxenio* procedure itself follows a set pattern but it may be initiated in many ways (cf. Bernard 1976:297), a factor that has undoubtedly contributed to its continued applicability in city life. In some cases neither the candidates nor their parents know one another, and in this "blind" *proxenio* the *proxenitis* is the only link, conveys all the information, and has a great deal of responsibility for the outcome. The introduction could be made by a sibling or close relative who may play the part of the *proxenitis*. Sometimes the parents of young people meet and themselves judge that a suitable match could be made, and a mutual acquaintance will then play the part of *proxenitis*. In all these cases the final decision depends upon the personal attraction of the candidates. Parents seldom desire to impose their will — forced marriage is generally agreed to be unacceptable — so that even if all other factors appear ideal, the match will fail in the absence of attraction. (One young man I knew had visited the home of 20 prospective brides without success, because either he or the girl was not sufficiently attracted.)

It is increasingly common for the proceedings to be initiated by a young person, usually the boy, after seeing or meeting a girl who appeals to him. Once the suggestion is made and approved by the parents, the usual *proxenio* procedure is followed. Today when couples say that they married "for love," they indicate that the initial suggestion was theirs, based on attraction, but in almost every case the formal *proxenio* took place. Clearly the chances of a match being concluded are higher when a degree of personal interest has already been established and the initiative comes from a young person, while the "blind" *proxenio* is less likely to have a successful outcome. Regardless of the way in which it is initiated, however, the *proxenio* follows the same stages, and its very formality preserves the self-interest of both parties, as well as their public face should the proposed match fail.

Once the suitability of the match has been established, a formal introduction takes place in the presence of the couples' parents and other close kin, together with the *proxenitis,* usually at the home of the girl (where her dowry may be covertly assessed). If the young people agree, a stage of negotiations follows in which material contributions to the marriage, essential for the existence and well-being of the family in the city, are discussed. The house is the chief item in the dowry contributed by the bride, its significance resting on the complementarity of husband's and wife's roles in subsequent family life. Once married, a woman is not expected to work, since the economic support of the family is the sole responsibility of the man. The provision of a house reflects *past* effort by the bride's family, who, in contrast, are concerned about the husband's *future* contribution, his employment, income, and prospects. In the parleying over material issues, antagonism may develop that can and often does affect relationships between affines after marriage.[5]

In view of common assumptions about city life, the vitality of the *proxenio* may be somewhat unexpected (cf. Vermeulen, in this volume), but it is explicable in the context of values that emphasize the permanence of the marriage bond and of family stability. The procedure admits a variety of contacts and accommodates personal choice within the conventional form. Consideration of the essential material preconditions for stable marriage is central to the *proxenio*. The necessity for calculated advantage is recognized together with that of individual attraction, and it is also realized that, in any particular match, material gain and emotional interest tend to be inversely proportionate. For this reason romantic love is deplored as an unsuitable basis for the establishment of secure family life.

THE DOWRY AND ITS EFFECTS

In this locality, and indeed all over the city, the dowry has not lost its importance. In taking the specific form of a "house" (or separate dwelling place), it represents the most costly allocation of resources for families with girls.[6]

The dowry usually includes a large variety of movable items (household linen, furnishings, and appliances), but it centers on the provision of a house, which is considered a precondition for her marriage. "When you have a house," people in Yerania say, "furniture and everything else can be found, but without it, everything is difficult" (*Epipla, ola yinontai otan yparchei spiti, otan then yparchei omos, ola einai dyskola*). A girl cannot expect to get married easily if her family does not provide some kind of separate residence where she will set up house after marriage. Conversely, a girl with a dowry dwelling but very little personal charm has a better chance of marriage than a girl without her own house. "Without a house a woman doesn't marry" (*Choris spiti i yineka then pantrevetai*), it is said, while people explain that "here in the city a house is absolutuly essential" (*edo stin poli to spiti einai to pio aparaitito*).[7] Statements of this nature together with other evidence suggest that particular urban conditions—a chronic shortage of housing, high land values, and limited resources—have induced the change in the dowry from movable items into a specific demand for a "house." In Asia Minor towns, however, gold coins, cash sums, and other movables constituted the customary provision among the older generation.

The dowry as a house is now a widespread expectation in both rural and

urban Greece and in Cyprus (Loizos 1975). The word "house" (*spiti*), however, designates a great variety of structures (villas, apartments, small
houses) depending on the economic stratum, so that in Yerania it may be no
more than a single room in the family home. In those cases where love pre-
vails and a girl marries without providing a dowry house, her family may be
relieved but not proud. The word describing such a bride, *xevrakoti*, translates significantly as "without pants," an uncomplimentary image casting as-
persions at her modesty. It is also seen as a failure of parental responsibility
(Kenna 1976:39, n.9), a view expressed vehemently in Yerania where even
the poorest families manage to provide some kind of shelter, however minimal, for their daughters.

Any explanation for emphasis on the house as a dowry must be set in
the context of past history and of urban conditions in Greece. The main cities
of Athens, Piraeus, and Thessalonika have suffered from severe housing
shortages for decades; fire destroyed large sections of Thessalonika in 1917,
and shortly afterward the influx of Asia Minor refugees, constituting a 20%
increase in population, created tremendous problems of absorption in various aspects of the country's life, while shelter itself continued as a focus of
refugee concern for over 40 years (see Pentzopoulos 1962:229ff.). The value
of urban home ownership has been further accentuated by postwar migration of villagers into the cities and the dissemination of urban values throughout the Greek countryside (see Sutton, in this volume). Since the dowry has
always constituted something of intrinsic worth, both material and symbolic, it is not surprising that city dwellers consider a house to be the most
suitable dowry.

Other factors that have undoubtedly also played a part in the emphasis
on a house can be given brief mention here. Certainly the notorious instability of the Greek currency over the past 50 years has had its effects, probably
more profound in areas such as Yerania, where economic hardship is longstanding. Numerous and drastic currency devaluations have resulted in a
skeptical attitude toward paper assets with a corresponding preference for real
estate investment. The value of home ownership as security is also related to
the absence of effective state welfare agencies. Cultural values, too, underline the integrity of independent family units, reflected in attitudes toward the
domestic realm: the head of the family should be head or master of the house
(*noikokyris*), while the position of tenant (*noikiaris*) is a dependent one, hence
inferior and abhorrent. Incommensurate pride and self-esteem are derived
from owning one's own home, no matter how small or humble.

The examination of historical demographic features provides another
dimension to the emphasis on dowry houses: a marked imbalance of the
sexes in critical age groups evidently has occurred at various times in the
past several decades. In the 1920s, for example, women over 16 years old
constituted over 62% of the population and men only 38% in four refugee

localities of Athens.[8] At that time the situation in these localities probably favored a "marriage strategy" where the most appropriate offering would be a house, given prevailing cultural values, the pressure of urban conditions, and a shortage of men. In the postwar period the relative shortage of marriageable men through selective labor migration abroad apparently results in a situation that continues "to favor men," since parents are having to provide increasingly expensive dowries.[9] Support for this interpretation comes from the people themselves, who often say, when discussing the grooms' dowry demands, "Nowadays it's the *men* who make the stipulations" (*Simera oi andres echoun tis apaitiseis*).

We have already noted the relative simplicity of modifying Yerania houses to provide additional living space. The ability to excavate under a house to create basement rooms was a most significant factor, for it potentially doubled living space. Given the premium on housing and the cultural prescription of dowry, it was both logical and convenient to subdivide the family residence on the marriage of daughters, providing each with separate quarters. The process took the following sequence: on the marriage of the first and second daughters, one or more rooms of the house were granted to them and the parents and unmarried children moved into the basement (which was considered unsuitable as dowry). For each new household, priority was given to a separate kitchen, usually of minimal size, provided in alcoves, on stairways, excavated under pavements, or added in the courtyard.[10] Finally, a small structure of two or three rooms would be erected in the courtyard (illegally and by the family itself) in order to provide dowry rooms for the younger daughters. In time even granddaughters' dowries were provided in this manner. In response to the need for living accommodation, it appears that sons are encouraged to marry early as they move into dowry houses provided by their wives and relinquish claims to the parental home (see Kenna 1976:29).

With minor variations a similar pattern is discernible throughout Yerania; indeed, over three-quarters of the houses have basement rooms excavated under them. Yerania's character today is largely a product of modifications to living arrangements that the prefabricated buildings allowed, and the social consequences of this housing flexibility have been marked. With the provision of separate living quarters in the bride's house, the bridegroom moves on marriage to live close to his wife's family; this residential group, living under one roof, does not, however, constitute a joint or extended family, for each marriage creates a separate household. Significantly in this densely populated situation, the precept of the independence of each conjugal unit is clear.

The history of one Yerania house, inhabited by the Yannides family, best illustrates this process through time. In 1928, when Yerania was established, the family of five members, parents, one daughter, and two sons, was

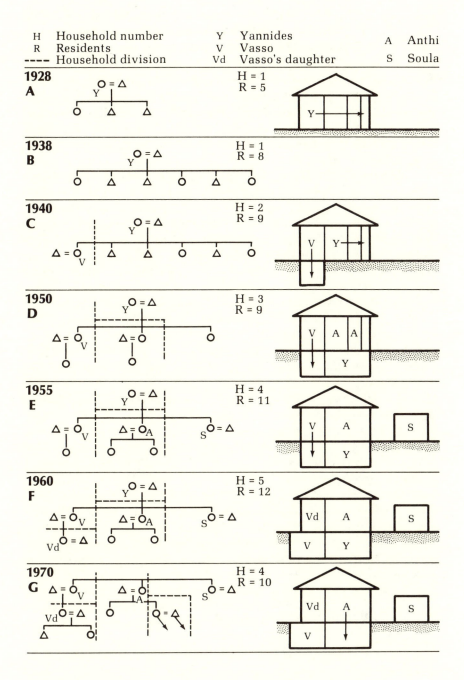

Figure 2. Domestic Cycle over Forty Years of the Yannides Family

given a house on a large central plot (Figure 2A). But within a few years another son and two daughters, Anthi and Soula, were born, so that ten years
later there were eight occupants in a single household (Figure 2B). Just before
1940 the first subdivision took place for the eldest daughter Vasso,
who was the first to marry. Her dowry consisted of the front room of the
house; when her husband, also from Yerania, moved into the dwelling, they
excavated a basement directly under the front room as their kitchen-living
room. The rest of the Yannides family occupied the remaining two rooms of
the house; thus in 1940 there were two households with nine persons resident in the dwelling (Figure 2C).

During the war years the picture changed considerably. The sons left
home, joined the Resistance, and later married (moving into dowry houses
provided by their wives). Vasso had a daughter, and the second sister, Anthi, was married, taking as her dowry the remaining rooms of the house.
The Yannides parents opened a second basement room at the back of the
house where they lived with the eldest girl, Soula. In 1950, when Anthi produced a child, the dwelling contained three separate households and nine
persons (Figure 2D).

Five years later Soula was ready for marriage. Two rooms were built in
the courtyard for her dowry, one as a bed-living room, the other as a kitchen.
Eleven persons now lived on the plot (since Anthi had produced another
child), and there were four households — the Yannides parents in the back
basement, and three married sisters in their respective dowry quarters (Figure 2E).

By 1960 Vasso's only child, a daughter, had reached a marriageable
age. As her parents had done before her, Vasso gave the front room of the
house to her daughter, and she moved down into the front basement with
her husband. Two small kitchen alcoves were excavated, partly under the
pavement, one for Vasso and one for her newly married daughter. Now at
its most crowded, there were five households and twelve persons on the plot.
Characteristically the older couples lived in basement rooms, while younger
married children occupied the original dwelling and additional courtyard
rooms (Figure 2F).

By 1970 the number of occupants and households was declining, for the
Yannides parents had died, as had Vasso's husband. Vasso's daughter, who
now had two children, was finding conditions too crowded in her portion of
the house (one room and a small kitchen alcove) and spoke of leaving.
Anthi's eldest daughter had married and left Yerania when her husband got
a job in Athens, but Anthi, her husband, and younger child were still there.
Soula had no children and lived with her husband in the courtyard house.
There were four separate households and ten residents at this time (Figure
2G).

In 1972 only six persons remained in three separate households. Vasso was alone in the front of the house, for her daughter and family had moved out. Anthi had taken over the back basement formerly occupied by their parents; her youngest daughter of 23 was ready for marriage and would be given the two upper rooms of the original dwelling, once Anthi's own dowry portion. Soula and her husband remained in the courtyard house.

Dowry apportionment, changing densities, and the fluctuating composition of the domestic group are well illustrated in this characteristic example. Obviously variations exist depending on particular family conditions, the number of children in the family (particularly daughters), the stage in the developmental cycle of the household, as well as economic conditions. In some cases, external factors such as the size of plot, as well as historical chance, resulted in houses being shared by unrelated families, thus diversifying the general pattern.

The characteristic composition of the domestic group in Yerania reflects the nature of dowry, which in turn may be seen as a response to an urban situation of high land values and shortage of housing, the absence of welfare provisions, and cultural values stressing family autonomy. Since extreme poverty in the past has restricted the choices open to Yerania families, the solution centered on the house (their main asset) where extra living quarters could be created by subdividing, by excavating under it, and by adding more rooms.[11] Particular pressures on housing in Yerania might suggest that it is a special case with limited relevance to general conditions in the city. On the contrary, I would argue that the situation in Yerania is of great interest because it provides a clear picture of family and domestic group relationships and highlights, on a small scale, characteristic patterns of urban residence.

In more affluent parts of the city the expectation that brides provide their own marriage residence is also prevalent, but different solutions have developed. The most common is for parents to build, in stages, a two- or three-story structure where each floor provides a self-contained apartment for a married daughter and parents respectively. In outlying suburbs where building plots are larger and planning regulations permit, daughters may be housed together in a two- or three-story building while parents may live in a separate cottage on the same land.

Although economic factors produce variation in the exact form of the dowry house in different parts of the city, the provision at marriage of separate living quarters by the bride's family results in a characteristic urban pattern, the close residential proximity of parents, their married daughters, unrelated sons-in-law, and unmarried children, either in the same structure, under the same roof, or on the same plot (see Zatz 1980). Yerania is a particular expression of this general pattern under severe economic constraints; in the developmental cycle of the family, periods of high densities occur that produce tension in relationships within local groups. For this very reason

Yerania is an instructive case, for here the major principles of family organization have been articulated with striking clarity.

RELATIONSHIPS IN THE DOMESTIC GROUP

Whereas the bride in many parts of Greece moves to her husband's home on marriage, in Yerania the bride remains near her own parents, sisters, and unmarried brothers, where she may derive support from close residential contract with her family of origin while achieving autonomy in her own household, subject, however, to her husband's authority (for some variations in postmarital residence, see Casselberry and Valavanes 1976, Kenna 1976).

In Yerania the autonomy of each household is a fundamental tenet of life; it is tangibly, and symbolically, represented by the construction of a separate cooking area that signifies the bride's independence in her newly formed family of marriage (Hirschon 1978:82; 1981). Kitchens are very rarely shared, and only then between mothers and sisters under extremely crowded conditions. Thus the number of kitchens usually reveals the number of households per dwelling.[12] In Yerania it is not unusual to find in one dwelling three, sometimes four, or even five kitchen areas. For example, one house with five separate "kitchens" had two in a single basement alcove. Koula and her married daughter Titsa both cooked here, using the same sink, but there were two gas stoves and two sets of kitchen equipment. The rear section of the house sheltered the families of three married sisters unrelated to Koula's family, each with a separate kitchen, two placed in the courtyard and one in the basement stairway. In these crowded dwellings household autonomy is preserved through careful organization, and the most important feature is that each housewife has her own realm, the living area and a separate kitchen that, no matter how small, is fully equipped and under her sole control. Women claim this is a most important factor in preserving residential harmony.

Obviously the size of household varies, and it may comprise only one or two individuals in the early and later stages of the developmental cycle, for example, an elderly widow or widower living on a pension or a newly married couple before the birth of children. In its middle stage the household consists of the nuclear family, whose size in the present period tends to be small. Families have been larger in the past and average family size has decreased in Yerania from 3.99 persons in 1930, to 3.77 in 1961, to 3.20 in 1971.[13]

Although the newly married couple forms an independent household (unlike the Sarakatsani), it is only after the birth of a child that the spouses gain full adult status as parents, the ultimate goal of marriage. The emphasis is not on many children but on fulfilling the purpose of conjugal life.[14] Now the duties of parenthood take priority over all other relationships, even the conjugal tie, as the child's welfare becomes the focus of attention for both husband and wife.

Children of both sexes are desired in Yerania. Even where girls' dowries lay so heavy a burden on the family's economic resources, parents stress that boys are not without their expenses, for they do not marry empty-handed. Mothers devote much time to the preparation of hand-worked articles for their sons as well as their daughters. But in the marriage of the son out of his parents' home they experience a loss. "A son is future without life" (*Einai mellon choris zoi*), for although a son continues the family name, he is effectively lost to them after marriage when he resides with his wife's family. Daughters, however, remain close to their parents and are seen as a comfort in old age.

Female Relationships. The primary effect of dowry provisions is clear; residential proximity allows the continuity of relationships between female kin. The close bond between mother and daughter may continue, reinforced now by their common experience as married women. Daughters tend to remain dependent on their mothers emotionally as well as for practical matters, particularly in pregnancy and in the postnatal period, when a mother's active support is essential. Even older married women may express this dependency, saying they would have difficulty being away from their mothers even for short periods. Marriage entails, however, a readjustment of obligations and loyalties: a separation of interests between mothers and daughters must develop after marriage, since they now belong to different households with their own living quarters.

With the emphasis on each nuclear family's independence, individual loyalties are redefined after marriage and the new family begins to take priority over the family of origin. Obligations to one's spouse and child are granted precedence over relationships with siblings or even parents. So it is inevitable that even the closest of relationships, those between mothers, daughters, and sisters, are replaced by those centered in the family of marriage.

Through childhood and adolescence sisters usually have close ties. After marriage their daily contact continues, since they live on the same plot and they often cooperate with shopping, caring for one another's children, and with household tasks. But the common identity that the sisters formerly shared has ended and each women becomes increasingly concerned with the welfare of her own family of marriage. Their relationship may acquire a strongly competitive tone centered on the success of husbands and the progress of children.

This pattern of residence affects, too, the relationship between female affines. Contrasts are frequently drawn between the daughter and the daughter-in-law (*nyphe,* also "bride"), always to the detriment of the latter. The position of greatest structural tension, of divided loyalty and conflicting ties, is that of the young married woman, who adds to her role of daughter that of *nyphe* to her husband's parents and siblings. In Yerania, parents are closely involved with their children (indeed, urban conditions may actually reinforce the potency of family bonds), so they undoubtedly feel the son's absence when he leaves home after marriage to live in the bride's dowry house, often under the same roof as her parents. Since he works during the week, his parents see little of him and inevitably dissatisfaction soon arises: his infrequent visits are attributed to the growing power of his wife, and any omissions are always her responsibility.

The daughter-in-law's role is clearly an invidious one—she must balance her own parents' expectations with those of her husband, and even when correct conduct is observed the daughter-in-law seldom gains credit. Sometimes, a woman who observes her obligations to in-laws is frustrated by her husband's indifference, or by his opposition to the time, money, or effort entailed. And the daughter-in-law who gets on well with her in-laws risks incurring her own parents' resentment and complaints about her neglect of them.

A particular point of tension, therefore, is the relationship of mother-in-law (*pethera*) and daughter-in-law (*nyphe*). The groom's mother is caught in ambivalent feelings for her son's marriage. She knows that the daughter-in-law's affections are centered in her own family of origin and she acknowledges the influence a wife has over a husband; for fear of losing contact with her son, she adopts a conciliatory attitude. One woman, somewhat of an expert on this subject with four married sons aged from their mid-forties to their mid-twenties, summed it up: "Daughters-in-law must be handled with kid gloves—everything depends upon them, what *they* say goes" (*Me ta gantia na tis echis—ola exartontai ap'aftes, o, ti tha poune yinetai*).

In many cases the difficult relationship of bride and mother-in-law originates in the period before marriage because mothers often feel that their sons deserve a larger dowry than what is offered. Such views stated before marriage may have long-lasting ill-effects, for the girl who was diplomatically pleasant before the event may reveal her resentment after the wedding; now the groom's parents show good will while she shows indifference, even hostility, secure in the presence of her family.

Male Relationships. The relationships of brothers and sisters in the family of origin can be contrasted: from relatively early ages boys have greater freedom of movement and association than their sisters, and, unlike girls, they separate early in pursuit of occupations and for army service and thus develop diverse contacts with non-kinsmen. After marriage they are dispersed to the homes of their wives where new relationships develop with affines and the other grooms who marry sisters. Significantly, perhaps, the relationship of *badzanakides* ("co-brothers-in-law") is notably amicable (see below, pp. 318–19).

Once married, brothers need to make special efforts to maintain contact, unlike the co-resident married sisters. Married brothers normally meet at formal family celebrations and they should visit one another's homes on name days; that of their father, in particular, is the time when all married siblings are expected to gather together with their families. But there is widespread acceptance that distance, together with the influence of the wife and her family, will predominate, so that men are usually seen as allied to their wives' families' interests. The weak relationship between brothers is often attributed to the power a wife has over her husband, but possibly this diffuse bond originates earlier, in the family of origin.

The residential proximity of the bride's close kin might suggest that the groom's position in his family of marriage is diminished. The question, arises, therefore, whether these in-marrying grooms are the urban equivalent of the rural *soghambros,* whose lower status in village situations has been noted. In Vasilika, for example, where the "in-marrying groom" is the exception, "the villagers say . . . that a *soghambros* is not 'master in his own house' " (Friedl 1962:65). In Yerania, however, men expect to marry into the wife's residence, nor does any stigma attach to this position, because the principle of male dominance is not challenged (see Duboulay 1974:126–28), and here the man has sole economic responsibility for the new family. Parents are expected to recognize a son-in-law's authority over their daughter immediately after marriage, the limitation on their own power being expressed in the saying "When you give your child away in marriage, he/she becomes 'master of the house'" *(Otan dineis to paidi sou stin pantria, noikokyris vinetai).* In Yerania the groom's superior position as head of the family, and with regard to his wife, remains the keystone of family relations.[15]

Indeed, it soon becomes evident in Yerania that the groom has the right to define his wife's activities, limit her contacts, and restrict her movements. His authority is undisputed despite the wife's parents' and siblings' presence in the same house (or on the same plot), provided his own conduct is socially acceptable. Co-resident women obviously have many opportunities for co-operation, but the groom may forbid his wife to help anyone, because her first obligation is to her own family. This authority is exercised only when open conflict occurs, but it is tacitly acknowledged as a sanction and regulates conduct between co-residents. A particular case provides a clear illustration of this principle.

In one corner house shared by four separate households (Figure 3) eight adults lived under crowded conditions because the small plot had been completely built over. One toilet and washbasin was shared by all and, not surprisingly, relationships were under some strain. The longest established

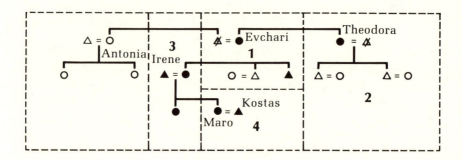

Ø Ⱥ	Deceased
O △	Resident elsewhere
● ▲	Resident in dwelling
- - - -	Households
(K)	Kitchens
(T)	Toilet/w.c.

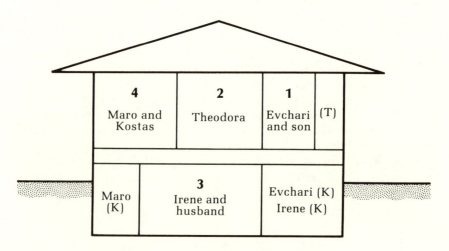

Figure 3. Co-residence and the Groom's Authority

households were those of two widowed sisters, Theodora (70), who kept house alone, since her sons had left the dwelling on marriage, and Evchari (63) with her unmarried son of 30. Evchari's only daughter, Irene (40), lived with her husband and an unmarried daughter in the basement, while the older daughter, Maro (23), lived in the front room of the house given to her at marriage (previously Irene's own dowry home).

Maro's husband Kostas was a metal-welder earning a good wage. They lived well, but the marriage of some five years was marred for they still had no children. One hot summer afternoon a disagreement between Kostas and his mother-in-law, Irene, became increasingly vituperative. When she produced the ultimate insult, "You are impotent!" *(Eisai anikanos)*, Kostas retaliated with some innuendo, "Ask your daughter if I'm impotent — she's the one who can't have children" *(Rota tin kori sou an eimai anikanos — ekeini einai pou then kanei paidia).* Thereafter Kostas ignored Irene entirely, forbade Maro contact with her family, and closed his home, the front room of the dwelling, where the family usually met in the evening to watch television.

Now a regular exodus took place at nightfall, as Evchari, Theodora, Irene, and her young daughter crossed the street to spend the evening at the home of Antonia, sister of Evchari's late husband; since the other two men, Maro's father and her mother's brother, were usually in the coffeeshops, Maro was left watching television alone or with her husband.

Two weeks after this incident Evchari's son (Maro's mother's brother) announced his engagement. Neighborhood speculation centered on Kostas's reaction, since the families of the engaged couple planned expensive formal celebrations, but he was unyielding — neither he nor Maro would attend. On the evening of the engagement party, a month later, he returned from work and, ignoring the family, ordered a tearful Maro to get ready and took her out to visit friends of his who lived in another district.

Weeks passed but Kostas showed no signs of relenting. Since Maro was not short of money nor was she being neglected, there were no grounds for family intervention. Her husband was within his rights in restricting her associations. Indeed, his reaction could even be justified in the light of his mother-in-law's injudicious conduct.

Clearly, then, the parents' ability to intervene in the life of a married daughter is limited, and their active mediation is acceptable only when the very foundations of the marriage are violated. Should a wife abandon her family or the husband prove shiftless, unable to support the family through some vice like gambling, the parents may arbitrate. Divorce proceedings might follow if reconciliation is impossible, but it is strictly a last resort, and it seems that the older generation seldom took this ultimate course even when a justifiable case existed.

In Yerania houses sounds carry through the partition walls, so ordinary conversation is audible from one room to another and disagreements can be closely followed. When quarrels between the spouses occur, the parents should remain neutral, for their duty is to support the marriage regardless of the objective justice of the situation. One mother related her distress hearing frequent quarrels between her daughter and son-in-law in the early years of their marriage: "I am a mother — but even so I never interfered" *(Mana eimai alla potes then anakatephtika)*. Ideally, a mother should maintain impartiality and respond only with exhortations to greater patience and fortitude *(ypomoni, kourayio)* when a daughter confides her problems. Similarly, if a parent's advice is sought, he or she should emphasize the spouse's positive qualities, the children, or whatever might bring about a reconciliation. The emphasis is always on maintaining stable family life. Indeed, the groom's position in crowded Yerania houses, firmly based on the precept of male authority, defines the autonomy of each conjugal unit and limits interference by others.

Another interesting aspect of local group relationships is the strong bond that often develops between the in-marrying grooms. These men who marry sisters, reciprocally called *badzanakides* (singular *badzanakis*), characteristically form friendships and often collaborate in various enterprises. It is commonly said that *badzanakides* are "better than brothers" *(o badzanakis einai kalyteros apo adelpho)*. The close proximity of their respective households where each is an independent family head, and where their wives are sisters, apparently promotes close, even affectionate ties.

Badzanakides may cooperate in business, get involved in joint investment (such as buying land), and give support in times of crisis. In one tragic incident when a man's wife was killed in an accident, it was his *badzanakis* who arranged the funeral, although the bereaved man had close kinsmen. Two other *badzanakides*, Stelios and Perikles, cooperated in helping their wives' brother Yannis, who owned a small tobacconist's shop and needed to supplement his income by driving a school bus. The *badzanakides* arranged to be free from their own jobs simultaneously each day to keep one another company and run the shop while Yannis did his driving job. Even in families where *badzanakides* do not reside together, they may visit one another without their wives; clearly, then, the men develop a relationship independent of the initial basis in their wives' kinship tie.

Interestingly, there is evidence that disagreement may arise more frequently between wives, who appear reluctant to extend cooperation between their families, while the husbands *(badzanakides)* seem willing to maintain a closer association. In societies with patrilocal extended households friction between nuclear families is usually attributed to the inability of *unrelated* wives to preserve harmony (Campbell 1964:71, Hammel 1968:15). In Yerania, even though the wives are close kin, often sisters, divisions between families appear to be maintained most often by the women. This was clear when, for example, Yiorgos and Christos finally gave up a joint family venture because of their wives' hesitation. They had planned to buy land on the island of Salamina, a popular holiday resort close to Piraeus, where together they could afford a much larger plot and a better house. The plan was abandoned when the sisters raised various objections, indicating their reluctance to a long-term commitment, although they were all on good terms. The close relationship of *badzanakides* may be expressed too in the face of their wives' hostility. When Prokopis's wife and her sister quarreled and canceled their joint carnival celebration, Prokopis was upset: "How can I not eat with my *badzanakis* tonight?" he complained, and sent his son to their home with a slice of bread on a plate, and greetings "to my *badzanakis.*"[16]

Examples of this kind are easily multiplied, all indications being that unrelated grooms develop ties of friendship and collaboration, independent of their wives' cooperation. Possibly their position as "strangers" in the local group where the sexual dichotomy is marked, together with earlier diffuse relationships in their natal household, and economic pressures, predispose the men to a smooth reorientation of relationships after marriage.

CONCLUSION

A revealing picture of urban family life is provided in this examination of Yerania, a locality settled for over 50 years by three to four generations of urban dwellers. Their pragmatic approach underlies the prevalence of the *proxenio,* a flexible form of "marriage by arrangement," in which matching of prospective spouses and of their contributions to the new household are central issues. Linked with this is an explicit emphasis on the permanence of the marriage bond and on family stability. The exigencies of urban life for these people, together with historical and demographic factors, have placed a premium on housing, enhanced, too, by cultural values regarding the family.

Dowry in Yerania takes the form of separate living quarters provided in the bride's family home. The resulting pattern of residence, a number of nuclear families related through females, does not, however, diminish the authority of the in-marrying grooms. Each conjugal unit is an autonomous household for which the husband has sole economic responsibility. The complementarity and dichotomy of male and female roles is clearly preserved in the locality where economic pressures have always been severe.

Many features of Yerania life have connotations of "traditionality" and might at first appear inconsistent with urban conditions. But the arranged marriage, the dowry, and the emphasis on family independence and male authority can be seen as culturally defined responses that have developed in particular conditions within this urban environment. Our knowledge of life in Yerania, therefore, challenges common expectations regarding social life in cities. One of these derives from a presumed polarity between "traditional" ways and "modernity," which assumes a necessary association between "modernity" (usually undefined but implicitly based on Western experience) and urban life. In this view, modern ways are city ways and vice-versa, and the corollary states that rural life is "traditional." Hence a decline in rural settlements must signal the final, if gradual, disappearance of "traditional" values and practices. "Modernity" and "tradition" are seen in this approach as mutually exclusive categories (cf. Bendix 1967), so that what appears in the urban context to be "traditional" is interpreted as some tenacious element of a doomed lifstyle or as part of a process of uneven social change with "cultural lag."

Evidence from Yerania can now be added to a growing number of empirical studies that support the contention, stated some 30 years ago but up to now insufficiently documented, that " . . . urbanization is not a single, unitary, universally similar process but assumes different forms and meanings, depending upon the prevailing historical, economic, social and cultural conditions" (Lewis 1962). Increasing anthropological interest in urban life in the Mediterranean will contribute to knowledge of cultural diversity and will, therefore, provide a broader framework for the understanding of general as well as specific processes of social life in cities.

NOTES

1. The scope and methods of inquiry were limited, to some extent, by the political conditions of the period. It was possible, however, to conduct a detailed survey of 62 households, which provided useful data and an adequate sample for analysis. Fieldwork covered 17 months in all, mainly in 1972 when I rented a room with a Yerania family. My contacts and knowledge of social life were by no means confined to Yerania or Nea Ephesus (pseudonyms) but extended throughout the surrounding districts, indeed far wider, as did the social links of local residents themselves. The term "locality" is appropriate, being open-ended, and avoids the connotations associated with "community" (see Leeds 1973, Weaver and White 1972). Thakurdesai's insights were invaluable in interpreting features of spatial organization. I am grateful to J. K. Campbell, P. Loizos, S. Ott, J. de Pina-Cabral, and L. Sciama for comments, and to S. Mitchell for diagrams.

2. The precarious economic status of many war-decimated families is vividly indicated here. Despite the pressures that have necessitated women's participation in the labor force over a long period, however, employment for married women is still not accepted, while jobs for unmarried girls are justified only as contributing to their dowries and hence as an aid to marriage. (The data for 1930 are to be found in an unpublished household survey, made available by staff at the Center for Social Policy, Piraeus, to whom I am grateful).

3. Other categories in 1972 were commerce (13%), employees (7%), seamen (3%), and professional (2%) (estimated from household survey). Unemployment was not a problem in this period of economic expansion, particularly with the boom in the construction industry (OECD 1972).

4. In this respect marriages in Yerania contrast with those from rural areas into towns where social and physical mobility is an explicit goal; see Friedl (1962:65–68; 1976) and Allen (1976:185).

5. In most families relationships between parents-in-law *(sympetheroi)*, and between the bride and the mother-in-law, are particularly fraught with distrust and antagonism. Those between co-brothers-in-law *(badzanakides)*, however, are notably pleasant (see pp. 318–19).

6. The marked preference for real estate investment in contemporary Greece noted by economists is undoubtedly associated with the provision of dowry houses, as well as reflecting lack of confidence in paper assets.

7. Marriage prestations do occur on both sides, since the groom is expected to contribute something toward the new household as well as personal gifts for the bride (gold jewelry, clothes). In this part of the city bedroom furnishing is usually his contribution.

8. In addition, the proportion of widows was striking, comprising 25% of the adult female refugee population, recorded in the report of the Refugee Settlement Commission (League of Nations 1926:176).

9. The significance of the demographic factor has been carefully examined by Loizos (1975) in the Greek Cypriot context. In mainland Greece it is clear that the dowry has suffered severe "inflation" in the period from the 1950s, when rapid emigration from Greece to other parts of Europe and the New World took place. The majority of migrants are young unmarried men, given the cultural restrictions on women's movements.

10. In the sample survey of 62 households, the average kitchen area was just over 3 square meters and four-fifths were actually under 2 square meters.

11. The period from the late 1960s was one of increasing affluence, and a greater variety of dowries were available (see Hirschon 1976:101–14). This chapter focuses on the present pattern of residential groupings, which resulted from a previous widespread solution to dowry.

12. There were 59 kitchens in the 62 households surveyed, two shared between widowed mothers and daughters, and a third where a widow had no kitchen but simply cooked in a corner of her room.

13. Calculated from unpublished census data. The decrease in average family size elsewhere in Greece has been demonstrated by Safilios-Rothschild (1969) and Vermeulen (1970:84).

14. The importance of childbearing for women and its symbolic correlates are discussed in Hirschon (1978).

15. The relationship between postmarital residence and the husband's authority is evidently subject to some ethnographic variation in Greece. I would suggest that the diminished status of the rural *soghambros* in parts of Greece, or even the "urban equivalent" in Exarchia (Zatz 1980), needs to be interpreted in terms of other factors, such as his relative economic dependence. (An extreme case of male subordination and "matriuxorilocality" in Galicia (Lisón Tolosana 1976:307–8) may also be seen in this light.) Evidence from Yerania and elsewhere (see Casselberry and Valavanes 1976:226, Dubisch 1973) would show that uxorilocal residence *per se* does not account for loss of male authority.

16. In Pisticci, where houses pass to daughters and female kin are concentrated together, Davis indicates only that men whose "wives are closely related to an offending woman" ought to intervene (1973:63), but is more specific in a later work: " . . . uxorilocal residence affects the composition of typically cooperating groups (a man with his father-in-law and wife's sisters' husbands)" (1977:168). The case of Yerania *badzanakides* may, therefore, have parallels elsewhere.

322 Urban Life in Mediterranean Europe

REFERENCES

Allen, Peter S.

1976   Aspida: A depopulated Manait community. In Muriel Dimen and Ernestine Friedl, eds., *Regional variation in modern Greece and Cyprus.* New York: New York Academy of Sciences, pp. 168–98.

Belmonte, Thomas

1979   *The broken fountain. New York:* Columbia University Press.

Bendix, Reinhard

1967   Tradition and modernity reconsidered. *Comparative Studies in Society and History* 9:292–346.

Bernard, H. Russell

1976   Kalymnos: The island of sponge fishermen. In Muriel Dimen and Ernestine Friedl, eds., *Regional variation in modern Greece and Cyprus.* New York: New York Academy of Sciences, pp. 291–307.

Campbell, John

1964   *Honour, family and patronage.* Oxford: Clarendon Press.

Casselberry, S. E., and N. Valavanes

1976   Matrilocal Greek peasants and a reconsideration of residence terminology. *American Ethnologist* 3:215–26.

Davis, John

1973   *Land and family in Pisticci.* London: Athlone Press.

1977   *People of the Mediterranean.* London: Routledge and Kegan Paul.

Dimen, Muriel, and Ernestine Friedl, eds.

1976   *Regional variation in modern Greece and Cyprus: Toward a perspective on the ethnography of Greece.* New York: New York Academy of Sciences.

Dubisch, Jill

1973   The domestic power of women in a Greek island village. *Studies in European Society* 1:23–33.

DuBoulay, Juliet

1974   *Portrait of a Greek mountain village.* Oxford: Clarendon Press.

Friedl, Ernestine

1962   *Vasilika: A village in modern Greece.* New York: Holt Rinehart and Winston.

1976   Kinship, class and selective migration. In John G. Peristiany, ed., *Mediterranean family structure.* Cambridge: Cambridge University Press, pp. 363–88.

Hammel, Eugene A.

1968   *Alternative social structures and ritual relations in the Balkans.* Englewood Cliffs, N.J.: Prentice-Hall.

Hirschon, Renée B.

1976   The social institutions of an urban locality of refugee origin in Piraeus. Ph.D. thesis, Oxford University.

1978   Open body/closed space: The transformation of female sexuality. In Shirley Ardener, ed., *Defining females: The nature of women in society.* London: Croom Helm, pp. 66–88.

1981   Essential objects and the sacred: Interior and exterior space in an urban Greek locality. In S. Ardener, ed., *Women and Space.* London: Croom Helm.

Hirschon, Renée B. and Thakurdesai

1970   Society, culture and spatial organization: An Athens community. *Ekistics* 30:187–96.

Kenna, Margaret
    1976   Houses, fields and graves: Property and ritual obligation on a Greek island. *Ethnology* 15:21–34.
League of Nations
    1926   *Greek refugee settlement.* Geneva.
Leeds, Anthony
    1973   Locality power in relation to supralocal power institutions. In Aidan Southall, ed., *Urban anthropology.* New York: Oxford University Press.
Lewis, Oscar
    1952   Urbanization without breakdown: A case study. *Scientific Monthly* 75: 31–41.
Lisón Tolosana, C.
    1976   The ethics of inheritance. In John G. Peristiany, ed., *Mediterranean family structure.* Cambridge: Cambridge University Press.
Loizos, Peter
    1975   Changes in property transfer among Greek Cypriot villagers. *Man* (n.s.) 10:503–23.
OECD
    1972   *Greece: Annual Economic Surveys.* Paris.
Pentzopoulos, Dimitri
    1962   *The Balkan exchange of minorities and its impact upon Greece.* Paris: Mouton.
Safilios-Rothschild, Constantina
    1969   Socio-psychological factors affecting fertility. *Journal of Marriage and the Family* 31:595–606.
Vermeulen, Cornelis J. J.
    1970   Families in urban Greece. Ph.D. thesis, Cornell University.
Weaver, Thomas, and Douglas White
    1972   Anthropological approaches to urban and complex society. In Thomas Weaver and Douglas White, eds., *The anthropology of urban environments.* Washington, D.C.: Society for Applied Anthropology:
Zatz, E. F.
    1980   The implications of housing for kinship relations in Exarchia. Paper presented at Modern Greek Studies Association Symposium, Philadelphia.

Contributors

Thomas Belmonte (b. 1946) majored in anthropology as an undergraduate at Hofstra University, where he studied with Alexander Lesser and Gitel Steed. He did graduate work at Columbia University, specializing in urban anthropology and Mediterranean studies under the direction of Conrad Arensberg. In 1974 he began a year of fieldwork among the urban poor in a central city neighborhood of Naples. His doctoral thesis was concerned with the impact of poverty upon social organization and character in a milieu that had been urban and poor for millennia. His book *The Broken Fountain* (1979) was an attempt to translate the major insights of field research into a form accessible to an educated readership and exemplifies its author's commitment to a literate, humanistic anthropology that can bridge the gap between science and art. Since 1978 Belmonte has been teaching at Hofstra University and has taught in the graduate programs in anthropology at Columbia University and the New School for Social Research. He plans to continue his studies of urban povety and temperament in a Latin American setting.

Jeremy Boissevain is professor of social anthropology at the University of Amsterdam. Born in London in 1928, he obtained his B.A. in 1952 (Haverford College, Pa.) and his Ph.D. in 1962 (London School of Economics). In between he served as chief of mission for the Cooperative for American Relief to Everywhere (CARE) in the Philippines, Japan, India, and Malta. He has taught at the universities of Montreal, Sussex, and Malta and carried out research in Malta, Sicily, and Montreal, where he has examined power relations, immigrant adjustment, and the impact of tourism. Besides many articles, his publications include *Saints and Fireworks* (1965), *Hal-Farrug* (1969), *The Italians of Montreal* (1970), *Friends of Friends* (1974), and (as co-editor) *Network Analysis* (1973) and *Beyond the Community* (1975). At present he is editing a book on European ethnic minorities and preparing research on small entrepreneurs.

Hans Buechler studied at the University of Geneva, Switzerland, at the Sorbonne in Paris, and at Columbia University, where he received his Ph.D. in 1966. He has carried out fieldwork in Bolivia, Ecuador, Spain, and Switzerland and is author of *The Masked Media: Fiestas and Social Interaction in the Bolivian Highlands* (1980) and co-author of *The Bolivian Aymara* (1971) and *Carmen: The Autobiography of a Spanish Galician Woman* (1981). An associate professor of anthropology at Syracuse University, he is currently interested in research into international migration in Europe and small-scale industries in urban Bolivia and Spain.

William A. Douglass received his Ph.D. in 1967 in social anthropology from the University of Chicago. He has conducted fieldwork in the Basque country of Spain, the Molise region of Italy, South America, the American West, and Australia. He is the coordinator of Basque studies for the University of Nevada, Reno, and is currently engaged in a comparative study of Spanish Basque and Abruzzese Italian migrant adaptation in Australia. His publications include *Death in Murelaga* (1969), *Echalar and Murelaga: Opportunity and Rural Depopulation in Two Spanish Basque Villages* (1975), *Amerikanuak: Basques in the New World* (with Jon Bilbao, 1975), and *Beltran, Basque Sheepman of the American West* (1979).

David D. Gregory, a cultural anthropologist specializing in the areas of political economy and demography, received his Ph.D. from the University of Pittsburgh in 1972. He has worked directly in the area of international manpower movements both in Mexico and Europe since 1963. He has received several Ford Foundation grants to study immigration in Europe and is the author of *The Andalusian Odyssey* (1978). He has also written on Mexican immigration for the Senate Judiciary Committee and the President's Select Commission on Immigration and Refugee Policy. He is currently an associate professor in the Department of Anthropology at Dartmouth College and the executive director of the Inter-American Council on Manpower and Development.

Renée B. Hirschon is senior lecturer in anthropology at Oxford Polytechnic, Oxford, England. She was born and educated in South Africa, and has studied at the University of Cape Town (B.A. 1963), the University of Chicago (1965–66), and Oxford University (D.Phil. 1976). Her doctoral research, on a locality of Asia Minor refugee origin in Piraeus, Greece, is currently being prepared for publication as a monograph. She has an active interest in women's studies and has published "Open Body/Closed Space: The Transformation of Female Sexuality" in *Defining Females* (1978), based on Greek material, and "Essential Objects and the Sacred: Interior and Exterior Space in an Urban Greek Locality" in *Women and Space* (1981). She is currently editing a book to be called *Women and Property, Women as Property.* Her other research interests include "ethnicity" and migration, social change and modernization, and the cultural organization of space. She has collaborated with architects, planners, and geographers in multidisciplinary research on urban settlements.

Michael Kenny did his undergraduate work in politics, philosophy, and economics and his graduate work in anthropology (with a D.Phil. in social anthropology) at Oxford University in England. His fieldwork has been conducted in Spain, Cuba, Miami, Mexico, and various cities in the United States. He is the author of one of the first urban anthropological monographs on Mediterranean Europe ever published, *A Spanish Tapestry: Town and Country in Castile* (1961). Two recent publications include *Inmigrantes, refugiados en México, siglo XX* (with others, 1979) and *Antropología médica en España* (with Jesus de Miguel, 1981). Currently he is professor of anthropology at the Catholic University of America in Washington, D.C. Migration, expatriate communities, cultural values, magic, witchcraft and religion, and peace studies and conflict resolution are his major research interests.

David I. Kertzer, born in 1948, received a B.A. from Brown and a Ph.D. in 1974 from Brandeis. He has been on the faculty of Bowdoin College since 1973. Kertzer's research on Italian social organization takes him to Italy regularly, especially to Bologna and Catania, where he served as Fulbright senior lecturer in 1978. His books include *Comrades and Christians: Religion and Political Struggle in Communist Italy* (1980), *Famiglia contadina e urbanizzazione* (1981), and *Age and Anthropological Theory* (co-edited with Jennie Keith, 1983). Kertzer's Italian research focuses on the impact of urbanization on family life in the Bologna area, and he is continuing his work on the relationship between politics and religion. Currently Kertzer is a Fellow at the Center for Advanced Study in the Behavioral Sciences, Stanford University.

Mary C. Knipmeyer was born in Kansas City, Mo., and went to college in Pittsburgh, Pa. She received her Ph.D. in 1979 from the Catholic University of America. Knipmeyer has specialized in psychological anthropology and has done fieldwork in the Washington, D.C., area and in southern Spain. Between 1974 and 1976 she studied gender identity and sex-role formation of preschool children in Granada, Spain. She maintains an interest in Spanish social stratification and in Mediterranean acculturation practices. Currently Knipmeyer is employed by the National Institutes of Health, Cancer Institute as an applied anthropologist.

Slavko Kremenšek was born in 1931 and studied history and ethnology at Ljubljana, Yugoslavia. He became a fellow at the Sociological Institute and a curator of the National Museum, both in Ljubljana, and studied for a year in Moscow. In 1960 he became an assistant professor in the Department of Ethnology of the University of Ljubljana, where he now is professor of ethnology. His books and monographs (in Serbo-Croatian) include *Zelena Jama as an Ethnological Problem* (1970), *The Slovene Student Movement 1919–1941*

(1972), the textbook *General Ethnology* (1973), and *Preface to the Ethnological Research of Ljubljana* (1980). He has also published a monograph in English, *Suburban Villagers: A Slovenian Case Study* (1979). Head of the long-term research project "The Way of Life of the Twentieth Century Slovene Population," Kremenšek's primary concerns are with the problems and theoretical orientation of Slovene ethnology.

Andrei Simić is currently an associate professor of anthropology and co-director of the Institute for Applied Anthropology at the University of Southern California. He has a B.A. in Slavic languages (with a minor in Romance languages), and received a Ph.D. in anthropology from the University of California at Berkeley in 1970. Among his numerous publications dealing with modernization and development are *The Peasant Urbanites* (1972) and *The Ethnology of Traditional and Complex Societies* (1975). He recently co-edited a volume dealing with aging in cross-cultural perspective, *Life's Career* (1977). Dr. Simić's current interests include the study of social gerontology, ethnic groups in the United States, and the problems of development in southern Europe and Latin America.

Michael Spangler (Northwestern University; University of Edinburgh, M.A. 1974; University of Wisconsin, M.W. 1975, Ph.D. 1979) has conducted fieldwork in the Italian-American community of Madison, Wisconsin, as well as his doctoral research in Belgrade, Yugoslavia. His doctoral thesis, entitled "Time and Social Change in a Yugoslav City," is concerned with time concepts and attitudes and their relation to economic and social development in Belgrade during the last one hundred years. His publications include "Future Time Perspective and Feeling Tone" in the *Journal of Social Psychology* (1978), and "Time Proverbs and Social Change in Belgrade, Yugoslavia" in *The Study of Time IV* (edited by J. T. Fraser, 1981). Spangler joined the State Department in 1979 as a foreign service officer and, beginning in August, 1982, will serve in Belgrade as an embassy economic officer. His current research interests center on social and economic development in Eastern Europe, urban labor organization, social stratification, and public policy studies.

Susan Buck Sutton is assistant professor of anthropology at Indiana University–Purdue University at Indianapolis. Her research interests include cities, migration, political and economic development, applied anthropology, and sex roles. She has conducted studies among migrants in Athens and elderly women in Nafplion, Greece. She has also studied Greek-Americans in a southern U.S. city and Hispanic migrant farmworkers in the Midwest. Sutton has worked in the administration of public housing and urban renewal projects in Massachusetts. She received her B.A. from Bryn

Mawr College in 1969 and her Ph.D. from the University of North Carolina at Chapel Hill in 1978.

Hans Vermeulen is lecturer in social anthropology, Department of European and Mediterranean Studies, University of Amsterdam. He received his training in anthropology at the State University at Utrecht, the Netherlands, and at Cornell University, Ithaca, N.Y. From 1964 to 1967 he worked as an assistant expert for UNESCO at the Social Sciences Centre in Athens; during this period he carried out research in the city. From 1975 to 1976 he did fieldwork in a Greek Macedonian village. His main interests are Mediterranean anthropology, ethnicity, and labor migration. He is currently directing a research project among immigrant minorities in the Netherlands. Two of his most recent publications are "Repressive Aspects in the Process of Outmigration: The Case of a Greek Macedonian Tobacco Village" in *Mediterranean Studies* (1979), and "Conflict and Peasant Protest in the History of a Macedonian Village, 1900–1936" in the *Greek Review of Social Research* (in press).

Index

Randall Library – UNCW
HT131 .U69 1983
NXWW
Urban life in Mediterranean Europe : anthropologic

304900276200X